Strategic Air Command in the UK

SAC Operations 1946-1992

Strategic Air Command
in the UK
SAC Operations 1946-1992

Robert S Hopkins III

First published in 2019 by
Hikoki Publications Ltd
1a Ringway Trading Est
Shadowmoss Rd
Manchester
M22 5LH
England

Email: enquiries@crecy.co.uk
www.crecy.co.uk

© Robert S Hopkins, III

Line drawings: © Chris Gibson
Layout by Russell Strong

ISBN 9 781902 109565

Printed in Malta by Melita Press

Front cover illustrations:

Top: Few SAC aircraft in England drew as much attention as the SR-71. Surprisingly, it had been in service for nearly a decade before it deployed to the UK, at first only for orientation missions and finally for operational reconnaissance sorties. 61-7967 departs RIAT on 21st July 1989. *Shaun Connor*

Bottom: In addition to the ubiquitous B-47 bomber, SAC operated nearly 100 specially modified ECM jamming aircraft. This Phase V EB-47E carried a two-man capsule in the bulged bomb bay in lieu of armament. *Augustine 'Gus' Letto*

Back cover illustrations:

Top: The first SAC bombers to visit the UK were B-29s. The 307th BG deployed to RAF Marham in 1948 during the Berlin Crisis, *sans* atomic weapons. *Terry Panopalis collection*

Middle left: The first KC-135A at RAF Greenham Common was 58-0074 on 14th August 1960. The jet-powered KC-135 was both an effective tanker for B-47s and B-52s, but an exciting addition to SAC's pantheon in England given the simultaneous rise of commercial jet travel. *Brian Baldwin*

Middle right: B-50s, including this one from the 328th BS, 93rd BG at Castle AFB, visited the UK only briefly, as they were quickly supplanted by B-47s and the type relegated to other missions. *Jim Webb collection*

Bottom: B-52G 59-2583 from the 320th BW was one of five Stratofortresses that took part in GIANT STRIKE X during 1980, although with less success than its predecessors in the RAF Bombing Competition in 1958 and 1960. *Chris Pocock via Brian Rogers*

Rear inside flap illustrations:

Top: Author photo. *Rob Hall*

Bottom: SAC fighters, such as F-84F 52-6608 from the 12th SFW, pioneered transoceanic deployments and tactical delivery of nuclear weapons. Their operational history was short-lived, as they were handed over to USAFE and TAC. *Terry Panopalis collection*

Half-title page: The KC-10 was SAC's 'Gucci Tanker' and was initially used to support CORONET fighter deployments to and from Europe rather than refuel SAC assets in the UK. Arguably its most important mission from England was Operation EL DORADO CANYON. *Adrian Balch*

Title page, top: When SAC sent an entire wing on a 90-day training rotation to England, it included the integral tanker squadron. In this case, 307th AREFS KC-97F 51-0381 arrived at RAF Greenham Common while the three B-47E squadrons flew to RAF Lakenheath. *Brian Baldwin*

Title page, bottom: A rare photo indeed. 40th BW B-47E 52-0404 departs RAF Greenham Common in 1958, likely after a REFLEX deployment. This was a TEE TOWN aircraft but the ECM pods have been removed, perhaps for use on the replacement B-47. *Brian Baldwin*

Contents

Acknowledgements 6

About the Book 8

Chapters

  1 The Yanks Are Here. 9

  2 A Difficult Beginning. 26

  3 The Jet Age. 47

  4 After Clearwater 68

  5 Wagging the Dog 92

  6 Eyes in English Skies 117

  7 Blackbirds 145

  8 Overlooked and Over Here 171

Epilogue: It's All About the Bombers 196

Appendices

  I SAC Bases in the UK 198

  II SAC Losses in the UK 216

Glossary 220

Index 222

The many barriers facing enthusiasts who recorded SAC's history in the UK on 9th November 1963: bad weather, high fences, limited access, the need to travel long distances on short notice in an old Isetta, a Vespa scooter, or hitchhiking, and plenty of security at a time when SAC consider all spotters to be spies. More than a few spent time in base police offices explaining their hobby!
Brian Baldwin

Acknowledgements

The idea for this book began over drinks and dinner with Neil Lewis and Tony Buttler in the Rose Pub at Baxterley while discussing topics that remained unaddressed by aviation historians. Although we understood that the subject of Strategic Air Command in the UK might initially have a very narrow appeal, we quickly agreed that SAC's presence in England constituted a major portion of SAC's history and strategic capability, as well as a significant period in the history of British strategic airpower and national security. Moreover, SAC's bomber legacy in the UK paralleled the career of Curtis LeMay from his days as a Colonel commanding the 305th BW in England during World War Two until the withdrawal of REFLEX ACTION alert B-47s in 1965, the same year LeMay retired as the four-star-general US Air Force Chief of Staff. We also agreed that SAC's tanker and reconnaissance missions were also inextricably linked to operations from England, and were far more widespread than just those at The 'Hall.

I have been the happy beneficiary of the gracious help and assistance by those who watched these events unfold firsthand, as well as those who supported my research efforts. Their photographs, many previously unpublished, offer a tantalizing glimpse into the halcyon days of early Cold War aviation. Brian Baldwin shared his trove of unpublished images thanks to the technical help of Darren Currie and the editorial assistance of Graham Luxton. Ken Delve provided contemporary airfield drawings. Mike Habermehl graciously allowed me to use photos from his vast collection. Rod Simpson not only provided his own images but allowed me to use some of those by George Pennick contained within the Air-Britain archives. Nick Stroud at *The Aviation Historian* kindly offered photos from his collection and enthusiastically supported this project, including publishing the story of the first B-47 deployment to the UK which is recounted in this volume. Images from the vast collection of the late Jamie Webb enhance this book. Mike Lombardi at the Boeing Archives graciously assisted with photos and content related to B-47s and other Boeing aircraft in the UK.

I am equally indebted to Rick Alexander, Adrian Balch, Steve Bond, Joe Bruch, Shaun Connor, Doug Gordon, Rob Hall, Steve Hill/EMCS, John Hughes, Dennis Jenkins, Colin Johnson, Brian Jones, Augustine 'Gus' Letto, Gordon Macadie, Steve Miller, Terry Panopalis, Jeff Peck, Brian 'Buck' Rogers, Ken Schmidt, Alan Scholefield, Greg Spahr and Richard Vandervord for allowing me to showcase their images, collections, and resources.

Given that so much of the historical content related to SAC in the UK is scattered across many sources, this book would not have been possible without the considerable research assistance and suggestions of many friends and colleagues. The late Bill Peake first introduced me to the addictive habit of 'spotting', the British Aviation Research Group (BARG), and their monthly missive *British Aviation Review*. Thanks to Bill I was able to establish friendships with many of the people who have contributed to this book. Many of them were the only witnesses to record these significant historical events, often hitchhiking vast distances to catch a glimpse of a rare visitor noted in a logbook.

Professor Ken Young of the Department of War Studies at King's College in London graciously provided documents, thoughtful analysis, and assistance in identifying primary source material. His book *The American Bomb in Brit-*

Mickey's Tea Bar was *the* place for enthusiasts at RAF Mildenhall to gather and swap data, photos, and rumors about all things aeroplane in the UK. Arguably without these informal efforts, much of SAC's history in England would be lost forever. *Lindsay Peacock*

ain: US Air Forces' Strategic Presence 1946-1964 is an invaluable scholarly reference for those seeking a 'deeper dive' into the political and military machinations during SAC's early years in the UK. Just before this book went to press we lost Ken to cancer. Hopefully this volume will reflect well on his considerable legacy and be of some comfort to Ioanna and his family. He will be missed.

Dave Wilton's research, published in *Aeromilt-aria*, as well as his helpful e-mails illuminated essential background of SAC bomber visits to the UK between the end of REFLEX ACTION and the disestablishment of SAC. Lennart Andersson provided material and comments on SAC reconnaissance flights in the Baltic. Archie DiFante at AFHRA oversaw SAFE PAPER efforts to accelerate access of relevant material. Master researcher and friend George Cully waded through endless pages of documents to find the missing details that tied together so many previously unknown operations or incomplete records, as did Bill Burr at the National Security Archives. Declassified SAC documents provided by Jeffrey Richelson, Matthew Aid, and Doug Keeney were equally invaluable. John Boyes provided background, photographs, and courtesy copies of his definitive books on the Thor program. Christina JM Goulter of the Sir Michael Howard Centre for the History of War and the King's Air Power Studies Research Group facilitated contacts with other scholars and encouraged fresh thinking on the national security implications of SAC's presence in England. Lindsay Peacock not only shared his extensive research on SAC flights in the UK but reviewed the manuscript for accuracy. Paul and Ali Crickmore hosted several visits to The Long Barn as Paul volunteered his expertise on SR-71 flights from the UK. Chris and Meng Pocock allowed me to stay in their guest room during research trips to the UK. Chris patiently commented on multiple drafts and clarified the many U-2 operations from England and Cyprus. Bob Archer discovered missing serial numbers, rare images, and verified the data that appears in this volume.

Jim Rotramel clarified the events of Operation EL DORADO CANYON.

This book would not have been possible without the pioneering research and perseverance of Colin Smith. Without his efforts so many of these events would be lost to history, their importance unknown, and the people who made them happen would be forgotten. I simply cannot thank Colin enough for his knowledge, advice, and friendship.

Once again Chris Gibson devoted time and patience to the maps, drawings, and overall editorial content, as well as encouragement and humor. Jeremy Pratt, Gill Richardson, and Charlotte Stear at Crécy graciously supported this book. Tom Ferris and Rob Hall deserve great credit for surviving my visits to Telford. Russell Strong did the magnificent layout work. Friday lunches with Jay Miller and his never-ending guest list were both motivational and relaxing. I could never have a better mentor as an aviation historian.

Above: Long before the days of digital cameras, photographers had to be ready with rolls of K64 and power winders to get 'that shot,' enduring sunburns and cold, driving rain.

Below: Being in the right place and time to get arrival images often meant taking great personal risk among wild beasts. Without this dedication, much of SAC's history in the UK would have gone unrecorded. *All: Lindsay Peacock*

Once again, my family has tolerated my research and writing habits. Thanks to Sarah, Mike and Olivia, Robert, Emily, and Christopher, as well as my parents LtCol Robert 'Hop' and Eula Mae Hopkins. My dad flew his 528th BS, 380th BW B-47 from Plattsburgh AFB to RAF Greenham Common when I was but a wee lad, although his most cherished memory of that trip was not about flying but getting a ticket to see Rex Harrison and Julie Andrews in the stage production of *My Fair Lady*. Finally, to my Anglophile wife Amy, I have at last written a book about English history. However far removed from the life of Lady Jane Grey it might be, I guess we have something historical in common after all.

Robert S Hopkins, III
Dallas, Texas
September 2019

About the book

In a perfect world every image in an aviation history book would be sharp, balanced color. It would show only the airplane, preferably in flight or in action on the ground. There would be no people in view (even ground crew, let alone civilians). Images taken more than 70 years ago, however, with small hand-held (even home built) black and white cameras may exist today only as faded or damaged prints. In an age where access to airfields (and SAC bases in particular) was rare and could result in arrest or the confiscation of the camera, many of the photos that remain today were taken at air shows. For purists, the presence of civilians meandering around (and in front of) an airplane would be sufficient to exclude the photo from inclusion in this book. I have taken an opposite point of view, and suggest that the historical importance of an image outweighs any imperfection in the quality of the print or its content. Indeed, many a spotter or enthusiast got his (or her) start wandering the tarmac at an air show or as a youngster staring in awe as the giant airplanes rumbled overhead. Moreover, many of the images published here show the British fascination with aeroplanes (to a far greater degree than their American cousins). This book is a history of SAC airplanes in the UK, not a coffee table picture book.

As the manuscript evolved there was a risk that it could easily become a yearly (if not monthly or even daily) list of unit visits with dense blocks of serial numbers, tail markings, and movements. These are certainly part of the history of SAC in England, but they do not make for a partic-

ularly interesting story. I have instead chosen to minimize text based on these data to allow for a greater number of images to be reproduced in larger size. Readers in search of these details are commended to Colin Smith's magnificent articles in the sadly defunct *British Aviation Review* (BAR) and *North American Military Aviation Review* (NAMAR), as well as his pieces in *Aeromilitaria*. Additional records appear in a variety of British magazines, notably those by Lindsay Peacock and Bob Archer in *Aviation News*.

By necessity there is some intersection of content in this book with my earlier *Spyflights*, KC-135, and B-47 books, although I have made every effort to minimize en masse blocks of text. To those who recognize this please accept my thanks for reading those books. To those who have yet to do so I trust the present volume will offer new insights and material.

Similarly, there may seem to be disproportionate coverage of some of the reconnaissance, fighter, Thor, or other subjects when compared with tanker or bomber operations. The former topics tended to be diverse in both scope and nature, often evolving over time. Peacetime tanker missions, on the other hand, were fairly routine with little variation. Devoting considerable 'real estate' to detailed but repetitive coverage of these latter operations adds little to either understanding their role or recognizing the contributions of those who flew and maintained them. No slight is intended.

In the absence of endnotes, material in 'quotes' reflects attribution of verbatim content or ideas by other writers or sources.

1 The Yanks are Here

After a week-long cruise aboard the RMS *Queen Mary*, the ground component of the 305th Bombardment Group (BG) arrived at Greenock, Scotland, on 12th September 1942, and promptly headed south to the East Midlands to replace the 97th BG at RAF Grafton Underwood. A month later, the 305th BG's Boeing B-17Fs arrived in England via Gander, Newfoundland, and Prestwick, Scotland. The Group was assigned to the Eighth Air Force's (AF) 40th Bombardment Wing (BW) and was under the command of newly promoted Colonel Curtis E LeMay. The four Bombardment Squadrons (BS) included the 364th BS, 365th BS, 366th BS, and the 422nd BS, and were soon in action, flying their first combat mission on 17th November 1942. Less than three weeks later, on 6th December, the 305th BG relocated en masse to RAF Chelveston, flying its first mission from there on 11th December to Rouen, France. Bad weather prevented bombing, but by 3rd January 1943, when the 305th BG attacked the submarine pens at St Nazaire, France, the Group had flown eight missions.

The 305th BG undertook its last combat mission on 25th April 1945, bombing the Skoda armament works in Pilsen, Czechoslovakia. By 'VE Day' on 8th May 1945, the 305th BG – one of the many American bomber units stationed in the UK – had flown 337 missions, 9,231 sorties, and dropped 22,362 tons of bombs against the loss of 158 aircraft and their crews. LeMay had been promoted twice to Major General and was reassigned to the Pacific theater to oversee the bombing of Japan.

Almost exactly 11 years later, the 305th BW from MacDill AFB, FL, returned to England at RAF Brize Norton in Oxfordshire during early September 1953. This was only the second overseas deployment for Strategic Air Command's (SAC) new Boeing B-47B, as the 305th BW replaced the 306th BW which had visited RAF Fairford from June through August 1953. The three squadrons (the 364th BS, 365th BS, and 366th BS) were accompanied by 305th Air Refueling Squadron (AREFS) Boeing KC-97G tankers which deployed to RAF Mildenhall in Suffolk. While in England, the 305th BW expe-

Colonel Curtis LeMay congratulates a 305th BG crew stationed at RAF Chelveston. LeMay and 'his' bombers would remain linked to the UK for the next 50 years.
Author's collection

rienced the same problems as the 306th BW: inadequate ultra-high frequency (UHF) radio and ground-controlled approach (GCA) facilities, bad weather complicating the use of both visual and electronic radar bomb scoring (RBS) ranges, notably at Heston, and the somewhat sorry condition of British bases in general. The 305th BW also visited RAF Lakenheath, RAF Greenham Common, and RAF Upper Heyford to assess their suitability for future B-47 operations as well as to introduce base personnel to the Stratojet. While at RAF Brize Norton the 305th BW planned to send 15 B-47s and five KC-97s to Sidi Slimane AB, French Morocco, but initially only one B-47 and the five KC-97s did so. On 2nd November, however, 41 B-47s finally managed to reach Sidi Slimane AB, returning to RAF Brize Norton over the next four days. The 305th BW jets departed for Florida in three waves in early December, flying nonstop with a single air refueling en route. By this time LeMay had received his fourth star and had been SAC's commanding general since October 1948.

The 305th BW next returned to England only briefly, with cumulative visits totaling less than a fortnight. Beginning in May 1961, the unit transitioned from B-47s to Convair B-58s at its new home at Bunker Hill AFB, IN. Although the two B-58 wings (comprising the 43rd BW at Little Rock AFB, AR, and the 305th BW) were authorized forward-base orientation missions known as ALARM BELL to Zaragoza AB and Morón AB in Spain as well as to the UK, actual visits to England by the Hustler were exceptionally rare. A lone 305th BW B-58A (61-2059) named *Greased Lightning* set a Tokyo-to-London speed record of 8 hours, 35 minutes for the 8,028nm (14,868km) flight before recovering into RAF Greenham Common on 16th October 1963, the first B-58 to visit the United Kingdom. A second 305th BW B-58 visit took place when 60-1117 arrived at RAF Brize Norton on 20th June 1964, departing the following day to RAF Upper Heyford and then returning to Bunker Hill AFB. The last recorded 305th BW B-58 visit to England took place from 7th-10th August 1964 when 60-1116 stopped at RAF Brize Norton and then RAF Upper Heyford. LeMay was now Chief of Staff of the US Air Force and had clashed repeatedly with US Secretary of Defense Robert S McNamara over the value of ballistic missiles versus strategic bombers. LeMay's distinguished military career ended when he retired on 1st February 1965.

During 1970, the 305th BW became the 305th Air Refueling Wing (AREFW) as its B-58s were retired, leaving only its Boeing KC-135A tankers and EC-135 airborne command posts in the years that followed. SAC Stratotankers had been frequent visitors to UK bases (usually in support of specific missions such as RB-47 and RC-135 operations), but regular European deployments went to the Spanish Tanker Task Force (STTF) at Torrejón AB, Spain. After the

Spanish government ejected the STTF in 1976, the KC-135s relocated to RAF Mildenhall with the establishment of the European Tanker Task Force (ETTF). From this time onward, KC-135s from the 305th AREFW joined other tankers in routine four-to-six-week deployments to the UK that continued until the new ETTF host unit – the 306th Strategic Wing (SW) – was inactivated on 31st March 1992, and replaced by the 100th AREFW. The now-retired Curtis LeMay had unwisely dabbled in national politics but then resumed his quiet life in Southern California. He died on 1st October 1990, unaware that 'his' Strategic Air Command would live only another 20 months.

***

Throughout its 46-year lifetime, Strategic Air Command and – to a large measure – Curtis LeMay were inextricably linked to ongoing deployments, basing, and operations in and from the United Kingdom. SAC bombers, continuing the American strategic bombing role that began with the US Army Air Force (USAAF) during World War II, were long-term 'guests' at British bases. Boeing B-29s, B-50s, and jet-powered B-47s undertook 90-day deployments and 'sat' alert, loaded with atomic weapons destined for targets in the Soviet Union and Warsaw Pact. These lengthy visits eventually shortened to three weeks when B-47s switched to REFLEX ACTION alert, improving the morale of US fliers while still filling the British countryside with noise and black smoke. The permanent bomber presence in the UK ended on 3rd April 1965 with the termination of REFLEX. Subsequent SAC bomber visits to England included Boeing B-52s plus rare trips by B-58s and General Dynamics FB-111s.

Although SAC's KB-29 and KC-97 tankers often accompanied bomber deployments to the UK, it was the KC-135 which became synonymous with the American air refueling mission in England. SAC tankers were tasked with refueling bombers en route to their targets in the USSR or during their post-strike egress to recovery bases in England. These tankers also supported US, British, and North Atlantic Treaty Organization (NATO) air operations throughout Europe, strategic reconnaissance flights, and transatlantic fighter 'drags'. For many British and European enthusiasts and photographers, a flight in a KC-135 to 'shoot' everything from B-52s to F-111s to the ubiquitous McDonnell Douglas F-4 was a once-in-a-lifetime experience as well as a positive public relations effort by SAC. Once joined by the McDonnell Doug-

las KC-10, SAC tankers in the UK took part in major combat support operations ranging from EL DORADO CANYON in 1986 to DESERT STORM in 1991.

If it was the duty of the tanker force in the UK to refuel SAC bombers en route to or from their targets in the Soviet Union, it fell to SAC's reconnaissance force operating from England to identify those targets and their defenses. North American RB-45s loaned from SAC and manned by Royal Air Force (RAF) crews conducted a handful of overflights of the USSR in 1952 and 1954, followed by a single SAC RB-47E overflight in 1954, collecting photo intelligence (PHOTINT) of prospective targets. Far more extensive were peripheral reconnaissance flights using RB-50s, RB-47s, RC-135s, Convair RB-36s, and Lockheed U-2s and SR-71s which also gathered electronic intelligence (ELINT) and communications intelligence (COMINT). Once fully integrated, these provided a detailed operational and electronic order of battle (EOB) of the USSR and its allies, allowing SAC planners to develop strike routes that avoided or minimized enemy defenses, as well as enabled other commands to identify enemy offensive capabilities. In addition, civilian and defense engineers used technical data derived from these missions in designing electronic countermeasures (ECM) to facilitate bomber penetration of hostile airspace. Finally, SAC U-2s and SR-71s participated in peacekeeping missions to verify multilateral compliance with cease-fire agreements.

Often overlooked but vitally essential to SAC's mission in the United Kingdom were assets that served only briefly, eventually supplanted by other commands. Building on the USAAF experience from World War II, SAC acquired fighters to escort its bombers on their strike missions. Severely limited in range, these Lockheed P-80s, North American F-82s, and Republic F-84s could not hope to cross the Atlantic Ocean while accompanying B-29s or B-50s, so SAC co-developed fighter air refueling procedures to allow its 'little friends' to reach the UK without multiple en route stops. Flying from bases in East Anglia, they could at last escort bombers to hostile airspace (but little more). In addition, SAC fighters provided a modest air defense of their English bases, and eventually acquired a very limited atomic strike role. SAC also had its own fleet of heavy lift transports to carry supplies, personnel, and atomic weapons to its forward bases in the UK. Douglas C-54s and C-124s, as well as C-97s, were regular visitors to the UK until the early 1960s when the Military Air Transport Service

Opposite, top: Vice CINCSAC Major General Thomas S Power greets the first 305th BW crew to arrive at RAF Brize Norton on 4th September. From (l) to (r) are Lieutenant Colonel Paul Von Ins, Captain Philip H Beagle, Power, Major C E Christie, Brigadier General James C Selser (7th AD Commander), and Staff Sergeant James Hacks. *USAF*

Opposite, bottom: KC-135A 63-8026 from the 305th AREFW visits RAF Fairford on 17th September 1978. Over the years, tankers acquired colorful tail markings and suffered through multiple overall color schemes. *Steve Bond via Adrian Balch*

For more than a few SAC personnel, deploying to England was an eye-opening experience. The aircraft commander (center) on this B-47 crew, however, may well have served on a bomber crew in the UK during the Second World War. The B-4 suitcase adds a nice public relations touch. *Photo BW90199 courtesy Boeing*

SAC's presence in the UK was the result of the longstanding friendship between Air Marshal Sir Arthur Tedder (l) and General 'Toohey' Spaatz (r). The informality gave both sides flexibility but led, at times, to unrealistic expectations. *Author's collection*

(MATS) took over these duties. Similarly, SAC was briefly responsible for an extensive aircrew survival and rescue program, with a small fleet of Douglas SC-47s operating from three UK bases. Finally, SAC's presence in the UK was more than 'just airplanes', as it had direct launch control authority over the RAF's Douglas Thor intermediate range ballistic missile (IRBM) force.

Ultimately, however, Strategic Air Command's mission in the United Kingdom was about its bombers and getting them to their targets in the Soviet Union throughout the Cold War. Plans to do this were well underway even before the end of the Second World War.

An Ambiguous Beginning

Strategic Air Command's presence in the United Kingdom was the result of integrating American and British political, organizational, and operational plans that began prior to 1945. Ken Young's *American Bomb in Britain* provides deep scholarly insight into the many complexities of this evolving association, and is highly recommended. Young argues that the Anglo-American '"special relationship" looked dramatically different when viewed through the American and the British lenses.' He shows that '...at every stage the initiative lay with the United States, simply because the Americans had the clear and unambiguous understanding of their national security interests that the British lacked. The British – ambivalent and equivocal – simply responded to American overtures, sometimes eagerly, sometimes reluctantly, sometimes in apparent absence of mind.' This disconnected Anglo-American foreign policy defined SAC's mission and impact in the UK, with often discordant consequences for both SAC and Great Britain.

The history of the Cold War US strategic bomber presence in the UK began with the 'deeply personal' relationship between General Carl A 'Toohey' Spaatz and Air Marshal Sir Arthur W Tedder. Having worked together during the Second World War, they established a high degree of mutual 'trust and respect' that led to 'an entirely informal arrangement' for US

basing rights in England. Indeed, according to a 30th January 1958 US Department of State letter, the American effort to procure bases in England was so discreet that in 1946 'Spaatz sent to the UK several of his officers, *in civilian clothes*, who under RAF auspices toured British air bases and in conjunction with the RAF selected certain fields whose runways could be strengthened and lengthened so that these bases could handle US B-29s in case of need' (emphasis added). This led to the arrival at RAF Marham in March 1946 of four Superfortresses from Air Proving Ground Command (APGC). These were part of Operation RUBY, which determined if B-29s could deliver the 11-ton Grand Slam bomb as well as validate prior assessments of British fields for use by SAC bombers.

On 9th August 1946, a Yugoslav Air Force Yakovlev Yak-3 forced US Army Air Force (USAAF) C-47A 43-15376 to land near the Yugoslavia-Italy border, claiming it had violated Yugoslavian air space. Ten days later another Yak-3 fired on and destroyed a C-47 near Bled, Yugoslavia. In response to these attacks, US President Harry S Truman directed that SAC flex its muscle in Europe as a 'warning' to the Soviet Union to 'behave' and to 'control' its client states in Eastern Europe. In mid-November, six B-29s from the 43rd BG at Davis-Monthan AFB deployed to Rhein-Main Airfield, West Germany. For nearly two weeks the B-29s 'flew along the border of Soviet-occupied territory,' visited the capital cities of friendly countries, and evaluated possible air bases for future use, including brief visits to the UK. Although none of these B-29s were configured to carry atomic weapons, the message was clear: the United States was prepared to use its atomic monopoly to protect its interests in Western Europe, and the notion of 'atomic diplomacy' was born.

SAC started full-time rotation of its B-29 units to Giebelstadt AB and Fürstenfeldbruck AB in West Germany beginning in June 1947 with the deployment of the 97th BG from Smoky Hill AFB, KS. Ten airplanes took part, which included side trips to the UK beginning 9th June as the 340th BS visited RAF Marham. Despite the initial survey efforts ordered by Spaatz and Tedder and evaluated under RUBY, the RAF fields were ill prepared to support B-29 operations. The implications for SAC operations from the UK were disappointing and of considerable concern to SAC planners. As war plans like FROLIC and OFFTACKLE assumed, invading Soviet ground forces would quickly overrun B-29s based in West Germany. Indeed, SAC considered all bases in Europe east of the Pyre-

nees as unsuitable given the potential for rapid capture by Soviet troops. Even Spain would not last long as advancing Soviet air forces would begin an aggressive bombing campaign against the Iberian Peninsula. For SAC, the only realistic option was England.

The 1948 Berlin Blockade prompted a slightly more formal agreement when Secretary of State for Foreign Affairs Ernest Bevin asked Truman to send bombers to the UK 'to beef up the general striking power available in Europe from Britain.' Bevin imagined that this would be only temporary, with the expectation that the B-29s would stay approximately 30 days and then return to the US. As British Secretary of State for Air Arthur Henderson noted on 28th June 1948, 'Units of the United States Air Force do not visit this country under a formal treaty but under informal and long-standing arrangements between the USAF and the RAF for visits of goodwill and training purposes. The B-29s at present at RAF stations are here to carry out long-distance flying training in Western Europe. It has not been decided how long they will stay. Other visits by United States squadrons will be made…'

With this handshake agreement in place, the US and UK began the slow development of the infrastructure necessary to support 'an accepted presence and rehearse operational procedures.' Funding this process, however, proved to be 'rather mysterious' according to the SAC history of operations in the UK, noting that 'many of the highly classified items that came over for the fields [at RAF Marham and RAF Scampton] were marked as household goods destined for a man who was not in the services!'

Prime Minister Clement Attlee (front right) further solidified the US-UK strategic bomber presence with President Harry Truman (front left). Secretary of State Dean Acheson (rear left) and Secretary of Defense George Marshall (rear right) look on, emphasizing the importance of the bases to US security. *NARA*

SAC's B-29s sent a clear message of American atomic capability. At the time, though, few knew that many of the B-29s in the UK, such as 44-62320 from the 2nd BG, did not have the SADDLETREE modification and could not carry atomic weapons. *via Bob Archer*

The number of SAC B-29s deploying to the UK and the frequency of these visits were intertwined with the delivery of the RAF's Washington bombers. Parking spaces were at a premium, leading to limits on American rotations. *Author's collection*

Organizationally, SAC's initial presence in the UK was equally ad hoc. Beginning on 2nd July 1948, the B-29 Task Force Command was established at RAF Marham. Two weeks later, this unit became the 3rd Air Division (AD) with Provisional (P) status under the command of Colonel Stanley T Wray. On 23rd August, Major General Leon W Johnson – a Medal of Honor recipient for his actions in the famous Ploesti oil field raids – assumed command of the 3rd AD. The unit relocated on 8th September to RAF Bushy Park near London, and again moved on 15th April 1949 to Victoria Park Estate at RAF South Ruislip. Senior officers considered command of SAC forces in the UK as a stepping stone to promotion and a successful career, so it was a highly desirable position.

Throughout the Berlin Blockade in 1948 and 1949, SAC began regular bomber deployments to England which not only 'bolstered Western European defenses' but evaluated each unit's mobility and operational preparedness. As the June 1951 SAC Mobility Planners Guide records, deployment of SAC 'forces at full war strength, with complete organizational equipment, as is required for sustained operations, would require from 60 to 90 days even under the most favorable, probable conditions.' This not only

defined how SAC would conduct operations from England but stipulated its organizational relationship with the UK. Mobility planning was based on 'constant and uniform' command and control procedures, 'continuity of effort' to facilitate the 'smoothest possible transition from peace to wartime', a ready command and supply 'nucleus' in place at forward bases, and required that deficiencies identified in peacetime be resolved as they arise rather than later when a crisis developed. For SAC planners, this meant total and exclusive SAC – not RAF – control over base personnel, facilities, and general logistics support at English bases with prepositioned supplies and equipment, and an *in situ* base complement awaiting the arrival of each rotating wing.

SAC stipulated at least four airfields were needed to meet its planned wartime operations. Each base required a runway measuring 9,000ft x 300ft (2,743m x 91m) and paved hardstands to accommodate 45 B-29s. The British approved this request on 26th August 1948, although it was not until nearly a year later that four initial bases were identified: RAF Brize Norton, RAF Upper Heyford, RAF Fairford, and RAF Greenham Common. These were in varying states of readiness, and the RAF hoped that American dollars would upgrade them for joint use. When it became clear that SAC's basing plans did not include room for the RAF's forthcoming eight squadrons of Washington B.1 (B-29) bombers, British officials balked at the original agreement and proposed instead RAF Marham, RAF Sculthorpe, and RAF Lakenheath, as well as Heathrow airport as an emergency wartime base. By the end of 1949, SAC operations were underway at these three interim locations (excluding Heathrow), with plans to relocate eventually to RAF Upper Heyford, RAF Brize Norton, RAF Fairford, and a fourth as-yet undecided wartime-only base.

Spiraling costs and bickering over who would pay for what further complicated matters, especially as the RAF lacked ready bases for its soon-to-arrive Washingtons. By early 1950, SAC agreed to limit its own B-29 operations primarily to RAF Lakenheath and RAF Sculthorpe while RAF Marham reverted to RAF control as it prepared to receive its first Washington on 22nd March 1950. Hardly just inter-service shuffling, the lack of space for the RAF bombers meant that SAC could not deploy more B-29s or its newer B-50s until additional bases were fully operational. Debate persisted over the 'four Oxford bases', and the British finally agreed to pay for upgrades to RAF Upper Heyford and RAF Brize Norton. Work began in

July 1950 at RAF Upper Heyford, with RAF Fairford and then RAF Brize Norton to follow in due course.

Problems of integrating SAC aircraft and personnel with English bases transcended bureaucratic disagreements among British and American officials. Simultaneous construction by the US Army Corps of Engineers and British firms proved challenging. Although Great Britain did not convert to metric units until 1965, there were still sufficient differences to create significant problems. Severe cold weather hampered outdoor work as well as aircraft maintenance due to lack of hangar space, and a nationwide coal shortage limited electrical power. This was further complicated by the difference in electrical voltage for construction tools, aircraft maintenance equipment, radios, lamps, and even medical gear, necessitating the added expense of large transformers. Shortages of aviation fuel were compounded by inadequate delivery methods from fuel depots to individual airfields. Tires and engines could not be changed due to the lack of suitable jacks or cranes, replacement propellers were in short supply, and there were no aircraft washing facilities. For crews, maintenance personnel, and wing staff the accommodations were austere, with no hot water, open-bay barracks with a single pot-bellied stove for heat, one or

Even as late as January 1954, when the 22nd AREFS KC-97s deployed to RAF Mildenhall, living conditions were, by some American standards, austere. Open-bay barracks – which LeMay had already eliminated in the US – were heated by a single stove and offered little respite for shift workers needing sleep while the ubiquitous poker game was underway at the next bunk. Still, there were some leisure opportunities, such as a visit to the famous Bird in Hand pub. *James Webb collection*

two dim light bulbs, and no recreation facilities. These conditions were little different from those encountered by US personnel in England just three years earlier during the Second World War. To be fair, however, most – if not all – of that preceding infrastructure was gone or in disrepair.

The outbreak of war in Korea in June 1950 added considerable urgency to these improvements, as some US officials feared that the fighting in Asia was merely a distracting prelude to war in Europe. Moving SAC bombers to England would send both a political and military signal to the Soviet Union that any invasion of Western Europe would provoke SAC's atomic wrath. Some 20 SAC units had rotated through the UK since 1948, and the expected addition of more units taxed the infrastructure and leadership to its limits.

Beyond strategic signaling and unit readiness, both the US and Great Britain focused considerable effort on the 'logistical, financial, and political considerations' that would be critical to maintaining SAC's forces in the UK. Several key issues were yet to be resolved, however, especially the expected duration of SAC's stay – Americans increasingly planned for a long-term (if not permanent) presence whereas the British considered this merely a temporary expedient. Moreover, planners from both sides of the Atlantic realized that SAC's English bases were highly vulnerable to Soviet attack (either pre-emptively or retaliatory), putting both SAC forces and the British public at risk. Even more nettlesome were the issues of storage and authority to use American atomic weapons.

Brigadier General Paul Cullen was the first commander of the 7th Air Division, created to oversee SAC operations in the UK. He and his staff were lost when the C-124 carrying them from Offutt AFB to England crashed in the Atlantic. *USAF*

The 7th Air Division

Other than the intercontinental B-36, SAC's remaining B-29 and B-50 force lacked the range to strike targets in the USSR from bases in the Zone of the Interior (ZI) within the Continental United States (CONUS). Even with aerial refueling, tankers would still need to be based abroad to refuel bombers en route to their targets. To meet its command and control requirements for these overseas bases, SAC formed two air divisions in early 1951. The 5th AD was activated at Offutt AFB, NE, under the command of Major General Archie J Old, Jr, prior to its relocation to French Morocco for operations in North Africa. Brigadier General Paul T Cullen commanded the 7th AD, which would replace the 3rd AD in England. The 7th AD had already activated on 20th March 1951 at RAF South Ruislip pending the arrival of Cullen and his staff from Offutt AFB, where he would '1) command…SAC units, personnel, and equipment in the UK; 2) command…UK bases occupied by SAC personnel; 3) [provide] normal base support with tenant units on SAC bases; 4) carry out [Commander-in-Chief, US Air Forces Europe (CINCUSAFE)] orders; and 5) coordinate with CINCUSAFE on all matters of joint interest.' Given these unambiguous responsibilities it was clear that SAC viewed its presence in the UK as long term and as the senior partner with both USAFE and the RAF. Tragically, Cullen never reached England. On 23rd March 1951, the C-124 carrying Cullen and his staff of approximately 50 crashed in the Atlantic Ocean west of Ireland. Debris was finally located some two weeks later, but the absence of survivors compelled Lieutenant General Curtis LeMay, SAC's Commanding General, to appoint Old as interim commander of the 7th AD. On 24th May 1951, LeMay assigned Major General John P McConnell as the 7th AD commander, and Old proceeded to take up his post as commander of the 5th AD in Morocco.

Among McConnell's first challenges was the resolution of the SAC base problem (see Appendix I). By mid 1952, the torpid pace of construction had earned LeMay's wrath. During a visit to England the newly promoted four-star general was furious over the lack of progress in completing a reconnaissance technical facility to process and analyze pre- and post-strike film. In an anecdote shared by then-Colonel Hewitt T Wheless, McConnell's deputy, LeMay asked 'McConnell to give him a date when it would be finished. General McConnell – after thinking a few minutes – picked a date out of the air about two months in the future. LeMay pulled out a pad, wrote the date down, turned to McConnell and said: "Fine. On that date you are fired if that facility is not completed".' Fortunately for McConnell the facility was barely completed by the deadline. He was eventually promoted to General and went on to serve both as one of SAC's Vice Commanders-in-Chief (CINCSAC) and as the Air Force Chief of Staff.

Except for RAF Greenham Common, the Midlands bases finally became operational in 1952, with RAF Upper Heyford hosting the first 'full wing' visit by 2nd BW B-50Ds in September (during prior movements, a wing's individual squadrons were often compelled to deploy to different bases due to limits in ramp space, support facilities, and billeting).

Arrival of the Stratojet

Routine arrivals of the B-47 beginning in 1953 further complicated the 'special relationship.' Their increasingly ubiquitous presence at SAC bases (and a few crashes) throughout the UK coupled with the legitimate concern they carried thermonuclear bombs, argues Young, 'fueled the fear of a nuclear accident [along with] resurgent anti-Americanism and the emergence, at the margins of public opinion, of a movement of nuclear resistance.' Once the USSR had produced sufficient atomic weapons and a medium-range bomber and ballistic missile force, both public and military assessments in Britain believed that 'few [civilians] would survive' a Soviet nuclear attack on the UK. It remained unclear, however, if Britain would eject SAC outright to prevent this, let alone invest the necessary resources to defend England against Soviet air strikes, conventional or otherwise. Indeed, Britain's own fledgling atomic program was problematic for SAC, as

the US sought to curtail the UK's nuclear weapons development (as it did unsuccessfully with France) by offering American-made atomic bombs and even the B-47 to deliver them. Although the RAF prudently declined the B-47 in favor of the indigenously designed V-force of Vickers Valiants, Avro Vulcans, and Handley Page Victors, US nuclear weapons were transferred to the RAF under Project E, although not without restrictions. For SAC, this meant that the Thor IRBMs operated by the RAF had an American on each RAF crew with one of two requisite launch keys. Consequently, the RAF could not launch an atomic weapon even if so directed by the Prime Minister but without American approval. In addition, RAF nuclear-armed bombers were 'assigned to [North Atlantic Treaty Organization (NATO)], and fell under the control not of British ministers, but of the [Supreme Allied Commander, Europe (SACEUR)]'.

Above: LeMay was a regular visitor to the UK, underscoring the importance of bases there to the success of SAC's Emergency War Plan.
Photo BW90189 courtesy Boeing

Below: Arrival of the B-47 in 1953 drew attention to the vulnerability of SAC bases to Soviet pre-emptive strikes and danger to the British public. B-47E 52-0448 visits RAF Sculthorpe in May 1962. *Adrian Balch*

SAC Has its Doubts

By 1956, senior SAC officials had become concerned about unfettered access to SAC bases in the UK. According to the 7th AD study 'Strategic and Political Dependability of SAC Bases in Britain,' they expressed fear that SAC bases 'are less reliable...than ever before,' worrying that 'it is only a matter of time before they will be denied to the US.' Indeed, in 1955 LeMay told British reporter Don Iddon in the London *Daily Mail* article 'The Great Deterrent' that 'the United States has no guarantee and no definite agreement that Great Britain will be at the side of the United States when the whistle blows.' SAC's commanders, nearly all of whom had served in England during the Second World War and considered its military leaders as both friends and colleagues, equated SAC with the Royal Navy. Major General Francis H 'Butch' Griswold, SAC's Vice Commander, said that 'SAC today is like the British Navy of the 19th-century. The Royal Navy kept the peace for almost 100 years, apart from minor wars, because it was so strong, so formidable, that no one dared challenge it... It was the great shield and barrier.' However, Griswold added, 'The feeling also here [at SAC headquarters] is that the RAF is inclined to have the lackadaisical attitude of "Let's have a bash, boys," and not be as scrupulously prepared as the Americans, with the result that the RAF accident rate is three times as high as that of the USAF.' However inaccurate this might have been, this perception was widespread among SAC's senior commanders.

Overseas bases were absolutely critical to SAC's mission, as noted American newspaper columnist Stewart Alsop wrote: the 'prime purposes of the Soviet's new ballistic missiles

are to intimidate the American allies who control LeMay's overseas bases; or, if need be, to destroy these bases in one vast, widespread, simultaneous missile strike.' According to Alsop, SAC was 'hopelessly dependent' on overseas bases which, if lost in a pre-emptive missile strike, would equate to losing 'four-fifths of [SAC's alert] B-47 force on the ground before the war even started.'

Aside from military anxiety raised by the deployment of Soviet ballistic missiles that could reach UK bases, by 1956 LeMay and his staff were concerned with 'the continued strength in Britain of a powerful left-wing movement which in the past two years has been moving closer and closer to a neutralist position in international relations.' Fears of a left-wing rapprochement with the Soviets prompted understandable concern that SAC would be evicted from its bases in the UK. After all, some wondered, the US presence in England would last only 'so long as it is needed in the general interest of world peace and security'. A British government that viewed SAC as an impediment to improved UK-Soviet relations (and hence 'world peace and security') would not hesitate to eliminate SAC bases.

Soviet pressure on the UK to do so was both constant and unequivocal. Soviet Deputy Premier Georgi Malenkov warned on 5th October 1952 that SAC bases in the UK placed Britain 'in a difficult, not to say dangerous position.' Soviet Defense Minister Marshal Georgi K Zhukov said in an 18th February 1956 speech that 'governments of states which have offered their territory for American military bases are playing with fire and are sacrificing the national interest of the peoples in their countries.' He added, 'they are subjecting their lives to a threat, because, according to the logic of armed battle,

Although SAC's bomber alert program began in 1958, the ability to launch atomic-armed bombers from the UK was always hostage to British political breezes. Fears of left-wing – even pro Soviet – policies risked the loss of SAC bases such as RAF Greenham Common, which hosted B-47E 53-2092 in July 1963. *Adrian Balch*

retaliatory blows must fall on bases independent of whose territory these bases are situated on.'

SAC's politically conservative leadership viewed this as 'air-atomic blackmail.' They warned that Welsh Labour Party leader and Shadow Foreign Secretary Aneurin 'Nye' Bevan was 'anti-American, if not personally, at least in policy.' They worried that the 'political grouping of pacifists, neutralists, and Marxists which collected under the banner of what has been called "Bevanism" was constantly seeking to embarrass the government over the issue of US bases,' placing the UK 'in mortal peril'.

The evolution of Britain's own strategic bomber and missile force, known as 'graduated deterrence', was equally troublesome to SAC planners. Once the UK had sufficient bombers and atomic weapons, it would no longer require SAC to provide a nuclear umbrella for the UK. Moreover, American and British foreign policy aims were drifting apart, further jeopardizing SAC's presence in the UK. Tory politicians and their conservative views, championed by the likes of Sir Winston Churchill, long an advocate of Anglo-American cooperation, were increasingly being replaced by those of Labour, which was 'moving more and more toward left-wing Bevanite thinking.' Interestingly, it was Labour Prime Minister Clement Attlee who first 'invited' SAC bombers to the UK in 1948, showing how far the Labour party had shifted its position.

The presence of American military personnel and their families also had an impact on the future of SAC bases. They represented the 'American way of life' which was notably different from that in Great Britain. Examples of their adverse effect on daily life in the UK, according to SAC's critics, included the 'raising of local rents, spreading immorality, showing off their tax-free possessions, and engaging in black market activities', but such claims appeared mostly in left-wing and communist newspapers. In the 10th December 1953 issue of *Daily Express*, Nye Bevan said 'The presence of American airmen is tolerated in Britain but not accepted. If their presence comes to be actively resented then they will have to withdraw... because a military base is useless if surrounded by a hostile population.' The more mainstream London *Sunday Dispatch* took a far different view in 1955. 'How convenient...to foist the blame for any and every moral lapse [in the UK] on our long-suffering and very patient guests,' the US Air Force. It added, 'We ought to be lost in wonder that 60,000 foreign nationals [out

Aneurin 'Nye' Bevan's socialist leanings worried SAC's commanders. Bevan represented a sizeable proportion of post-war Britons who were weary of war and sought domestic quality of life improvements rather than what they saw as entanglements with the US that risked yet another war, this time with erstwhile ally the Soviet Union. *Author's collection*

of a population of 51 million], most of whom don't want to be here, have fitted in so peacefully and pleasantly in the 20 or so areas where their bases are built,' concluding that '...never in history has a large foreign armed force settled in a country with so little of the moral and economic upset traditionally connected with "licentious soldiery".' Colonel Ervin Wursten, the 7th AD commander prior to its 1965 inactivation, agreed, telling a group of Britons who served to enhance Anglo-American relations, 'The efforts made by the British to make us welcome here – welcome at their own expense and initiative – have no counterpart in any other area where SAC forces are stationed overseas.'

Ironically, the most notable expression of anti-SAC attitudes during its early years in the UK came from the sabotage on 23rd July 1950 of 301st BG B-29s at RAF Lakenheath by four British Army guards. Two were eventually convicted of slicing tires with their bayonets, as well as damaging batteries and other components, leading to a hasty effort to provide better security for its bases – RAF Lakenheath lacked even so much as a fence around the airplanes. US records dryly note that this was merely an act of vandalism by 'two drunken soldiers, with no political motive, only pique at their sergeant.' This disingenuous description masked the reality that the vandalized airplanes included SILVERPLATE/SADDLETREE/GEM B-29s ready to be loaded with Mark IV atomic bombs as part of the US response to the outbreak of the Korean War. One can only imagine the consequences if the B-29s were so configured!

SAC concluded that despite these many military and political challenges, 'it is very unlikely that [Great Britain] would break the air-atomic alliance which has done so much to keep the world at peace in the past ten years. Britain

SILVERPLATE and SADDLETREE

Although the B-29 was the logical choice to carry the atomic bomb, it required considerable modifications to do so. The prototype was B-29 42-6259, and the changes were undertaken at Wright Field, OH, beginning in December 1943. The most significant modification was extension of the bomb bay to accommodate the 'Thin Man' (precursor to the 'Little Boy') which was 17ft (5.2m) long and could not fit inside the standard B-29 bomb bay. Wright removed the fuselage section between the two existing bomb bays and installed suspension and release mechanisms for 'Fat Man' and 'Little Boy'. The resulting bomb bay was 33ft (10m) long and used a pair of extended bomb bay doors.

Between October and November 1944, the Glenn L Martin plant at Omaha, NE, delivered 17 modified B-29s under Project 98146-S, known as SILVERPLATE. Three of these were used for drop testing at

Los Alamos, NM, and the remaining 14 were assigned to the 393rd BS for crew familiarization and training. Additional modifications included an improved Wright R-3350-41 engine, enhanced loading, monitoring, and dropping mechanisms, and removal of all gun turrets (except the tail gunner) to save weight. SILVERPLATE B-29s delivered directly from Omaha were identified as B-29-36-MO aircraft to distinguish them from standard B-29-35-MO bombers.

By the end of 1945, 46 SILVERPLATE B-29s had been produced. On 26th July 1946 an additional 19 B-29s were slated for conversion to provide the newly formed Strategic Air Command with a more robust atomic strike force. Less than a year later, on 12th May 1947, the name SILVERPLATE was deemed compromised and all subsequent work related to modifying B-29s to carry atomic bombs used the code name

SADDLETREE. During January 1948, the JCS directed the conversion of 225 additional SADDLETREE aircraft, including 80 B-29s plus B-50s and B-36s. On 16th April 1948, the overall code name for modifying airplanes to carry and drop atomic weapons changed to GEM, although the 80 B-29s previously identified for modification remained known as SADDLETREE. GEM also incorporated winterization for the B-29s and the RURALIST receiver air refueling capability. In the end, there were 65 SILVERPLATE B-29s and 80 SADDLETREE B-29s.

Beginning in April 1951, additional atomic modifications were made to SAC bombers (including the new B-47) as part of the ON TOP program.

Source: Richard H Campbell, *The Silverplate Bombers: A History and Registry of the Enola Gay and Other B-29s Configured to Carry Atomic Bombs* (Jefferson, NC: McFarland, 2005).

today is still America's most dependable ally in Europe.' However, 'an economic or political crisis might place the leadership of Great Britain in the hands of men who are not sympathetic to the presence of US forces in the country... [which] rests on purely informal grounds and could be terminated almost as easily as it was established.' Surprisingly, the challenge to sympathy for the American military presence in England came not from a change in British leadership, but from the results of an American presidential election.

Gold Flow

John Fitzgerald Kennedy's defeat of Richard Milhous Nixon in November 1960 created a contradiction in US policy toward American military forces abroad. Democrat Kennedy campaigned hard by claiming that Republican Nixon was 'soft' on defense, despite being the conservative vice president for former General of the Army and two-term president Dwight D Eisenhower. Kennedy promised to increase America's already significant military strength to contain growing Soviet power. He also had strong ties to England, as his father Joseph P Kennedy, Sr, served as the US Ambassador to the Court of St James from 1938 to 1940.

Paying for Kennedy's expensive military build-up proved problematic. His 'Whiz Kid' Secretary of Defense Robert S McNamara and his Secretary of the Treasury C Douglas Dillon argued that US bases abroad actually hurt defense spending by needlessly sending

American gold abroad to pay their rent. They proposed the CLEARWATER program designed to reduce the number of US overseas forces and bases and hence curtail the outflow of gold, including bases in England. This continued after Kennedy's assassination in 1963 and his succession by Vice President Lyndon B Johnson.

There was more to the reduction of SAC forces in the UK than pinching pennies. McNamara viewed the manned strategic bomber as a weapon of the past, costly to develop and expensive to operate. He saw ICBMs stationed at bases within the United States as the nuclear delivery system of the future. Indeed, on 15th March 1964, the number of SAC ICBMs on alert exceeded the number of SAC bombers on alert. For McNamara, the B-47 was the ideal solution to all of these challenges. By retiring the Stratojet as part of the FAST FLY program, he could slash SAC's bomber force by nearly 1,000 airplanes, cut operational spending at home, and reduce the gold flow problem abroad, resulting in the departure of B-47s from the UK at the beginning of April 1965 and the concurrent termination of SAC's REFLEX ACTION.

It is surprising that the CLEARWATER efforts to reduce American spending abroad and the FAST FLY program to eliminate the B-47 fleet failed to provoke more strident opposition by LeMay (as Air Force Chief of Staff) and General Thomas S Power (as CINCSAC). Although Power tried in vain to keep his B-47s, both he and LeMay understood the vulnerability of SAC bases abroad, especially in the UK. As early as 1955 LeMay wrote 'by 1960 the Soviets will have

1,000 ballistic medium range missiles [1,300nm (2,408km)] which will give them adequate weapon coverage of all our UK, Spain, and Mediterranean bases, as well as Thule, Keflavik, and the Alaskan complex.' The missiles, with 'a 3-mile CEP [circular error probable] with a 3 MT [megaton] yield', could be launched with little warning, so 'tankers and bombers within missile range will probably be [quickly] lost and the bases rendered untenable.' He concluded that this 'causes me to question our dependence on these bases to support the strike force. Certainly from 1960 onward we must plan to launch our alert forces from the relatively more secure ZI and Canadian bases.' LeMay clearly understood that one of the vulnerabilities of SAC's offensive capability was its reliance on bases in the UK, and he held no illusions that SAC's bomber presence in England would be permanent.

It is noteworthy that CLEARWATER was not undertaken at the behest of the British government or to satisfy any British political or security goals; rather, it was a unilateral American decision. Although this removed permanent strategic bomber bases from the UK and the threat they posed to the British public as targets for Soviet attacks, American nuclear weapons remained in England in the form of tactical bombs for use by USAFE aircraft. SAC's tanker and reconnaissance forces also remained in the UK, which attenuated – but did not eliminate – British concerns about its authority over the operations of American aircraft from its soil and public worries about antagonizing the USSR to such a degree that it placed British bases and their civilian neighbors at risk. As Young says, '…in their preparedness to contain Soviet expansionism through encirclement with bases, the United States demonstrated unambiguous resolve and clear values. While accepting a part in this global role, the British response was nonetheless characterized by equivocation in its expression, by ambiguity of purpose and by ambivalent impulses toward both ally and adversary. In that respect, the "special relationship" was profoundly asymmetrical.'

Nuclear Authority

In the event of war, the British government had only the 'assurance' of US 'consultations' prior to the launch of SAC bombers from English bases. While this was certainly practicable in cases of gradual escalation leading to any pre-emptive or retaliatory strike, it was effectively meaningless in the case of a 'bolt from

the blue' Soviet attack on the United States. Such an attack by Soviet bombers detected only at the last minute (or by soon-to-be deployed ICBMs such as the SS-6 *Sapwood*) would leave SAC with very little time to 'launch on warning,' and certainly without any meaningful time to consult with the Prime Minister (PM). The author's father was a B-47 pilot on REFLEX ACTION alert in the UK, and was told in no uncertain terms that because of the extreme vulnerability of the SAC bases, in the event of an attack on the United States the B-47s in England would launch immediately without regard for British decisions. There simply was insufficient time for the PM to assemble the cabinet, let alone Parliament, to debate a course of action separate from a pre-approved SAC operational plan. In any case, it was wholly unreasonable for British politicians to believe that England could remain unscathed and unaffected by a general nuclear war between the US and the USSR. In short, by casting its lot in with the US at the onset of the Cold War, England had consigned itself to share the fate of America irrespective of what British politicians and the public thought.

Establishing just when the first American atomic weapons arrived in the UK has proved challenging. According to the US Department of State, 'at the time of the Berlin blockade and the commencement of the Berlin Airlift [1948], on RAF request to SAC, SAC units *with nuclear weapons* were brought to the UK' (emphasis added). None of the B-29s deployed to the UK as part of Operation FERRYBOAT, however, had the SILVERPLATE/SADDLETREE/GEM modification to carry atomic bombs, so this is certainly wrong. A message from the USAF Air Staff and an unpublished memoir by US Air Force Major Curtis L Miragon quoted in Young's *American Bomb in Britain* more accurately elucidate the

US Secretary of Defense Robert McNamara saw the elimination of the B-47 fleet as the solution to both excessive bleeding of American gold abroad and the reduction of SAC's bomber force, replaced by ICBMs. This effectively ended SAC's bomber presence in the UK.
Author's collection

With the onset of the Korean War, President Truman authorized the deployment of two nuclear-capable wings to the UK. B-50D 48-0095 from the 97th BW (top) and 49-0360 from the 93rd BW (bottom) both relocated to England in the event the USSR planned to invade Western Europe. Both brought atomic weapons with them. *Author's collection; Photo P-12159 courtesy Boeing*

initial arrival of American atomic weapons in the UK. In response to the outbreak of the Korean War, President Truman approved on 11th July 1950 the deployment of GEM-configured B-50s from the 97th BG at Biggs AFB, TX, to RAF Sculthorpe and the 93rd BG at Castle AFB, CA, to RAF Mildenhall. The 97th BG B-50s traveled first to Kirtland AFB, NM, where each collected a single Mark IV atomic bomb minus its plutonium core. The 93rd BG B-50s staged via Goose AB, Labrador, where they were similarly armed. Consequently, the first atomic weapons in the UK (unusable without their cores) likely arrived with the 97th BG B-50s, followed by those from the 93rd BG. SILVERPLATE/ SADDLETREE B-29s from the 301st BW at Barksdale AFB, LA, were already on temporary duty (TDY) at RAF Lakenheath, and these were reportedly supplied (but not necessarily armed) with Mark IVs via C-124s.

Beginning in 1952, the United States and Great Britain laid out specific – if not ambiguous – procedures for the employment of American nuclear weapons from British bases. In a 9th January 1952 communiqué following talks between Prime Minister Churchill and President Truman, the two countries agreed that 'the use of these bases in an emergency would be a matter for joint decision by His Majesty's Government and the United States Government in the light of circumstances prevailing at the time.' According to declassified documents, there were two general sets of circumstances: strategic warning and tactical warning. In the former, there were clear indications of a Soviet intention to attack, whereas in the latter there were radar returns or other indicators that an attack was 'underway or has occurred'. With sufficient strategic warning, the 'Prime Minister and the President of the United States [would] consult together [by phone] regarding a joint decision to commit [SAC's nuclear-equipped] attack retaliatory forces based in the United Kingdom.' In the case of tactical warning, the two leaders would 'speak personally' before ordering SAC bombers in England into the air, but there were other considerations in play. With an attack 'underway or [having] occurred', the CINCSAC could 'launch his Alert Force under "Positive Control" procedure, which [proceeded] on pre-arranged routes toward targets, but [would] not pass beyond a specified line [the 'Fail-Safe' point] without further definite instructions' (this explains the 'launch-on-warning' of the author's father and his B-47).

Following a 9th March 1953 conversation between Truman and new Prime Minister Anthony Eden, American obligations expanded to consult with the Prime Minister 'prior to US use of any nuclear weapon' anywhere in the world. Truman told Eden that 'in the event of increased tension or the threat of war, [the US would] take every possible step to consult with Britain and our allies.' By 1958, this was more fully codified with the Murphy-Dean Agreement of 7th June, which stipulated that 'such use in an emergency shall be a matter for joint decision by the two Governments in the light of the circumstances at the time,' almost verbatim from the original Truman-Churchill agreement of 1952. A 30th July 1976 letter at the President Gerald R Ford Library from newly elected British Prime Minister L James Callaghan demonstrated the unwavering commitment by both sides to honor this 1958 agreement: '…it has been the practice whenever the office of the United States President or British Prime Minister has changed hands to reaffirm the understandings between our two governments with regard to consultation on the use of nuclear weapons.' Ford replied, 'I am pleased to confirm the United States Government will regard the Memorandum of Understandings…as remaining in effect.' Although there were some exceptions related to US ballistic missile submarines or naval vessels in British territorial waters, British Strike Command aircraft carrying British nuclear weapons, and NATO-dedicated assets, the impact was unequivocal: use of SAC's nuclear armada in the UK was subject to joint consultation by the American President and the British Prime Minister. Practically, under tactical warning, this meant the decision would be made on-the-spot by the PM without opportunity for consultation with the cabinet.

Despite this diplomatic language, there remained a significant loophole in these agreements. In each case, there was only the requirement for 'consultation', which is far different from 'consent'. There is no as-yet declassified procedure that covers the possibility the PM might have rejected the use of SAC forces launched from English bases. Once they were airborne, it is inconceivable that the US would honor this disapproval and recall its bombers to England while the rest of SAC's bombers

and ICBMs were already heading toward the USSR and British bases were minutes away from annihilation by Soviet missiles. Nonetheless, the Dean-Murphy Agreement provided at least a *pro forma* sense of British control over its sovereignty.

Endgame

After 1965, SAC's presence in the United Kingdom was defined almost exclusively by its reconnaissance forces – notably RB-47s, RC-135s, U-2s and Lockheed TR-1s, and the crowd-pleasing SR-71 – and its KC-135 and KC-10 tankers. Although these were clearly not combatants, they served as icons of both SAC's nuclear strike mission and American conventional military operations, especially in Southeast Asia. The loss of the Central Intelligence Agency's (CIA) U-2 on 1st May 1960 followed by the loss of a SAC RB-47H on 1st July 1960 (the latter departed from RAF Brize Norton) profoundly influenced the way the British government exercised its authority over SAC reconnaissance missions launched from British bases, including those overseas.

English sympathies toward American military operations in general soured as the war in Vietnam dragged on with little hope for either a decisive American victory or a peaceful resolution that guaranteed South Vietnamese legitimacy. Labour Prime Minister J Harold Wilson disliked US President Lyndon Johnson (the feeling was mutual), and Wilson's Cold War view that the fighting in Vietnam was intended to contain the spread of communism clashed with the increasing left-wing perspective of the Labour Party that Vietnam was a war of national liberation. Wilson's Tory successor Edward R G 'Ted' Heath did little to alter the British public's opposition to the war. Consequently, any US military base in England, including SAC tanker and reconnaissance bases, quickly became a lightning rod for anti-war and anti-American protests. By the 1980s, many of the indigenous anti-war protests by groups such as the Campaign for Nuclear Disarmament (CND) which had focused on eliminating nuclear weapons during the 1950s and 1960s, had been supplemented by Soviet-funded anti-American groups as well as an expansion of the CND by entities such as the Molesworth People's Peace Camp and women's groups such as the Greenham Common Women's Peace Camp. These organizations primarily opposed the placement of US tactical nuclear-equipped Ground Launched Cruise Missiles (GLCM) in England that were not

After the elimination of bomber alert in the UK in 1965, SAC reconnaissance and tanker operations remained as the visible reminder of its ongoing presence through 1992. Perhaps the most popular was the combination of the SR-71 and its KC-135Q tankers.
Bob Archer (top), Adrian Balch (bottom)

assigned to SAC, so did not specifically target SAC's tanker or reconnaissance bases (although the women at RAF Greenham Common were treated to an early morning wake-up call by a departing SR-71 upon which they had previously splashed red paint).

Despite these public tensions over the presence of American military forces in the UK, Her Majesty's Government (HMG) approved the use in April 1986 of RAF Fairford and RAF Mildenhall for tanker operations in support of F-111s launched from RAF Lakenheath and EF-111s based at RAF Upper Heyford to strike targets in Libya as part of Operation EL DORADO CANYON.

In conjunction with British Operation Granby in Iraq, SAC tankers in the UK refueled hundreds of airplanes crossing the Atlantic in both directions as part of Operations DESERT SHIELD and DESERT STORM in 1990 and 1991. A small contingent of B-52s flew combat missions against Iraqi Republican Guard ground forces from RAF Fairford during DESERT STORM.

The summer of 1991 saw a groundswell of popular support for military aviation in the UK following the successful operations in Iraq, with SAC aircraft attending air shows and static displays throughout England. Unbeknownst to most Britons (and even Americans), plans

KC-10A 82-0191 was one of the 20 Extenders used to support Operation EL DORADO CANYON. Their larger fuel capacity and ability to be refueled in flight made them a better choice than the KC-135.
Author's collection

were underway in Washington, DC, to completely reorganize the US Air Force, beginning with the dissolution of Strategic Air Command. SAC's storied ground-alert bombers and ICBMs were removed from their traditional continuous 15-minute reaction posture on 27th September 1991. SAC's 100th AREFW relocated to RAF Mildenhall on 1st February 1992, replacing the ETTF (it had previously been the 100th BG at RAF Thorpe Abbotts from 1942-1945 where it earned the ignominious legacy of the 'Bloody Hundredth'). SAC was formally deactivated on 31st May 1992, and its B-1s and B-52s were reassigned to Air Combat Command (ACC). Most of its KC-135s and all of its KC-10s were distributed to Air Mobility Command (AMC), although the 100th AREFW's KC-135s remained in England but were henceforth assigned to USAFE's Third Air Force.

Between the end of the Second World War in 1945 and the end of the Cold War in 1992, the United States and Strategic Air Command developed a working arrangement with the British government and the Royal Air Force. At times it was collaborative and functional, at times it was problematic and troublesome. For SAC the 'special relationship' provided the means to project America's atomic air armada against targets in the USSR using its medium-range bombers pending the accessibility of true intercontinental bombers and ICBMs.

Once these bombers were in service, the role of SAC bases in the UK shifted to post-strike recovery and reconstitution. In addition, these bases provided bomber aerial refueling support and strategic reconnaissance capabilities essential to fulfilling SAC's nuclear strike mission. For the British, the benefits of SAC bases were less obvious, partly because of evolving British policies at home and abroad, and partly because they understood that meeting SAC's operational requirements necessitated at least partial subjugation of British sovereignty.

The British Chiefs of Staff articulated this dilemma in a 24th August 1951 letter to Air Chief Marshal Sir William Elliott, seconded to Washington to liaise with senior American military and political officials: 'You should make it quite clear to the [US] Joint Chiefs that, however much they wish to, they cannot keep their hands free in this matter, which is one of life or death to this country. The United Kingdom is not an American aircraft carrier conveniently anchored off the coast of Europe. We are their only really solid Ally – in the long run as indispensable to them as they are to us – and we intend to be treated as such. And in this matter, more perhaps than any other strategic matter, we insist on having an agreed policy thought out in advance.' Despite this insistence from London, initial American war plans assumed absolute British acquiescence.

Resplendent in D-Day 75th anniversary heritage markings in June 2019, KC-135R 62-3551 of the 'Bloody Hundredth' reflects the legacy that binds the 100th BG at RAF Thorpe Abbotts during the Second World War and the 100th AREFW and the sunset of tanker operations in the UK. *Bob Archer*

2 A Difficult Beginning

The evidence was overwhelming, and President Harry Truman knew it was time to act. Soviet warships on 'naval exercises' in the Black Sea forced their way through the Bosphorus and Dardenelles to enter the Aegean Sea. With fifth-columnists and sleeper agents already in place, the Turkish and Greek governments quickly rolled over and allowed the Soviet navy unfettered access to the Mediterranean Sea as Bulgarian and Soviet ground forces crossed into northern Greece. Soviet tanks and troops moved quickly into Austria bound for northeast Italy, again benefitting from communist sympathizers in Rome. A strong Soviet armored force drove deep into West Germany, with two thrusts aimed at the industrial Ruhr and toward Denmark. To support this, the Soviet Baltic fleet – again purporting to be conducting an exercise – sailed for the Kattegat and the Danish capital. The Soviet North Sea fleet, recently starting a trip to Albania (of all places) for a show of 'fraternal proletariat friendship' and now just passing the southern tip of Norway, diverted eastward to the Skaggerak to meet the Baltic fleet and capture the narrow access to the Baltic Sea. Soviet Tupolev Tu-4 *Bull* bombers dropped conventional weapons on US and NATO bases in West Germany and the capital at Bonn. Other NATO bases and capitals were next. The Soviet invasion of Western Europe had begun.

Throughout the day President Truman conferred with his senior military and political advisors. Surprisingly, Secretary of State Dean Acheson argued for restraint until the Soviet's actual intentions were clear. Secretary of Defense Louis Johnson warned that the intent was obvious – global domination by the communists through the invasion of Europe. Air Force Chief of Staff General Hoyt S Vandenberg echoed Johnson's perspective, and counseled Truman to launch the American war plan against the USSR. Given that it would take several days just for US strategic forces to be ready to attack, diplomats could still work to curtail (and hopefully rollback) Soviet military aggression against the West. Truman agreed with Vandenberg, who ordered Strategic Air Command's Commanding General to execute the Emergency War Plan (EWP). Lieutenant General Curtis E LeMay complied, and established Monday, 24th April 1950, as 'E-Day.'

The US Joint Chiefs of Staff (JCS) briefed Truman on two EWP plans – TROJAN and OFFTACKLE – to strike 70 and 123 Soviet 'industrial centers', respectively. Truman approved their recommendation to implement OFFTACKLE. Only 60 out of 123 targets for this EWP had been positively located, so SAC RB-29s would have to undertake pre-strike reconnaissance over the vast expanse of the Soviet Union in order to find the remaining 63.

SAC B-29s and RAF Washingtons were not the only 'Stratofortresses' in Europe capable of attacking hostile forces. Soviet Tu-4 *Bulls* were capable of striking British bases, and SAC planners expected them to do so en masse.
via Yefim Gordon

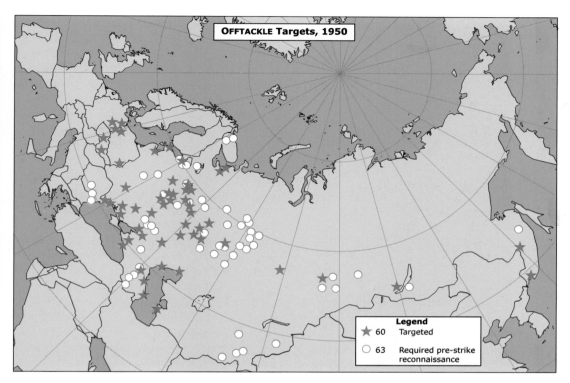

OFFTACKLE Targets, 1950

Legend
★ 60 Targeted
○ 63 Required pre-strike reconnaissance

Truman called British Prime Minister Clement Attlee to notify him of America's response, while Vandenberg contacted Air Chief Marshal Sir John C Slessor, the RAF Chief of the Air Staff, to alert him to the impending arrival of SAC's bomber force. Top Secret messages quickly clogged the telegraph lines between SAC Headquarters near Omaha, NE, and SAC bases around the United States. Commanders from Georgia to California recalled all personnel while 'wrench turners' worked feverishly to make every airplane flyable. Most ominously, the guardians of America's atomic arsenal prepared as many of the 200+ Mark IV and Mark VI atom bombs then available for handover to SAC bombers and transports that would carry them to forward bases for impending use against targets in the Soviet Union.

By Tuesday, mass movements of SAC aircraft were well underway across the US.[1] B-29s from the vaunted 509th BG at Walker AFB, NM, and the 301st BG at Barksdale AFB, LA, headed to Kindley AB, Bermuda, for refueling prior to their final departure for the UK. A few units deployed to Eielson AFB in Alaska (it was not a state at this time). In all, a total of seven Bombardment Groups, one Fighter Group (FG), one Reconnaissance Group (RG), and five atom-bomb assembly teams were en route to eight destinations in England via staging bases at Goose AB and EA Harmon AFB (both in Labrador, Canada), Andrews AFB, MD, Kindley AB, and Lajes Field, the Azores. The first airplanes arrived in the UK on Thursday, E+3. By Saturday, every unit (aside from stragglers) was in place.

NOTE

1 Source: 'Commander's Conference, United States Air Force', Ramey Air Force Base, 25-26-27 April 1950, TOP SECRET, 21 April 1950. Declassified 1 December 2006, National Archives and Records Agency (NARA)

B-29s such as 42-93951 from the 2nd BG at Hunter AFB would be among those sent to English bases as part of the OFFTACKLE war plan. Non-SADDLETREE bombers like this one would carry only conventional weapons and function as decoys for the atomic carriers.
via Bob Archer

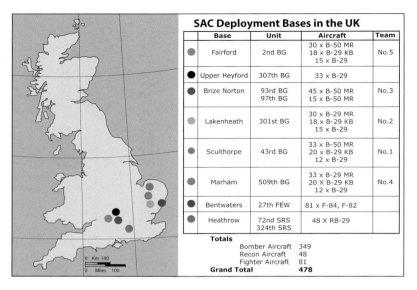

SAC Deployment Bases in the UK

	Base	Unit	Aircraft	Team
●	Fairford	2nd BG	30 x B-50 MR 18 x B-29 KB 15 x B-29	No.5
●	Upper Heyford	307th BG	33 x B-29	
●	Brize Norton	93rd BG 97th BG	45 x B-50 MR 15 x B-50 MR	No.3
●	Lakenheath	301st BG	30 x B-29 MR 18 x B-29 KB 15 x B-29	No.2
●	Sculthorpe	43rd BG	33 x B-50 MR 20 x B-29 KB 12 x B-29	No.1
●	Marham	509th BG	33 x B-29 MR 20 x B-29 KB 12 x B-29	No.4
●	Bentwaters	27th FEW	81 x F-84, F-82	
●	Heathrow	72nd SRS 324th SRS	48 X RB-29	

Totals

Bomber Aircraft	349	
Recon Aircraft	48	
Fighter Aircraft	81	
Grand Total	**478**	

NOTE

2 B-29MR indicated 'modified ruralist' aircraft. Although this appears in some SAC documents, this designation was not used on the aircraft record cards. It is used here to distinguish these receiver-equipped B-29s from standard B-29As.

On paper, this 'English Armada' included 186 of the planned 225 GEM (previously SILVERPLATE and SADDLETREE) atomic-capable 'B-29MRs'[2] and B-50A/Ds, 87 conventional B-29As, 76 KB-29M tankers, 48 RB-29A reconnaissance airplanes, and 81 F-82s and F-84 fighters supported by 17 C-54s and 10 C-97s. In addition, a handful of SAC's 27 new B-36s would launch from Eielson AFB, Goose AB, or Rapid City AFB, SD, and recover in England or the Middle East. In reality, however, the numbers were much less. Shortages of parts and skilled maintenance personnel limited the in-service rate of SAC's aircraft at times to as low as 51% across the command. How many operationally ready airplanes actually reached England was unknown to SAC's commanders, but was likely around 300 (little more than half of the planned 505), the result of maintenance issues, breakdowns, and the inevitability of a few crashes along the way.

Once in England, crews tried to sleep, eat, and study their EWP missions while their airplanes were refueled, armed, and repaired as needed. Low maintenance reliability was not the only concern of SAC war planners. Although flight crew experience had improved since the February 1949 series of MAXIMUM EFFORT missions against targets that included the infamous 'raid' on Dayton, OH, there was still a considerable way to go before reaching the operational levels expected by LeMay. SAC planners were equally concerned about the RAF staging bases. Three of them – RAF Fairford, RAF Upper Heyford, and RAF Brize Norton – had 6,000ft (1,829m) runways which were 'inadequate for B-29 operations and extremely marginal for B-50s.' The runway at RAF Bentwaters was 'inadequate' for F-84Es 'operating with four external fuel tanks,' essential to provide the range necessary to accompany SAC bombers (none of the F-84s at the time were actually configured to carry four external tanks, but this did not obviate the problem). In all cases, plans were underway to lengthen the runways, but 'considerable time' would be required to complete this work. With war at hand, these plans were moot. Lodging and messing facilities for arriving SAC personnel, as well as support equipment were sufficient only at RAF Lakenheath, RAF Sculthorpe, and RAF Marham. Security at all bases was limited to 'only a few 50 calibre guns and no concrete plans…for fighter cover and ground troops for protection against sabotage.' SAC estimated that it would take '30 days warning to set up an antiaircraft defense for the bases.' Fuel lines that connected tank farms with air bases were not in use, compelling delivery by lorries and railroads, both of which were inefficient and vulnerable to attack by saboteurs and fifth columnists.

Early in the morning on E+6, Sunday, 30th April, 201 B-29 and B-50 bombers carrying both atomic and conventional bombs, as well as KB-29 tankers, departed from RAF Fairford and RAF Brize Norton. Of these, 112 flew northeast, approaching the USSR from 'South-

SAC would launch its B-36s from bases in the US, Alaska, and Guam to strike Soviet targets during OFFTACKLE. Many of these would recover to England for reconstitution and second strikes. *via Dennis Jenkins*

Air refueling was essential to SAC's EWP. Early methods, such as the looped-hose seen here with 7th BG KB-29M 45-21788 (upper) refueling a 509th BG B-29MR (lower), were risky and led to SAC's adoption of the 'flying boom' on its KB-29Ps, KC-97s, KC-135s, and KC-10s. *Photo BW38524 courtesy Boeing*

ern Scandinavia and Southern Finland', with penetration of the Soviet border 'occurring in the area northeast of Leningrad.' The remaining 89 headed southeast, crossing 'Central France, Central Italy, and the Southern Balkans,' entering Soviet airspace along the 'Black Sea area.' Mission timing was critical to ensure that 'the northern force [crossed] Southern Scandinavia [just as] the southern force [crossed] Greece', enabling the simultaneous penetration of Soviet borders between 1905Z and 1950Z [7:05-7:50 PM, Greenwich Mean Time (GMT or Zulu)] to overwhelm Soviet air defenses

and command and control facilities. Given the added distance involved, the southern force did not benefit from fighter escort. SAC had estimated the need for four fighter groups to cover OFFTACKLE bombers, but the additional requirement to provide air base defense cover back in the UK meant that the lone SAC fighter wing that deployed was woefully inadequate.

The two prongs aimed at 29 'target areas', with the first attacks using conventional weapons to hit peripheral targets such as air defense bases that hosted interceptors and rudimentary

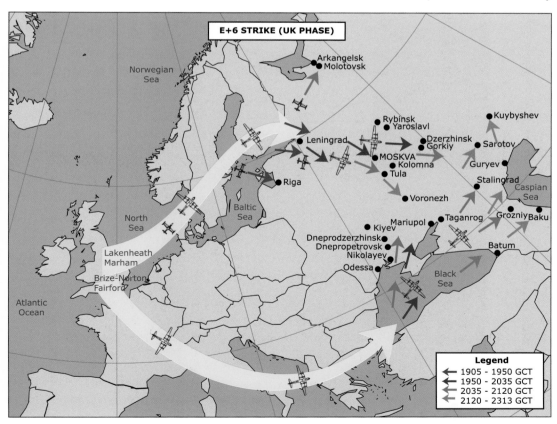

OFFTACKLE dispensed with dense bomber formations in favor of carefully timed cells of 4 or 5 B-29s with conventional weapons to attack Soviet defenses while screening a lone atom bomb carrier. *Jim Webb collection*

early warning radars. Some 45 minutes later, additional strikes on seven target areas took place, including the first with atomic weapons. Five more areas were attacked over the next hour, with the final target group struck by midnight in London (0300Z in Moscow).

Each bomber cell included only a *single* 'A-carrier' plus two to four conventionally armed bombers, flying one minute apart. The B-29s carrying standard high-explosive (HE) bombs attacked Soviet defenses and priority targets such as military bases, railyards and transiting facilities, and areas easily suited for collateral destruction by the ensuing fire from HE explosions (interestingly, none of SAC's bombers attacked invading Soviet ground forces in Europe). Moreover, they functioned as bait or decoys to attract Soviet fighters, allowing the lone atom bomber to continue unimpeded.

Following their missions, the surviving northern bombers returned to England while the surviving southern bombers withdrew 'to staging bases in the Middle East,' notably Dhahran in Saudi Arabia, Karachi in Pakistan, and Cairo in Egypt. Without knowing how many aircraft survived the first strike, SAC planners prepared for a second wave of attacks launched from these forward bases to take place 'not later than E+9' – Wednesday 3rd May. Doubts about the availability of fuel, maintenance, and even weapons at these staging bases meant that many of the aircraft which launched from the UK were of questionable use for a return strike.

SAC also was keenly aware that its English bases were highly vulnerable, especially in the face of Soviet attacks launched from captured bases in Western Europe. Planners optimistically wrote, 'If United Kingdom bases remain tenable, it is planned to complete strikes against 123 targets within a period of 30 days.' Unlike the Second World War, there were no mass-produced bombers, tankers, and fighters to replace those lost in combat. Unconverted B-29s could not substitute for GEM B-29s or B-50s, limiting the number of targets to be struck by atomic weapons. Even the quantity of Mk IV and Mark VI atom bombs was limited, and SAC could ill afford to lose any from ineffective missions, combat losses, missed targets, or even flying accidents (for example, a GEM B-36 on a routine flight jettisoned its Mk IV in the Pacific Ocean before crashing in British Columbia on 15th February 1950). Post-strike BDA and pre-strike reconnaissance of new targets for a second strike were equally problematic. SAC estimated these missions would require 750 sorties using four wings, double the number of RB-29s deployed to England.

Based on the results of prior exercises, SAC imagined that only 49% of all OFFTACKLE bombs would actually hit their targets, with a circular error probable (CEP) of between 2,500-3,000ft (762-914m). Using Hiroshima-scale damage planning for the atom bomb, this resulted in only 32% of targets being 'completely destroyed', 37% of targets 'moderately to severely damaged,' and an amazingly high 17% of targets 'with no appreciable damage' whatsoever. Conventional bomb damage was even worse. America's initial atomic strike on the Soviet Union, conducted almost exclusively from bases in the United Kingdom, was of dubious success.

The Reality

Despite SAC's optimistic plans to fulfill OFFTACKLE, the reality for this imaginary scenario was far different. Early US war plans such as PINCHER assumed the pace of any war with the USSR would be similar to that of the Second World War. For the first *12 months* of such a war, the US and its allies would devote their resources to halting Soviet advances while maintaining control of Sicily, Cyprus, Western Turkey, and the British Isles. Over the next 12 months the West would reduce Soviet war potential by conventional strategic bombing deep within the USSR. From E+24 to E+36 months, the US and NATO would somehow repeat the German invasion of Western Russia – this time successfully – forcing the capitulation of the Soviet leadership, followed by another 12 months consolidating control over an occupied (but suddenly free and astonishingly democratic) Russia.

Initial US war plans that utilized atomic bombs, such as BROILER and FROLIC, were far too idealistic given the shortage of 'special weapons' and long-range airplanes to deliver them. For example, FROLIC, which was approved on 17th March 1948, warned 'of the grave military weakness of the United States' based on these inadequacies. The plan called for the delivery of atom bombs on the USSR beginning on E+15 *days* (as opposed to PINCHER's *months*) from bases in the UK and on E+30 days from the base at Karachi. With only 56 Mark IV bombs, approximately 100 SILVERPLATE B-29s, and some 90 qualified crews available in 1948, the logistics alone of FROLIC were grossly unrealistic. As historian Steven T Ross notes in his 1996 book *American War Plans, 1945-1950*, even with atomic weapons FROLIC planners were especially doubtful of their ability 'to secure the British Isles as a strategic base complex.' Without access to British bases and extensive fuel stocks, the chances of success for any war plan against the USSR were abysmally low.

The ensuing OFFTACKLE plan, submitted on 8th November 1949, recognized similar weaknesses, especially of inadequate airplanes and spare parts, as well as the projected shortage of aviation fuel. Although OFFTACKLE discounted the threat of a Soviet sea-borne invasion of the British Isles, it was downright alarmist at the prospect of Soviet air attacks against England. US and Allied planners calculated that by E+2 months the USSR would drop between 12-16,000 tons of bombs *per month* and conduct 11,000 fighter sorties against Great Britain. To defend against this threat required 144

antiaircraft regiments and 1,152 fighters. Britain could muster only 107 antiaircraft regiments and 232 fighters, with the difference made up of American guns and airplanes pulled from other key regions, effectively yielding those areas to Soviet forces. Much to the chagrin of the US Navy, joint war planners assumed that its carriers would be assigned to protect England, placing them at considerable risk while operating in the narrow confines of the North Sea adjacent to Britain or off the west coast of France given the limited range of Navy fighters.

OFFTACKLE initially called for SAC to begin atomic bombing as soon as sufficient bombers and bombs were available and in place. By E+3 months, SAC would strike 104 Soviet cities with 220 atom bombs, with 72 special weapons held in reserve. Planners naively expected that additional atomic bombs and newly built B-36 and B-50 bombers could be produced at rates approaching those at the height of the Second World War. In addition, they ignored the issue of SAC conducting bombing operations from England against Western European targets captured by the Soviets and Russian targets west of the Urals *in addition to* simultaneous commitments to bomb targets in the Soviet Far East and the newly problematic 'Red China' from bases in the Pacific. With its limited bombers, atomic weapons, and poor operational readiness, SAC could barely fulfill its atomic strike mission from the UK let alone mount a global atomic air offensive.

In a 1950 iteration, produced following the 29th August 1949 detonation of a Soviet atomic bomb, OFFTACKLE (which subsequently became DROPSHOT) called for an additional 19 American and seven British heavy and medium bombardment groups totaling 780 bombers (twice SAC's existing inventory), 144 photo reconnaissance aircraft, and 72 weather reconnaissance airplanes to support the BRAVO mis-

The shortage of atomic weapons, SILVERPLATE/SADDLETREE B-29s to carry them, and the number of qualified crews limited SAC's nuclear strike capability. In an atomic war, there would be no mass production of replacement weapons or bombers. *Author's collection*

Right: SAC lacked an organic weather capability such as this WB-29, forcing it to use a small number of its limited strike aircraft as weather scouts until the arrival of the RB-47K. *Author's collection*

sion, the 'blunting' of any Soviet atomic strike force poised against the United States and its allies. Some 75-100 atom bombs would be dropped on atomic research and assembly points, storage and transit facilities, and heavy bomber bases, nearly none of which were even known to target planners. In addition, DROPSHOT directed attacks on the Soviet power grid and industrial base to cripple Soviet wartime production. Again, these target locations were hardly known and there were insufficient airplanes and atom bombs in the US arsenal to satisfy global strikes against the USSR. Indeed, during the first 30 days of DROPSHOT, SAC and RAF Bomber Command airplanes were envis-

aged to drop 453 atom bombs on Soviet targets. When DROPSHOT was first proposed there was a total of 512 bombers in SAC (with an in-service rate below 60%) and only 159 special weapons in the world. With the exception of the new B-36 (which suffered from considerable teething problems) SAC's bombers lacked the range to reach targets from the United States, requiring forward deployed bases in the United Kingdom, North Africa, the Middle East, Guam, and Okinawa. With US policy clearly favoring the reconstruction and defense of Western Europe, English air bases were the only solution to support a strategic air armada.

TYPES OF BOMBER DEPLOYMENT TO THE UK

SAC bomber deployments to the United Kingdom evolved considerably. Beginning in 1946, 'casual' visits from bases in West Germany shifted to lengthy rotations of entire wings, then reduced in number and frequency to orientation trips, and finally ended in 1991 with combat operations not against the USSR but against Iraq. In most cases, only one specific type of airplane was involved.

Group Deployments – Early visits, usually by portions of bomb groups (sometimes just a few airplanes) for familiarization with UK operations. Both a diplomatic show of force (most famously during 1946 and 1948) and a 'goodwill' public relations effort.

90-Day Rotations – Mass movement of entire groups (or wings after mid 1950), often three squadrons totaling 45+ bombers as well as an accompanying squadron of KB-29 or KC-97 tankers, to British bases for a three-month tour of temporary duty (TDY). This program demonstrated SAC's ability to relocate medium bombers and their supporting units (such as maintenance) from US

bases to forward areas on short notice in preparation for strikes against Soviet and Warsaw Pact targets. Initial rotations carried atomic bombs minus their nuclear components, but these were later stockpiled in the UK for arriving bombers.

Post-Strike Exercises – B-36 recovery in the UK after a simulated strike launched from US bases to targets in Europe. These did not carry nuclear weapons or components Although B-47 units conducted similar missions, this was the only type of routine deployment by B-36s to the UK.

REFLEX ACTION – A small number of B-47s (2-3 airplanes) from multiple wings deployed weekly to SAC bases in the UK (as well as North Africa) for 21 days, resulting in a maximum of 6 airplanes from a specific wing at each base always on alert. Rotating aircraft did not carry nuclear weapons or components, but were loaded and placed in a 'cocked' configuration upon arrival.

ALARM BELL – B-52, and rarely B-58, orientation visits for post-strike familiarization by SAC ground crews and

weaponeers in the UK. No nuclear weapons were carried. These differed from B-36 post-strike exercises in that ALARM BELL was usually a direct flight from the US to the UK (or Spain, thence to England) and did not include a simulated strike on a European target. In later years, these were largely 'incentive' flights for SAC bomber crews to visit the UK (something which their co-located tanker crews did on a regular basis, leading to decreased morale among bomber crews that had deployed only to Southeast Asia).

BUSY BREWER/WARRIOR – SAC commitment to support NATO conventional operations in Europe. Deployments were not limited to UK bases, and included visits to other NATO installations while some performed non-stop round-trip sorties from bases in the continental US.

DESERT STORM – Ten B-52Gs deployed to RAF Fairford (in conjunction with those to Morón AB, Spain) to conduct strike operations against Iraq as part of Operation DESERT STORM.

One of the first SAC B-29s in England was 44-84096 from the 341st BS, 97th BW, seen in June 1947 at RAF Marham. This was a 'courtesy' visit as the unit was then deployed to Fürstenfeldbruck AB in West Germany. This base was too close to Soviet ground forces, so SAC wisely sought to relocate its bombers to the UK. *via Steve Bond*

Berlin '48

Beginning in 1946, SAC's European bomber deployments rotated to Fürstenfeldbruck AB and Wiesbaden AB in West Germany, although a handful of these B-29s occasionally crossed the Channel to the UK for brief 'orientation' and 'goodwill' visits beginning in June 1947, and again in April 1948. Post-war stresses between East and West boiled over two months later into an international crisis that prompted the first operational deployment of SAC bombers to England.

Following the end of the war in Europe, the Allies created a *de facto* partition of the remains of the German Reich. The Soviet Union controlled the eastern half, including the capital of Berlin. Britain and the United States were responsible for 'Bizonia' in the west, which later became 'Trizonia' with the addition of France. Berlin was similarly partitioned, with ground access from the western zones by rail. As tensions increased between the USSR and the West over economic and political matters related to Germany, its partitioning, and the reconstruction of Europe via the Marshall Plan, the Soviets began regulating access to Berlin. By March 1948 these issues resulted in Soviet restrictions on rail movement from the West into Berlin. On 24th June a currency crisis led the Soviets to impose a complete ban on travel to and from Berlin, and the following day they blockaded all food deliveries to West Berlin.

American leaders rejected an initial plan by then-US Air Forces Europe (USAFE) Commander Lieutenant General LeMay that called for 301st BG B-29s, on deployment in West Germany, to threaten Soviet airfields while ground forces moved toward Berlin. Instead, General Lucius D Clay, Commander-in-Chief, US Forces in Europe and military governor of the American zone in West Germany, directed an airlift of food, coal, medicine, and other supplies via the three air corridors to Berlin. LeMay obliged, and ordered the start of the Berlin Airlift on 26th June.

Concurrently, SAC's commander, General George C Kenney, alerted B-29s from the 28th BG and 307th BG for deployment to the UK. By July, plans were in place to put 60 B-29s in England – 30 at RAF Scampton, 20 at RAF Marham, and 10 at RAF Waddington as part of Operation FERRYBOAT. The 307th BG reached

Above: B-29s from the 307th BG reached RAF Marham in July 1948 as part of Operation FERRYBOAT, sharing the ramp with RAF Lincolns during the Berlin Crisis. None of these were configured to carry atomic weapons, but the message was clear. *Terry Panopalis collection*

Top and middle: The arrival of SAC's Superfortresses prompted no end of interest by the British, in this case a 353rd BS, 301st BG B-29. A planned visit in 1950 by the King and Queen was canceled because a US officer 'contracted polio,' but it was more likely a security issue related to the start of the Korean War. *Jim Webb collection*

Below: The 301st BG sent 30 B-29s from Smoky Hill AFB to RAF Scampton beginning in October 1948. B-29s from the 32nd BS had yellow tail markings and nose gear doors, while those from the 353rd used blue. *Jim Webb collection*

RAF Marham during 16th-19th July, and the 28th BG arrived at RAF Scampton between 17th-19th July. There were concerns that the runway at RAF Scampton was too short to allow the B-29s to operate at maximum gross weight, limiting their range, so the 20 B-29s at RAF Marham were apparently allocated to the farthest targets. To ensure that the Soviet leadership understood American resolve, B-29s took part in a mass flyover of British cities on 29th July. Distinguished visitors to RAF Marham included General Vandenberg and US Secretary of the Air Force W Stuart Symington, underscoring the importance of SAC's bomber force in American diplomacy. [It is worth noting that *none* of these B-29s were SADDLETREE/ GEM configured. Two 509th BG Stratofortresses (44-86430 and 44-27300) had previously stopped at RAF Manston in March 1948 and were the first atomic-capable – but unarmed – B-29s in England.]

Additional B-29s deployed to the UK in August when the 2nd BG arrived at RAF Lakenheath, prompting an inspection by Air Marshal Tedder. The 28th BG departed for South Dakota in October, and was promptly replaced by the 301st BG at RAF Scampton, bringing the total number of B-29s in England to nine squadrons.

SAC flew practice missions to bombing ranges at Heligoland, Otmore in Oxfordshire, and Wainfleet in Lincolnshire. November saw additional arrivals, with the 97th BG split between RAF Marham and RAF Waddington and the 22nd BG at RAF Lakenheath. Crowded ramps and the earlier concerns about the runway at RAF Scampton prompted plans to relocate the B-29s there and at RAF Waddington to RAF Sculthorpe in 1949. These operations were not without risk, as three B-29s were lost in England and one during its return to America while passing through the Azores.

Although tensions over Berlin decreased in 1949, SAC bomber rotations continued, including the first deployment to RAF Sculthorpe in February with 92nd BG B-29s. It is worth emphasizing that all of these (and subsequent) movements until 1958 were 'training rotations' and airplanes were not placed 'on alert' when they arrived in the UK. Should the situation require, they could be prepared for the EWP mission and launched if and when so directed. Most notable among these movements was the arrival a week before the end of the Berlin Airlift on 12th May 1949 of the entire 509th BG from Roswell AFB, one of SAC's two atomic-capable units, with two squadrons at RAF

SAC BOMBER UNIT ROTATIONS TO THE UK, 1948-1953

From	To	Unit	Aircraft	Deployment Base(s)
17 Jul 48	4 Nov 48	307th BG	B-29A	RAF Marham, RAF Waddington
18 Jul 48	18 Oct 48	28th BG	B-29A	RAF Scampton
11 Aug 48	17 Nov 48	2nd BG	B-29A	RAF Lakenheath
19 Oct 48	19 Jan 49	301st BG	B-29A	RAF Scampton
4 Nov 48	17 Feb 49	97th BG	B-29A	RAF Marham, RAF Waddington
19 Nov 48	14 Feb 49	22nd BG	B-29A	RAF Lakenheath
9 Feb 49	18 May 49	92nd BG	B-29A	RAF Sculthorpe
17 Feb 49	10 Apr 49	307th BG	B-29A	RAF Lakenheath, RAF Marham
4 May 49	30 Aug 49	509th BG	B-29A	RAF Lakenheath, RAF Marham
18 May 49	18 Aug 49	98th BG	B-29A	RAF Sculthorpe
20 Aug 49	18 Nov 49	43rd BG	B-50A	RAF Sculthorpe, RAF Marham, RAF Lakenheath
20 Nov 49	18 Feb 50	22nd BG	B-29A	RAF Lakenheath, RAF Marham
21 Feb 50	15 May 50	2nd BG	B-29A, B-50D	RAF Sculthorpe, RAF Marham, RAF Lakenheath
19 May 50	1 Dec 50	301st BW	B-29A	RAF Lakenheath, RAF Sculthorpe, RAF Bassingbourn
15 Jul 50	1 Feb 51	93rd BW	B-50D	RAF Mildenhall, RAF Marham, RAF Wyton, RAF Fairford, RAF Lakenheath
20 Jul 50	9 Feb 51	97th BW	B-50D	RAF Sculthorpe, RAF Wyton, RAF Waddington, RAF Valley, RAF Oakington, RAF Bassingbourn
4 Feb 51	4 May 51	509th BW	B-29A, B-50D	RAF Mildenhall, RAF Lakenheath, RAF Sculthorpe
4 May 51	31 Aug 51	2nd BW	B-50D	RAF Mildenhall, RAF Bassingbourn, RAF Wyton
5 Sep 51	4 Dec 51	22nd BW	B-29A	RAF Sculthorpe, RAF Wyton, RAF Lakenheath, RAF Mildenhall
6 Dec 51	6 Mar 52	93rd BW	B-50D	RAF Lakenheath, RAF Mildenhall
15 Mar 52	11 Jun 52	97th BW	B-50D	RAF Lakenheath
4 Jun 52	2 Sep 52	509th BW	B-50D	RAF Lakenheath, RAF Mildenhall
10 Oct 52	4 Dec 52	2nd BW	B-50D	RAF Upper Heyford
3 Dec 52	4 Mar 53	301st BW	B-29A	RAF Brize Norton, RAF Upper Heyford
10 Mar 53	5 Jun 53	43rd BW	B-50A	RAF Brize Norton

Above: Interestingly, when the 2nd BG deployed to England in February 1950, it brought 24 B-50As and 6 B-29, including 42-65274 *Bad Penny*. The Group returned to Georgia in May, just prior to the beginning of the Korean War. *Author's collection (top), via Bob Archer (middle and bottom)*

Below: B-50Ds were increasingly common after 1950, but other than RB-50s were gone from English skies by June 1953. *Alan Scholefield*

Marham and one at RAF Lakenheath. All 31 of these were SADDLETREE/GEM configured for air refueling as well as capable of carrying atomic bombs. From 25th June through 3rd July, these B-29s served as 'attacking forces' in Operation Foil, an RAF air defense exercise. Unfortunately, SAC's B-29s were suffering from engine problems, grounding much of the fleet. Consequently, the 509th BG was replaced in August by SAC's other atomic-capable unit, the 43rd BG and 21 of its GEM B-50As. Once again, SAC hosted multiple high-profile visitors at its bases in Britain, including the Queen Mother at RAF Sculthorpe, along with British Secretary of State for Air Arthur Henderson and 'Father of the RAF' Lord Trenchard at RAF Marham.

Although these two deployments involved atomic-capable B-29s and B-50s, no weapons were transferred to the UK for their use. Moreover, the influence of SAC's bomber presence in England on the outcome of the Berlin Crisis has never been quantified. In the minds of SAC's commanders as well as American and British officials the bombers certainly contributed to its peaceful resolution. 'Atomic diplomacy', however defined, seemed to work, and would be used again in 1950 with the outbreak of war on the other side of the world.

Atomic Weapons Arrive

As the sun rose in Korea on 25th June 1950, a heavy artillery barrage by communist Democratic People's Republic of Korea preceded an invasion of the Republic of Korea all along the 38th Parallel dividing the two countries. South Korean forces were ill prepared for the onslaught, and two days later the capitol Seoul fell to North Korean invaders. Despite an immediate call by the United Nations Security Council to provide military assistance to defend South Korea, it was not until 27th June that the Truman administration, satisfied that an American response would not provoke a Soviet military reaction in Asia, approved the deployment of US ground, naval, and air forces to South Korea.

SAC's B-29 deployments to the UK during the 1948 Berlin Crisis provided operational experience to move B-29s and B-36 – this time including atomic weapons – from the ZI to Japan and Guam. Concerns among senior administration officials, however, raised the possibility that the outbreak of war on the Korean peninsula was merely a diversion for an impending Soviet attack on Western Europe. There was scant evidence to support this claim, but SAC responded by sending two atomic-

SAC ATOMIC WEAPONS IN THE UK

Storing atomic weapons in the UK fell to innocuously named Aviation Field Depot Squadrons (AFDS), which were later redesignated as Aviation Depot Squadrons (ADS), and ultimately to the more appropriately labeled Munitions Maintenance Squadrons (MMS). As bases were added or removed from the Emergency War Plan (EWP) these units relocated accordingly. Construction of these facilities had begun by 1949 as the first atomic-capable bombardment groups began rotating to England, and were located at RAF Lakenheath, RAF Sculthorpe, and RAF Marham.

The mission of these squadrons was to support SAC's 'special weapons program', specifically to 'maintain operational proficiency in the storage, surveillance, handling, assembly, and loading of atomic weapons.' They also provided training in 'atomic, biological, and chemical warfare' defenses. One unit, the 99th ADS, had the unique requirement to 'equip and train

assigned detachments to receive, maintain, and retain custody and operational release, on proper authority, US weapons and missile re-entry vehicles, which [were] allocated to RAF Bomber Command.' In addition to their atomic weapons, these units also coordinated the acquisition and storage of conventional high-explosive (HE) bombs provided by the RAF.

Despite – or perhaps because of – the extremely sensitive nature of their mission, these squadrons suffered from the same ills as other SAC units in the UK. The 2nd AFDS, for example, reported in October 1952 that personnel complained of 'low morale' due to excessive additional duties such as 'change-of-quarters, kitchen police, officer-of-the-day, mess checker, and [conducting] various inventories.' These precluded personnel from 'regular assignments for excessive lengths of time.' The following month the 8th AFDS undertook a 'severe crackdown on personnel who [had] bad debts'.

Atomic weapons did not arrive in the UK until July 1950 following the start of the Korean War. They were carried by B-50As of the 97th BG and 93rd BG, which brought them from storage facilities in the US and Canada. Atomic-capable B-29s from the 301st BG were already in the UK at the onset of the war, although the question remains as to how any atomic weapons they might have used were delivered to the UK. At least one source suggests there were 89 atomic weapons (minus their nuclear cores) in the UK by the end of July 1950. As the two deployed B-50 units totaled some 80 airplanes, one explanation might be the rotation from the US of specific B-50s as they underwent upgrades, with additional weapons brought during these singular movements. Other sources show that SAC's newly acquired C-124s arrived at RAF Lakenheath in late July, quite possibly carrying additional Mark IVs, which appears to be a far more likely explanation.

B-29s from the 92nd BG deployed to RAF Sculthorpe in February 1949, transiting via Kindley AB, but with several diversions to RAF Lyneham and RAF St Eval.
Photo HS1556 courtesy Boeing

The 22nd BG sent B-29s to the UK in 1949 and again in 1951 following its deployment to Kadena AB in 1950 (seen here) for combat operations in Korea. While in the UK during 1949, the unit provided familiarization training for future RAF Washington crews.
Photo HS1560-1 courtesy Boeing

SAC ATOMIC DEPOTS IN THE UK

Base	Unit	From	To	Weapons Stored as of 30 June 1958*
RAF Brize Norton	4th AFDS	6 Jul 51	8 Nov 54	
RAF Brize Norton	4th ADS	8 Nov 54	15 Oct 55	
RAF Brize Norton	2nd ADS	6 Jun 56	1 Jul 60	Mk 6, Mk 36 Mod 1
RAF Brize Norton	2nd MMS	1 Jul 60	Mar 65	
RAF Bruntingthorpe	Det 1 11th ADS	n/a	1 Feb 59	
RAF Bruntingthorpe	80th ADS	1 Feb 59	1 Sep 59	
RAF Chelveston	Det 1 ? ADS	n/a	1 Feb 59	
RAF Chelveston	? ADS	1 Feb 59	1 Sep 59	
RAF Fairford	2nd AFDS	19 May 51	8 Nov 54	
RAF Fairford	2nd ADS	8 Nov 54	6 Jun 56	
RAF Fairford	Det 1 1st ADS	Oct 57	1 Jun 58	
RAF Fairford	Det 1 4th ADS	1 Jun 58	1 Dec 58	Mk 36 Mod 1
RAF Fairford	Det 1 2nd ADS	1 Dec 58	1 Jan 59	
RAF Fairford	9th ADS	1 Jan 59	1 Jul 60	
RAF Fairford	9th MMS	1 Jul 60	Jun 64	
RAF Greenham Common	Det 1 8th AFDS	n/a	15 Oct 53	
RAF Greenham Common	8th AFDS	16 Oct 53	14 Jun 54	
RAF Greenham Common	4th ADS	15 Oct 55	1 Jul 60	Mk 6, Mk 39 Mod 0, Mk 36 Mod 1
RAF Greenham Common	4th MMS	1 Jul 60	Jun 64	
RAF Lakenheath	8th AFDS	26 Nov 51	16 Oct 53	
RAF Lakenheath	8th AFDS	14 Jun 54	8 Nov 54	
RAF Lakenheath	8th AFDS	8 Nov 54	14 Apr 55	
RAF Lakenheath	8th ADS	14 Apr 55	1 Oct 59	Mk 6, Mk 7 Mod 5†
RAF Mildenhall	Det 1 8th ADS	n/a	1 Feb 59	Mk 39 Mod 0
RAF Mildenhall	19th ADS	1 Feb 59	1 Sep 59	
RAF Upper Heyford	1st AFDS	19 May 51	8 Nov 54	
RAF Upper Heyford	1st ADS	8 Nov 54	1 May 58	
RAF Upper Heyford	Det 2 1st ADS	1 Jun 58	1 Dec 58	None recorded
RAF Upper Heyford	11th ADS	1 Dec 58	1 Jul 60	
RAF Upper Heyford	11th MMS	1 Jul 60	30 Apr 65	
Joint SAC-UK Atomic Weapons Depots				
RAF Lakenheath	99th ADS	23 May 58	20 Dec 63	
RAF Honington (V-Bombers)	Det X 99th ADS	1 Jun 58	1 Jul 61	
RAF Marham (V-Bombers)	Det Y 99th ADS	1 Jun 58	20 Dec 63	
RAF Waddington (V-Bombers)	Det Z 99th ADS	1 Jun 58	30 Mar 62	
RAF Feltwell Sites (Thor IRBMs)	Det Q 99th ADS	1 Oct 59	1 Jul 60	
	Det Q 99th MMS	1 Jul 60	1 Apr 63	
RAF Hemswell Sites (Thor IRBMs)	Det R 99th ADS	1 Oct 59	1 Jul 60	
	Det R 99th MMS	1 Jul 60	5 May 63	
RAF Driffield Sites (Thor IRBMs)	Det S 99th ADS	1 Oct 59	1 Jul 60	
	Det S 99th MMS	1 Jul 60	1963	
RAF North Luffenham Sites (Thor IRBMs)	Det T 99th ADS	1 Oct 59	1 Jul 60	
	Det T 99th MMS	1 Jul 60	15 Aug 63	

* Source: *History of the Strategic Air Command, 1 January - 30 June 1958*, SAC Historical Study No 73, Vol I, pp 89-90. Declassified under FOIA 95-33 by Hans M Kristensen; † Mk 7 stored for CINCEUR; ‡ No nuclear material; MMS = Munitions Maintenance Squadron; AFDS = Aviation Field Depot Squadron; ADS = Aviation Depot Squadron

capable B-50 units to the UK just in case, bringing their atomic bombs with them.

The 301st BG had previously arrived at RAF Lakenheath on 15th May, with an additional squadron reaching RAF Sculthorpe three days later. This was the first time that a full total of 45 bombers plus a refueling squadron had rotated to the UK. Following the outbreak of war, the 301st BG prepared for imminent operations, although only with conventional weapons. A

planned trip by King George VI and Queen Elizabeth (the same Queen Mother) to inspect the B-29s at RAF Lakenheath on 26th June was cancelled, ostensibly because an American officer there had contracted polio, likely used as a smoke screen for sudden security increases.

The 97th BG from Biggs AFB was the first SAC bomber unit to deploy to the UK in response to the Korean War, as well as being the initial rotation of the B-50D to England. The airplanes

OTHER SAC ATOMIC WEAPONS DEPOTS

Base	Unit	From	To	Weapons Stored as of 30 June 1958*
Torrejón AB, Spain	1st ADS	1 May 58	1 Jul 60	Mk 6, Mk 36 Mod 1
	1st MMS	1 Jul 60	30 Apr 65	
Andersen AFB, Guam	3rd ADS	27 May 51	30 Jun 60	Mk 6, Mk 39 Mod 0, Mk 36 Mod 1
	3rd MMS	1 Jul 60	30 Sep 72	
Sidi Slimane AB, French Morocco	5th ADS	1952	30 Jun 63	Mk 6, Mk 36 Mod 1
Nouasseur AB, French Morocco	6th ADS	Feb 53	30 Jun 63	Mk 6, Mk 36 Mod 1, Mk 7 Mod 4 and 5
Goose AB, Labrador‡	7th ADS	16 Nov 50	n/a	Mk 6§
Ben Guerir AB, French Morocco	10th AFDS	30 Oct 54	30 Jun 63	Mk 6, Mk 36 Mod 1
Sandia Base/Kirtland AFB, NM‡	3rd AFDS	16 Nov 50	26 May 51	
	11th AFDS	n/a	20 Oct 52	
Limestone AFB, ME‡	11th AFDS	20 Oct 52	18 Nov 53	
Thule AB, Greenland	11th ADS	n/a	n/a	Mk6, Mk36 Mod 1§
Kadena AB, Okinawa	12th ADS	n/a	1 Oct 59	Mk 6, Mk 39 Mod 0
Zaragoza AB, Spain	13th ADS	12 Mar 58	1 Jul 60	Mk 6, Mk 39 Mod 0
	13th MMS	1 Jul 60	30 Jun 64	
Eielson AFB, AK	14th ADS	27 Jul 56	n/a	Mk 6, Mk 39 Mod 0, Mk 36 Mod 1
Morón AB, Spain	15th ADS	n/a	31 Mar 65	Mk 36 Mod 1
Elmendorf AFB, AK	73rd ADS	18 May 59	n/a	

* Source: *History of the Strategic Air Command, 1 January - 30 June 1958*, SAC Historical Study No 73, Vol I, pp 89-90. Declassified under FOIA 95-33 by Hans M Kristensen; ‡ Weapons from these facilities were collected by SAC bombers en route to the UK; § No nuclear material; MMS = Munitions Maintenance Squadron; AFDS = Aviation Field Depot Squadron; ADS = Aviation Depot Squadron

arrived at RAF Sculthorpe beginning 15th July, although they subsequently moved to six other bases during their stay. The 93rd BG at Castle AFB brought its B-50Ds to RAF Mildenhall at the same time, and likewise rotated through multiple bases in England. Interestingly, the 93rd BG swapped its initial 40-plus B-50s throughout its stay for newer airplanes. In all, the 93rd BG rotation accounted for some 80 B-50Ds until their departure in January 1951. To evaluate the suitability of RAF Fairford as an emergency base, nine of the 93rd BG B-50Ds were detached there on 30th December, with a Douglas C-47 serving as the ground station. They departed for RAF Marham on 4th January.

Both B-50D units were replaced in early 1951 with B-29s and B-50Ds from the 509th BW scattered across RAF Lakenheath, RAF Sculthorpe, and RAF Mildenhall. A declassified SAC history reveals the complexity of these rotations. The 509th BW was alerted on 26th January to deploy as part of its EWP mission with a training emphasis on achieving the 'range, profile, weight, bombing altitude, composition, timing, and navigation' needed to strike its targets from bases in the UK. In particular, crews would focus on 'Special Weapons exercises and air-to-air refueling.' The advance team left Roswell AFB on 29th January, with the planned departure 'E-Day' scheduled for 31st January. B-29s from the 393rd BS departed on E+1, with the other squadrons following on E+2 and E+3, totaling 24 B-29MRs, nine standard B-29s, four B-50s, and 20 KB-29M tankers. Of these, 51 flew the southern route via Kindley AB and Lajes, with five taking the northern route. Some 1,877 personnel and 346,000 lb (156,943kg) traveled via civilian and MATS transports. In addition, six MATS and one SAC C-54 carried en route support and maintenance teams, unit essential equipment (UEE), and supplies necessary for the trans-Atlantic trip. These 'leapfrogged' the bombers as they made en route stops. Finally, a lone C-54 was used as a weather reconnaissance and control airplane.

What these bombers did while deployed to England is increasingly known thanks to declassified documents. B-50Ds from the 2nd BW, for example, arrived in May 1951 at RAF Wyton,

While at RAF Sculthorpe, B-29 42-65357 participated in three monthly 'maximum effort' exercises, with the 98th BG peaking at an impressive 140 sorties in June 1949.
Photo G1929-1 courtesy Boeing

Right: GEM-configured B-50s from the 97th BW at Biggs AFB deployed via Sandia at Kirtland AFB to collect atomic weapons en route to the UK at the start of the Korean War.
Photo P12281

Below: Crews and airplanes from the 97th BW frequently relocated among seven English bases, no doubt creating a security nightmare for those responsible for the Wing's atomic weapons.
Photo P12205

Opposite page: English weather complicated the task of both flight and maintenance crews. Filling up a B-50 with AvGas was a laborious process.
Photo P12206

Modern notions of an 'alert scramble takeoff' simply didn't exist in 1950. Launches were no different than those of B-17s or B-24s from England in the 1940s, and took hours of preparation and execution.
Photo P12208

The 97th BW returned to Biggs AFB in February 1951, their atomic diplomacy mission fulfilled. The deployment gave SAC valuable experience in the mass movement of atomic strike wings overseas.
Photo P12216
All courtesy Boeing

RAF Mildenhall, and RAF Bassingbourn. While in England, the unit practiced 'six-cell' bombing missions. In these, Alfa, Baker, Charlie, Dog, and Echo cells each had four conventionally equipped B-50s, while Fox was composed of two B-50s with atomic bombs and two 'support' aircraft. Each cell relied heavily on electronic countermeasures (ECM), achieving 'some success' in spot jamming and chaff drops, rendering early-warning, ground-controlled intercept, and gun-laying radars sufficiently ineffective to allow the two Fox atom bombers to penetrate enemy defenses. They also highlighted weaknesses in the B-50's AN/APQ-24 bombing and navigational radar.

The 2nd BW also took part in the NATO OMBRELLE exercise, simulating a surprise Soviet attack across Germany and west of the Rhine River. B-50s 'attacked' targets in Europe to test interceptor coordination among USAFE and NATO forces. Some 287 fighters reacted to the B-50s, but the unit reported 'little or no fighter

interference' while completing its missions. During June, the unit participated in the JUNE BUG training exercise, which stressed formation flying, fighter rendezvous, air refueling, camera gunnery, and night cell tactics, achieving a 98% training effectiveness rating. For example, the B-50s successfully hit 251 radar bombing targets (only 225 were needed to achieve a 'passing' score), resulting in a circular error average CEA of 7,584ft (2,311m) and a CEP of 5,700ft (1,737m). Although the number of targets struck was certainly impressive, the error distances were still far from ideal, reflecting both the progress SAC had made since the dismal days of the late 1940s and the goal it had yet to achieve. Most importantly, these results highlighted the need for better target briefing materials, photo mosaics, town plans, and detailed charts. This would necessitate more reconnaissance units and pre-strike missions as early as E+72 hours.

B-29s from the 22nd BW and B-50s from the 93rd BW rotated to the UK in late 1951. In fact, these continuing rotations were hardly necessary, as the feared Soviet invasion never materialized. Indeed, the 22nd BW was the last non-atomic-capable unit to deploy to England. Nonetheless, these movements gave SAC units the peacetime operational experience it required should war erupt. Consequently, SAC placed considerable emphasis on continuing these full-unit training rotations to England.

Perhaps the most significant event of 1951 was the first UK visit by SAC's giant Peacemaker. B-36Ds from the 7th BG and the 11th BG at Carswell AFB, TX, arrived at RAF Lakenheath, supported by three C-124s carrying parts, supplies, and 195 personnel. This was intended to be the initial assessment of the B-36D under simulated EWP conditions, specifically to 'evalu-

ate airspeed and compression tactics for heavy bombardment aircraft, and to evaluate select crew capability for bombing unfamiliar targets.' A dozen B-36s departed Carswell AFB on 15th January, but heavy snow and bad weather meant that only six of these were able reach Limestone AFB, ME, to refuel and continue to England. Icing forced the remaining six B-36s and two C-97s to return to Carswell AFB. Those that continued reached their target on Heligoland (five hit it successfully) and then onward to the Heston Bomb Plot in Middlesex, achieving a disappointing CEP of 7,593ft (2,314m). They landed at RAF Lakenheath on 16th January, and returned to Carswell AFB on 21st January. Post-mission analysis identified several key shortcomings, most notably icing of the B-36's jet engines during the post-takeoff climb. Additional 7th BW B-36Ds passed through RAF Lakenheath during 29th June through 3rd July. All three (44-92049, 44-92072, and 49-2659) made a low-level pass over London while en route to the Paris Air Show on 1st July, returning to RAF Lakenheath later in the day.

Both of these B-36 deployments were essentially public relations affairs, with the first operational deployment taking place late in the year. Beginning 25th October 1951, seven 28th SRW RB-36Ds operated from RAF Sculthorpe with three goals: '1) to determine the 28th SRW's capability to conduct a simulation of its assigned war plans, 2) to test the RB-36's complete reconnaissance function from initial takeoff through pre-strike staging in the UK, and 3) to test the adequacy of strategic support' for B-36 overseas operations. The airplanes departed Rapid City AFB (it was renamed Ellsworth AFB in 1953) on 23rd October, staging to Goose AB. From there, they flew a simulated photo reconnaissance and strike mission

B-36D 44-92034 from the 11th BG was one of the first six Peacemakers to visit the UK. B-36s were slated for post-strike reconstitution in England, necessitating occasional short stays to familiarize crews with English bases. *via Nick Stroud/TAH*

to French Morocco, landing at RAF Sculthorpe. As the RB-36s passed London they dropped the target radar file imagery by parachute to personnel on the ground at Heathrow Airport, who then delivered it to the reconnaissance technical squadron at RAF West Drayton for analysis. Overall, the 'mission was successful and the Eighth AF felt that it increased the capabilities of the Wing to perform its War Plan mission more than any mission to date.'

For some reason B-36 visits to the UK seemed plagued by misfortune. On 27th January 1952, for example, B-36D 44-92042 arrived at RAF Boscombe Down with four of its 10 engines shut down. Dense fog and inadequate GCA facilities forced B-36H 51-5719 to overshoot RAF Fairford on 7th October 1953. Low on fuel, the crew bailed out and the airplane crashed into a cow field in Wiltshire. This entirely avoidable loss highlighted both the rigidity of SAC procedures and the technological limits of aerial navigation. As British researcher Colin Smith records, "Favorable tail winds had brought the 7th BW aircraft to the UK three hours earlier than planned but, due to the specific demands of their [Unit Simulated Combat

On 1st July 1951, Londoners were treated to the unforgettable sound of three 7th BW B-36Ds en route to overfly the Paris Air Show. Readers need only watch the Jimmy Stewart film *Strategic Air Command* to experience this for themselves. *via Nick Stroud/TAH*

B-36 STAGING EXERCISES TO THE UK, 1951-1956*

From	To	Unit	Aircraft	Deployment Base(s)
16 Jan 51	22 Jan 51	7th/11th BG	B-36D	RAF Lakenheath
29 Jun 51	3 Jul 51	7th BW	B-36D	RAF Lakenheath (Paris Air Show on 1 July)
25 Oct 51	6 Nov 51	28th SRW	RB-36D	RAF Sculthorpe
26 Jan 52		7th BW	B-36D/F	RAF Boscombe Down
27 Jun 52	30 Jun 52	11th BW	B-36D/F/H	RAF Brize Norton
25 Jul 52	31 Jul 52	28th SRW	RB-36H	RAF Upper Heyford
6 Feb 53	14 Feb 53	7th BW	B-36D	RAF Fairford
18 May 54	20 May 54	28th SRW	RB-36H	RAF Fairford
17 Jun 54	26 Jun 54	5th SRW	RB-36H	RAF Upper Heyford
16 Sep 54	23 Sep 54	42nd BW	B-36D/H/J	RAF Upper Heyford, RAF Burtonwood
29 Mar 55	8 Apr 55	42nd BW	B-36D/H/J	RAF Upper Heyford PORT CALL
18 Sep 55	18 Oct 55	42nd BW	B-36D/H/J	Unverified
18 Oct 56	25 Oct 56	11th BW	B-36H/J	RAF Burtonwood

* Excludes ROUNDOUT reconnaissance deployments

With R4360 engines 1, 2, and 6 plus an unspecified jet engine shut down, 44-92034 landed adjacent to the A303 road well short of the runway at RAF Boscombe Down. It was repaired and returned to Carswell AFB. *via Nick Stroud/TAH*

The immense size of this 5th SRW RB-36, seen at RAF Fairford during the winter of 1952-53, shows the concern associated with moving the airplane around British bases. This planning paid off when B-52s arrived. *via Nick Stroud/TAH*

Mission (USCM)], the unit was required to fly a triangular pattern over the UK rather than land early at Fairford. By the time the landings were authorized, visibility had deteriorated at Fairford and … GCA radar landings had become necessary. As the GCAs got underway some aircraft carried out missed approaches and were obliged to rejoin the stack. With 17 machines involved and the GCA facility allegedly limited to approaches as 15-minute intervals, some were soon in trouble with low fuel states. For whatever reason, air traffic control was initially either reluctant or unable to divert aircraft to RAF Brize Norton until the situation became desperate,' resulting in the loss of 51-5719. Deployment crashes on 14th February and 5th August 1953 claimed two more B-36s.

Arguably the most significant result of the B-36 post-strike visits to the UK were the lessons learned in handling very large bombers, invaluable in preparing for SAC B-52 operations.

A Change in Plans

By 1952, SAC was fully committed to integrating its operations in the United Kingdom into its EWP. Plans were underway to increase its total wartime presence in England from 599 to 1,543 aircraft, including 130 post-strike B-36s. The activation of USAFE's 49th AD at RAF Sculthorpe added 35 B-45s and 96 F-84s from Tactical Air Command's (TAC) GALE plan for wartime operations in the UK, complicating SAC's deployments. Shuffling SAC and TAC aircraft around in England during peacetime – known as HOGMANAY in 1952 – led to competition between the commands for limited airfield real estate, especially given the many challenges associated with base construction.

A core component of these new plans was the anticipated introduction of the new jet-powered B-47 into SAC's inventory to replace B-29 and B-50 piston-powered bombers. Plagued

Top: Quite possibly the last B-36 visit to England was RB-36F 49-2720 from the 72nd BW, seen at RAF Greenham Common on 5th September 1957. At the time, the 72nd BW was conducting training flights between Ramey AFB, PR, and Nouasseur AB in preparation for the CURTAIN RAISER airborne nuclear alert test beginning in January 1958. Why it ended up in the UK remains a mystery. *Brian Baldwin*

Upper: Unusual visitors to the UK included 92nd BW B-36D 44-92081 (the last B-36B conversion) *sans* the unit's 'circle W' tail marking. The 92nd BW previously deployed to England in 1949 with its B-29s. *Author's collection*

Lower and bottom: The first visit of a B-36 to the UK was a cause for considerable interest. After 7th BW B-36D 49-2658 arrived at RAF Lakenheath on 16th January 1951, it consumed not only a huge portion of the ramp but overwhelmed the billeting and messing facilities with its large crew. For size comparison, note the RAF Gloster Meteor F.4 next to the nose. *via Nick Stroud/TAHS (top), via Dennis Jenkins (left, right)*

Top and below:
The B-36 was the star attraction at air shows, especially if visitors could take a peek inside the 'Aluminum Overcast'. The airplane's unique sound would soon give way to the scream of the B-47 and its jet engines. *Mike Hooks via Nick Stroud/TAH*

by production delays and shortcomings, the B-47 lacked the range to fly from bases in the ZI to targets in the USSR. Consequently, the B-47, upon which SAC was betting its future mission capability, required either air refueling or forward basing. LeMay opted for both, and planned to deploy B-47s to bases in England and North Africa, with co-located tankers to refuel them after completing their EWP mission upon returning to the UK or French Morocco for reconstitution. Although not significantly different from B-29 and B-50 missions, the sheer number of planned B-47s (nearly 2,000) meant that British ramp space would be at a premium.

B-50 training rotations and B-36 post-strike missions to the UK continued throughout 1952, but the 3rd December 1952 deployment of the 301st BW was the final Superfortress visit to

the UK. Some 30 B-29s went to RAF Upper Heyford and 16 to RAF Brize Norton during the bitterly cold winter of 1952-53. The unit relocated a portion of these airplanes to a much warmer Wheelus AB, Libya, for a USCM exercise, but unfortunately lost 44-27261 on 2nd February 1953 in a takeoff crash there. The final SAC B-29 departed the UK and returned to Barksdale AFB on 10th March 1953. That same month the final SAC B-50 deployment to England took place with the arrival of 43rd BW B-50As at RAF Brize Norton beginning 9th March 1953. They returned to Davis-Monthan AFB, AZ, from 5th-12th June and, like the B-29s, were promptly stored or scrapped.

RB-36 visits to the UK – excluding ROUNDOUT photo reconnaissance missions – continued in 1954 for multiple 'special maneuvers' and exercises including CAN DO and CHERRY PIE. The March 1955 PORT CALL exercise brought 19 B-36Ds, B-36Hs, and B-36Js from the 42nd BW to RAF Upper Heyford. Starting 18th October 1956, 16 B-36Hs and B-36Js from the 11th BW spent a week at RAF Burtonwood, preceding both the Hungarian uprising and the outbreak of hostilities in the Suez Crisis by a matter of days. With the end of this deployment, SAC piston-powered bomber rotations to the UK were over, replaced by the B-47 for both full-wing training rotations and, beginning in 1958, REFLEX ACTION ground alert. The many shortcomings, failures, and successes of these early rotations showed SAC's planners how to relocate its medium bomber fleet successfully to bases in England. Unfortunately, neither SAC nor its English bases were ready for the transition from prop to jet.

3 The Jet Age

High above the skies of North Korea, the performance of the MiG-15 *Fagot* stunned SAC's commanders. This new jet-powered fighter proved brutally efficient in attacking and destroying B-29s conducting traditional daylight bombing raids of North Korean targets. Shortly after 9:00AM on 23rd October 1951, nine B-29s from the 307th BW struck a target near Namsi AB in the heart of 'MiG Alley'. Some 38 MiG-15s, commanded by Soviet pilot Colonel Alexsandr Pavolvich Smorchkov, launched to intercept the bombers. Despite an escort of F-84s and North American F-86s, the MiGs flew directly into the bomber formation, with Soviet pilot Major Dmitrii Pavlovich Os'kin claiming one Superfortress on his first pass. More MiG-15s joined the fray resulting in a 15-minute aerial battle eventually involving 182 airplanes. A second and third B-29 quickly fell to MiG-15s. Ultimately six of the nine B-29s were lost, either in combat or trying to land while badly damaged from flak and MiGs, 'the highest percentage of United States bombers ever lost on a major mission.'

During October 1951 alone, nine Superfortresses were shot down and four more damaged beyond repair. Despite claims that these fateful missions compelled the end of B-29 daylight attacks and the switch exclusively to night bombing, in fact they 'solidified and accelerated plans that had been in the works for years.' As former B-29 pilot Earl J McGill writes in *Black Tuesday Over Namsi: B-29s vs MiGs – The Forgotten Air Battle of the Korean War, 23rd October 1951*, his detailed study of the engagement, 'Namsi and other bombing missions verified what strategic warfare planners had suspected, that the slower propeller-driven bombers of the pre-jet age could no longer be relied on to deliver bombs on the target.' B-29s, B-50s, and the B-36 'were no longer viewed as viable deterrents to nuclear war.'

Although fully aware of the potential of new jet fighters (including SAC's own), events over the Korean Peninsula reaffirmed the urgency of plans to replace SAC's lumbering piston-powered B-29s, B-50s, and B-36s with jet-powered B-45s and B-47s. Tests against both of these new jets, however, with a North Korean defector's MiG-15 revealed even their vulnerability to jet interceptors. Although the B-47 was fast enough to outrun the MiG-15 in a tail chase, it was still in grave danger from a front quadrant or pursuit curve attack.

The Stratojet, however, had more than its share of troubles. Maligned as the perfect bomber should war break out with Canada or Mexico, the B-47 – upon which SAC based its near-term operational future – simply could not reach targets in the USSR when launched from bases in the United States without at least one air refueling. Even then they lacked the range to reach post-strike bases for reconstitution. Problems with refueling jet-powered B-47 from piston-powered KC-97s – ranging from technical issues to incompatible speeds to lack of crew mastery – made in-flight refueling a risk that SAC planners struggled to mitigate. With the operational debut of the jet-powered KC-135 Stratotanker still at least five years away, SAC elected to use the same temporary solution for the B-47 as they had for its B-29 and B-50 force: forward basing in the United Kingdom, North Africa, and Guam.

Early plans called for 195 B-47s and 65 RB-47s at English bases during any pre-war buildup, reaching 390 B-47s and 130 RB-47s by the time war erupted. In January 1953, SAC sought to validate these plans by deploying 306th BW

An 'enemy fighter' shot down B-29A 44-62073 on 8th November 1952 during a night bombing mission. SAC operations in Korea reaffirmed the need for a high-speed, high-altitude jet bomber to evade Soviet MiGs. *Author's collection*

Above: Colonel Mike McCoy led the 306th BW on the B-47's first deployment to the UK. It is unknown if he flew B-47B 50-0008 *The Real McCoy!* on either his initial assessment visit to England or on the full deployment. *Photo HS5665 courtesy Boeing*

during SKY TRY: '...certain important deficiency areas, principally in the bombing and defensive armament systems, imposing serious limitation on the aircraft's combat effectiveness. ... Until the B-47 is equipped with an acceptable armament system with which to defend itself against the type of interceptor attack which will probably be used against it [the B-47 still lacked tail guns at the time], the aircraft will be forced to operate under a serious tactical penalty.'

Despite the many shortcomings identified during SKY TRY, SAC commanders were sufficiently encouraged by the B-47's performance to move ahead with its first overseas deployment. On 7th March 1953, SAC directed the 306th BW to prepare for the initial 90-day rotation to the UK.

Off to England

Colonel Michael N W McCoy, the flamboyant commander of the 306th BW, led an initial pair of B-47Bs from MacDill AFB to RAF Fairford. Departing 6th April 1953, they stopped at Limestone AFB for refueling, and then proceeded to England, setting an unofficial speed record of 553.8mph (891kmh) en route. The two airplanes did not reach RAF Fairford, however, diverting to RAF Brize Norton on 7th April when the crews' anti-exposure suits caused hyperthermia. The two eventually visited other bases, including RAF Lakenheath on 14th April.

What McCoy found was problematic. The runway at RAF Fairford was indeed the req-

B-47Bs from MacDill AFB, FL, to the UK in May. LeMay rejected this proposal, however, as 'premature' due to the lack of combat-ready crews and because the 306th BW had yet to execute a successful simulated EWP evaluation.

Efforts to assess the operational readiness of the newly delivered B-47 had been planned since August 1952 but were repeatedly deferred due to delivery delays, logistics issues, and lack of combat-ready crews. Project SKY TRY finally took place from 22nd January through 19th February 1953. Results were surprisingly good. Out of the total of 150 planned sorties, 126 (84%) were effective over the target, and 109 (72.7%) finished the mission completely. Commanders were warned, however, about being overly optimistic as the B-47's performance

48

uisite 10,000ft (3,048m) in length but had no overruns. Lines were hastily painted 100ft (30.5m) from each end of the runway to create these overruns, which reduced the overall length to 9,800ft (2,987m) with resulting penalties in fuel load and takeoff performance. As with earlier B-29 and B-50 deployments, UHF radios were still largely non-existent, and GCA facilities remained 'primitive' by SAC standards. McCoy returned to Florida on 21st April to oversee final preparations for the deployment, which garnered considerable press attention. On 22nd May Air Force Vice Chief of Staff General Nathan F Twining announced that B-47s would deploy to England 'as part of

the Air Force's established program for maintaining the mobility of Strategic Air Command.'

McCoy led the full Wing's deployment to RAF Fairford, with the 45 B-47Bs departing Mac-Dill AFB in three waves on 2nd, 3rd, and 4th June. Some 22 KC-97Es from the 306th AREFS deployed to EA Harmon AFB where they could refuel any en route B-47 in case of emergency, but no air refueling was otherwise planned for the trip to England. Each B-47 routed through Limestone AFB, with 15 reaching RAF Fairford on 4th June, 12 on 5th June, 16 on 6th June, and the final two stragglers arrived on the 7th of June. Several set unofficial speed records along the way.

Opposite, bottom: B-47B 51-2323 was just six months old when it passed through Limestone AFB en route to England during June 1953 (seen here). Note the absence of tail guns. The early B-47s were hardly combat ready. *Photo courtesy Boeing*

Above and left: Following their refueling at Limestone AFB, a number of the 306th BW B-47Bs set unofficial speed records for the trans-Atlantic crossing. Note special nacelle markings on the second B-47, as well as those on *Sa-Gua* (Cherokee for 'first' or 'one'). *Photos BW90076 and BW90077 courtesy Boeing*

Above: Success at last, as 51-2271 lands at RAF Fairford for the first time. Conditions were Spartan and not conducive to mission effectiveness for the complex and sensitive jet bomber. *Photo BW90190 courtesy Boeing*

Right and below: However idyllic the deployment to RAF Fairford might have appeared, the gutted house was an apt metaphor for the poor conditions the 306th BW found in England just eight years after the end of the Second World War. *Harold Siegfried (upper), photo courtesy Boeing (lower)*

Bright and shiny in the summer English sun, 51-2206 sports the red squadron tail band and hi-visibility red wing markings. *Harold Siegfried*

With the landing gear retraction already under way, 51-2295 *Cheri-Lynn* departs RAF Fairford for MacDill AFB. 'Success' of the mission came from identifying the many weaknesses in both the B-47 and British bases. *Photo HS920 courtesy Boeing*

Once in the UK, the B-47s flew frequently to familiarize crews with the English environment and ground support personnel with the new airplane. Each crew typically flew every three days, accruing some 50 hours of flight time each month. Weather was an unexpected problem, with unseasonal fog forcing the Wing to lower the daytime approach minima from 1,000ft (305m) ceiling and 2nm (3.7km) visibility to just 300ft (91m) and ¾nm (1.4km). The runway at RAF Fairford remained a source of serious concern. Given its rough finish and the presence of stiff crosswinds, crews worried about dragging an outboard engine pod or excessive bumps damaging the airplane's sensitive electronics. Radar aborts were frequent, although how many were caused by rough taxiways and runways remains unknown. Crew accommodations were 'austere' and overcrowding commonplace. Stockpiles of JP-4 jet fuel were inadequate but quickly overcome. Unplanned 'bounces' by friendly fighters were forbidden, and the B-47s were prohibited from any flight operations closer than 300nm (556km) from the USSR or communist-bloc areas.

On 29th-30th June, the Wing took part in Operation BIG LEAGUE, designed to test the wing's capability against continental targets. Results were poor, largely due to weather, resulting in additional training missions in July, producing the desired results during a simulated EWP mission flown on 16th July. All 44 planned launches took place, with 40 sorties 'effective' over the target. The following week the unit flew Exercise WORLD SERIES with similar results.

The B-47's highly publicized trip to the UK received LeMay's personal attention while visiting England from 13th May through 16th June, followed by Vice CINCSAC Major General Thomas S Power from 24th August through 7th September. Six of the Wing's B-47Bs relocated to Nouasseur AB in French Morocco on 12th August under Operation SAFARI to evaluate those facilities. All of the 306th BW's jets returned directly to MacDill AFB in three waves departing on 4th, 5th, and 6th September, with each B-47 air refueled en route. Overall, the Stratojet's foreign debut was a public relations success, sadly marred by the loss of B-47B 51-2267 on 2nd July at RAF Upper Heyford. Moreover, there were still significant operational issues to resolve.

Second to None

Addressing these problems fell to the 305th BW, also from MacDill AFB, when 45 of its B-47Bs flew to RAF Brize Norton. Of these, 12 arrived on 4th September, 14 on 5th September, 16 on 6th September, and the final three on 7th September, with 22 KC-97Gs from the 305th AREFS proceeding to RAF Mildenhall. The 305th BW experienced the same problems as the 306th BW: inadequate UHF radio and GCA facilities, bad weather complicating the use of both visual and radar RBS ranges, and the deteriorated state of British bases in general. Consequently, visual bombing practice took place at the Ksar-es-Souk range and the Marrakesh RBS site in Morocco. B-47Bs visited RAF Lakenheath, RAF Greenham Common, and RAF Upper Heyford to assess their suitability for future B-47 operations as well as to introduce base personnel to the Stratojet.

The Wing originally planned to send 15 B-47s and five KC-97s to Sidi Slimane AB, but only one B-47 and the five KC-97s made the trip. On 2nd November, a gaggle of 41 B-47s finally managed to reach Sidi Slimane AB, returning to RAF Brize Norton over the next four days. The jets finally departed for Florida in three tranches, with 16 on 5th December, 15 on 6th December, and 14 on 7th December. They flew nonstop with one air refueling en route, although strong headwinds on 6th December forced 11 diversions into Hunter AFB, GA, Langley AFB, VA, and Limestone AFB.

By the end of 1953, the 22nd BW had completed plans for its first high-profile deployment to England. Plans called for 10 of its new B-47Es to fly nonstop from March AFB to RAF Upper Heyford using in-flight refueling, with the remaining 35 jets routing through Limestone AFB. The unit's KC-97s would fly from March AFB to Griffiss AFB and then to RAF Mildenhall. Poor weather – both in Maine and in the UK – played havoc with the deployment.

The first 15 B-47s departed March AFB on 3rd December and arrived at Limestone AFB, but severe fog in the UK prevented them from flying the next leg to RAF Upper Heyford. Fog remained a problem and these Stratojets were grounded at Limestone AFB until 11th December, when just eight managed to depart for England. Of these, five reached Upper Heyford and three diverted to RAF Brize Norton and RAF Mildenhall. On the same day, the remaining 30 B-47s, including those scheduled to fly nonstop from March AFB to RAF Upper Heyford, arrived at Limestone AFB. Once again, RAF

Upper Heyford was closed due to extreme fog, prompting SAC to request permission to launch the B-47s now stranded at Limestone AFB with the intent to reach England but with the ability to divert to Sidi Slimane AB should weather preclude landing in the UK. Accordingly, 20 of the 37 B-47s then at Limestone AFB prepared to depart on 19th December, but while awaiting take-off suffered unanticipated wing icing. The base's lone de-icing truck could clean only five B-47s, which managed to get away before the take-off deadline.

As if this 'goat rope' were not sufficiently troublesome, SAC approved the launch of the remaining 32 B-47s from Limestone AFB in small groups, destined for any available UK base or Sidi Slimane AB should a diversion be necessary. On 21st December, 20 B-47s left Limestone in doublets and triplets, leaving 12 on the ground in Maine because of mechanical problems. Efforts to launch these the following day failed when bad weather again struck Limestone AFB. The weather finally co-operated on 24th December, by which time 34 jets reached their ultimate destination at RAF Upper Heyford. Eleven came from Limestone AFB, nine from Sidi Slimane AB, seven from RAF Brize Norton, and the remaining seven from RAF Mildenhall. The final jets arrived at RAF Upper Heyford on Christmas Day, the last of these was B-47E 52-0024, ending what had turned into a 23-day outbound deployment!

These lessons were not lost on SAC planners who had failed to account for more than one deicer at Limestone AFB or the impact of bad weather not only on the mission aircraft but also on the C-54, C-97, and C-124 support airplanes. The weather minima of 1,500ft (457m) ceilings with 3nm (5.6km) visibility required in the UK prior to launching trans-Atlantic flights were often unobtainable, preventing arrivals from the US or local operations in general. In addition, the 22nd BW had just converted from B-47Bs to B-47Es, and many of the newer airplanes had been sitting idle for weeks in the warmer climate at Davis-Monthan AFB, as well as their new home base in sunny southern California. Arriving in the cold, snow, and icy conditions at Limestone AFB seriously undermined their ability to operate in all weather conditions without degradation, an issue which significantly worried SAC planners. SAC's ability to wage war was clearly hostage to the vagaries of English weather.

During January 1954, 15 B-47s and 10 KC-97s from the 22nd BW deployed to Wheelus AB for an exercise. On 17th February, 44 B-47Es

Opposite page: A crew from the 320th BW stows their baggage (and swag) in the unused RATO compartment on YRB-47B 51-2365 prior to returning from RAF Brize Norton in September 1954. *Terry Panopalis collection*

According to press releases, Colonel David Burchinal (AC), Major Forrest McCoy (N), Captain Stephen Franco (CP), and Major Pat Earhart (spare pilot) set a record long-duration flight in a 320th BW YRB-47B because of inclement weather. In reality, Burchinal (who commanded the 43rd BW) had planned the flight to evaluate the B-47's ability to remain airborne for extended periods. *Author's collection*

and 22 KC-97s deployed to Sidi Slimane AB and Wheelus AB to take part in a HIGH GEAR exercise (also known as QUICK SWITCH) along with 33 B-47s from the 301st BW already present at Sidi Slimane AB (52-0023 had crashed in the UK on 8th February, reducing the 22nd BW jets by one). These rotations to North Africa were essential to maximize the exposure of B-47 crews and support personnel to all available overseas bases prior to the start of any conflict. They also had the effect of raising morale of crews who suffered through a rough deployment and a cold and foggy stay England, and were 'rewarded' with the better weather in North Africa, although winter there could be equally fickle.

The return trip to March AFB was less disruptive, with most of the 22nd BW B-47s reaching home between 3rd and 7th March 1954. Interestingly, when the 321st BW brought its B-47Bs from Pinecastle AFB to England in December 1954, its commanders wisely chose to fly first to Sidi Slimane AB, where the crews spent the night instead of trying to fly directly to RAF Lakenheath amid the unpredictability of British winter weather.

Toward a Routine Presence

Planned changes in 1954 to the EWP and unplanned events in England led to significant alterations in SAC's efforts to establish a regular B-47 operational presence in the UK. Most notable among these was the shift from using British bases as the origin of atomic strikes against the USSR to using them as post-strike bases following their initial launch from ZI bases. In addition to the planned 90-day B-47 rotations, the 68th BW from Lake Charles AFB assessed a 45-day visit from 14th June through 7th August. Results of this shorter duration were not surprising: better morale associated with briefer deployment and a lower degradation of the unit's EWP preparedness. Unfortunately, the wing lost two B-47s while in the UK which badly undermined their otherwise improved spirits. Finally, the failure of the runway at RAF Greenham Common in March 1954 compelled the urgent and unplanned relocation by April of the 303rd BW to RAF Fairford. Similarly, RAF Mildenhall closed for runway repair in June.

Among the more interesting B-47 visits to the UK in 1954 was the 320th BW from March AFB. The Wing brought 44 YRB-47Bs and a lone B-47B to RAF Brize Norton beginning 3rd June. Although designated as reconnaissance aircraft,

these functioned as standard B-47B bombers. During July they served as targets for the annual Dividend UK air defense exercise, and the following month flew to Crete and Turkey on a 'highly classified survey flight' to assess potential post-strike bases there. Another highlight was the record-setting flight of YRB-47B 51-2062. Allegedly due to inclement weather, from 17th-19th November 43rd BW Commander Colonel David A Burchinal and crew of three flew nonstop roundtrip from Sidi Slimane AB to RAF Fairford twice, logging a total of 21,163nm (39,194km) over 47:35 hours with nine air refuelings. Burchinal later admitted this was a planned evaluation of lengthy flights rather than an acci-

dent of weather, particularly as Burchinal's 43rd BW operated B-47Es rather than YRB-47Bs. The 340th BW later brought its own YRB-47Bs and B-47Bs to RAF Lakenheath in September 1955, the final visit of this type to the UK.

Training rotations to the UK continued throughout 1955 amid what seemed to be an endless list of special exercises such as TAR PAIL, TOP DRAWER, and PICKET FENCE. Post-strike deployments included OPEN MIND, SIGN BOARD, and BOILER MAKER, extremely demanding events. BOILER MAKER, for example, involved both the 43rd BW and the 303rd BW, totaling 64 B-47Es. Crews were required to 'undertake a gunnery mission, day formation flying, a 55,000 lb (24,948kg) refueling and a simulated 40,000 lb (18,144kg) refueling, a grid navigation leg, two recorded radar bomb scoring runs and a radar camera attack. ... Each formation leader was scheduled to fly a day celestial navigation mission and two "electronic rendezvous" missions (presumably radio-silent tankings).'

Unique operations in 1955 included the 9th BW at RAF Fairford flying 40 LOBSTER POT sorties, a '20-crew exercise to saturate' RAF Brize Norton's radar approach control and to evaluate the base's ability to handle 'special weapons.' In addition, the 9th BW joined the 310th BW at RAF Upper Heyford in flights to Garder-

moen AB and Sola AB in Norway. YUKON JAKE was intended to familiarize SAC bomber and tanker crews with EWP operations from Norway following a 1952 agreement. These ended in October 1955 when a KC-97 was 'unable to leave the runway [at Gardermoen AB] due to construction work' forcing it to taxi around for nearly an hour until it finally 'parked in front of the control tower.' Mightily displeased, the Norwegian commander at Gardermoen AB sent a message to cancel the planned visit the next day by two 340th BW YRB-47Bs from RAF Lakenheath. Unfortunately, the Norwegians sent the message to RAF Bomber Command – not SAC – so the two YRB-47Bs arrived unannounced (and undesired) at Gardermoen AB and were forced to divert to Sola AB, where they were joined by the errant KC-97.

Improvements to the B-47's combat range, 'absolute' confidence in air-to-air refueling, and optimistic assumptions about the range of the B-52 resulted in changes to SAC's view that British bases were no longer required for pre-strike or staging operations, but were instead to be used primarily for post-strike support and reconstitution (refueling and rearming). Beginning in October 1955, SAC identified 'Main Bases' from which B-47s would launch EWP strikes, 'Post-Strike Bases' to which aircraft would return for reconstitution following an EWP strike, and 'War-Only Standby Bases' to be opened in the event others were unusable. The main B-47 bases included RAF Brize Norton, RAF Greenham Common, RAF Upper Heyford, and RAF Lakenheath. Post-strike bases were RAF Fairford, RAF Mildenhall, and RAF Chelveston. The war-only bases were RAF Homewood Park (actually London's Heathrow airport – SAC assigned it this spurious name 'to disguise its...presence in the EWP pending completion of Stansted [airport] as a tanker base'), RAF Lindholme, and RAF Full Sutton. SAC's requirements for the main and post-strike bases meant that they would need to be visited at least twice a year by B-47 units and that the runways be at least 10,000ft (3,048m) long with additional 1,000ft (305m) overruns at each end. These requirements led to tensions with the UK's Air Ministry as it was forced to requisition private property or re-route local roads to lengthen runways and build overruns needed by the B-47.

Beginning 14th July 1955, RAF Upper Heyford hosted the 376th BW from Lockbourne AFB, OH. Among the 43 aircraft that made the trip were highly secretive BLUE CRADLE EB-47E ECM jammers. Some 45 B-47Es were initially modi-

SAC BOMBER UNIT ROTATIONS TO THE UK, 1953-1958

From	To	Unit	Aircraft	Deployment Base(s)
11 Jun 53	7 Sep 53	306th BW	B-47B	RAF Fairford
4 Sep 53	5 Dec 53	305th BW	B-47B	RAF Brize Norton
7 Dec 53	5 Mar 54	22nd BW	B-47E	RAF Upper Heyford
4 Mar 54	5 Jun 54	303rd BW	B-47E	RAF Greenham Common, RAF Fairford
3 Jun 54	4 Sep 54	320th BW	YRB-47B*	RAF Brize Norton
14 Jun 54	7 Aug 54	68th BW	B-47E	RAF Fairford
5 Sep 54	10 Dec 54	43rd BW	B-47E	RAF Fairford
9 Dec 54	5 Mar 55	321st BW	B-47B	RAF Lakenheath
10 Mar 55	8 Jun 55	310th BW	B-47E	RAF Upper Heyford
23 May 55	11 Jul 55	9th BW	B-47E	RAF Fairford
9 Jun 55	9 Sep 55	40th BW	B-47E	RAF Lakenheath
14 Jul 55	14 Oct 55	376th BW	B-47E†	RAF Upper Heyford
13 Sep 55	3 Nov 55	340th BW	YRB-47B* B-47B	RAF Lakenheath
11 Nov 55	29 Jan 56	98th BW	B-47E	RAF Lakenheath
26 Jan 56	30 Apr 56	509th BW	B-47E	RAF Upper Heyford
5 May 56	4 Jul 56	97th BW	B-47E	RAF Upper Heyford
7 Jul 56	5 Oct 56	307th BW	B-47E	RAF Lakenheath
3 Oct 56	9 Jan 57	310th BW	B-47E	RAF Greenham Common
3 Jan 57	5 Apr 57	384th BW	B-47E	RAF Brize Norton
3 Apr 57	3 Jul 57	380th BW	B-47E	RAF Brize Norton
1 Jul 57	1 Oct 57	40th BW	B-47E	RAF Greenham Common
27 Sep 57	8 Jan 58	68th BW	B-47E	RAF Brize Norton
29 Dec 57	1 Apr 58	100th BW	B-47E	RAF Brize Norton

* Bomber configuration only; † Includes first BLUE CRADLE deployment

fied (six more were subsequently converted) to carry a 7,000lb (3,175kg) bomb-bay pod configured with a variety of barrage jammers and chaff dispensers. One or two of these would lead each group of strike B-47s to jam Soviet radars. The following year, the first nine Phase V ECM jamming EB-47Es from the 509th BW (one aircraft) and the 307th BW (eight jets) arrived at RAF Upper Heyford and RAF Lakenheath, respectively. These differed from the BLUE CRADLE jammers by carrying two electronic warfare officers (EWOs) in a capsule in the bomb bay rather than an unmanned pod (both of these were later redesignated as EB-47Es, but for clarity are listed here as such irrespective of date).

At the end of 1955, the 98th BW conducted two unusual missions during its deployment to the UK. Beginning 7th November, 43 B-47Es participated in SADDLE ROCK which involved a 'special weapons exercise' at Lincoln AFB followed by a mass night air refueling in the North East Air Command (NEAC) area and finished with camera-scored bombings against UK targets before landing at RAF Lakenheath. This was the first 'cradle to grave' simulation of a post-strike recovery EWP mission, complete with weapons (!), mass refueling, and simulated strikes to reach the UK. In the second mission on 5th December, 10 of the wing's B-47Es flew back to the United States as part of the TEXAS LEAGUE test of US Air Defense Command (ADC) units in the US and Canada. These B-47s returned to RAF Lakenheath on 9th December.

By 1956, 90-day B-47 rotations to and from England were fairly common, although there were the occasional glitches due to weather, mechanical failures, and accidents. Operational exercises in the UK benefitted from an occasional sense of humor. For example, on 13th August 1956 the 307th BW took part in Operation PINK LADY. Target 'Bravo' was the top of the bell tower at the Tower of London and Target 'Golf' was

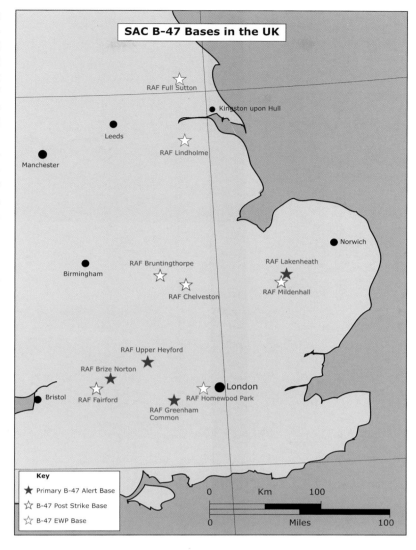

the 'center of the bridge [near] Windsor Castle.' In another incident involving a 98th BW B-47, a T-59 'shape' – the facsimile of the Mark VI atomic bomb – failed to drop over the oceanic bomb range. Instead, it 'plopped' unceremoniously onto the bomb doors, a situation which the crew finally understood as the B-47 neared

To meet its ECM penetration requirements, SAC procured the BLUE CRADLE EB-47E. It carried an unmanned bomb-bay pod with pre-set barrage jammers and additional chaff. 52-0396 was one of the first to visit at RAF Upper Heyford in July 1955. *via Bob Archer*

Top and below:
The Phase V ECM EB-47Es could be distinguished by the bulged bomb bay containing two electronic warfare officers. Figuratively speaking, these airplanes were decoys designed to jam enemy radars and, as a last resort, draw hostile fire away from the bombers.
Adrian Balch collection (upper), Augustine 'Gus' Letto (lower)

Having a B-47 at an air show was, by 19th May 1956 when 51-5214 was displayed at RAF Upper Heyford, an unusual occurrence. SAC understood the value of positive public relations, but this conflicted with its obsessive security.
Adrian Balch

While deployed to RAF Upper Heyford in 1956, 97th BW B-47E 51-2404 made a trip to RAF Greenham Common to join its 97th AREFS KC-97s for the 19th May Armed Forces Day.
Brian Baldwin

RAF Lakenheath. The crew pulled the emergency bomb release handle and the 'shape' finally dropped onto a homeowner's garden leaving a 30ft x 15ft x 14ft (9m x 4.6m x 4.3m) crater which proved quite expensive to repair. A similar event took place on 3rd March 1958 in Ashton Keynes involving the accidental jettisoning of a wing tank from a 100th BW B-47E.

In November 1956 Israel attacked Egyptian forces in the Sinai in response to Egypt closing the Straits of Tiran to Israeli shipping, and both France and Britain attacked Egypt following its nationalization of the Suez Canal. Out of fear that Soviet forces might intervene on behalf of Egypt and Syria, President Eisenhower was initially cautious in responding. Once he determined that the USSR was not inclined to send troops to bases in Syria, he authorized SAC to undertake a show of force, establishing a 'war readiness posture that fell just short of complete mobilization for war.' The Suez Crisis had surprisingly little effect, however, on SAC operations in the UK.

The 310th BW had previously deployed 45 B-47Es on 3rd October from Smoky Hill AFB, KS, to RAF Greenham Common in Operation LUCKY BOY, the first such rotation there since the March 1954 runway failure. The Wing went on full alert as the Middle East crisis developed, with minimal local flight operations. This reduced flying pleased the local residents who had justifiably complained about the excessive noise the B-47s produced. Nonetheless, SAC exercises such as POWER HOUSE and ROAD BLOCK sent a clear message to Soviet leaders that the United States would not tolerate any Soviet attack on Britain or France in retaliation for their actions against Egypt. General LeMay visited the unit on 13th December, and the Wing returned to Smoky Hill AFB on 9th January 1957.

Yet another crisis arose in the Middle East during July 1958 in Lebanon. Sectarian tensions

between Lebanese President Camille Chamoun, a Christian, and the increasing majority of the Muslim population led to a national strike and efforts to overthrow Chamoun in an armed rebellion. On 14th July, a coup in Iraq killed the pro-Western King Faisal, a sign which Eisenhower took as indicative of Soviet-backed efforts to destabilize the Middle East. On the same day Chamoun appealed to the US to intervene under the Eisenhower Doctrine to maintain Lebanon's independence.

SAC went to an elevated state of alert beginning 15th July. Although no additional B-47 units deployed to the UK or North Africa, within 130 hours SAC was at its peak of 396 B-47s and 10 Phase V ECM B-47s on alert, including those in England. This 'show of force' proved successful and the alert ended on 30th July. SAC had a lesser-known conventional role in the crisis. An undetermined number (almost certainly six) of the 310th BW B-47s at RAF Mildenhall and 10 B-47s from the 68th BW at RAF Fairford could be configured with internal conventional bomb racks. Operations Plan 1-58, known as BLUE BAT

B-47 crews faced adversity with good humor, substituting a sports car for an unavailable Jeep at RAF Fairford in 1953. Rumors abound of a B-47 crew bringing an MG home in their bomb bay. Photo courtesy Boeing

The 310th BW's B-47Es (including 52-0304) flew to RAF Greenham Common in October 1956. As such, the Wing was part of the American diplomatic signaling associated with the Suez Crisis the following month. Mike Hooks via Nick Stroud/TAHS

and believed to provide conventional bombing in Lebanon, began on 15th July and lasted through 25th October 1958. Further details are not known. Interestingly, in a 1970 interview, former SAC Vice Commander Lieutenant General Griswold said of these show-of-force efforts, 'I don't think they had much effect, really,' so their actual impact on US-Soviet tensions remains unclear.

REFLEX

Prior to 1954, SAC's offensive doctrine was based on the massive forward deployment of its bombers to staging bases for attacks on the USSR. Recognizing that these bases would be vulnerable to Soviet pre-emptive strikes, operations such as PAUL REVERE, HIGH GEAR, FULL HOUSE, and LEAP FROG evaluated the ability of B-47s to fly directly from ZI bases to Soviet targets while utilizing air refueling and then recover to forward bases for post-strike regeneration. LeMay approved a 'quick strike' capability to evaluate the ability of a modest bomber force to launch within a few hours of notification. Given 12 hours of warning, SAC could launch 180 B-47s. That number jumped to 880 with 48 hours of warning. Acutely aware that a surprise Soviet attack on SAC bases – an atomic Pearl Harbor – would be the end of America's strike force, on 5th October 1955 LeMay requested to start a ground alert program which Air Force Chief of Staff General Nathan F Twining agreed to 'in principle' on 14th December. The Air Council endorsed this in March 1956, but final

approval for a ground alert force was not given until December 1957. SAC's ultimate goal was to have one-third of its force on continuous alert with a 15-minute reaction time by 1st July 1960.

The ground alert program in the CONUS offered an important lesson for overseas bases. Rather than deploying entire wings of B-47s plus their tankers and support aircraft for 90 days at a time, SAC recognized the value in placing a smaller number of B-47s on alert and rotating them more frequently. As Smith concisely notes, 'full-wing TDYs were cumbersome, expensive, tactically questionable, and, in isolation, certainly could not meet the exercise requirements of all the bases in the UK, Spain, and Morocco, Moreover, one or two rotational training Wing [deployments] were not the most appropriate retaliatory threat to the developing Soviet ballistic missile force.' Consequently, Operation REFLEX ACTION began on 1st July 1957 at Sidi Slimane AB. Results were positive, with only 'irritating' rather than 'critical' problems encountered such as inadequate housing and messing and shortage of maintenance personnel. Nonetheless, SAC was sufficiently impressed,

As the history of SAC's alert program recounts, overseas REFLEX operations proved far more valuable than maintaining only CONUS alert. The benefits of REFLEX included 'the need to keep some aircraft [overseas] due to political considerations; the necessity of attacking Soviet targets as soon as possible after initial warning; the limited number of tankers availa-

REFLEX deployments were typically three Stratojets from the same wing, compared to prior massive 45-ship rotations. 528th BS, 380th BW B-47E 53-3368 formates en route to RAF Greenham Common. *First Lieutenant Robert 'Hop' Hopkins*

ble to the command did not permit launching the entire force from ZI bases; and because the very existence of these forces posed difficult targeting problems for an attacker who must hit them and ZI bases simultaneously to effect a surprise attack.'

REFLEX also resulted in a considerable savings. Deploying the 307th BW from Lincoln AFB, for example, involved moving 45 airplanes, 1,600 personnel, and 190 tons of cargo, plus other fixed expenses at a total cost of $42,428,000. REFLEX reduced the deployment cost alone by nearly 40%. Regular rotations of 45 B-47s plus their KC-97 tankers allowed little room for aborts or missed refueling, risking diversions or worse. For REFLEX operations, however, only two or three B-47s from a single unit would deploy at a given time (four B-47s were lost during deployment flights prior to the establishment of REFLEX, with only two lost after 1958). Initially, these were intended to carry their own atomic weapons from the ZI. Events such as the 11th March 1958 jettisoning of a nuclear bomb near Mars Bluff, SC, by 2nd BW B-47E 53-1876 en route from Hunter AFB to England forced the reconsideration of this policy, and deploying aircraft were unarmed.

Upon arrival the B-47s underwent a thorough maintenance check, strike cameras were loaded with film, and they received their EWP fuel load. Once moved to the alert ramp, they were configured with rocket-assisted takeoff (RATO) racks, chaff, 20mm ammunition for their tail guns, approach and drag chutes, water alcohol, liquid oxygen, and a Mk 39 nuclear weapon. The incoming crew then 'cocked' the airplane on alert and had the remainder of the day off for rest. The following day they began their 22-day alert cycle – 14 days on alert and 7 days off alert, then returned to their CONUS base. In 1962 this changed to a 28-day tour with three weeks on alert separated by two rest periods of three-and-one-half days each. Prior to assuming alert, newly arrived crews were tested on their knowledge of tactical doctrine and positive control procedures, with anything less than a perfect score resulting in a sudden, shameful return to their home station. This was a real worry, as in 1959 B-47 pilots TDY to Eielson AFB for simulated EWP exercises scored a dismal average of 65% and observers 63% on their tactical doctrine test (the Task Force Commander scored 64%).

Alert exercises were fairly common, both to test reaction times and to stress the gravitas of the REFLEX alert mission. There were four exercises used throughout SAC. During an

B-47 crews had ample time during REFLEX deployments to see the sights, whether in England or elsewhere in Europe (thanks to ongoing MATS flights to the Continent). Three weeks away from home was far more tolerable than the three-month rotations. *Photo BW90194 courtesy Boeing*

Alpha alert, most common at British bases, 'Crews proceeded to their aircraft, completed the engine check list, called the wing control room [Command Post] and informed them they were ready to start engines. The control room logged the time and the crew recocked the aircraft. Goal for this alert was E [Execution time] plus 19 minutes.' Bravo alerts were a bit less frequent, and created a lot of smoke and noise as crews 'started engines, ground crews signaled clear to taxi, and the crews called the control room. The control room acknowledged the call and the aircraft was recocked. The goal was E plus 22 minutes.' Far less frequent but even more impressive was 'the Mover,' or Cocoa alert, where the 'aircraft assumed its proper position in the taxi order and proceeded

View from the front seat of a Cocoa alert. This was essential not only to test reaction time, but to acculturate the crews to both procedures and the emotional sensation of preparing to go to nuclear war. *Augustine 'Gus' Letto*

to the takeoff runway. When the green light was received the lead aircraft simulated take-off by applying full power then cutting back after reaching 50 knots. The lead aircraft then returned to the parking area [as] the other aircraft simulated takeoff at one-minute intervals. Goal for the lead aircraft to start its simulated takeoff was E plus 30 minutes [SAC documents refer to 'Cocoa', 'Coco', and even 'Coca'].' The final alert notification was Delta, 'an actual takeoff. Goal was E plus 30 minutes.' There is no record of this actually happening in the UK (or elsewhere) as it would have involved the launch of B-47s using RATO, the jettisoning of the two expended large, metal RATO racks, and crowded flying in full EWP configuration, including nuclear weapons, over British towns and cities. Oddly, 7th AD's commanders had to convince CINCSAC General Power that even a *test* of Delta alerts in the UK was 'unacceptably dangerous.'

REFLEX in Practice

In typical SAC fashion, the 7th AD received the Operations Order (OpOrd) establishing REFLEX ACTION in the UK on 16th September 1957 with the expectation that it would have an initial alert force ready in just two weeks. On 1st October, nine B-47Es from the 68th BW at RAF Brize Norton were placed on full alert in preparation for the anticipated REFLEX alert to begin in January 1958. Original plans called for B-47s from SAC's 2nd Air Force (AF) and 8th AF to provide 15 B-47s apiece, with six wings responsible for five B-47s each to RAF Fairford (2nd AF) and RAF Greenham Common (8th AF). Each cadre of five would arrive on a Tuesday, Wednesday, or Thursday, sit alert for seven days, and then depart the following Wednesday, Thursday, or Friday. This proved cumbersome, especially following the addition of RAF Brize Norton as the third UK REFLEX base.

Right and below: B-47E 53-1923 and EB-47E 53-1963 from the 100th BW were among the final wing of B-47s to undertake a 90-day rotation in 1958. They both later returned for REFLEX alert. *Bob Archer (top), via John Hughes (bottom)*

The last 90-day rotation to England ended in April 1958 as the 100th BW flew its B-47s back to Pease AFB. In the end, REFLEX eliminated the quarterly mass deployments but resulted in constant movements. During *each week* in June 1958, for example, 81 alert aircraft overseas conducted 162 deployments and redeployments. At least 20 Lajes-based KC-97s provided en route air refueling for these B-47s as part of Operation SHORT PUNT. By 1st July there were 194 B-47s and four Phase V B-47 ECM jets on alert in both CONUS and overseas. SAC decreased the reaction time for all alert aircraft to 20 minutes (already in effect overseas, and down from two hours in the ZI) for the first aircraft to launch with subsequent takeoffs at one-minute intervals.

As of January 1959, seven UK bases supported REFLEX alert under the program name WILDCAT and hosted 42 B-47s, including six 301st BW Phase V Capsule ECM aircraft at RAF Brize Norton. The decision in 1959 by the French government to remove all NATO nuclear-capable aircraft from French bases meant that three tactical fighter wings were forced to relocate to West Germany and the UK. Four of SAC's B-47 bases – RAF Bruntingthorpe, RAF Chelveston, RAF Lakenheath, and RAF Mildenhall – transferred to USAFE's 3rd AF to support the influx of tactical fighters. This resulted in shuffles among the remaining three B-47 REFLEX bases and the withdrawal of all Phase V ECM aircraft from the UK to Pease AFB [eight ECM aircraft returned in 1960, with four each to RAF Upper Heyford (BLUE CRADLE) and RAF Greenham Common (Phase V)]. By the end of 1959 there were only 24 B-47s on alert in the UK.

Compiling a complete accounting of specific units and REFLEX bases in the UK has proven

UK REFLEX ALERT BASES

Base	Code Name
RAF Fairford	WILDCAT – ALPHA
RAF Greenham Common	WILDCAT – BRAVO
RAF Brize Norton	WILDCAT – CHARLIE
RAF Mildenhall	WILDCAT – DELTA
RAF Chelveston	WILDCAT – ECHO
RAF Bruntingthorpe	WILDCAT – FOXTROT
RAF Upper Heyford	WILDCAT – GOLF

to be a Herculean task. Alternate bases were sometimes used briefly as primary venues were briefly closed for runway or other maintenance. Wings occasionally used more than one REFLEX base at a time due to overcrowding. Moreover, the number of B-47s ranged from six to nine at four primary bases. Identifying specific tail numbers has been difficult to nail down as they often rotated to and from England without being observed, or returned unnoticed to the United States for the MILK BOTTLE structural integrity modification or any of the extensive upgrade programs to the B-47 fleet.

The 1961 Berlin Crisis resulted not only in a halt to planned deactivation of a half dozen B-47 units but an increase during July in the number of B-47s on alert in the UK. Each base typically had three B-47s added to its alert force, and the total reached 39 B-47s. In addition, all 16 of the Phase V and BLUE CRADLE EB-47E ECM airplanes on overseas alert were in the UK. Total numbers increased further by August 1962 with 48 B-47Es and 20 EB-47Es on alert. The onset of the Cuban Missile Crisis in October 1962 saw the temporary cessation of new deployments to the UK, but an augmented total of 56 B-47Es and 22 EB-47Es on

These 310th BW REFLEX jets are seen in 1958 on alert at the north side of RAF Greenham Common in the aftermath of a tragic 28th February accident. A jettisoned fuel tank destroyed B-47E 53-6204 on the south side, forcing SAC to disperse its aircraft more widely around the base. *Brian Baldwin*

SAC B-47 REFLEX ACTION Deployments to the UK

RAF Base and Unit	From	To	Comments
RAF Fairford WILDCAT ALPHA			3919th CSG inactivated 26 Jun 64
2nd BW	7 Jan 58	6 Apr 58	
308th BW	7 Jan 58	6 Apr 58	
384th BW	7 Jan 58	30 Jun 58	Unit REFLEX transferred to Morón AB
68th BW	21 Jun 58	31 Jul 62	
96th BW	15 Jul 61	1 Apr 62	Unit redesignated
96th SAW	1 Apr 62	31 Jul 62	Unit REFLEX transferred to RAF Greenham Common
340th BW	1 Aug 62	30 Jun 63	Unit converted to B-52
40th BW	1 Jul 63	1 Feb 64	Unit redesignated
40th SAW	1 Feb 64	31 Mar 64	Unit REFLEX transferred to RAF Brize Norton
376th BW	1 Apr 64	31 May 64	BLUE CRADLE REFLEX transferred from RAF Upper Heyford
RAF Greenham Common WILDCAT BRAVO			3909th CSG inactivated 30 Jun 64
98th BW	7 Jan 58	30 Jun 58	
307th BW	7 Jan 58	30 Jun 58	
310th BW	7 Jan 58	30 Jun 58	Unit REFLEX transferred to RAF Mildenhall
40th BW	1 Jul 58	13 Jan 59	
380th BW	5 Jan 59	30 Jun 59	
341st BW	1 Jul 59	1 Apr 61	Unit inactivated on 25 Jun 61
301st BW	1 Apr 60	31 Jul 62	Phase V REFLEX transferred to RAF Brize Norton
96th BW	28 Mar 61	1 Apr 62	Unit redesignated
96th SAW	1 Apr 62	18 Feb 63	Unit converted to B-52
307th BW	1 Aug 62	30 Jun 63	Unit REFLEX transferred to Zaragosa AB
384th BW	1 Jul 63	31 Mar 64	Unit inactivated on 1 Sep 64
301st BW	1 Apr 64	1 Jun 64	Phase V REFLEX transferred from RAF Brize Norton; unit converted to KC-135
RAF Brize Norton WILDCAT CHARLIE			3920th SW inactivated 31 Mar 65
2nd BW	6 Apr 58	12 Jul 59	
308th BW	6 Apr 58	30 Jun 58	REFLEX transferred to Nouasseur AB
301st BW	31 Jul 58	9 Jan 59	Phase V REFLEX relocated to RAF Chelveston
100th BW	13 Jul 59	31 Aug 60	Unit relocated from RAF Bruntingthorpe
380th BW	30 Aug 60	15 Sep 64	Unit redesignated
100th BW	15 Jul 61	31 Jul 62	
301st BW	1 Aug 62	31 Mar 64	Phase V REFLEX relocated from and to RAF Greenham Common
40th SAW	1 Apr 64	30 Jun 64	Unit inactivated on 1 Sep 64
310th SAW	1 Jul 64	31 Dec 64	Unit inactivated on 25 Jun 65
380th SAW	15 Sep 64	31 Mar 65	Last jet out 53-1884 on 3 Apr 65
RAF Mildenhall WILDCAT DELTA			3913rd CSG inactivated 1 Sep 59
310th BW	26 Jun 58	30 Jun 59	
340th BW	Apr 59	Jul 59	Occasional supplements to 310th BW
44th BW	1 Jul 59	1 Aug 59	Unit REFLEX transferred to RAF Upper Heyford
RAF Chelveston WILDCAT ECHO			3914th CSG inactivated 1 Sep 59
301st BW	5 Jan 59	25 Jul 59	
376th BW			Unit slated for Jul 59 – any deployment unconfirmed
RAF Bruntingthorpe WILDCAT FOXTROT			3912th CSG inactivated 1 Sep 59
100th BW	9 Jan 59	12 Jul 59	Unit REFLEX transferred to RAF Brize Norton
96th BW	9 Jul 59	23 Jul 59	Temporary coverage
RAF Upper Heyford WILDCAT GOLF			3918th SW inactivated 8 Feb 65
98th BW	5 Jan 59	1 Aug 59	
44th BW	1 Aug 59	1 Jan 60	
98th BW	1 Jan 60	30 Jun 63	Unit REFLEX transferred to Zaragosa AB
376th BW	1 Apr 60	31 Mar 64	BLUE CRADLE; Unit REFLEX transferred to RAF Fairford
509th BW	1 Jul 63	31 Mar 65	
380th SAW	1 Apr 64	30 Sep 64	
310th SAW	1 Oct 64	31 Dec 64	

CSG = Combat Support Group

96th BW B-47Es 52-0537 and 52-0466 were on alert at RAF Fairford and 98th BW B-47E 52-0503 was at RAF Brize Norton during the 1961 Berlin Crisis, President Kennedy's first test of international brinkmanship and a harbinger of what would happen in 1962. *via Bob Archer*

Bottom: From January through June 1958, the 310th BW pulled REFLEX alert at RAF Greenham Common. On 30th June, the wing relocated its REFLEX commitment to RAF Mildenhall, demonstrating the challenges in tracking these deployments. *Brian Baldwin*

Aside from operational costs for each deployment, overseas bases incurred considerable infrastructure expenses. The CLEARWATER program was intended to reduce these by eliminating REFLEX at, among other locations, RAF Brize Norton. *Augustine 'Gus' Letto*

alert in England. By the end of the year these had decreased to the previous levels of 48 and 20, respectively.

A top concern for President John Kennedy's administration was the issue of 'gold flow', which referred to US payments to other countries in exchange for basing rights. By 1963, this affected SAC REFLEX operations in the UK, Spain, and North Africa, leading to the CLEARWATER initiative to reduce or eliminate these expenses, saving $21 million annually. CLEARWATER would

remove all reflex B-47s from the UK and Spain (on paper this translated to 40 aircraft each) by 1st April 1965. Affected bases would be RAF Brize Norton (returned to the UK) and RAF Upper Heyford (retained as a dispersal base) in the UK, and Morón AB and Torrejón AB in Spain.

There was more to the demise of the B-47's overseas alert basing than gold flow. As early as 1959, SAC was keenly aware that to be tactically viable in the 1965-1970 period the B-47

Aircraft turnover between units complicated identifying REFLEX units. 53-2351 wears the distinctive arrow of the 509th BW, but in fact it had just been transferred to the 380th BW and then sent to England while still in older markings. *Brian Baldwin*

Trailing its distinctive drogue and braking chutes, 53-1958 from the 307th BW lands at RAF Greenham Common on 10th August 1962. Lincoln AFB was home to the 98th and 307th, both of which suffered misfortune during their REFLEX deployments to Spain and England, respectively. *Brian Baldwin*

The TEE TOWN B-47E was arguably the ultimate Stratojet, incorporating the latest equipment as well as twin ECM pods, seen at RAF Upper Heyford in August 1963. *Adrian Balch*

On arrival in the UK, REFLEX crews would cock their airplane for alert. Aside from fuel, ammunition, nuclear weapons, and necessary maintenance, the pilots would set up their flash curtains for takeoff. Once airborne, they would remain closed except for air refueling. *Adrian Balch*

Alert was unaffected by rainy English weather. The flaps were already extended to takeoff position and the crew entry door open. One wonders how many crewmen were stung by bees that found a home inside the cockpit. *Adrian Balch*

On a hot summer day in England (even with RATO), the Stratojet used every inch of runway. If the rack failed to jettison, the drag and weight compromised the mission, and the sortie was cancelled. EB-47E 53-2126 at RAF Brize Norton on 13th July 1963. *Adrian Balch*

would have to be extensively modified with decoy missiles, air-to-surface missiles, and the AN/ALQ-27 ECM suite for defense suppression as well as enhanced low-level modifications such as an improved radar altimeter, a terrain avoidance system, and further structural integrity measures. All of these carried a significant range/fuel penalty, not to mention considerable cost. Under both Presidents Eisenhower and Kennedy, however, the Air Force budget simply did not allow for these expensive and questionably valuable 'end-of-life' improvements. Combined with CLEARWATER and Secretary of Defense McNamara's vision that ICBMs should replace bombers in America's nuclear deterrent force, the B-47's days were numbered, both abroad and at home.

Untenable Bases and Bombers

SAC's first significant participation in wargaming was a 1955 inter-service exercise at Maxwell AFB, AL, represented by SAC's Deputy Director of Plans, Brigadier General William H Blanchard. According to the 1959 SAC History, its commanders quickly became firm believers in using war games to 'point out shortcomings in present and future programs, and to seek changes in [SAC's] programmed force.' A 'Red Team', composed of Plans and Intelligence personnel, played the part of Soviet forces while a 'Blue Team' was made up of Operations officers. One of the most significant results of these annual wargames was the establishment of SAC's dispersal and ground alert programs which relied in part on overseas bases in England and elsewhere.

In late 1958, the wargaming team compared SAC's projected 1962 force with the National Intelligence Estimate (NIE) for the USSR in three scenarios: 1) a Soviet surprise attack on the US and its allies, 2) a Soviet attack with 15 minutes of warning, and 3) a US first strike under duress on the Soviet Union. SAC commanders believed that the no-notice event was most likely, with the initial attack warning coming 'from missiles impacting in the US.' Results of this first scenario were abysmal. 'The SAC force was decimated although its bombers were in a ground alert posture. Its [available post-attack] retaliation [force] consisted of [just] 26 bombers, 41 tankers, and 19 ICBMs. Of this force, [only] 22 bombers and 9 ICBMs reached the Soviet Union' where they faced 'about 9,000 defensive aircraft.' The report concluded, 'It was a grim picture. Under conditions of no warning SAC's retaliatory capability would not

deter' a Soviet attack, and, SAC's commanders feared, Soviet leaders knew this and were planning accordingly. The solution, SAC's commander General Power argued, was the long-range B-52 'with necessary tanker support capable of *sustained airborne alert* operations with multiple weapons to follow the missile attack' [emphasis added].

At the end of 1959, SAC had '88 B-47s… on alert at 17 bases outside' of the CONUS, including the UK, North Africa, Alaska, and Guam, with the first B-47 ready to be airborne 'no later than 20 minutes after receipt of the execution message, with subsequent aircraft following at one-minute intervals.' Despite their importance as staging bases, 'real symbols of American armed strength,' and their complication of 'the Soviet's targeting problems,' the value of these overseas Stratojets and their tankers 'for the future was declining coincidently with increased Soviet IRBM and missile-launching submarine strength.' By 1962, SAC's commanders argued, these bombers and their bases abroad would be 'untenable'. Irrespective of budgetary constraints on B-47 upgrades or the CLEARWATER basing reductions, overseas bases – particularly those in the UK, Spain, and North Africa – were of questionable strategic value. SAC's future alert force would be based in the CONUS and would recover to bases in the UK (if they still existed), the Middle East, and Southwest Asia.

Wargaming projections aside, by the end of 1963 there were just 39 B-47Es and 20 EB-47Es remaining on alert in the UK. On 1st July 1964 SAC eliminated REFLEX at RAF Fairford and RAF Greenham Common, both of which reverted to the UK, and the 10 BLUE CRADLE EB-47Es returned to Lockbourne AFB. This reduced the total number of alert B-47s in the UK to 30. Further CLEARWATER reductions spelled the end of UK alert, despite strong protests from CINCSAC General Power who told Congress 'I cannot endorse a proposal which eliminates a vital SIOP capability when adequate replacement [in this case the B-58] is not available.' Nonetheless, REFLEX ended with the departure on 3rd April 1965 of 380th SAW B-47E 53-1884 from RAF Brize Norton back to Plattsburgh AFB. TEE TOWN B-47E 52-0473 (with two external fuselage ECM pods) from the 509th BW departed RAF Upper Heyford for Pease AFB on 4th April, as did TEE TOWN 52-0199 leaving on 5th April. After 1965, SAC's bomber and tanker presence in England had become insignificant compared to its heyday just a decade before, but it was not gone altogether.

The farewell parade for SAC's departure from RAF Greenham Common took place on 5th May 1964. The Third Air Force band led the three squadrons from the 3909th CSG down Northbrook Street to the Market Place in Newbury. Many Britons were saddened to see SAC leave.
Brian Baldwin

B-47E 53-1884 taxis out to the runway at RAF Brize Norton for the final 380th BW flight back to Plattsburgh AFB on 3rd April 1965.
Brian Jones

With the end of REFLEX in 1965, the B-47's signature black exhaust and ear-splitting roar came to a similar end in the UK. RB-47s would continue to fly in English skies for another two years.
Brian Jones

4 After Clearwater

With the 1965 end of SAC B-47 bomber alert in the UK and the general reduction of US forces in Europe as part of President Kennedy's CLEARWATER economic initiative, there would be no more mass bomber deployments to England. This did not entirely eliminate the presence of SAC's strike force in Albion, as B-52s were infrequent visitors taking part in occasional exercises, incentive and familiarization flights, and static displays at British air shows. Introducing the B-52 to English bases, however, was no simple matter. During 1957, SAC began investing funds to improve RAF Brize Norton, RAF Upper Heyford, RAF Fairford, and RAF Greenham Common to accommodate the Stratofortress. This included strengthening and widening the runways and taxiways to meet the B-52's increased gross weight (nearly double that of the B-47) as well as its outrigger landing gear. There were no plans to base B-52s (or KC-135s for that matter) in the UK; rather, the intent was to prepare SAC bases in England for post-strike reconstitution – much like missions by the soon-to-retire B-36s – where B-52s would launch from bases in the US, fly to and strike their targets in the USSR and Eastern Europe, and then recover in the UK for refueling and rearming in preparation for second strikes.

Even before these extensive construction programs were underway, the first B-52 arrived in the UK. Operation POWER FLITE was a high-visibility demonstration of SAC's global reach that combined the command's new B-52 with its worldwide air refueling capability. Five B-52Bs assigned to the 93rd BW at Castle AFB took part in a non-stop 'round-the-world mission. Two of these were airborne spares and, while over French Morocco, would be directed to recover into England as the remaining three completed their non-stop eastbound return to Castle AFB. The flight of five departed California on 16th January 1957, but icing of the air refueling receptacle on B-52B 53-0396 (call sign *Runner 22*) prevented it from taking on fuel during the first refueling, forcing it to divert into Goose AB, Labrador (it also suffered an outrigger gear malfunction after takeoff, but this was eventually resolved). As this jet was planned to continue on the global flight it was replaced by the first air spare (53-0397, call sign *Runner 44*). Over North Africa the airborne

POWER FLITE demonstrated SAC's global reach by air refueling its new B-52s. Five departed Castle AFB, but one diverted to Goose AB unable to refuel. The remaining spare was relieved, and became the first B-52 to land in the UK. *Jim Webb collection*

The crew of *Runner 55* was the first of many B-52 crewdogs to visit the UK. From (l) to (r) Major Ben H Clements, aircraft commander, Major Robert J Jones, pilot, Captain Donald L Taylor, pilot, Captain Harmon R Sage, navigator, Major Ernest C Skorheim, navigator, Captain Hays F Griffin, navigator, First Lieutenant Walter D Cooke, ECM operator, Staff Sergeant Albert T Aroney, gunner, and Staff Sergeant Thomas A Rouch, crew chief. *Author's collection*

commander Major General Archie Old (aboard 53-0394, call sign *Runner 11*) notified the crew of B-52B 53-0395 (call sign *Runner 55*) that they were no longer needed and should proceed to RAF Brize Norton, landing there on 17th January, with RAF Lakenheath and RAF Greenham Common as alternates. The three remaining B-52Bs (including 53-0398, call sign *Runner 33*) completed the global circumnavigation.

On the following day B-52B 53-0395, conspicuously named the *City of Turlock* (a town near Castle AFB), was the star attraction for briefings given to RAF Chief of the Air Staff Air Chief Marshal Sir Dermot A Boyle and Air Officer Commanding Bomber Command Air Marshal Sir Harry 'Broady' Broadhurst, as well as the press. It departed for home on 21st January. Interestingly, the *City of Turlock* was the first B-52 'to land anywhere outside North America,' recognizing that 53-0396 which diverted to Goose AB was the first B-52 to land outside the United States.

The following year saw the first arrival in quantity when six B-52Ds from the 92nd BW at Fairchild AFB flew to RAF Brize Norton to participate in the annual RAF bombing competition. Plans to deploy 22 B-52s from the 42nd BW in February 1958 to participate in the ROUGH GAME EWP exercise were canceled for 'tactical and financial' reasons.

ALARM BELL

With the B-52's increasing importance to SAC's strike mission, by the end of 1958 it was essential to give flight crews first-hand experience in operating to and from overseas recovery bases (although many were former B-47 fliers with plenty of REFLEX experience), as well as to train personnel at the recovery bases in post-strike

refueling, maintenance, and weapons handling in the new airplane. Moreover, these trips were highly prized by SAC personnel as 'incentive training flights' to overseas locations in lieu of the 'routine' drudgery of ground alert, CHROME DOME airborne alert flights, and round-robin flights to and from the SAC base in the US. This prompted the 1958 ALARM BELL program to Europe (primarily England and Spain) and the GLASS BRICK program to the Far East. Declassified histories show that the 28th BW at Ellsworth AFB and the 6th BW from Walker AFB were the first to send B-52s to the UK during January 1959, followed with a return visit by the 6th BW in June. Curiously, there are no sighting reports of any of these airplanes.

UK ALARM BELL deployments were definitely more noticeable during 1960, including B-52Ds, B-52Fs, and B-52Gs from several strategic wings. At least a dozen B-52s arrived in England the following year. By the first half of 1962, B-52 visits reached one or two per month with the final airplane noted around 12th August. SAC flying activity in the UK abated almost entirely during the October Cuban Missile Crisis as alert

Newspaper clipping from the *Oxford Mail* folded into the 93rd BW History for January 1957 showing B-52B 53-0395 *City of Turlock* at RAF Brize Norton. *Author's collection*

GREATEST ACHIEVEMENT IN U.S. AVIATION

B-52 ALARM BELL visits included 5-6 or more airplanes a month across the four Midland bases through 1965, although some months saw an absence of Stratofortresses. Silver schemes were not well covered due to security and limits to access as compared to later B-52 deployments.

On 11th January 1962, 4136th SW B-52H 60-0040 set 11 world records during its non-stop, unrefueled flight from Kadena AB, Okinawa, to Torrejón AB, Spain, a distance of 12,532 miles (20,168km). Seen two years later at RAF Greenham Common and while part of the 450th BW, it bears the mission's name *Persian Rug*. Sadly, it crashed on 6th December 1988.

B-52Cs, such as 54-2686 from the 99th BW at Westover AFB, were very rare visitors to England, in large part because of their comparatively limited operational numbers.
All three photos: Brian Baldwin

In March 1964, each of the four Midland bases had a B-52 visitor. This 'Grand Slam' happened only once, and included B-52D 56-0604 from the 416th BW, still wearing the 4128th SW emblem.
via John Hughes

One of the more frequent visitors to the UK was the 410th BW from K I Sawyer AFB. B-52H 60-0033 was noted at RAF Greenham Common on 21st March 1964, and the unit sent a handful of additional B-52s to five GIANT STRIKE competitions. *Brian Baldwin*

An essential part of the ALARM BELL missions was ground crew familiarization with the Stratofortress, especially post-strike reconstitution. B-52G 58-0226 from the 465th BW at Robins AFB attracts some basic maintenance attention. *Brian Baldwin*

A number of early B-52 bases were eventually transferred to other commands, and are seldom associated with SAC, such as B-52F 57-0143 from the 454th BW at Columbus AFB. *Brian Baldwin*

B-47s were ready to launch, with no B-52 ALARM BELL exercises through the end of December. In fact, it was nearly a year before the next B-52 deployment on 30th August 1963 when 5th BW B-52G 57-6487 from Travis AFB, CA, arrived at RAF Brize Norton. At least 15 were seen during the last four months of 1963. It was not until March 1964 that any B-52s reached RAF Upper Heyford. Interestingly, during the weekend of 21st March, SAC's four primary bases 'simultaneously hosted a B-52', the first such occasion. The last ALARM BELL deployments to RAF Fairford and RAF Greenham Common took place in April 1964 prior to their closure. Dozens of B-52Gs and B-52Hs continued to make weekend (and occasionally mid-week) trips to RAF Brize Norton through early 1965.

The last B-52 incentive flights to the UK took place in March 1965, with 72nd BW B-52G 57-6468 visiting RAF Brize Norton on 14th March, and 28th BW B-52D 55-0675 at RAF Upper Heyford from 19th-20th March. Interestingly, the latter was the first B-52 to be seen in England with the 'O' prefix to the serial, indicating that it was 'obsolete' and at least 10 years old.

B-52D 55-0080 from the 340th BW at Bergstrom AFB was one of a few SAC bombers from that Texas base to visit the UK. *Brian Baldwin*

Relatively easy off-base access to photograph B-52s at RAF Greenham Common made enthusiasts happy, but created security nightmares for local munitions units practicing uploading of nuclear weapons. *Brian Baldwin*

The last ALARM BELL B-52D visit was by 28th BW 55-0675. The 'D models' would be back a decade later as part BUSY BREWER, albeit in SEA camouflage. *Adrian Balch collection*

B-52G 58-0191 from the 456th BW. Four years later, the author's father added this airplane to his logbook while at Beale AFB. Many SAC fliers had more than one tour to the UK in different airplane types. *via John Hughes*

Hustlers and Swing Wings

During 1961, SAC developed plans for REFLEX ACTION deployment of B-58s to Zaragoza AB, Spain, to begin 1st July 1963. These alert lines did not come to fruition, and the two B-58 wings took part instead in ALARM BELL training missions. The first such arrival in the UK was a 43rd BW B-58 at RAF Brize Norton on 27th-28th January 1964, with perhaps as many as 12 additional B-58s coming to England through the end of 1964.

One notable B-58 appearance was not an ALARM BELL flight but the arrival of 305th BW Hustler 61-2059 *Greased Lightning* on 16th October 1963 at RAF Greenham Common following its record-setting flight from Kadena AB, Okinawa, for the Tokyo-London record. (According to the 24th October 1963 issue of *Flight International*, the airplane was named simply *Can Do*, the 305th BW motto, and did not bear the name *Greased Lightning*, which was apparently the mission name and was later applied to the B-58). Similarly, B-58A 59-2440 from the 43rd BW was the star attraction at the 16th-18th May 1969 Armed Forces Day open house at RAF Mildenhall. The B-58 retired in January 1970 without an extensive history of overseas deployments beyond

KNOWN B-58 HUSTLERS IN THE UK

Date	Serial	Unit	Location	Comments
16 Oct 63	61-2059	305th BW	RAF Greenham Common	*Can Do, Greased Lightning*
27 Jan 64		43rd BW	RAF Brize Norton	
19 Feb 64	59-2442	43rd BW	RAF Brize Norton	*Little Rascal*
19 Feb 64			RAF Brize Norton	
May 64			RAF Brize Norton	
May 64			RAF Brize Norton	
May 64			RAF Brize Norton	
May 64			RAF Brize Norton	
20 Jun 64	60-1117	305th BW	RAF Brize Norton	to RAF Upper Heyford
20 Jul 64	59-2457	43rd BW	RAF Brize Norton	
7 Aug 64	60-1116	305th BW	RAF Brize Norton	to RAF Upper Heyford
22 Sep 64			RAF Brize Norton	
16 May 69	59-2440	43rd BW	RAF Mildenhall	

Total number of aircraft = 13

occasional trips to Guam, England, and Spain.

After a convoluted series of cancellations and politically charged competitions during the early 1960s, SAC's future strategic bomber morphed from the North American XB-70 into the General Dynamics FB-111A, with the concurrent derivation of the Advanced Manned Strategic Aircraft (AMSA) into the Rockwell B-1A and subsequently the B-1B. Forward basing of alert FB-111s in the UK would have been an appropriate option given the airplane's comparatively limited range (akin to the B-47),

Despite its historic significance, photos of the arrival and visit of B-58A 61-2059 *Greased Lightning* have proven elusive. Fortunately, the airplane has been preserved, seen here in 1978 at the SAC Museum in Bellevue, NE. *Lindsay Peacock*

B-58A 59-2440 was the last Hustler to visit the UK when it arrived at RAF Mildenhall on 16th May 1969. The B-58's post-strike recovery was limited by fuel, making England an unlikely reconstitution venue. *Adrian Balch collection*

FB-111A UK DEPLOYMENTS*

Deployment	From	To	Host Base	Units	Aircraft	Serial
GIANT STRIKE III	18 Mar 71	27 Apr 71	RAF Marham	340th BG	FB-111A	68-0246
				509th BW	FB-111A	68-0266
TEA PARTY / NATO Tactical Fighter Meet	30 Jul 86	9 Aug 86	RAF Waddington	509th BW	FB-111A	67-7196
				509th BW	FB-111A	68-0257
				509th BW	FB-111A	68-0267
				509th BW	FB-111A	68-0273
				509th BW	FB-111A	68-0275
NATO Tiger Meet	4 Sep 86	8 Sep 86	RAF Upper Heyford	509th BW	FB-111A	67-7193

* Excludes display aircraft

but the FB-111 was not operational prior to the 1965 cessation of SAC alert operations in the UK. The FB-111 was likewise slated for upgrade into the FB-111H, addressing (in part) its predecessor's limited SIOP range and payload, but this never took place. In either case, the presence of SAC's variable-geometry bombers in the UK was extremely limited.

Two FB-111As made their first visit to the UK at RAF Marham for the 1971 GIANT STRIKE III RAF bombing competition (one each from the 509th BW at Pease AFB, NH, and the 340th BG at Carswell AFB), although they did not participate beyond 'demonstration missions.' In addition, SAC's FB-111s took part in the 1986 NATO Tactical Fighter Meet, arriving initially at RAF Lakenheath on 19th July for 'in-theater indoctrination', followed by their relocation on 30th July to RAF Waddington for the Meet. They returned home to Pease AFB on 9th August. A lone 393rd BS, 509th BW FB-111A deployed to RAF Upper Heyford 4th-8th September 1986 for the NATO Tiger Meet. Finally, FB-111s were occasional static display aircraft at RAF Mildenhall's *Air Fête* and RAF Fairford's Royal International Air Tattoo (RIAT).

Although not a SAC asset, the first B-1 to visit the UK was from the Air Force Flight Test Cen-

Right: 68-0246 was the sole FB-111A from the 340th BG at Carswell AFB to attend the April 1971 GIANT STRIKE III competition at RAF Marham. The unit was inactivated in December 1971. *Adrian Balch collection*

Right and bottom: Interestingly, SAC's FB-111As did not participate in the traditional 'bombing' competition held by the RAF. Instead, they made a single 1986 visit to the NATO Tactical Fighter Meet at RAF Waddington, and the Tiger Meet at RAF Upper Heyford. *Hubert Barnich via Bob Archer (upper), Bob Archer (lower)*

Upper, lower and below: Prior to SAC's disestablishment in 1992, B-1B visits to the UK were effectively ceremonial to attend air shows. The 319th BW at Grand Forks AFB sent the first four, beginning with 86-0114 at RAF Mildenhall (top). RAF Fairford hosted two more, including 86-0111 *Ace in the Hole* (middle). RIAT proved an ideal location to expose the British public to the B-1B's considerable engine noise.
Bob Archer (top, middle), Adrian Balch (bottom)

Left: Less than two weeks after the demise of SAC, 384th BW B-1B 85-0080 visited RAF Boscombe Down. Future 'Bone' deployments would be from ACC units with traditional fighter tail codes.
Adrian Balch

Right: With plenty to crow about, crews from the 6th BW pose in front of B-52E 56-0651, one of six that won 1960 RAF Bombing and Navigation Competition.

Below: Top crew for the 1960 event, seen standing in front of B-52E 56-0711 *The Enchanted Lady,* is 40th BS crew S-72 (l) to (r) Major John Q Wise, aircraft commander, First Lieutenant Stephen P Meyers, pilot, Captain Leonard L Kunko, radar navigator, Captain Joseph F Ingenloff, navigator, Captain Leon A Barry, electronic warfare officer, and Master Sergeant Henry A Hatch, gunner. *Jim Webb collection*

ter (AFFTC) at Edwards AFB, CA, when B-1A 76-0174 arrived for the 1982 Society of British Aerospace Companies (SBAC) display at RAE Farnborough. The first SAC B-1Bs (86-0114 and 86-0119 from the 319th BW, Grand Forks AFB, ND) visited RAF Mildenhall in May 1989 for the *Air Fête,* followed by two others (86-0111 and 86-0123, also from the 319th BW) two months later at RIAT. Other displays included RAF Leuchars (1989), RAF Mildenhall, A&AEE Boscombe Down, and RAF Leuchars (1990), and again at RAF Mildenhall, RAF Fairford, and RAF Leuchars (1991).

SAC's FB-111As were either retired by 1991 or handed over to Air Combat Command (ACC) and converted to F-111Gs, with some later transferred to the Royal Australian Air Force (RAAF). With the disestablishment of SAC in 1992, all subsequent B-1B visits to the UK were undertaken by those assigned to ACC.

RAF Bombing Competition

Beginning in 1948 Strategic Air Command hosted a bombing and navigation competition to boost morale while enhancing operational readiness. Known as the 'SAC Bombing Com-

petition' from 1948-49 and the 'SAC Bombing and Navigation Competition' from 1951 through 1992, this annual event was routinely referred to simply as 'Bomb Comp.' Beginning in 1951 (there was no competition in 1950 due to the Korean War) RAF B-29 Washingtons deployed to MacDill AFB, FL, to participate. That same year two SAC B-29 units reciprocated the invitation, taking part in the RAF Strike Command's Bombing and Navigation Competition and placing first in the Visual Bombing category. Through 1960, SAC bombers visited England six more times for this competition, with B-52Ds from the 92nd BW, Fairchild AFB, WA, and B-52Es from the 6th BW, Walker AFB, NM, claiming top prizes in 1958 and 1960, respectively.

During 1967 SAC resumed participation in the RAF competition at RAF Marham in GIANT STRIKE I. This was surprising as SAC's combat commitments in Southeast Asia prompted cancelation of its own GIANT VOICE 'Bomb Comp' in 1967 (as well as 1968, 1972, and 1973). Most notable among the initial GIANT STRIKE competitors was B-52H 60-0008, emblazoned with huge nose art reading 'Dear Rocky, not to win is a very Bad Thing.' 'Rocky' was Colonel Gordon F Goyt, the commander of the 19th BW.

Opposite page, top: The first SAC B-52s to participate in GIANT STRIKE I included the best wings from each of the three SAC Air Forces. B-52F 57-0039 from the 93rd BW did not carry '15' on the tail as did the B-52Hs from the 8th and 2nd AF.

Upper: Arguably the most well-known GIANT STRIKE competitor was 19th BW B-52H 60-0008, famous for an admonition to win the competition emblazoned on the forward fuselage. A gold circle to the left reads '8th AF Golden Bomber Wing, Jan 61-Feb 61, Jan 65-Jul 65.'

Left and right: Despite the endearing encouragement on the left side of the airplane, 60-0008 was in fact named the *Flamingo Flier* with 'Homestead, Fla' and 'Florida City, Fla' surrounding the blue water and green state of Florida.

Bottom: Sporting blue cowlings and external tank noses with white stars and a red '2' in 1967, 449th BW B-52H 60-0049 returned to RAF Marham for GIANT STRIKE IX in 1979, although with the 28th BW. *All photos Jeff Peck via Adrian Balch*

This page:

By the time B-52s arrived at RAF Marham for GIANT STRIKE II they had acquired the SIOP camouflage. B-52H 61-0016 from the 319th BW was part of the four wings that jointly won the Blue Steel Trophy. *Terry Panopalis collection*

Four B-52s made up the team for GIANT STRIKE III, including 2nd BW B-52G 59-2583. A B-52H from the 410th BW took home the Blue Steel Trophy. *Terry Panopalis collection*

The 410th BW took part in five RAF Bombing Competitions, including GIANT STRIKE V in 1973. The Wing used six different airplanes, with two in 1981. *Richard Vandervord*

EARLY SAC PARTICIPATION IN RAF BOMBING COMPETITIONS

From	To	Unit(s)	Aircraft	Comments
12 Dec 51	18 Dec 51	7th BW 9th BW 11th BW 93rd BW 301st BW	B-36 B-29 B-36 B-50 B-29	9th BW and 301st BW won first place in Visual Bombing
Jul 52	Jul 52	509th BW	B-50	Second place in Visual Bombing
Dec 52	Dec 52	301st BW	B-29	First place in Blind (radar) Bombing
Sep 53	Sep 53			
Nov 53	Nov 53	2nd BW	B-50	First place in Blind (radar) Bombing
14 May 58	20 May 58	92nd BW	B-52D x 6	Best Unit Award in Combined Bombing & Navigation; Best Crew Award in Bombing; Best Crew Award in Bombing and Navigation
1 May 60	3 May 60	6th BW	B-52E x 6	Best Unit Award in Combined Bombing & Navigation; Best Crew Award in Bombing; Best Crew Award in Bombing and Navigation

RAF BOMBING COMPETITION B-52s

1958 – 92nd BW B-52D		
55-0112	56-0584	56-0667
56-0599	56-0674	56-0668

1960 – 6th BW B-52E		
56-0638	56-0651	56-0707
56-0640	56-0655	56-0711

Opposite, top: SAC's color scheme and small numbers complicated identifying specific B-52s. During GIANT STRIKE V, 60-0004 from the 319th BW was often parked adjacent to 61-0014, leading to some confusion among spotters. *Richard Vandervord*

Below, upper: GIANT STRIKE VII, known by the RAF as Double Top 77, hosted the usual four B-52s, but temporary parking arrangements made for an interesting photo of B-52H 60-0015 from the 410th BW. *Richard Vandervord*

Below, lower: 449th BW B-52H 60-0025 placed second in the Blue Steel Trophy points in 1977. Over the next four years B-52 performance failed to earn any top places, perhaps reflecting a general malaise within SAC. *Richard Vandervord*

Bottom and inset: In an effort to add some historic color to SAC's presence at GIANT STRIKE X, 379th BW B-52G 58-0189 wore the Triangle K associated with its Second World War heritage as the 379th BG at RAF Kimbolton. The 97th BW at Blytheville AFB ('Hooterville') adorned the tail with an Arkansas Razorback. The 68th and 320th BWs were more restrained, using only the Wing emblem, although the 320th added the Milky Way. The 2nd BW had no special markings. *Brian Rogers collection, 68th BW Chris Pocock via Brian Rogers*

Top: Nose art on 5th BW B-52H 60-0046 reads 'Magicians Best in SAC', while 410th BW 61-0028 shows Michigan's Upper Peninsula and the words 'Someplace Special.' Full 410th BW markings were in tribute to its participation from England in D-Day. GIANT STRIKE XI proved to be anything but magical or special for SAC. *Terry Panopalis collection (upper), author's collection (lower)*

Below: Yosemite Sam adorns B-52H 60-0026 from the 319th BW 'Red River Raiders' during the final GIANT STRIKE competition in 1981. *Author's collection*

Left: In the spirit of all exchange operations, SAC crewdogs managed to 'zap' Vickers Valiant XD818 on display at RAF Marham in 1981. This was particularly humiliating, as XD818 was the only airplane at the base that had actually delivered a live hydrogen bomb. On 15th May 1957 it dropped Britain's first H-bomb in Operation Short Granite. The airplane has since been relocated and restored at RAF Museum Cosford. *Ken Schmidt*

GIANT STRIKE B-52 DEPLOYMENTS

SAC Designation	RAF Designation	From*	To*	Units	Aircraft	Serial	Comments
GIANT STRIKE I		4 Mar 67	20 Mar 67	19th BW	B-52H	60-0008	
				93rd BW	B-52F	57-0039	
				449th BW	B-52H	60-0049	
GIANT STRIKE II	Double Top 70	8 Apr 70	11 May 70	2nd BW	B-52G	59-2583	Joint team won the Blue Steel Trophy
				319th BW	B-52H	61-0016	
				320th BW	B-52G	58-0158	
				379th BW	B-52H	60-0037	
GIANT STRIKE III	Double Top 71	18 Mar 71	27 Apr 71	2nd BW	B-52G	59-2583	410th BW won the Blue Steel Trophy
				320th BW	B-52G	57-6500	
				379th BW	B-52H	60-0019	
				410th BW	B-52H	60-0024	
				340th BG	FB-111A	68-0246†	
				509th BW	FB-111A	68-0266†	
GIANT STRIKE IV	Double Top 72	13 Apr 72	24 May 72	2nd BW	B-52G	57-6509	28th BW won the Blue Steel Trophy
				17th BW	B-52H	61-0002	
				28th BW	B-52G	59-2580	
				449th BW	B-52H	60-0013	
GIANT STRIKE V	Double Top 73	28 Mar 73	9 May 73	5th BW	B-52H	60-0021	SAC crews placed 2nd, 7th, 8th, and 9th overall
				17th BW	B-52H	60-0012	
				319th BW	B-52H	60-0004	
				410th BW	B-52H	61-0014	
GIANT STRIKE VI	Double Top 76	5 Mar 76	16 Apr 76	2nd BW	B-52G	57-6505	320th BW won the Blue Steel Trophy and the Camrose Trophy
				92nd BW	B-52G	58-0181	
				97th BW	B-52G	58-0207	
				320th BW	B-52G	59-2589	
GIANT STRIKE VII	Double Top 77	14 Apr 77	20 May 77	5th BW	B-52H	60-0030	449th BW second in Blue Steel Trophy points
				319th BW	B-52H	60-0054	
				410th BW	B-52H	60-0015	
				449th BW	B-52H	60-0025	
GIANT STRIKE VIII	Double Top 78	7 Jun 78	7 Jul 78	2nd BW	B-52G	57-6503	
				2nd BW	B-52G	59-2584	
				92nd BW	B-52G	57-6503	
				379th BW	B-52G	58-0206	
GIANT STRIKE IX	Double Top 79	5 Jun 79	30 Jun 79	28th BW	B-52H	60-0049	
				28th BW	B-52H	61-0003	
				319th BW	B-52H	60-0054	
				410th BW	B-52H	60-0058	
GIANT STRIKE X	Double Top 80	23 Jun 80	2 Aug 80	2nd BW	B-52G	59-2577	
				68th BW	B-52G	58-0193	
				97th BW	B-52G	59-2580	
				320th BW	B-52G	59-2583	
				379th BW	B-52G	58-0189	
GIANT STRIKE XI	Double Top 81	6 Jun 81	21 Jul 81	5th BW	B-52H	60-0046	Out of 22 teams, SAC's B-52 wings ranked 13th, 19th, and 22nd
				319th BW	B-52H	60-0026	
				319th BW	B-52H	61-0022	
				410th BW	B-52H	60-0057	
				410th BW	B-52H	61-0028	

* Dates are for deployment to the UK, not the actual competition; † Did not compete

Despite this admonition, the SAC bombers came home empty handed. These were also believed to be the last uncamouflaged B-52s to make an appearance in the UK.

Subsequent GIANT STRIKE participants were chosen based on their performance in the preceding year's GIANT VOICE competition. This strategy paid off as a joint team won the Blue Steel Trophy in 1970, as did the 410th BW during GIANT STRIKE III held in 1971. A B-52G crew from the 28th BW won the Blue Steel Trophy again in 1972, but SAC failed to win any trophies during GIANT STRIKE V in 1973. Post-war domestic American criticism of SAC competitions precluded visits in 1974 and 1975. After returning for GIANT STRIKE VI in 1976, the 320th BW won both the Blue Steel and Camrose Trophies, the latter awarded for the most points accrued in low-level bombing (not bridge!). Misfortune struck the 1977 GIANT STRIKE teams when ground radar bomb scoring (RBS) equipment failed, necessitating scoring by means of aircraft-based vertical bombing photography. As the B-52H was not 'adequately equipped' to do this, the best that SAC could muster was a second-place finish by the 449th BW. B-52s fared little better in following years, culminating in finishes only in the bottom half during GIANT STRIKE XI during 1981. This was SAC's final year of participation, yielding a last place finish out of 22 crews.

SAC Conventional Support to Europe

Concerns among US military leaders in 1976 that Warsaw Pact forces were increasingly capable of rapidly overrunning NATO forces and occupying West Germany or other European nations, and that the US would not authorize the use of tactical nuclear weapons to repel them, prompted conventional warfare solutions. CINCSAC General Russell E Dougherty and CINCUSAFE General Richard H Ellis (who replaced Dougherty as CINCSAC on 1st August 1977) proposed sending two squadrons of B-52Ds and up to 30 additional KC-135s to RAF Greenham Common, RAF Fairford, or RAF Sculthorpe for conventional bombing of European targets, much as they had done in Southeast Asia. According to the 1977 SAC Reconnaissance History, at the onset of hostilities B-52Ds would 'strike Communist artillery tanks and troops as they made their initial move westward to attack NATO land forces.' Subsequent B-52 missions would include 'interdiction both in the vicinity of the battle area and beyond its forward edge; airfield attack; defense suppression; sea surveillance; and antishipping.' In addition to the B-52Ds, this would later utilize a portion of the B-52G fleet configured for conventional bombing. This notably excluded SAC's nuclear-only B-52Hs, although the 28th BW at Ellsworth AFB, SD, flew three B-52Hs on 16th April 1980 in BUSY BREWER 80-9 (without landing in the UK), earning the wrath of CINCSAC General Ellis who promptly canceled two additional missions as these assets

were committed to SAC's dedicated Strategic Projection Force (SPF).

The 1976 GIANT BATTLE proof-of-concept evaluation of Ellis' proposal took place in conjunction with the NATO TEAMWORK exercise, and was SAC's 'first overseas contingency deployment to a forward operating base since the Vietnam War'. Four 7th BW B-52Ds from Carswell AFB conducted sorties from RAF Upper Heyford from 16th–27th September 1976. These flights proved both successful (especially in low-level European training) and popular to crews, so plans were developed for recurring visits to European bases as well as non-stop, round-robin CERTAIN SENTINEL missions from the continental US to the strategic training range near Ramstein AB, FRG. These were known as BUSY BREWER (CERTAIN SENTINEL missions were later similarly renamed). The first of these began in May 1979 as BUSY BREWER 79-1 with three B-52Ds from the 96th BW at Dyess AFB, TX, arriving at RAF Upper Heyford to participate in NATO's FLINTLOCK and DAWN PATROL exercises. A number of these deployments also acted as targets for the RAF's Priory air defense exercises. Among the many NATO exercises which included BUSY BREWER B-52Ds were BOTANY BAY, COLD FIRE, DISPLAY DETERMINATION, OPEN GATE, DAMSEL FAIR, CLOUDY CHORUS, BROWN FALCON, POOP DECK, and OCEAN SAFARI.

The final B-52D deployment to the UK was BUSY BREWER 82B, from 23rd April through 14th May 1982 (the last B-52D flight in the UK took place on 8th October 1983 with the delivery of ex-7th BW 56-0689 to the Imperial War Museum at Duxford). Subsequent BUSY BREWER

missions were undertaken by B-52Gs, beginning with the arrival at arrival at RAF Marham on 27th May 1982 of three B-52Gs from the 2nd BW at Barksdale AFB, in support of multiple NATO exercises, including NORTHERN WEDDING and BOLD GUARD. During BUSY BREWER 85B, three B-52Gs (out of seven at RAF Fairford) from the 42nd BW and the 320th BW at Mather AFB, CA, deployed on 19th-23rd September from England to Sidi Slimane AB, Morocco. This was the first visit by SAC bombers to the Moroccan base since their 1963 withdrawal.

A number of BUSY BREWER B-52s served double duty for air shows and fly-bys in the UK and throughout Europe during their time in England. One interesting B-52G visitor to RAF Mildenhall from 18th-27th August 1986 was 59-2570, believed to have conducted AGM-84 Harpoon demonstration flights off northern Scotland.

On 22nd June 1986, General John T 'Jack' Chain replaced General Larry D Welch as CINCSAC. For many SAC personnel and alumni accustomed to LeMay's rigid and dogmatic

Below: The first BUSY BREWER deployment began on 9th May 1979, with the arrival of B-52D 56-0659 at RAF Upper Heyford. For many SAC crews it was their first overseas deployment after the end of SEA missions.
John Hughes

way of doing things, having yet another former 'free-style' fighter pilot leading the bomber command was controversial. Chain incorporated many of his Tactical Air Command (TAC) experiences, including colorful cloth nametags on flying suits, re-introduction of nose art on airplanes, and an emphasis on SAC as a 'warrior' command (denigrated by some as 'worrier')

rather than as a stagnant organization defined exclusively by its SIOP alert role. Beginning in 1988, BUSY BREWER referred to the NATO-support mission tasking, while the deployments themselves became BUSY WARRIOR and the exercise name became MIGHTY WARRIOR. The first of these saw three 42nd BW and two 320th BW B-52Gs arrive at RAF Fairford beginning 30th August

BUSY BREWER/WARRIOR **B-52 UK DEPLOYMENTS***

Deployment	From	To	Host Base	Units	Aircraft	Serials
GIANT BATTLE†	16 Sep 76	27 Sep 76	RAF Upper Heyford	7th BW	B-52D	55-0090, 55-0671, 56-0672, 56-0673
BUSY BREWER 79-1	9 May 79	23 May 79	RAF Upper Heyford	96th BW	B-52D	55-0107, 55-0677, 56-0659
BUSY BREWER 79-2	11 Sep 79	8 Oct 79	RAF Marham	7th BW	B-52D	55-0067, 56-0679, 56-0683
BUSY BREWER 80-2	6 Dec 79		canceled	22nd BW	B-52D	
BUSY BREWER	23 Apr 80	19 May 80	RAF Marham	22nd BW	B-52D	55-0071, 55-0080, 56-0694
BUSY BREWER	10 Jun 80	16 Jun 80	RAF Fairford	7th BW	B-52D	55-0073, 56-0600, 56-0658
BUSY BREWER	15 Jul 80	18 Jul 80	RAF Upper Heyford	96th BW	B-52D	55-0677, 56-0585
BUSY BREWER	25 Aug 80	29 Aug 80	RAF Brize Norton	22nd BW	B-52D	56-0606, 56-0617, 56-0671
BUSY BREWER	10 Sep 80	15 Oct 80	RAF Brize Norton	96th BW	B-52D	55-0677, 56-0659, 56-0676
BUSY BREWER 81A‡	11 Nov 80	18 Nov 80	RAF Upper Heyford	7th BW	B-52D	55-0090, 55-0113, 56-0698
BUSY BREWER 81B	2 Dec 80	8 Dec 80	RAF Brize Norton	22nd BW	B-52D	55-0062, 55-0079, 56-0612
BUSY BREWER 81C	2 Apr 81	16 Apr 81	RAF Brize Norton	96th BW	B-52D	55-0105, 56-0585, 56-0686
BUSY BREWER 81D	24 Apr 81	15 May 81	RAF Brize Norton	7th BW	B-52D	56-0600, 56-0679, 56-0690
BUSY BREWER 81E	5 Jun 81	26 Jun 81	RAF Upper Heyford	22nd BW	B-52D	55-0079, 55-0088, 56-0606
BUSY BREWER 81F	1 Sep 81	15 Oct 81	RAF Marham	22nd BW	B-52D	55-0075, 55-0079, 56-0606
BUSY BREWER 81G	10 Sep 81	25 Sep 81	RAF Marham	96th BW	B-52D	55-0107, 56-0689
BUSY BREWER 82A	20 Oct 81	13 Nov 81	RAF Fairford	7th BW	B-52D	55-0069, 55-0070, 56-0690
BUSY BREWER 82B	23 Apr 82	14 May 82	RAF Marham	22nd BW	B-52D	55-0090, 55-0091, 56-0629
BUSY BREWER 82C	27 May 82	9 Jun 82	RAF Marham	2nd BW	B-52G	57-6518, 58-0167, 59-2594
BUSY BREWER 82D	7 Sep 82	11 Oct 82	RAF Fairford	19th BW / 42nd BW	B-52G / B-52G	58-0172, 58-0192, 58-0197 / 58-0207, 58-0236
BUSY BREWER 83A	Jun 83		canceled			
BUSY BREWER 83B	12 Sep 83	12 Oct 83	RAF Brize Norton	2nd BW	B-52G	59-2588, 59-2596, 59-2599
BUSY BREWER 84A	24 Apr 84	18 May 84	RAF Upper Heyford	2nd BW / 320th BW	B-52G / B-52G	58-0250 / 57-6478, 58-0213
BUSY BREWER 84C	13 Sep 84	12 Oct 84	RAF Fairford	2nd BW	B-52G	57-6520, 58-0253, 59-2599
BUSY BREWER 85A	24 May 85	20 Jun 85	RAF Fairford	2nd BW	B-52G	57-6489, 57-6506, 57-6512, 57-6519, 58-0210, 59-2586, 59-2599
BUSY BREWER 85B	6 Sep 85	11 Oct 85	RAF Fairford	42nd BW / 320th BW	B-52G / B-52G	57-6468, 57-6476, 57-0258, 59-2565, 59-2596, 57-6469, 58-0226
BUSY BREWER 86B	29 Aug 86	6 Oct 86	RAF Fairford	2nd BW	B-52G	58-0216, 58-0240, 59-2569
BUSY BREWER 87A	1 May 87	8 Jun 87	RAF Fairford	42nd BW	B-52G	57-6510, 58-0172, 58-0202, 58-0240, 58-0241, 59-2576
BUSY BREWER 87C	1 Sep 87	5 Oct 87	RAF Fairford	2nd BW / 42nd BW	B-52G	58-0216, 58-0218, 59-2586 / 58-0172, 58-0224, 59-2596
BUSY BREWER / MIGHTY WARRIOR 88-1	30 Aug 88	19 Sep 88	RAF Fairford	42nd BW / 320th BW	B-52G	58-0195, 58-0226, 58-0235 / 58-0213, 58-0255
BUSY WARRIOR	18 Apr 89	21 Apr 89	RAF Fairford	42nd BW	B-52G	58-0241, 59-2595
MIGHTY WARRIOR	7 Sep 89	25 Sep 89	RAF Fairford	2nd BW / 42nd BW	B-52G	58-0180, 58-0216, 58-0233, 59-2565, 59-2570, 58-0232, 58-0240
BUSY WARRIOR 90-1	19 Apr 90	30 Apr 90	RAF Fairford	2nd BW	B-52G	58-0212, 58-0256, 59-2598
MIGHTY WARRIOR	12 Jun 90	25 Jun 90	RAF Fairford	2nd BW	B-52G	58-0202, 58-0258, 59-2565, 59-2570, 59-2588
BUSY WARRIOR	29 Aug 91	14 Sep 91	RAF Fairford	42nd BW	B-52G	58-0195, 58-0206, 58-0216, 58-0218, 58-0226
BUSY WARRIOR	6 Mar 92	19 Mar 92	RAF Fairford	42nd BW	B-52G	58-0195, 58-0216, 58-0226, 58-0230, 58-0255

* Excludes diversions and transient aircraft; † Proof of concept deployment for BUSY BREWER; ‡ Numbers based on FY

Opposite page:
The intent of SAC's BUSY BREWER visits was to provide USAFE with additional conventional bombing assets, as its precision strike aircraft – such as F-111E 68-0022 – were primarily allocated to nuclear missions. *Richard Vandervord*

RAF Fairford initially hosted the least number of B-52D BUSY BREWER deployments – just two – including 56-0658 from the 7th BW in 1980. After 1984, all remaining B-52G deployments went exclusively to RAF Fairford.
Adrian Balch

The last B-52D to fly into the UK was 56-0689, when it was delivered to the Imperial War Museum at Duxford on 8th October 1983. After a sunny photo call, it is now inside the American display there.
Adrian Balch

The 2nd BW sent three B-52Gs to RAF Marham for BUSY BREWER 82C, including 57-6518. Henceforth the deployments would only utilize B-52Gs.
Adrian Balch

A number of B-52s made solo trips to the UK, where they often appeared at air shows. Rarely, one of these would carry AGM-28 Hound Dog missiles, as with B-52H 60-0043 at RAF Mildenhall in 1971.
Rick Alexander

Under CINCSAC General John T 'Jack' Chain, BUSY BREWER missions alternated with MIGHTY WARRIOR deployments. The first of these included five B-52Gs from the 2nd BW and two from the 42nd BW, all to RAF Fairford.
Adrian Balch

for MIGHTY WARRIOR 88-1. A brief (18th-21st April 1989) BUSY WARRIOR deployment, again to RAF Fairford, followed with two 42nd BW B-52Gs.

The second MIGHTY WARRIOR exercise took place in September 1989, and merits a brief summary as SAC billed it at the time as the 'largest conventional exercise in SAC history.' All nine B-52, two FB-111, and two B-1 bomb wings assigned to Eighth Air Force deployed to seven US and three European bases. The overall scenario was based on the NATO command post exercise WINTEX-CIMEX 89. Bomb wings that relocated to Europe would 'change operational

control' (CHOP) from SAC to NATO. Following the airlift phase from 5th-11th September, 68 bombers conducted strikes against targets in both Europe and the US. SAC's Eighth Air Force staff relocated to 'NATO's primary war headquarters in Mons, Belgium' to familiarize themselves with 'NATO command and control procedures and how best to integrate SAC bomber participation.' Sorties from European bases, including RAF Fairford, included simulated targets in southern and central Europe as well as the Mediterranean and North Seas, dropping both live and concrete-filled bombs.

2nd BW B-52G 58-0258 took part in the last MIGHTY WARRIOR deployment in June 1990. Two months later, Iraq invaded Kuwait and the next B-52Gs deployed to the UK would be in combat. *Richard Vandervord*

B-52s also conducted mine laying, surveillance, and other maritime sorties, notably AGM-84 Harpoon launches. Interestingly, two 42nd BW B-52Gs relocated from RAF Fairford to RAF St Mawgan from 11th-21st September for the SHARP SPEAR portion of the overall NATO exercise.

The ensuing June 1990 MIGHTY WARRIOR deployment proved to be SAC's last peacetime exercise, as the Iraqi invasion of Kuwait in August prompted Operations DESERT SHIELD and DESERT STORM. After the cessation of hostilities in March 1991, a variety of B-52s and B-1s crossed 'The Pond' for static displays at airshows in the UK, France, Belgium, Spain, and even the Soviet Union. The first BUSY WARRIOR rotation following DESERT STORM took place from 29th August through 14th September 1991, again to RAF Fairford, with B-52Gs from the 42nd BW. The same unit participated in the next – and final – BUSY WARRIOR deployment from 6th-19th March 1992. With the disestablishment of SAC on 1st June 1992, future B-52 operations in the UK would be under the aegis of Air Combat Command but their missions remain largely unchanged.

To War

Over more than four decades SAC bombers deployed to the United Kingdom in preparation for atomic strikes against the Soviet Union and its allies. Despite often fluctuating international tensions, these airplanes were never used in anger. With little more than a year before SAC's retirement, B-52s operating from England were finally used in combat, albeit with conventional weapons and against targets not in the USSR but in the Middle East.

Iraqi forces invaded Kuwait on 2nd August 1990. Concerns that Iraq would continue moving into Saudi Arabia prompted the Saudi government to invoke American defense assistance. US forces began arriving in 'the Kingdom' on 7th August and were largely defensive in nature – McDonnell Douglas F-15s, RC-135s, and Boeing E-3s. Plans to deploy a contingent of B-52s to Saudi Arabia were put in abeyance for fear that their strictly offensive role might be seen by Iraqi President Saddam Hussein as provocative and lead to an immediate Iraqi invasion against the as-yet-incomplete US preparations. Consequently, SAC began its B-52 buildup during Operation DESERT SHIELD with the 4300th BW(P) at NSF Diego Garcia in the Indian Ocean, with additional reserves assigned to the 1500th SW(P) at Andersen AFB, Guam. Only B-52Gs were used, with B-52Hs remaining on SIOP alert. According to the post-war analysis *Gulf War Air Power Survey* (GWAPS), the 'objective of the B-52 role was psychological. It was to undermine the morale of Iraqi ground forces through periodic bombardment.'

With the onset of combat in Operation DESERT STORM beginning 17th January 1991, six B-52s relocated to the 1708th BW(P) at King Abdul Aziz IAP, Jeddah, Saudi Arabia ('Club Jed'). The need for additional B-52s prompted the hasty establishment of the 801st BW(P) at Morón AB and the 806th BW(P) at RAF Fairford. The Wing staff for the 806th BW(P) was seconded from the 97th BW at Eaker AFB, AR, with the first of an eventual 10 airplanes arriving on 5th February. RAF Fairford crews came from the 62nd BS, 2nd BW at Barksdale AFB, 328th Bombardment Training Squadron (BTS), 93rd BW at Castle AFB, 524th BS, 379th BW at Wurtsmith AFB, MI, and the 668th BS, 416th BW at Griffiss AFB, NY. Deployed airplanes were also spread across multiple units, with one from the 2nd BW, two from the 416th BW (their conspicuous Statue

Above: The 806th BW(P) commander took the notion of security to the limit, ordering that all visible unit markings be painted over, notably the large Statue of Liberty tail markings on the two 416th BW jets. Several of the 379th BW jets retained their Triangle K markings, however. *Bob Archer*

Below: B-52G 58-0182 prepares to depart for a strike mission on 17th February. It later carried the name *Courage* as well as *What's Up Doc*, but without any accompanying additional artwork. *Bob Archer*

Opposite, top: Unit markings on the jets at RAF Fairford were confusing, at best. 58-0237 was assigned to the 379th BW and had the Triangle K tail marking. It retained the 93rd BW unit emblem from its assignment there just prior to the war. As early as 1989 it carried *Daffy's Destruction* nose art, which had been painted over here and then carried the name *Blytheville Storm* in the crew chief's name plate. *Bob Archer*

of Liberty tail art painted out), and seven from the 379th BW. All of these were 1B-52G-777 enhanced conventional modification package jets. Of these, three arrived from Morón AB (on 5th, 23rd, and 24th February) while one relocated to Morón AB (22nd February). The Wing became operational on 8th February.

Combat missions began on 9th February, and typically involved three- and four-ship formations. Given the distances involved – approximately 2,540nm (4,089km) each way, totaling 5,080nm (8,178km) – the total flight time averaged 16 hours. Tankers from the 807th

Middle: Just as they have for decades, bomb loaders sent their personal messages to the recipients. Not everyone in the UK shared this dark humor, with concerns about jettisoning bombs over populated areas or provoking Iraqi retaliatory attacks in England. *Bob Archer*

Bottom: 2nd BW B-52G 58-0245 *Equipoise II* departs for a mission on 19th February. The 16-hour flights over a period of two weeks provoked debate within SAC over the value of these strikes. *Lindsay Peacock*

AREFS(P) at Mont de Marsan AB, France, and the 803rd AREFS(P) at Hellenikon AB (Athens IAP), Greece, supported the missions. Other than the occasional maintenance or weather diversions, the 'Royal Gloucester Air Force' operations were unremarkable. There was, however, some consternation that any bombs jettisoned by a departing B-52 experiencing an emergency might harm civilians nearby or shipping in the Bristol channel (an existing RAF jettison area). Alan Williams, Member of Parliament (MP) for Swansea West, noted in a Parliamentary discussion that the jettison area was some 100 miles (160km) from RAF Fairford, and the intervening route overflew 1.5 million people, all subject to the dropping of 108 x 500 lb (227kg) bombs 'in a pattern one mile long and half a mile wide.' Fortunately, there were no untoward incidents.

The final mission from RAF Fairford took place on 27th February. Over 15 days the 806th BW(P) flew 62 sorties while accruing nearly

Right: 59-2589 is refueled while sharing ramp space with 58-0247. The 379th BW from Wurtsmith AFB flew 38 sorties from RAF Fairford, although the top airplane was 57-6498 from the 416th BW with 11 sorties.
Lindsay Peacock

Below: Armed and ready (note bombs and tail guns pointed upward), 58-0182 awaits its next combat sortie. SAC's B-52Gs flew DESERT STORM missions from England, Spain, Saudi Arabia, and Diego Garcia.
Lindsay Peacock

Opposite page: 58-0247 clears the active runway at RAF Fairford. Wing tanks are still full of ice-cold fuel and have frosted over in the humid English air, giving the appearance of being painted white. Underwing frost is barely visible.
Lindsay Peacock

The final B-52 mission of the war was an 18-ship strike on 27th February to Taji. As crews were landing in England and Jeddah, US President George H W Bush was announcing the cessation of hostilities.
Lindsay Peacock

1,000 hours of flying and combat time, and delivering 1,158t of munitions, including 2,193 Mk117 and 560 Mk82 high explosive bombs and 255 CBU-71/87/98 cluster bombs, comprising 4% of the total B-52G weapons dropped. B-52G 57-6498 from the 416th BW logged the most sorties (11) and the most hours (177.1).

The small number of weapons delivered over just two weeks raises interesting questions about why the 806th BW(P) was even established, especially given the additional tanker demands for each sortie. Perhaps the reason was political. Nicholas Ridley (MP for Cirencester and Tewkesbury where RAF Fairford is located) noted 'how appreciative the majority of the population are that the Americans have stationed their forces here in order to protect our troops who are at risk in the Gulf by bomb-

ing Iraqi military targets.' Such support could be (and was) easily undertaken by Coalition aircraft based elsewhere, but having a B-52 combat presence in the UK may have given the public a visible political reassurance that Britain was doing even more than its already sizeable role in Operation Granby. An entirely opposite view expressed by Jonathan Sayeed (MP for Bristol East) – similar to one commonly adduced during the height of the Cold War – argued 'that the people of Bristol would prefer B-52s to drop their bombs *in extremis* in the Bristol channel rather than that, in years to come, Saddam Hussein should drop a nuclear bomb in Bristol.'

The 806th BW(P)'s B-52 departed RAF Fairford between 1st-9th March 1991. SAC's brief B-52 combat operations from the United Kingdom were over.

DESERT STORM B-52G OPERATIONS FROM RAF FAIRFORD

Home Unit	Serial	Name	Arrived	Call Sign	Departed	Call Sign	Sorties*	Total Hours*	Comments
2nd BW	58-0245	*Equipoise II*	5 Feb 91	*Brew 70*	9 Mar 91	*Jambo 10*	9	133	From Morón AB
379th BW†	58-0168	*Treasure Hunter*	23 Feb 91	*Shiva 11*	28 Feb 91	*Doom 69*	2	33.8	From Morón AB
	58-0182	*What's Up Doc? Courage*	5 Feb 91	*Quite 31*	22 Feb 91	*Shiva 11*	6	87.2	To Morón AB‡
	58-0204	*Special Delivery*	5 Feb 91	*Quite 23*	5 Mar 91	*Shiva 33*	6	86.5	
	58-0237	*Daffy's Destruction Blytheville Storm*	6 Feb 91	*Grim 53*	9 Mar 91	*Jambo 09*	10	145.1	
	58-0247		6 Feb 91	*Juror 33*	9 Mar 91	*Coho 03*	3	51.9	
	59-2579		24 Feb 91	*Thump 01*	9 Mar 91	*Coho 01*	2	31.3	From Morón AB
	59-2589		6 Feb 91	*Juror 22*	1 Mar 91	*Shiva 11*	9	133.8	
416th BW	57-6498	*Ace in the Hole*	5 Feb 91	*Grim 51*	8 Mar 91	*Griff 01*	11	177.1	
	58-0231	*High Roller*	5 Feb 91	*Grim 52*	8 Mar 91	*Griff 02*	4	61.5	
Total							**62**	**941.2**	

* Sortie count and total hours are from RAF Fairford only.
† 379th BW B-52G 59-2591 *Sweet Revenge* reportedly deployed to RAF Fairford, but details of any operational flying there have not been verified.
‡ 58-1082 returned from Morón AB to RAF Fairford for redeployment on 9 Mar 91 to Wurtsmith AFB as *Coho 02* along with 59-2579 and 58-0247.

5 'Wagging the Dog'

In an 18th July 1955 letter that began 'Dear Curt,' Second Air Force Commander Major General Frank A Armstrong warned General LeMay in no uncertain terms about the new B-47's absolute dependency on air refueling. 'If we lose our refueling bases we cannot strike... We "go" provided we can refuel. We "stay home" if we cannot.' Armstrong made a compelling case for the importance of tanker bases in Canada, North Africa, and in the UK. He added that SAC's recent LONG HAUL exercise, which simulated an attack on the Soviet Union from MacDill AFB, was a 'hand to mouth operation' that required three aerial refuelings per B-47 with a high likelihood of at least one tanker lost prior to refueling, crippling the bomber's range and rendering it incapable of reaching its target. Without an extensive tanker force (by some SAC estimates a 2:1 or even 3:1 tanker-to-bomber ratio) deployed at US and overseas bases, SAC's bombers could not complete their initial strike, let alone recover into post-strike bases in the UK, North Africa, and Southwest Asia for pre-planned follow-up attacks. In short, Armstrong concluded, 'the tail is wagging the dog.' SAC's nuclear strike capability was utterly dependent not on its bombers but on an inadequate tanker force with insufficient forward bases, a deficiency that could no longer be tolerated.

Beginning in March 1946, SAC's bomber inventory included 148 B-29s operated by six bomb groups, with additional B-29s assigned through 1947 and 1948, and new B-50s and B-36s expected to enter service in 1948. Neither the B-29 nor the B-50 had intercontinental range (the B-36's operational future was then uncertain), so forward bomber basing in Allied nations was essential for coverage of all target areas. In mid-1948 the Air Force was concerned that given the need to reach these distant targets, 'an aircraft of acceptable size could not be built to perform its mission at the desired range *unless air-to-air in-flight refueling were employed* [emphasis added],' but noted that an extensive modification program was already under way to provide tankers and receivers in the near future. Some 92 B-29s were converted into KB-29M tankers (code-named SUPERMAN), and 74 B-29MRs, 57 B-50As, and 44 RB-50Bs modified into receivers (code-named RURALIST). The 43rd AREFS and 509th AREFS became the

SAC TANKER UNIT ROTATIONS TO THE UK, 1949-1957

From	To	Unit	Aircraft	Deployment Base(s)
3 May 49	30 Aug 49	509th AREFS	KB-29M	Lakenheath, Marham
16 Aug 49	16 Nov 49	43rd AREFS	KB-29M	Sculthorpe, Lakenheath, Marham
6 Apr 50	15 May 50	2nd AREFS	KB-29M	Sculthorpe, Lakenheath, Marham
15 May 50	30 Nov 50	301st AREFS*	KB-29M	Lakenheath, Burtonwood
19 Jan 51	20 Mar 52	91st AREFS	KB-29P	Manston, Sculthorpe
1 Feb 51	4 May 51	509th AREFS	KB-29M	Wyton
4 May 51	31 Aug 51	2nd AREFS	KB-29P	Lakenheath
6 Dec 51	6 Mar 52	93rd AREFS	KB-29P	Upper Heyford
15 Mar 52	11 Jun 52	97th AREFS	KB-29P	Upper Heyford
4 Jun 52	2 Sep 52	509th AREFS	KB-29P	Upper Heyford
10 Sep 52	4 Dec 52	2nd AREFS	KB-29P	Lakenheath
3 Dec 52	4 Mar 53	301st AREFS	KB-29M	Lakenheath
10 Mar 53	5 Jun 53	43rd AREFS	KB-29M	Lakenheath
11 Jun 53	7 Sep 53	306th AREFS	KC-97E	Mildenhall
4 Sep 53	5 Dec 53	305th AREFS	KC-97G	Mildenhall
7 Dec 53	5 Mar 54	22nd AREFS	KC-97F	Mildenhall
4 Mar 54	5 Jun 54	303rd AREFS	KC-97G	Mildenhall
3 Jun 54	4 Sep 54	320th AREFS	KC-97F	Lakenheath
5 Sep 54	10 Dec 54	43rd AREFS	KC-97G	Lakenheath
9 Dec 54	5 Mar 55	321st AREFS	KC-97F KC-97G	Brize Norton
10 Mar 55	8 Jun 55	310th AREFS	KC-97F KC-97G	Brize Norton
9 Jun 55	9 Sep 55	40th AREFS	KC-97F KC-97G	Brize Norton
13 Sep 55	3 Nov 55	340th AREFS	KC-97F KC-97G	Lakenheath
11 Nov 55	29 Jan 56	98th AREFS	KC-97G	Lakenheath
26 Jan 56	30 Apr 56	509th AREFS	KC-97G	Lakenheath
5 May 56	4 Jul 56	97th AREFS	KC-97G	Greenham Common
7 Jul 56	5 Oct 56	307th AREFS	KC-97F KC-97G	Greenham Common
3 Oct 56	9 Jan 57	310th AREFS	KC-97F KC-97G	Upper Heyford
4 Jan 57	11 Apr 57	100th AREFS	KC-97F KC-97G	Greenham Common
3 Apr 57	3 Jul 57	380th AREFS	KC-97F KC-97G	Mildenhall
26 Nov 57	10 Dec 57	310th AREFS	KC-97G	East Kirkby†

* First full tanker unit deployment;   † Tanker support for IRON BAR

first air refueling units in the US Air Force on 19th July 1948, and the first KB-29M was delivered to the 43rd AREFS later the same year.

Tankers in the UK

The first recorded visit of SAC tankers to the UK took place in early May 1949 when 11 newly converted KB-29Ms from the 509th AREFS joined B-29s at detachments at RAF Marham and RAF Lakenheath, beginning the long association of co-located tanker support for 90-day bomber training rotations. Among these KB-29Ms were 44-87781, 45-21701, 45-21785, and 45-21865, all noted at RAF Lakenheath. The hose-reel-equipped SUPERMAN KB-29Ms were still a novelty, so considerable time was spent practicing aerial refueling with the 509th BG RURALIST B-29MRs. At this time

trans-Atlantic deployments to the UK were not air refueled but instead 'island-hopped' via Lajes in the Azores, Keflavik, Iceland, and Kindley AB, Bermuda, although a few of the SADDLETREE B-29s did attempt non-stop air-refueled crossings. Few operational details of the

Above: KB-29M 44-69981 was one of 16 301st BW hose-reel tankers *in situ* at RAF Lakenheath when the Korean War erupted in 1950. Some 27 of the Wing's 45 B-29s had received the SADDLETREE modification and were ready to deliver atomic bombs.

Middle: 2nd AREFS KB-29Ps 44-83993 and 44-69693 deployed to RAF Lakenheath from Hunter AFB in May 1951 as part of Operation REDHEAD. Among their duties was refueling proficiency for F-84Gs from the 137th FBW, Oklahoma ANG, based at Chaumont, France. *All three: Jim Webb collection*

Bottom: In March 1952, the 97th AREFS brought the first full complement of KB-29Ps to RAF Upper Heyford (including 44-69701) to refuel the Wing's three B-50D squadrons at RAF Lakenheath and RAF Mildenhall. *Gordon Macadie*

Top: Seen preparing to depart Walker AFB for RAF Upper Heyford in June 1952 are KB-29Ps 44-84071 and 44-84049, plus an unidentified third airplane. 44-84071 wears the boom ruddevator code C-25, first applied for this deployment. *Museum of Flight, Jim Webb collection*

Above and right: The final B-29MR deployment was supported by KB-29Ms from the 301st AREFS from December 1952 to March 1953. Nose art, such as *Panic Wagon* on 44-69815 was rare and reflected the pride of tanker crews who often felt overlooked in SAC's bomber worldview. *via Bob Archer (upper), Jim Webb collection (lower)*

The 43rd BW brought the last bomber hose-reel refuelers to the UK in February 1953. KB-29M 45-21713 and unidentified B-50A *Up 'N Atom* receive a distinguished RAF visitor on the ramp at RAF Lakenheath. 43rd BW KB-29M 44-69710 *Homogenized Ethyl* was not part of this deployment, but later returned as a 55th AREFS aircraft to refuel RB-50Gs. *Jim Webb collection*

Often mistaken for SAC KB-29s, TAC briefly operated colorfully adorned KB-29Ps with the 420th AREFS from RAF Sculthorpe from 1955 until December 1956, when it transitioned to KB-50s.
Mike Hooks via Nick Stroud/TAH

1949 509th BG deployment have been declassified (understandable as it was one of only two atomic-capable units at the time), but records show that KB-29M 44-87770 belly landed at RAF Marham, where it was eventually stricken and later used for fire practice.

Additional KB-29Ms, including those from the 43rd AREFS, departed for England in August and again in September 1949 as the 509th BG was replaced by RURALIST B-50As from the 43rd BG. At least nine visiting KB-29Ms have been identified, with three (44-87680, 45-21700, and 45-21713) deployed to RAF Lakenheath, two to RAF Sculthorpe, and three to RAF Marham. The lack of ramp space at British bases made it necessary to split each bomb group deployment among two or three locations, with a handful of tankers accompanying each bomb squadron. These assignments were not fixed, however, as squadrons and individual airplanes bounced between bases with alarming frequency. Long-range training flights continued in April 1950 when several RURALIST B-50As from the 2nd BG flew a goodwill mission from the UK to South Africa.

The first full-unit tanker deployment to the UK took place from May through November 1950 when at least 16 KB-29Ms from the 301st AREFS arrived at RAF Lakenheath and RAF Sculthorpe (previous movements had not included all of the tanker squadron's airplanes). During June 1951, the unit supported B-29MRs from the 352nd BS and 353rd BS in a major air refueling training exercise. That same month SAC tankers in the UK experienced another first when two boom-equipped KB-29Ps (44-89823 and 44-89858) from the 93rd BW at Castle AFB arrived at RAF Mildenhall, joining the 93rd BW GEM/ON TOP B-50Ds there, as these were configured with the in-flight refueling (IFR) receptacle rather than the hose-reel system. KB-29P deployments became more frequent as the boom-capable B-50Ds

entered service, as well as the need to provide tanker support for boom-capable F-84Gs flying across the Atlantic and in Europe. The following year saw the first use of RAF Upper Heyford as a tanker base when it hosted 19 KB-29Ps from the 97th AREFS as the 97th BW's B-50Ds located to RAF Lakenheath, replaced by the 509th AREFS for its 90-day training rotation from June through September 1952.

The final RURALIST B-29MR deployment to the UK took place from December 1952 through March 1953 when 20 KB-29Ms from the 301st AREFS accompanied the 301st BW to RAF Lakenheath. Upon their return to the US, most of the KB-29Ms were scrapped. The 'last Superfortress TDY to the UK' involved RURALIST B-50As and 15 KB-29Ms from the 43rd BW, the latter deployed to RAF Lakenheath from March through June 1953. Subsequent tanker deployments used KC-97s in lieu of KB-29s to accompany the forthcoming B-47 rotations.

Refueling SAC's Jet Bombers

KC-97 rotations to the UK began with the initial B-47 deployment from MacDill AFB to RAF Fairford. Twenty-two KC-97Es from the 306th AREFS, 306th BW arrived at RAF Mildenhall during 4th-9th June 1953. Two of these (51-0199 and 51-0205) were not officially part of the deployment and remained in the UK for an undetermined period, quite possibly as 'large theater transports' for the 7th AD. This was the only KC-97E deployment to the UK, as the airplanes were not well liked by their crews due to poor engine reliability. When the 305th BG replaced the 306th BG in September 1953, the 305th AREFS brought 20 new KC-97Gs to RAF Mildenhall.

Joint KC-97/B-47 operations in the UK quickly became routine, especially the massive shuttle deployments between England and French

Morocco. On 2nd November 1953, for example, 14 KC-97Gs from the 305th AREFS refueled 41 B-47s from the 305th BW en route to Sidi Slimane AB; the KC-97s recovered at Nouasseur AB. They all returned to the UK in several groups over the next four days, carrying out the NOVEMBER MOON unit simulated combat mission (USCM) during the return flight. Three months later. all 22 of the 22nd AREFS KC-97s refueled all 44 of the 22nd BW's B-47Es during the QUICK SWITCH EWP mission from the UK to North Africa (one KC-97 was damaged upon landing and remained at Nouasseur AB for repairs until May 1955). Not all bomber wing deployments to the UK saw their tanker squadrons go there as well. When the 68th BW B-47Es deployed from Lake Charles AFB, LA, to RAF Fairford in June 1954, the 68th AREFS relocated its KC-97Es directly to Nouasseur AB.

These early deployments of three bomb squadrons and the tanker squadron from a single bomb wing validated SAC's early war plans. They showed that B-47s could first relo-

306th AREFS KC-97E DEPLOYMENT, 1953

KC-97Es				
51-0199*	51-0212	51-0222	51-0232	51-0237
51-0205*	51-0213	51-0223	51-0233	51-0238
51-0206	51-0215	51-0226	51-0235	51-0239
51-0208	51-0217	51-0228	51-0236	51-0240
51-0209	51-0218			

* Reassigned to 7th AD once in the UK

cate to an overseas location with the assistance of KC-97 tankers, then refuel and arm with weapons already *in situ*. The B-47s would then launch from bases in England, strike their targets in the Soviet Union, refuel, and recover at North African and other bases to be reconstituted for second-strike missions thanks to SAC's 'unsung' tankers. By practicing these missions in peacetime using the same crews from the same wings as would be used in wartime, SAC bombers and tankers developed the operational expertise that LeMay found lacking when he took over SAC in 1948.

The first KC-97s to arrive in the UK en masse were those from the 306th AREFS. Originally slated to operate from RAF Lakenheath, they deployed instead to RAF Mildenhall, including 51-0228, seen here unloading passengers in June 1953. *Jim Webb collection*

Poor engine reliability of the 306th AREFS KC-97Es hampered initial deployment of the type, and they were seen only once again in the UK. 51-0223 *Last Resort* undergoes engine repair. *Jim Webb collection*

Inclement weather proved to be the bane of trans-Atlantic B-47 deployments, as crews from the 22nd BW discovered during their initial rotation in December 1953. Departures from March AFB began on 3rd December, with 10 B-47s slated to fly non-stop via air refueling to RAF Upper Heyford. Bad weather forced the bombers to land at Limestone AFB, where heavy snow brought the deployment to a halt. The last B-47 finally arrived in England on Christmas Day, 25th December. The accompanying KC-97s were scheduled to route via EA Harmon AFB in Newfoundland to RAF Upper Heyford, and via Griffiss AFB to RAF Mildenhall. Similarly, snow, adverse winds, and icing forced the KC-97s to divert to Prestwick, Scotland, and RAF St Eval, with the last tanker arriving in the UK on 26th December, a nearly three-week transit from California to England (the same misfortune hampered the July 1957 deployment of the 40th BW, although with summer storms).

The KC-97s did more than simply refuel associated B-47 squadrons en route to and from overseas bases or flying carefully scripted USCMs. Between 1st-5th November 1953, 305th AREFS KC-97s participated in HARVEST MOON, a US Army ground exercise, although it is unclear if they refueled USAFE fighters or served in a transport role. During early February 1955, the 321st BW conducted OPEN MIND, an operational test which evaluated the 'adequacy and validity of planning factors involved' with a wing's ability to undertake 'quick strike capability', an intellectual forerunner to ground alert. To support this evaluation, the 321st AREFS maintained four KC-97s on strip alert at RAF Brize Norton for 18 days, ready to launch with no warning to refuel inbound B-47s following their simulated strikes. At the same time, the 321st AREFS sent 10 KC-97s to Lajes in the Azores in support of SAC's 5th AD operations from North Africa.

Aerial refueling was essential to B-47 flights between the UK and North Africa. 22nd AREFS KC-97F 51-0281 leads a flight of three from RAF Mildenhall in January 1954. *Jim Webb collection*

In what was arguably the longest deployment to the UK, 22nd AREFS KC-97Fs were delayed by bad weather, with many diverting into Prestwick (including 51-0287, seen here). *Jim Webb collection*

SAC's change in the EWP meant that its tanker basing would be optimized for early aerial refueling of striking bombers, meaning KC-97Gs such as 53-0327 would be located in Canada rather than England. *Henry Brown via Jim Webb*

In another example from mid-1955, KC-97s from the 310th AREFS were overtaxed in their support of 310th BW B-47 operations from RAF Upper Heyford. The bombers flew routine missions to and from Sidi Slimane AB as well as YUKON JAKE sorties to Gardermoen and Sola in Norway, putting heavy demands on the tanker squadron at RAF Brize Norton. On top of this, the 310th AREFS supported SNEAK PLAY, the deployment of SAC's 27th Strategic Fighter Wing (SFW) to RAF Sturgate. An engine fire on KC-97G 53-0110 (call sign *Bracer 14*) led to its loss on 4th May 1955 some 90nm (167km) southwest of Iceland.

Other non-bomber missions were equally fraught with unhappy results. In early October 1955, KC-97s from the 340th AREFS took part in MABELS DIARY, an exercise to provide in-flight refueling training for Republic F-84Gs from the Royal Norwegian Air Force. Logistical issues and a notable communication disconnect between SAC and Norwegian officials resulted in the cancellation of YUKON JAKE sorties. During September 1955, the 340th AREFS dedicated six of its KC-97s to refuel the trans-Atlantic MOBILE ABLE movement of Tactical Air Command's (TAC) 405th Fighter Bomber Wing (FBW) F-84Fs from Langley AFB, VA, to RAF Burtonwood. No doubt this extra flying proved popular with the KC-97 crews, but SAC planners recognized the stress this placed on its 'bomber-dedicated' tanker force to meet TAC's fighter movements. TAC had just accepted the KB-50J tanker to fulfill its air refueling requirements, but these would be short lived and the source of ongoing tension between SAC and TAC. When SAC retired its KC-97s and transferred them to the Air National Guard (ANG), they replaced the KB-50s for TAC refueling, although the KC-97s later returned to Europe as part of CREEK PARTY.

A Change in Strategy

By 1957 the prospective deployment of Soviet intermediate range ballistic missiles to Eastern Europe – coupled with an increase in the number of Soviet bombers that could reach England – highlighted a critical weakness in SAC's EWP. Moving B-47s from the US to staging bases in the UK where they would be fueled and armed prior to attacking the USSR rendered them vulnerable to Soviet pre-emptive attacks that would eliminate British bases. Without these bases there could be no B-47 strikes. Test programs like HIGH GEAR and LEAP FROG evaluated the potential of B-47 missions with an early aerial refueling flown directly from ZI bases to Soviet targets followed by recovery to forward 'un-pre-empted' bases for post-strike regeneration. The success of these evaluations contributed to the 1957 implementation of SAC's ground alert program in the United States (including Guam), England, North Africa, and Spain, which significantly changed SAC tanker commitments to the UK. Indeed, plans were underway to eliminate the 'peacetime and wartime tanker mission in the UK' entirely by FY59.

Maintaining the existing KC-97 and growing KC-135 fleets in England significantly reduced the number of tankers in the ZI needed to refuel outbound ground alert bombers over Canada and the North Atlantic. Consequently, SAC decided to detach only a handful of tankers to the UK from units that were already TDY to North Africa. New tanker bases in Spain and Turkey, along with existing facilities in Dhahran and Wheelus AB in Libya, acquired much of the tanker force previously located in the UK. These units would refuel post-strike B-47s en route to their reconstitution bases. In January 1957, for example, 19 KC-97s from the 100th AREFS deployed to Dhah-

SAC STRIP ALERT TANKER DEPLOYMENTS TO THE UK

Base / Unit	From	To	Comments
RAF Brize Norton			
90th AREFS	4 Jan 58	4 Apr 58	2 strip alert TDY from Lajes
308th AREFS	2 Apr 58	2 Jul 58	2 strip alert TDY from Lajes
19th AREFS	23 Jul 58	3 Oct 58	2 strip alert TDY from Lajes
306th AREFS	23 Jul 58	5 Oct 58	4 strip alert TDY from Thule AB during Lebanon Crisis
70th AREFS	30 Sep 58	12 Dec 59	2 strip alert TDY from Lajes
340th AREFS	5 Jan 59	10 Apr 59	2 strip alert TDY from Lajes
55th AREFS	4 Feb 59	1 Dec 62	Det 1, 55th SRW (numbers varied)
90th AREFS	5 Oct 59	14 Jan 60	2 strip alert TDY from Lajes; transferred from RAF Upper Heyford
91st AREFS	4 Jan 60	9 Apr 60	1 strip alert TDY from Lajes; second KC-97 at Morón AB
321st AREFS	6 Apr 60	13 Jul 60	1 strip alert TDY from Lajes
301st AREFS	11 Jul 60	12 Oct 60	1 strip alert TDY from Lajes
70th AREFS	5 Oct 60	11 Nov 61	1 strip alert TDY from Lajes
340th AREFS	3 Jan 61	4 Mar 61	1 strip alert TDY from Lajes, transferred to RAF Greenham Common
306th AREFS	29 Apr 61	12 Jul 61	1 strip alert TDY from Lajes; transferred from RAF Greenham Common
91st AREFS	6 Jul 61	10 Oct 61	1 strip alert TDY from Lajes
321st AREFS	3 Oct 61	9 Jan 62	1 strip alert TDY from Lajes
44th AREFS	8 Jan 62	20 Apr 62	1 strip alert TDY from Lajes
307th AREFS	17 Apr 62	31 Jul 62	1 strip alert TDY from Lajes
70th AREFS	31 Jul 62	28 Sep 62	1 strip alert TDY from Lajes
98th AREFS	2 Oct 62	7 Jan 63	1 strip alert TDY from Lajes (withdrawn in Cuban crisis)
19th AREFS	16 Dec 62	31 Dec 62	TDY from Lajes; 1 strip alert support for 1 B-52 from Westover AFB
305th AREFS	5 Jan 63	8 Apr 63	1 strip alert TDY from Lajes
11th AREFS	2 Apr 63	10 Jul 63	1 strip alert TDY from Lajes
44th AREFS	1 Jul 63	2 Sep 63	1 strip alert TDY from Lajes
RAF Fairford			
19th AREFS	16 Dec 62	31 Dec 63	TDY from Lajes; 1 strip alert support for 1 B-52 from Westover AFB
RAF Greenham Common			
376th AREFS	4 Oct 57	10 Jan 58	Det 1 from Ben Guerir AB
44th AREFS	24 Aug 58	30 Aug 58	6 from RAF Mildenhall and Ben Guerir AB for BOOT CAMP
340th AREFS	4 Mar 61	26 Mar 61	1 strip alert TDY from Lajes; transferred from RAF Brize Norton
306th AREFS	28 Mar 61	29 Apr 61	1 strip alert TDY from Lajes, transferred to RAF Brize Norton
384th AREFS	16 Dec 62	10 Feb 63	1 strip alert support for 1 B-52 from Westover AFB
100th AREFS	16 Feb 63	31 Dec 63	1 strip alert support for 1 B-47 from Pease AFB
RAF Mildenhall			
91st AREFS	8 Apr 54	9 May 54	5 KC-97s to support GREEN GARTER
44th AREFS	27 Jun 57	11 Oct 57	Det 1, 5 from Ben Guerir AB
RAF Upper Heyford			
340th AREFS	5 Jan 59	10 Apr 59	Strip alert TDY from Lajes
98th AREFS	6 Apr 59	8 Jul 59	2 strip alert TDY from Lajes
307th AREFS	8 Jul 59	11 Nov 59	2 strip alert TDY from Lajes
90th AREFS	5 Oct 59	14 Jan 60	2 strip alert TDY from Lajes; transferred to RAF Brize Norton
384th AREFS	16 Dec 62	10 Feb 63	1 strip alert support for 1 B-52 from Westover AFB
509th AREFS	10 Feb 63	31 Dec 63	1 strip alert support for 1 B-47 from Pease AFB
44th AREFS	1 Jul 63	6 Oct 63	1 strip alert TDY from Lajes
384th AREFS	8 Oct 63	2 Feb 64	1 strip alert TDY from Lajes
19th AREFS	1 Jan 64	1 Jun 64	1 strip alert from Otis AFB
509th AREFS	1 Jan 64	1 Jun 64	1 strip alert from Pease AFB
100th AREFS	1 Jan 64	1 Jun 64	1 strip alert from Pease AFB

TDY = Temporary duty

ran to refuel 384th BW B-47s recovering from simulated strike missions that departed from RAF Brize Norton, as well as the POWER FLITE global circumnavigation mission by three B-52s.

The reduced tanker presence in the UK began in earnest during July 1957, when five KC-97Gs from the 44th AREFS cycled from Ben Guerir AB to RAF Mildenhall. By the time this modest detachment was replaced in October, it had flown 82 sorties (of which 63 were air refueling). The same squadron also sent KC-97s to RAF Greenham Common in support of BOOT CAMP, a proof-of-concept evaluation of B-47 post-strike operations at bases in Turkey, Saudi Arabia, and Libya. The 376th AREFS replaced the 44th AREFS in October, and through January 1958 was scheduled to fly 85 sorties (including 75 air refueling flights) and completed 73 of these. Clearly, fewer tankers in the UK meant more flying for the few KC-97s on detachment there. Ironically, this reduction in UK tankers took place during the long-planned and massive IRON BAR exercise from 25th November through 10th December 1957 involving five wings of RB-/B-47s.

Air refueling in support of IRON BAR was a mixed bag, reflecting the limits of SAC's idealized planning. On the first day (25th November) only nine of the 20 KC-97s from the 310th AREFS at Schilling AFB, KS, were able to depart the US for RAF East Kirkby due to higher-than-normal runway temperatures. The following day the remaining 11 attempted to reach RAF East Kirkby but three suffered engine problems, Of the other eight, only two reached England with the remainder diverting due to lack of fuel. By 30th November, all of the KC-97s from the 310th AREFS had finally reached RAF East Kirkby, with local tanker sorties finally taking place. Considering that IRON BAR was extensively pre-planned and had more than sufficient time to prepare for the specified departure day, its actual rag-tag implementation was an inauspicious omen for the reality of no-notice alert launches. It also emphasized the need for a more reliable tanker and refueling strategy.

The December 1957 implementation of ground alert at SAC bases in the United States had its counterpart in the UK, Spain, and North Africa with the introduction of REFLEX ACTION B-47 ground alert. Although the increase in B-47 deployment frequency (weekly rather than every 90 days) from multiple home bases in the ZI to British REFLEX bases might appear to require more refueling support, the lower number of B-47s involved in each transit (originally 15 and eventually as low as three per week per wing) paled in comparison to the massive single-base 45-aircraft wing rotations and in-country flights

of prior training deployments. Consequently, SAC tanker operations in the UK dwindled accordingly. Moreover, the end of SAC's fighter mission in July 1957 also reduced the need for large numbers of KC-97s in the UK.

During January 1958 the 376th AREFS returned to the US from Ben Guerir AB, as did its five KC-97s detached to RAF Mildenhall. At the same time, a complete squadron of KC-97 began rotating monthly through Lajes, with two of these deployed to the UK for a period of 21 days in what became known as the SHORT PUNT 'strip alert'. On occasion, additional KC-97s were relocated to England in support of special no-notice exercises such as ROUGH GAME and SNOW FLURRY which involved many of the REFLEX ACTION B-47s in the UK. The KC-97 strip alert program ended in 1964.

Enter the Stratotanker

The performance mismatch between the KC-97 and the B-47 not only complicated the ability to refuel the Stratojet during its EWP mission, it endangered the bomber and its crew. With the planned introduction of the B-52, this risky incompatibility between piston-powered tanker and jet-powered bomber would only increase. To resolve this, SAC wisely acquired the KC-135A, which entered service in June 1957. The Stratotanker made its first visit to the UK a year later, and its presence there has been uninterrupted for more than 60 years.

Sadly, this initial trip was marred by tragedy. A flight of four KC-135As from the 99th AREFS, 4050th AREFW at Westover AFB, MA, planned to establish a New York-to-London

Above: For a variety of reasons, SAC moved its KC-97 operations from the UK to Lajes Field. A handful of KC-97s would rotate between the Azores and British bases, although this eventually dwindled to a strip alert tanker for emergency refueling of any SAC, USAFE, or NATO aircraft. *Jim Webb collection*

19th AREFS KC-97G 53-3816 was among the very few KC-97s on alert at RAF Fairford to support a B-52 alert sortie from Westover AFB in the US. *Photo P17600 courtesy Boeing*

Clockwise from top left: An inseparable pair: without the KC-97, the B-47 lacked the range to reach its target. Despite many incompatibilities, the techniques and procedures they developed served SAC for the remainder of its operational history. KC-97G 53-0169 at RAF Greenham Common on 31st August 1963. *John Hughes*

Eventually SAC abandoned the widespread distinctive markings such as tail bands and wing emblems, leaving its KC-97s fairly innocuous. *Mike Hooks via Nick Stroud/TAH*

It was commonplace for a wing to deploy its tankers to a separate base than its bombers, largely because of ramp space limits. On 10th May 1956, 97th AREFS KC-97G 52-2695 operated from RAF Greenham Common while the B-47s were at RAF Upper Heyford. *Brian Baldwin*

KC-97G 52-2692 wears the smaller U S Air Force title in May 1956. At the time, SAC was transitioning to larger titles (see photograph on page 56 for comparison). *Brian Baldwin*

305th AREFS KC-97G 52-0830 was deployed to Ben Guerir AB in French Morocco, but is seen at RAF Greenham Common. Tankers dragged B-47s in both directions, as well as functioned as transports between continents. *Brian Baldwin*

Bad weather would not inhibit launching on SAC's EWP mission, but it hampered training operations and, of course, landing. RAF Greenham Common was 'socked in' on 3rd November 1963. *John Hughes*

Wearing a fresh coat of conspicuity paint on the tail and wingtips, KC-97G 52-2678 basks in the sun at an Open Day. This paint faded and peeled, and was eventually deleted on all US aircraft. *Mike Hooks via Nick Stroud/TAH*

speed record as part of TOP SAIL, departing the US on the evening of 27th June 1958. The third airplane (56-3599 TOP SAIL Cocoa) crashed on takeoff, killing all 15 aboard. The lead KC-135A (56-3630 TOP SAIL Alpha), followed by KC-135A (56-3637 TOP SAIL Bravo) set the record of 5 hours 29 minutes 14.64 seconds with an average speed of 630mph (1,014km/h), arriving at RAF Brize Norton on 28th June. They returned to Westover AFB the following day, establishing the westbound record of 5 hours, 53 minutes, 12 seconds at an average speed of 587mph (945km/h).

KC-135 trips to the UK were sporadic until 1960, and were predominantly associated with the rotation of REFLEX ACTION crews or the delivery of urgently needed supplies and materiel. The first KC-135A strip alert began at RAF Brize Norton on 2nd February 1960 with the arrival of 96th AREFS KC-135A 56-3658 from Altus AFB, OK, quite possibly in support of the STEEL

TRAP and later CHROME DOME airborne nuclear alert program (records show these tankers were *not* part of SAC's ground alert program). Subsequent rotations that year were also undertaken by the 96th AREFS as well as the 68th AREFS, 305th BW at Bunker Hill AFB, but the detachment was inactivated by year's end. KC-135s also took part in the 13th April 1960 YORKTOWN FIFTY deployment of six B-52Es from the 6th BW at Walker AFB, NM, to participate in the annual RAF Bombing and Navigation Competition, but did not, apparently, land in the UK.

One notable KC-135 – 57-2589 – assigned to the 34th AREFS, 4231st SW at Offutt AFB made its first trip to RAF Brize Norton on 26th May 1961. Although it was indeed a tanker, its role as the personal aircraft of the CINCSAC, in this case General Thomas S Power, emphasized its transport usage rather than its air refueling mission. It remained a regular visitor to the UK until the dissolution of SAC in 1992.

Early KC-135A visits to the UK were largely for orientation and occasionally transport of parts and personnel to REFLEX units, but were not on alert. *Jim Webb collection*

By 1963 a number of KC-135As seen in England, including 57-1504 at RAF Greenham Common, had the vertical stabilizer extension, but remained unpainted. *Author's collection*

The 68th AREFS from Bunker Hill AFB was an infrequent visitor to RAF Brize Norton. Its KC-135As were present for a month or so followed by lengthy absences, suggesting support for missions other than REFLEX. *Jim Webb collection*

Top: RAF Brize Norton often served as an overnight terminus for KC-135 flights carrying personnel to the UK and Spain for REFLEX alert. *Jim Webb collection*

Upper: Although B-47s had six engines, it often seemed to those living near airfields as if the KC-135 was louder during approach and landing. *John Hughes*

Lower: KC-135s deployed to the UK did not provide regular refueling for CHROME DOME nuclear airborne alert. This tasking was assigned instead to those KC-135s in Spain. *Jim Webb collection*

Below: KC-135 cell formations were commonplace, but 58-0078 is much closer and higher than the standard separation. While overseas, crews 'expanded the envelope' for normal operations. *Jim Webb collection*

Tanker operations during the 1962 Cuban Missile Crisis were almost non-existent, but 6th AREFS KC-135A 58-0041 departed RAF Brize Norton on 21st October, likely to support the increased alert in the UK. *Jim Webb collection*

The KC-135 presence in the UK changed in 1962 with the establishment of another detachment (or perhaps the reactivation of the prior unit) at RAF Brize Norton, beginning with the January arrival of KC-135A 59-1495 from the 905th AREFS, 4133rd SW at Grand Forks AFB, ND and 59-1449 from the 916th AREFS, 5th BW at Travis AFB, CA. These were replaced irregularly until October, when the detachment appears to have been closed as a consequence of the Cuban Missile Crisis, although four KC-135As were later noted at RAF Brize Norton between February and May 1963, with at least one on strip alert. By August 1963 this had become a single-ship alert.

Stratotanker missions from England were not exclusively devoted to SAC support, as at least five airplanes provided aerial refueling for USAFE's DAILY DOUBLE exercise during July 1963. KC-135s were seldom seen at other British bases except for RAF Greenham Common, which hosted weekday transient airplanes that dropped off REFLEX ACTION crews or other cargo, often while en route to the Spanish Tanker Task Force (see below). Five KC-135s were noted at RAF Greenham Common during October for the *Greased Lightning* B-58 record-setting flight.

By January 1964 the KC-97G strip alert program had been reduced to a single airplane at RAF Upper Heyford. Moreover, the Lajes TDY unit had closed, so each tanker came directly from home units until 30th June 1964, when the KC-97G strip alert program ended completely. The last strip alert KC-97 is believed to have been 53-0191, noted on 28th June prior to its departure. KC-135s were seen more frequently at RAF Brize Norton and RAF Greenham Common, but these were not part of any formal tanker deployments to the UK. A burst of KC-135 activity at RAF Brize Norton in late February 1965 (10 jets noted) is likely related to the termination of the REFLEX ACTION program and the return of support personnel and equipment to B-47 bases in the ZI.

One little-known but interesting KC-135 operation from RAF Upper Heyford was BILLY BOY. With the accelerated withdrawal of the Vickers Valiant tankers, the RAF was without any means to refuel the alert English Electric Lightnings as well as the 29 Squadron Gloster Javelins at RAF Akrotiri, Cyprus, pending the arrival of the first converted Handley Page Victor tanker. Three dedicated KC-135s arrived at RAF Upper Heyford on 24th March 1965, with the first UK proficiency missions starting on 5th April. One KC-135 relocated to Incirlik AB, Turkey, to refuel the Javelins beginning 29th April, just a day after the first Victor tanker was delivered to the RAF. The Victors were declared operational in August, bringing BILLY BOY to an end.

Spain or England?

With the elimination of the SAC tanker mission in the UK in the late 1950s, a small number of KC-135s deployed regularly to the 3970th SW at Torrejón AB, and later to the 3973rd SW at Morón AB, Spain, locations considered 'safe' from hostile air attack and 'guarded' by the Pyrenees Mountains from hostile ground attack. This formed the basis of the Spanish Tanker Task Force (STTF). On 25th June 1966, the STTF was reassigned – but not relocated – to the 98th SW at RAF Upper Heyford. The 98th SW did not have any KC-135s or crews of its own, and all aircraft were deployed to Spain on a rotational TDY basis for approximately 28 days. Normally four KC-135s were assigned,

Below: Wearing the unit's distinctive 'Ramrod' nickname, 99th AREFS KC-135A 62-3499 remains in the natural metal scheme on 29th June 1969 at RAF Upper Heyford. Over the next two decades, KC-135s would wear multiple color schemes, not all of which were well received. *John Hughes*

Above: Water injection increased the KC-135A's takeoff thrust but led to dense black exhaust and extraordinary noise. 62-3538 from the 509th AREFS 'starts the water' at RAF Mildenhall. *Author's collection*

Below: In late 1977, the Air National Guard and the Air Force Reserve deployed its first KC-135As to RAF Mildenhall. Over the next 15 years, ANG and AFRES tankers became an indispensable part of the ETTF. 57-1468 and 57-1505 were the first of many, seen here on 24th and 22nd October 1977, respectively. *Both: Bob Archer*

but a fifth tanker was added in March 1968. The 98th SW moved from RAF Upper Heyford to RAF Mildenhall on 1st April 1970.

By 1974 the Spanish government sought to evict the STTF from Torrejón AB, claiming that excessive operations there caused havoc with airspace around Madrid. The reality was Spain's unwillingness to risk an oil embargo by Arab nations for any support of the United States in the wake of the 1973 Arab-Israeli War. USAFE strongly objected to relocating the STTF to England, and wanted the new base to remain in Spain, preferably at either Zaragoza AB or Morón AB. The final agreement, signed on 24th January 1976, allowed only a small detachment at Zaragoza AB while the remaining KC-135s relocated to RAF Mildenhall.

Control of the newly renamed European Tanker Task Force (ETTF) passed on 15th August 1976 to the 306th SW at Ramstein AB, West

Bottom: Although a clear 'cause and effect' relationship has yet to be verified, the presence of colorful tail markings on ANG KC-135s may well have cleared the way for similar schemes on SAC's Stratotankers. *Author's collection*

Opposite, top: The first KC-10 to arrive in the UK was 79-0434, caught on 31st May 1981 at RAF Mildenhall. The Extender did not compete with the KC-135s from the ETTF, as its primary role was trans-Atlantic fighter drags and NATO orientation missions. *Bob Archer collection*

Germany, which assumed operational control of all SAC tanker and reconnaissance operations in Europe. On 1st July 1978, the 306th SW relocated to RAF Mildenhall, where it remained until it was inactivated on 31st March 1992 and replaced by the 100th AREFW.

Following the 1976 transfer of control, two new KC-135 squadrons deployed to RAF Mildenhall. KC-135A 57-1468 from the 336th AREFS, 452nd AREFW of the Air Force Reserve (AFRES) at March AFB, CA arrived on 13th October, and KC-135A 57-1505 from the 132nd AREFS, 101st AREFW of the Air National Guard (ANG) at Bangor, ME, landed on 22nd October, becoming the first reserve component KC-135s to visit the UK. SAC had just recently approved the transfer of KC-135s to replace the ANG KC-97s, and those units were reassigned to SAC. Guard and Reserve KC-135s remained regular visitors to English bases, and were par-

ticularly notable for their often-impressive color schemes and immaculate appearance.

Just five years later SAC's newest tanker, McDonnell Douglas KC-10A 79-0434 from the 32nd AREFS, 2nd BW, at Barksdale AFB, made its initial arrival at RAF Mildenhall on 30th May 1981 after dragging LTV A-7Ds from the 125th TFS, 138th TFW of the Oklahoma ANG from

Upper: Named *The Shocker,* prototype KC-135R 61-0293 made its initial trip to the UK on 23rd November 1983. It had previously been in England both as an airborne command post and a refuelable tanker.

Lower: On occasion the weather in Blighty cooperated, with the clouds parting after a rainstorm to highlight the 410th BW rainbow on KC-135A 60-0314 on 19th July 1987.

Bottom: The 'Shamu' whale scheme was ill-considered. Aside from making it nearly impossible to see unit markings, it was a heat sink, raising the internal temperature of the KC-135 while on the ground. 340th AREFW KC-135R 63-7993 soaks up the sun at RAF Mildenhall on 31st March 1989.
All: Bob Archer

Tulsa, OK, to RAF Wittering. It remained at RAF Mildenhall until 2nd June, when it departed for the Paris Air Show, and finally returned to the US on 12th June along with its 'SLUF chicks' in tow. During the SAC years, KC-10s were mostly associated with trans-Atlantic deployments rather than TDY rotations to England, so were frequent but not lengthy visitors to the UK.

Two years later the first KC-135R visited England. This re-engined tanker had improved fuel offload capacity and was significantly quieter than its 'steam jet' predecessors. Although active duty KC-135As and re-engined KC-135Es from the ANG and AFRES continued to rotate to the UK, their days were numbered. In addition, most were painted in the 'Shamu' dark grey scheme, reportedly the pet project of an unnamed SAC general who argued that it would better protect them while operating over Europe in support of NATO forces. Needless to say, it failed to do so as the KC-135s flew over the sands of Southwest Asia.

The Reconnaissance Missions

Just as SAC's early bombers were constrained by their limited range, SAC's evolving strategic reconnaissance operations were equally circumscribed by their lack of 'reach,' especially given their lengthy missions. RB-29s and RB-50s could fly long distances from overseas bases to reach their areas of interest and loiter, but then lacked the fuel to return. RB-45s were equipped with gas-guzzling jet engines which prevented both long-range and long-endurance missions. Although RB-36s had the necessary range, they were ill suited to regular intelligence operations along the periphery of the communist bloc by virtue of their 'highly secret' dual nuclear capability. Consequently, aerial refueling was

essential to the success of SAC reconnaissance operations, especially those conducted from bases in the United Kingdom.

The first formal deployment of KB-29Ps took place in January 1951 when four 91st AREFS airplanes accompanied an equal number of 91st SRW RB-45Cs to RAF Manston and later RAF Sculthorpe. These KB-29Ps supported the 17th April 1952 RAF JU JITSU overflight of the USSR. On 28th April 1954 the same unit, now flying KC-97Fs and deployed to RAF Mildenhall, refueled the JU JITSU II RAF overflight, in addition to training flights from England of 91st SRW RB-47Es as part of Operation GREEN GARTER. One of these RB-47Es undertook a dramatic overflight of the Murmansk region on 4th May, nearly running out of fuel while returning to England. As with the identity of the RB-47E, the KC-97 that refueled the damaged airplane at just 3,000ft (914m) over England is unknown, but was one of five recorded at RAF Mildenhall (51-0375, 51-0378, 51-0386, 51-0387, and 51-0388).

Similarly, KB-29Ms from the 55th AREFS at Ramey AFB, PR, supported 343rd Strategic Reconnaissance Squadron (SRS) RB-50 peripheral reconnaissance missions. In March 1952, KB-29M 44-27340 was the first to deploy to RAF Mildenhall, returning to Ramey AFB in May. The KB-29s accompanied the RB-50s 'to the northern Norway area, undertook a refueling, returned to the UK, and then later met the returning RB-50 for another in-flight top-up.' Interestingly, the KB-29Ms and the RB-50s were the last hose-reel tankers and receivers in the Air Force at the time.

Subsequent 55th AREFS visits to RAF Mildenhall (including a second tanker) resumed from May 1953 through 6th June 1954 when the runway closed for repairs, and the detachment

KB-29Ps from the 91st AREFS refueled both SAC and RAF RB-45s operating from RAF Scampton, including the clandestine JU JITSU I overflights. *Photo P12846 courtesy Boeing*

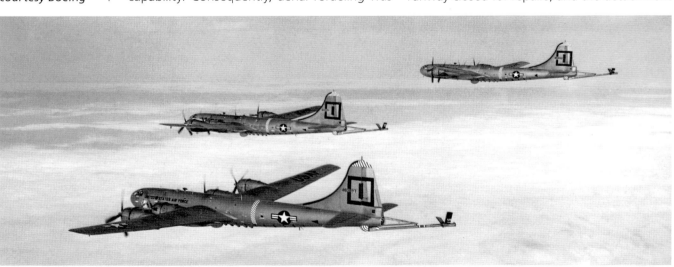

Top: 44-69729
Tillie the Tanker
was among
the 55th AREFS
KB-29Ms
operating from
RAF Mildenhall
that refueled
SAC's clandestine
RB-50G ELINT
collectors. *Jim
Webb collection*

Left and below:
EC-135C 63-8047
from the 2nd ACCS
at Offutt AFB was
one of just a few
of SAC's airborne
command posts
to visit the UK.
EC-135G 63-8001
from the 4th
ACCS at Ellsworth
AFB was another
rare guest. *Both:
Author's collection*

relocated to RAF Lakenheath. Changes to SAC's reconnaissance force in June 1956 affected tanker operations from the United Kingdom as RB-47Hs replaced RB-50Gs for the ELINT mission. This required a change in supporting tankers, as the RB-47Hs used the boom rather than the RB-50G's looped-hose method. As such, KC-97s from the 55th AREFS returned to RAF Mildenhall on 15th June 1956 as Detachment (Det) 1, 55th SRW, and relocated again in January 1958 to RAF Brize Norton, where it served as the dedicated air refueling unit in support of 55th SRW ERB-/RB-47H operations from there.

The 55th AREFS was replaced on 1st January 1960 with a monthly KC-135 rotation. The first of these was 57-1442 from the 96th AREFS at Altus AFB, OK. The loss of RB-47H 53-4281 on 1st July 1960 led to the suspension

of reconnaissance operations from the UK, but a KC-135 remained at OL-1 until 8th October, when 57-1457 from the 68th AREFS returned to Bunker Hill AFB. It was replaced by 55th AREFS KC-97G 53-0286. This was assigned only to strip alert duties, and did not refuel any operational RB-47 sorties. After OL-1 returned to the UK in 1961, the refueling mission was reassigned to KC-135s deployed to the STTF.

Six KC-135As arrived at RAF Brize Norton during August and September 1961, ahead of the announced resumption of Soviet atmospheric testing of nuclear weapons at Novaya Zemlya. These refueled the associated RB-47Hs and RB-47Ks of the 55th SRW rather than SPEED LIGHT JKC-135A 55-3127, which had not been modified with an IFR capability. One of these KC-135As also served as a radio relay airplane

The tanker that might have been. Although Boeing pitched the 747 for use as a tanker, SAC acquired four E-4 National Emergency Airborne Command Posts. Despite its regular appearances in support of the US President and Secretary of Defense, SAC's E-4s had no operational mission in the UK. 1st ACCS 75-0125 visited RAF Fairford on 9th June 1984. *Bob Archer collection*

for 55-3127 while it was on station off Novaya Zemlya (at the same time six other KC-135As took part in the STAIR STEP deployment of ANG F-86s and F-84s to France, although not as tankers but as radio relay airborne command posts). GARLIC SALT KC-135A nuclear sampling aircraft (55-3121, 59-1465, and 59-1514) began air-refueled operations from the UK in 1963, requiring tanker support, along with OFFICE BOY KC-135A-IIs in 1964.

With SAC's departure from RAF Brize Norton planned for January 1965, its KC-135 was reassigned to Det 1 for RB-47 refueling, beginning with 61-0307 followed by 56-3620 in February. This lasted only until 30th August 1965 when tanker support was once again transferred to the STTF at Morón AB. Following the June 1966 reassignment of the STTF to the 98th SW

at RAF Upper Heyford, Det 1, 98th SW coordinated air refueling operations for SAC RC-135 reconnaissance missions including BURNING CANDY, BURNING PIPE, and GARLIC SALT/PROUD ELTON, as well as emergency standby requirements for KC-135R BRIAR PATCH reconnaissance missions. Det 1, 98th SW tanker support relocated to RAF Mildenhall in April 1970, and subsequent tanker support for SAC reconnaissance operations from the UK was almost exclusively from 'the Hall,' including dedicated KC-135Q (and later KC-10) missions to refuel the Lockheed SR-71.

In addition to tankers dedicated to air refueling SAC's reconnaissance assets, 'tankers' from SAC's airborne command post squadrons visited the UK on an extremely rare basis. Although fully capable to function as tankers, they did not serve in this capacity. Rather, these

Two of the five 305th AREFW refuelable KC-135As at RAF Mildenhall on 19th April 1980, the day before they further deployed to Cairo West AB. Three of the five would be refueled in flight, then proceed to refuel the C-141s returning with the freed hostages. *Bob Archer*

visits were similar to the earlier ALARM BELL incentive flights. Nonetheless, they were occasionally confused with the USAFE SILK PURSE airborne command posts, and have even been referred to as 'special mission tankers,' a euphemism that translates roughly into 'no idea what these really are or why they're here' in England!

Combat Missions

It is both ironic and reassuring that the only two combat refueling missions flown by SAC tankers from the UK involved brief contingency operations rather than the general nuclear war between East and West for which they trained. The British connection in the first of these was not well known – likely by intention – as the KC-135s involved deployed to an advanced loca-

tion rather than operated from bases in England. In the second case, it was difficult – if not impossible – to hide the considerable (and noisy) tanker involvement from RAF Fairford and RAF Mildenhall from the British public (and spotters!).

In November 1979 Iranian students seized the American embassy in Tehran in response to the admission of the deposed Shah of Iran, Mohammed Reza Pahlavi, to New York for cancer treatment. The students held the staff hostage, and negotiations failed to resolve the impasse. President James E 'Jimmy' Carter authorized an ambitious military rescue attempt in April 1980. Operation EAGLE CLAW was a complicated two-day plan involving US Air Force special mission EC-/MC-/AC-130s and C-141s, as well as US Navy RH-53D helicopters and US Army Rangers and elite Delta Force per-

Washington ANG KC-135A 57-1425 refueled both groups of 'special mission' C-130s as they crossed the Pond en route to the Middle East. On the first night it was joined by 58-0036, and 379th BW 60-0317 for the second night (seen here on 13th April at RAF Mildenhall).
Bob Archer

sonnel. After establishing a clandestine base (Desert One) in Iran on the first day, the actual rescue would take place from an advanced locale (Desert Two) on the second day, with the freed hostages flown by helicopter from downtown Tehran to nearby Manzariyeh AB (captured by the Rangers), where they would be evacuated by Lockheed C-141Bs. Refueling the special mission C-130s and the C-141s involved KC-135s that deployed via the UK to Cairo West AB, Egypt.

Primary tankers for the mission were the refuelable KC-135As ('RT-135s'). all from the 305th AREFW at Grissom AFB, IN. Three of these [58-0018, 60-0362 (a previous UK visitor as an RC-135D), and 61-0293 (a UK SILK PURSE airborne command post alumnus)] left RAF Mildenhall on 21st April for Cairo West AB. That night, KC-135A 57-1425 of the 116th AREFS, 141st AREFW (Washington ANG) and 58-0036 of the 19th BW departed RAF Mildenhall to Lajes Field, and refueled a low-level [9,000ft (2,743m)] formation of 'C-130s' en route from the southeast US to Egypt. The tankers returned to England the following day. Two more RT-135s (58-0011 and 58-0126) left RAF Mildenhall for Cairo on 22nd April. In addition, KC-135A 60-0317 from the 379th BW and the same Washington ANG tanker refueled another low-level formation of 'C-130s' destined for Egypt, returning to RAF Mildenhall on 23rd April.

The rescue operation began on 24th April, and quickly fell apart. Mechanical problems with the RH-53s resulted in the decision to abort the mission (a minimum of six were needed, but only five were available). During the departure from Desert One, an RH-53 clipped an EC-130E, sparking an ensuing conflagration of exploding fuel and ammunition, killing eight US personnel. The remaining four RH-53s were abandoned and the American forces departed the site in the five operational C-130s. These were critically low on fuel, so were air refueled by the RT-135s as they all recovered to Cairo West AB.

EL DORADO CANYON **KC-135s AND KC-10s**

KC-135s				
56-3603	58-0050	58-0126	61-0295	63-8878
56-3615	58-0073	60-0357	63-8018	63-8884
58-0018	58-0124			

KC-10s				
79-1710	82-0191	83-0077	84-0188	85-0029
79-1712	82-0193	83-0078	84-0190	85-0030
79-1713	83-0075	83-0080	84-0191	85-0031
79-1949	83-0076	84-0186	85-0027	86-0027

EL DORADO CANYON

Ongoing tensions between the United States and Libya erupted into open conflict in March 1986, when the US sank the Libyan corvette *Ain Zaquit* in the Gulf of Sidra. Libyan leader Muammar Ghaddafi called for global reprisals against Americans. Two weeks later, a bomb planted by Libyan-backed terrorists exploded in the *La Belle* discothèque in West Berlin, killing three (including two American soldiers) and injuring some 230. In response, US President Ronald Reagan ordered an attack on Libyan military facilities by USAFE F-111s from the UK and by US Navy carrier forces in the Mediterranean. Although Operation EL DORADO CANYON did not explicitly target Ghaddafi, Reagan would not have been disappointed if he had been killed; however, Italian Prime Minister Benedetto 'Bettino' Craxi warned Ghaddafi at the last minute, allowing him to escape.

The longest combat aerial refueling operation from the UK began on Friday, 11th April 1986, with the arrival of seven KC-10s at RAF Mildenhall, with four additional Extenders reaching RAF Fairford from Zaragoza AB. By Sunday, the number of KC-10s in the UK 'nearly doubled,' mostly from the 22nd AREFW at March AFB along with a smattering from the 2nd BW at Barksdale AFB and the 68th Air Refueling Group at Seymour Johnson AFB, NC. The 11th Strategic Group (SG) at RAF Fairford hosted seven KC-10s in addition to two KC-135As, while RAF Mildenhall's ramps were packed with 12 KC-10s, six KC-135As, one KC-135E, and one KC-135Q selected for the mission.

KC-10s served as the primary mission refueling aircraft given their larger fuel offload capability than KC-135s, as well as their ability to be refueled in flight. As multiple NATO and allied nations refused overflight permission for the strikes from England, the 24 PAVE TACK-equipped General Dynamics F-111F strike aircraft from the 48th Tactical Fighter Wing (TFW) at RAF Lakenheath and the six EF-111A electronic countermeasure (ECM) jets from the 20th TFW at RAF Upper Heyford were forced to fly a 6,400nm (11,853km) mission track around the Iberian Peninsula, through the Straits of Gibraltar, and thence to Libya, returning via the same route [this distance was 200nm (370km) short of the 1982 RAF 'Black Buck' Vulcan bombing missions of the Falklands].

The need for multiple refuelings was complicated by F-111 crews having only a few months of experience refueling from KC-10s, which had begun regular European theater operations in January 1986. To mitigate this, each F-111 crew was assigned to a specific 'mother tanker' throughout the entire mission. This would familiarize each F-111 pilot with a single KC-10 boom operator over the course of the 13-hour mission with five planned radio-silent air refuelings. This procedure worked well during Operation GHOST RIDER, the October 1985 dress rehearsal by 20th TFW F-111Es for EL DORADO CANYON, although tanker crews were not particularly enamored by this arrangement.

There were three F-111 refuelings scheduled on the way down and two during the return trip, with two KC-10 refuelings in both directions. However, as they approached their 'drop off' points near Sicily, the F-111s continuously cycled through the KC-10s to keep topped off with fuel. When they returned to the tankers after the mission they were all low on fuel and latched onto the first tanker they could find, which led to some initial confusion as to who was where and who had been lost. In addition, the F-111s did not use their transponders or other radio emitters to prevent any ground radar observers from inferring that this was anything other than a large tanker exercise.

Because of the short runway at RAF Mildenhall [9,219ft (2,810m)], the KC-10s were unable to take off with a full load and had to be topped off by UK-based KC-135s as they headed southwest past France, again similar

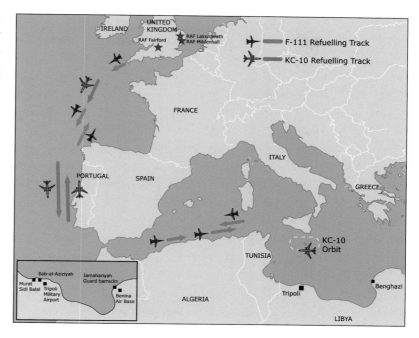

to the Black Buck mission and its cascading Victor tanker refuelings. [At least four air-refuelable KC-135As from the 305th AREFW at Grissom AFB (58-0018, 58-0124, 58-0126, and 60-0357) were in Spain, but these are known to have supported potential MC-130 rescue missions should a strike aircraft have gone down inside Libya. They may have had a secondary role to refuel any of the KC-10s., although they were not used for this.]

KC-135As from RAF Mildenhall included 2nd BW 56-3603 and 5th BW 63-8878 (seen just prior to the mission). Their tasking was to 'top off' the KC-10s to maximum fuel loads, constrained by runway length. *Bob Archer*

The first KC-10 to launch was 2nd BW 83-0077, which served as the airborne command post for the mission, carrying senior commanders from the flying wings and USAFE. *William R Peake*

So it Begins

Tanker departures began on 14th April at 1709Z with the launch of six KC-135A/Qs (in sequence 56-3603, 63-8878, 58-0050, 58-0073, 63-8884, and 61-0295) from RAF Mildenhall. Some 15 minutes later, 10 KC-10s departed (in sequence 83-0077, 85-0030, 85-0027, 79-1712, 86-0027, 85-0031, 84-0191, 82-0191, 79-1710, and 85-0029). The first KC-10A to depart – 83-0077 – was the airborne mission command post, configured with additional radios. On board were Colonel Lynn T Berringer, 306th SW commander, Colonel Sam W Westbrook, III, 48th TFW commander, and Major General David W Forgan, the USAFE Deputy Chief of Staff for Operations and airborne mission commander for Operation EL DORADO CANYON.

The first F-111F departed RAF Lakenheath at 1735Z. RAF Fairford tanker departures began at 1815Z with KC-10 83-0080 followed by five KC-10s and KC-135s (in sequence: KC-10s 82-0193 and 83-0076, KC-135s 63-8018 and 56-3615, and then KC-10 84-0186). The lead KC-10 made the short flight over to RAF Upper Heyford where the EF-111As took off and rejoined on it for the long flight south. Three additional KC-10s departed between 1934Z and 1955Z (79-1713, 83-0078, and 79-1949). These were 'reliability' tankers; the third one topped off the other two which then served as airborne spares in case one of the primary tankers broke. These then orbited over the Mediterranean Sea to provide extra fuel if needed. The two KC-135s from RAF Fairford refueled the first KC-10 launched from RAF Fairford, which was the EF-111 mother ship, before returning there around 2115Z. The second RAF Fairford KC-10 was the airborne spare for the first one, and was refueled by the third KC-10. Following the first aerial refueling, the airborne spares –

six F-111Fs and one EF-111A – returned to the UK. They were supported by KC-135A 58-0073 in case any of them required fuel.

Following anywhere from three to four actual air refuelings per airplane, the strike package reached Libya. The KC-10s established anchor orbits south of Sicily, ready to refuel the post-strike USAFE aircraft prior to the long haul back to England. The US Navy aircraft at the east end of the Gulf of Sidra were supported organically by Grumman KA-6D Intruder tankers from the USS *America* and USS *Coral Sea*.

Standoff jamming of surface-to-air missiles (SAM) by EF-111As began at 2352Z and continued for about 20 minutes, supported by an EA-6B from the USS *America*. Meanwhile, radar site suppression in support of the F-111F attacks began at 2355Z with LTV A-7Es from VA-46 launching 16 AGM-88A HARM anti-radiation missiles while VA-72 A-7Es launched eight AGM-45 Shrikes. The main strike was scheduled for 0000Z on 15th April, with the F-111Fs attacking targets in the vicinity of Tripoli and US Navy jets attacking in and near Benghazi. By 0013Z all US strike aircraft (minus F-111F 70-2389 *Karma 52* which had been shot down) were 'feet wet' and the F-111Fs headed for their KC-10 tankers orbiting over the Mediterranean Sea. These aircraft loitered for nearly an hour in their orbit areas pending any signs of the two missing crewmembers who, unfortunately, had perished.

The six RAF Mildenhall KC-135s that had refueled the mothership KC-10s returned between 2126Z and 2349Z. The four RAF Mildenhall KC-10s that refueled the motherships returned around midnight. The mission KC-10s arrived home between 0549Z and 0744Z (in sequence 84-0191, 82-0191, 85-0029, 85-0030, and 83-0077), with the last two having been aloft for 14.3 hours. The reliability KC-10s (84-0188 and 84-0190) returned to RAF Mildenhall

Left: 63-8018 was one of two KC-135As to depart from RAF Fairford, along with four KC-10s. *Steve Edwards*

Below: 96th BW KC-135A 58-0073 was dedicated to refueling the airborne spare F-111Fs and EF-111As. Once the main package had completed its first refueling, these spares returned to RAF Lakenheath and RAF Upper Heyford, respectively. *Bob Archer*

Left and below: After more than 14 hours, the final KC-10s (including 84-0191) returned to their English bases, with 79-1713 among the last to land. EL DORADO CANYON utilized 33% of the entire KC-10 fleet, demonstrating its value to long-range strike operations. *Author's collection*

around 0620Z. The EF-111A escorts began landing at RAF Fairford at 0408Z with 83-0076, followed by 79-1949 at 0516Z, with 82-0193 and 83-0080 around 0650Z, and 79-1713 and 83-0078 straggling in by 0955Z.

The KC-10 armada 'remained intact' at RAF Fairford until 22nd April in case that subsequent strikes would be ordered. In any event, there were no additional attacks, but the KC-10s and KC-135Qs were nonetheless busy refueling SR-71 battle damage assessment missions. Most of the KC-10s at RAF Fairford were gone by 25th April. The 15 KC-10s at RAF Mildenhall remained in place until 26th April, when they slowly returned home or relocated to other locations, leaving just 83-0077 and 83-0079 by 1st May.

***

The August 1990 Iraqi invasion of Kuwait sparked arguably the largest trans-Atlantic movement of aircraft since the onset of the Cold War. The initial deployment of additional RC-135s and E-3s to Saudi Arabia benefitted from KC-135s based in England. As the DESERT SHIELD defensive build-up continued, the relocation of entire wings of F-15s, General Dynamics F-16s, Lockheed F-117s, a variety of special-mission C-130s, and sundry Lockheed C-141s and C-5s were all refueled or replaced by dozens of KC-135s from or passing through RAF Mildenhall. At times, most of Scottish airspace was one giant air refueling track. When the DESERT STORM offensive to reclaim Kuwait began in January 1991, British-based KC-135s and KC-10s were even busier – in both directions – refuel-

ing transports hauling replacement personnel and war materiel to the Middle East, as well as those that were returning empty to the US. A few even served as 'trash haulers' to get vital equipment and people to bases in theater or in a medical evacuation role. At the height of the pre-war buildup, there were upwards of 50 KC-135s at RAF Mildenhall alone.

This single event, more than any other, dramatically altered the nature of American tanker operations, especially those flying from the UK. A year later, SAC would be gone, and its tankers redistributed to Air Mobility Command (AMC) where they would see dual use as air refuelers and transports. More importantly, SAC's former bomber and tanker fleets would be in constant combat for decades to come, not in a thermonuclear environment but in support of conventional warfare in Southeastern Europe, parts of Africa, the Middle East, and Southwest Asia. Tankers based in Britain increasingly refueled a far greater proportion of fighters and special-mission receivers than bombers. Moreover, the demand for tankers located in-theater created the need for detachments or provisional units closer to the receivers and their targets, reducing the need for an expansive Tanker Task Force in the UK. Indeed, RAF Mildenhall is slated to close in 2024 and the US tanker presence in England will be relocated after 75 years to Germany. Throughout these changes, the essential demand for aerial refueling to accomplish all of these missions meant that SAC's tankers – for 50 of those 75 years – remained the tail that wagged the dog.

The end of an era. The last KC-135A in the UK was 62-3539 departing RAF Mildenhall on 17th November 1993. The last 'water burner' was KC-135Q 58-0046 (seen here) which left on 19th December 1994. *Bob Archer*

6 Eyes in English Skies

When Strategic Air Command was founded on 21st March 1946 it was seen by many as just a bomber organization, and throughout its 46-year history SAC became synonymous with B-36s, B-47s, and B-52s. Without adequate target knowledge, however, SAC's bombers were an empty threat. In recognition of this critical gap, SAC's founding charter specified that America's bomber command would also 'conduct maximum range reconnaissance over land or sea either independently or in cooperation with land and naval forces.' This intelligence would benefit not only military and civilian policy makers, but would satisfy SAC's global targeting requirements as well. Most importantly, aerial intelligence would provide the margin needed for America to learn of an impending attack – no doubt with atomic weapons – allowing US leaders and SAC to respond accordingly.

Just as it did by deploying its bombers to England, SAC appreciated that it would be equally valuable to send its reconnaissance aircraft to the United Kingdom in support of what would become the US Peacetime Aerial Reconnaissance Program (PARPRO). From there, these camera- and electronic-gizmo-laden converted bombers could easily cover Western Europe, where most military and civilian leaders believed any Soviet attack would begin. Moreover, SAC reconnaissance assets in England could monitor the North Atlantic – especially the critical Greenland-Iceland-United Kingdom (GIUK) Gap – through which Soviet offensive naval forces would pass into the Atlantic Ocean or would put SAC bombers and tankers en route to their targets at risk from naval anti-aircraft fire or SAMs. From England, SAC's electronic 'ferrets' could easily patrol the East-West border between the Federal Republic of Germany (FRG-West Germany) and the German Democratic Republic (GDR-East Germany), as well as the periphery of the USSR or in the Baltic Sea, collecting the electronic signatures of early warning (EW) and targeting radars that could detect and destroy SAC's bombers. British bases

Reconnaissance missions spanned the entire history of SAC operations in the UK. In later years, 55th SRW BIG TEAM RC-135C 64-14841 collected ELINT, while 6th SW RIVET BRASS RC-135D 60-0356 primarily collected COMINT. *Adrian Balch*

TYPES OF INTELLIGENCE

Although there are many different types of intelligence, these are the primary 'INTs' associated with SAC reconnaissance aircraft.

COMINT (COMmunications INTelligence) – functional intelligence processed from voice, visual, and electronic communications, telephone, telegraph, television, facsimile, and satellite sources

ELINT (ELectronic INTelligence) – technical and intelligence information derived from foreign noncommunications electromagnetic radiations emanating from other than atomic detonations or radioactive sources

NUDINT (NUclear Detonation INTelligence) – intelligence derived from the collection and analysis of radiation and other effects resulting from radioactive sources

MASINT (Measurement And Signature INTelligence) – scientific and technical intelligence information obtained by quantitative and qualitative analysis of data (metric, angle, spatial, wavelength, time dependence, modulation, plasma, and hydromagnetic) derived from specific technical sensors for the purpose of identifying any distinctive features associate with the source, emitter, or sender and to facilitate subsequent identification and/or measurement of the same

PHOTINT (PHOTographic INTelligence) – processed information obtained from all forms of photography, film or electronic, including satellite (currently called **IMINT** for IMagery INTelligence)

SIGINT (SIGnals INTelligence) – intelligence combining COMINT and ELINT

Definitions are from official US intelligence agency (NSA, CIA, JCS, etc) references, cited in Leo D Carl, The International Dictionary of Intelligence (McLean, VA: International Defense Consultant Services, 1990)

Although they were perhaps best known for their missions in the Far East, RB-29s such as 44-61929 *El Diablo II* conducted reconnaissance flights from the UK during the 1948 Berlin Crisis and at the outset of the Korean War in 1950. *Terry Panopalis collection*

were also effectively halfway between the US and key deployment venues in the Middle East, most notably Adana AB (renamed Incirlik AB on 28th February 1958) in Turkey or Dhahran AB in Saudi Arabia. From these forward bases, SAC ferrets could create an electronic order of battle (EOB) for the southern approaches to the USSR, and camera-equipped assets could identify potential post-strike recovery bases. Finally, the SAC reconnaissance presence in the UK was linked to one of the most important intelligence-sharing arrangements in the Cold War, part of the 'Special Relationship' between the United States and Great Britain.

Despite all of these advantages, there were periods of significant strain on the relationship, with some in British leadership roles concerned that the American presence invited, at worst, a Soviet pre-emptive attack during periods of heightened tensions to eliminate SAC aircraft, or, at least, undermined 'cordial' relations between the UK and the USSR. This issue was

not unique to reconnaissance aircraft, however, and mirrored the same situation with SAC bombers on English soil. It did carry a far greater sense of imminence and urgency, especially after the 1st May 1960 U-2 Incident and the 1st July 1960 Soviet attack that resulted in the loss of a SAC RB-47H launched from RAF Brize Norton. Indeed, records of Parliamentary debates and questions show considerable hostility by some Members toward these bases and operations. Nonetheless, the overall British response to these criticisms resulted in a 'workable arrangement' that allowed SAC operations to continue while ensuring British sovereignty and final approval.

Early Years

What is believed to be the first SAC reconnaissance visit in the UK began with four RB-29As from the 16th Photo Reconnaissance Squadron (PRS) of the 91st Strategic Reconnaissance Group (SRG) from McGuire AFB, NJ, that had been deployed to Fürstenfeldbruck AB in West Germany. During October and November 1948, these RB-29s visited RAF Scampton. While in England they conducted a four-day trip to Dakar, Senegal. After returning from Africa, RB-29A 44-61999 crashed on 3rd November at Higher Shelf Stones, Wig Point, Bleaklow in Derbyshire, killing all 13 aboard (this should not be confused with the loss of 307th BW B-29 44-86356 at Lajes Field in the Azores the same day). The remaining 91st SRG RB-29s departed RAF Scampton on 24th November for McGuire AFB via Lajes.

Reconnaissance deployments to England resumed on 22nd December 1949 when the first RB-29A from the 23rd Strategic Reconnaissance Squadron (Photographic) [SRS(P)], 5th SRG at Fairfield-Suisun AFB, CA, arrived at

RB-29A 44-61999 came to grief as it clipped a short rise during the type's first deployment to England in 1948. Bad weather proved a challenge both to mission success and safe flying. *Rob Hall*

RAF Sculthorpe. Ultimately, a dozen airplanes arrived after extensive delays. While in England the RB-29s conducted local exercises as well as five 'long-range' flights to Dhahran AB, and were intercepted en route by Malta-based RAF de Havilland Vampires. All 12 departed for home on 6th March 1950, with 10 passing through Lajes and the other two returning via Keflavik.

On 25th June 1950 North Korean troops invaded South Korea. For many American military and political leaders this was seen as merely a diversion for what they believed would be a forthcoming Soviet invasion of Western Europe. At the outbreak of the Korean war, RB-29As from the 72nd SRS(P), 5th Strategic Reconnaissance Wing (SRW) at Fairfield-Suisun AFB were at RAF Sculthorpe, having arrived there from 27th-30th May for a routine deployment. One of these reached England in dramatic fashion, landing safely with one engine feathered and the other engine on the same side on fire! In conjunction with other *in situ* reconnaissance assets in Europe and North Africa, the 72nd SRS(P) RB-29s found no indicators of an imminent war on the Continent. Soviet naval exercises in the Black Sea, for example, were determined to be preplanned, benign, and not suggestive of any wider Soviet effort.

A substantial mishap occurred on 7th June when RB-29A 42-94081 crashed into the sea some 20nm (37km) east of Cromer. It was on an air-sea gunnery training exercise when the forward top turret accidentally shot out the #4 engine while flying just 500ft (152m) above the water. Eight of the 11 crewmembers were able to bail out before the airplane ditched, but only five survived. On 16th July the 72nd SRS(P) RB-29s relocated to RAF Marham, and by the end of the month moved to RAF Burtonwood. Tragedy again struck the unit with the loss of RB-29A 45-21763 on 11th August at RAF Mildenhall. The remaining airplanes returned to California on 15th November 1950 in preparation for the unit's conversion to Convair RB-36s.

Operation ROUNDOUT

The first significant SAC reconnaissance deployment to the UK began on 19th January 1951 when 11 Boeing RB-50Es from the 38th SRS, 55th SRW at Ramey AFB, PR, deployed to RAF Bassingbourn. These were configured for PHOTINT collection and flew sorties along the East-West border in Europe. Within 'a matter of hours' of their arrival in England, five airplanes flew their first mission covering 15 out of 21 targets. Sustained operational readiness, however, proved to be a challenge. For the third mission, flown on 30th January, nine RB-50s were scheduled to launch. Of these, two were ground aborts and one aborted half-way through its flight. The remaining six photographed 18 of 21 targets. Nagging maintenance issues detracted from the overall success of the program. During March, for example, RB-50E 47-0123 suffered a runaway turbocharger, forcing replacement of the engine and propeller, and 47-0126 lost nose wheel steering upon landing, with one propeller damaged by gravel as the airplane veered violently off the runway.

These photographic missions predated what – by early 1952 – would become known as Operation ROUNDOUT, the 'collection of radar and aerial photography of strategic western European targets which might fall under enemy control in the event of war.' SAC planners recognized that they had very limited photography of potential Soviet targets (mostly ex-Luftwaffe materials captured after the war), severely hampering SAC's ability to locate and destroy key Soviet targets. Consequently, SAC planners understood the need for accurate PHOTINT of potential targets in friendly Western European nations under the assumption that Soviet forces would capture them and it would become necessary to destroy them to prevent their use to support Soviet industrial output, as well as for the conduct of any liberation operations. During March 1951, for example, RB-50Es specifically photographed 13 European airfields.

RB-50Es from the 38th SRS, 55th SRW left the warmer climes of Puerto Rico for chilly England in January 1951 for an extended PHOTINT mission that would eventually become the ongoing Operation ROUNDOUT. 47-0124 would later be converted for COMINT collection. *AFHRA via George Cully*

ROUNDOUT DEPLOYMENTS TO THE UK, 1952-1954

From	To	Unit	Aircraft	Deployment Base(s)
8 Apr 52	7 Aug 52	55th SRW	RB-50E	RAF Sculthorpe, RAF Upper Heyford
9 Aug 52	9 Nov 52	111th SRW	RB-29/A/F	RAF Lakenheath
2 Sep 52	8 Dec 52	28th SRW	RB-36H	RAF Fairford
12 Dec 52	12 Mar 53	5th SRW	RB-36F	RAF Fairford
20 Mar 53	23 Apr 53	28th SRW	RB-36H	RAF Fairford, RAF Lakenheath
19 Jun 53	20 Sep 53	5th SRW	RB-36H	RAF Brize Norton, RAF Lakenheath
20 Sep 53	15 Dec 53	28th SRW	RB-36H	RAF Lakenheath
19 May 54	15 Aug 54	99th SRW	RB-36F	RAF Fairford
13 Sep 54	3 Nov 54	26th SRW	RB-47E	RAF Upper Heyford

Phase I ROUNDOUT missions overflew West Germany to provide post-war images, as well the United Kingdom. Phase II flights covered 31 targets in France, Italy, Sweden, and Holland, with Phase III sorties expanding to Belgium, Portugal, and North Africa, as well as photographing countries previously overflown [one Convair RB-36 pilot recalls mapping all of Portugal in a single pass from north to south while flying at 26,000ft (7,925m)].

ROUNDOUT sorties flew no closer than 30nm (56km) to the borders of communist-bloc countries (SAC requested permission to fly up to the border, but this was rejected). RB-36 crews were instructed to remain at least 200nm (370km) from communist-bloc nations to prevent the Soviets from collecting radar data about the airplane – or worse should one crash. There are no known ROUNDOUT overflights of 'denied territory.' It is not clear that the governments of all the friendly European nations that were overflown consented to the missions, or were even aware of their true purpose. Crews were prepared for the 'the worst.' During April 1951, 38th SRS RB-50 gunners fired 15,700 rounds during practice flights while in the UK.

Beginning 8th April 1952, eight 38th SRS RB-50Es returned to RAF Sculthorpe and later to RAF Upper Heyford in the first deployment specifically associated with Operation ROUNDOUT.

Of the eight RB-50Es, 47-0128 and 47-0131 were configured with a 100in (254cm) focal length camera for oblique photography well beyond the borders of East and West, collecting PHOTINT of communist-bloc territory while still in friendly airspace. This deployment ended on 7th August 1952 and the RB-50s returned to their new home at Forbes AFB, KS.

Another eight RB-50Es returned to RAF Mildenhall from 24th June-22nd September 1953. Declassified records of this deployment suggest the broad scope of the ROUNDOUT mission. There were '93 large scale, 92 small scale, and 96 radar targets plus 217 prime vertical and 217 split vertical flight lines for charts and mosaics.' By the end of the deployment, the RB-50s had flown 741 hours and logged 58 sorties while acquiring 14,505nm (26,863km) of 'acceptable photography and radar coverage.' Bad weather hampered the success of the mission, with 18 days in July, 21 days in August, and six days in September considered 'poor', precluding aerial photography. Overall the project achieved 81% 'overall acceptability'. During a mission on 27th July, the RB-50E was subject to 'radio jamming of a homing beacon,' but 'the jamming station was never pinpointed.'

The majority of ROUNDOUT missions were flown by RB-36Hs from the 5th SRW (23rd SRS, 31st SRS, and 72nd SRS) at Travis AFB (previously named Fairfield-Suisun AFB), and the 28th SRW (77th SRS, 717th SRS, and 718th SRS) at Rapid City AFB beginning in November 1952. The units rotated frequently and to different bases. For example, in May 1953 RB-36Hs from the 28th SRW (Rapid City AFB was renamed Ellsworth AFB on 8th June 1953) arrived at RAF Lakenheath from RAF Fairford. These were replaced on 19th June by four 5th SRW RB-36Hs at RAF Brize Norton, which returned to Travis AFB on 22nd July. By August 1953 there were at least eight 5th SRW RB-36Hs at RAF Laken-

SAC got out of the RB-50 PHOTINT and mapping business, transferring its aircraft to the APCS. Ultimately SAC's PHOTINT collection would fall to its high fliers, such as RB-47Es, RB-57Ds, U-2s, and SR-71s. *Terry Panopalis collection*

51-5753 was among the first 28th SRW RB-36Hs to deploy in 1953 to RAF Lakenheath for ROUNDOUT missions. By the time this image was taken, it had been transferred to the 72nd SRW and its flying days were nearly over. *Author's collection*

Primary RB-36 ROUNDOUT units were the 28th SRW and the 5th SRW, which alternated sending airplanes to RAF Lakenheath. During August 1953, 5th SRW RB-36H 52-1384 was one of 13 that visited England. *via Dennis Jenkins*

heath, although Travis-based 52-1369 crashed in the Atlantic Ocean west of Ireland on 5th August en route to England [misfortune also affected the 28th SRW with the loss of the deputy commander of the 717th SRS while in C-47D 43-48803 which collided with a Royal Norwegian Air Force (RNoAF) Republic F-84G on 10th July 1953 near Sola AB]. This deployment ended on 28th September, having been relieved on 20th September by the 28th SRW which remained in the UK until 15th December, returning to South Dakota in January 1954.

RAF Fairford hosted the final RB-36 ROUNDOUT deployment, including 99th SRW RB-36F 49-2708. The entire program lasted some two years. *via Dennis Jenkins*

The rules for RB-36s and RB-47Es during ROUNDOUT were clear: avoid hostile territory by at least 225nm. There is some debate if all ROUNDOUT flights were armed, but crews from the 28th SRW took no chances and maintained the guns in top condition. ECM antennae would have been of interest to the Soviets if an airplane was lost. via *Dennis Jenkins*

Seven 99th SRW RB-36Fs from Fairchild AFB replaced the 28th SRW by flying to RAF Fairford on 19th May 1954. These left in July and were replaced by others from the 99th SRW which departed England on 15th August, followed by the detachment's closure on 20th August. (It is worth noting that not all RB-36 visits to the UK were reconnaissance related, as the RB-36 retained atomic strike capability as well as its PHOTINT and ELINT roles.)

During September and October 1954, RB-47Es from the 26th SRW from Lockbourne AFB deployed to RAF Upper Heyford as part of ROUNDOUT to acquire imagery of Norway. As with the RB-36s, the RB-47Es were prohibited from operating any closer than 225nm (417km) from the Soviet border or that of its satellites (which was ironic given that a 91st SRW RB-47E had overflown the USSR in May 1954). While over the North Sea the RB-47Es also served as targets for interceptor practice by Norwegian fighters. This level of comity did not extend to international candor should an RB-47 be forced

to land in Norway for any reason: 'crews will be briefed to refer to their mission as a "routine navigational training mission" *being particularly cautious not to mention the fact that reconnaissance work is being done*' [emphasis in original]. In addition to the flights over Norway, the 26th SRW undertook concurrent overflights of Iceland as part of OpOrd 143-54. This also provided information 'on the Soviet fishing fleet'. SAC intelligence officers noted that these ships, which averaged 250 in number, carried a variety of shipborne EW radars typically found on Soviet naval vessels. Photographs of these 'fishing trawlers' would reveal their military capability in the vital GIUK Gap. US interceptors based in Iceland, however, were not authorized to conduct practice intercepts on the RB-47Es. Landing in Iceland was strongly discouraged, as SAC feared genuine attempts to sabotage the aircraft or subvert the crew (ROUNDOUT crews were briefed on arrival about local threats, 'with special emphasis being placed on Communistic and subversive activities'). The 26th SRW RB-47s returned to Ohio from 28th-30th October.

In addition to the ROUNDOUT RB-36s and RB-47s that collected PHOTINT, RB-50Fs from the 338th SRS, 55th SRW at Ramey AFB visited the UK on missions related to target mapping. The RB-50F was configured with the Short-range Navigation (SHORAN) system for electronic mapping and geodetic work. Beginning 6th April 1953, four RB-50Fs arrived at RAF Lakenheath. These relocated to RAF Mildenhall on 21st April and were joined by two others (47-0121 and 47-0142) from Wheelus AB in July 1953, where they flew 12 'effective sorties' over 224 hours. During May 1954 the RB-50F mapping mission was transferred to the Military Air Transport Service (MATS), and all subsequent RB-50F visits were not SAC assets.

Photo mapping was entering a new technological phase in 1953, when SAC sent its RB-50Fs to England to use SHORAN and other electronic mapping aids. 47-0138 wears the Circle V tail markings of the 55th SRW. *Terry Panopalis collection*

RB-50Fs from the 338th SRS, 55th SRW conducted mapping missions from RAF Lakenheath, although on paper they were assigned to the 1370th PMG. By 1964, when this image was taken, there was no doubt they were no longer SAC assets. *Terry Panopalis collection*

Amid the many SAC aircraft that visited the UK in support of Operation ROUNDOUT, a small number of RB-29s, RB-50s, and RB-36s took part in ELINT collection. Their presence in the UK and over Europe would have been easily conflated with the PHOTINT mission, providing further cover for their clandestine missions ranging from the Barents Sea to the Black Sea. Perhaps the first ELINT-configured airplanes in the UK were two 343rd SRS RB-50Gs (47-0145 and 47-0153), which visited Detachment (Det) 2 of the 55th SRW at RAF Mildenhall from January through May 1952 as part of the SAM SPADE overall ELINT collection program. On 9th August 1952, four Air National Guard (ANG) ELINT RB-29As (44-61680 and 44-61981), RB-29 (42-21773) and 'RB-29F' (45-21859) [B-29A temporarily modified for 'Arctic tests', a euphemism for Alaskan reconnaissance] of the 111th SRW at Fairchild AFB departed for the UK (the 111th SRW was an active-duty component of the Pennsylvania ANG). These remained at RAF Lakenheath until 9th November. Addi-

tional ELINT assets arrived at RAF Lakenheath from Ramey AFB on 17th August in the form of two RB-50Gs (47-0150 and 47-0154) from the 343rd SRS, 55th SRW. These were replaced in February 1953 by another pair (47-0133 and 47-0143). Sometime during 1952, according to one pilot's memoir, a 28th SRW RB-36H conducted an ELINT flight from the Baltic Sea to

RB-50G 47-0161 *Caribbean Queen* diverted into Prestwick following a landing gear issue. These were regularly refueled by KB-29Ms on their ELINT missions 'to northern areas,' and were the last looped-hose receivers in the UK. *Gordon Macadie*

Vienna, Austria. This was reportedly the first time 'the Russians had seen a B-36 on radar,' and the crew was instructed 'not to do anything foolish.' An on-board Russian-speaking crewmember determined that the Russians were very excited by the RB-36's flight, which was able to collect ELINT on a new frequency hopping Soviet radar. So much for SAC's 200nm restriction!

Five 343rd SRS ELINT RB-50Gs shuttled regularly to Det 2, 55th SRW at RAF Mildenhall from March 1953 through June 1954. Between 13th August and 20th September, two of these took part in Project STATEHOUSE, accomplishing just two sorties. The RB-50Gs relocated to RAF Lakenheath (along with three other newly arrived airplanes) following the closure of RAF Mildenhall's runway for badly needed repairs. This also spelled the end for Det 2, as well as some changes in the RB-50G's ownership. On 1st April 1954, the 340th BS at Biggs AFB, TX, acquired the remnants of the 55th SRW reconnaissance fleet as that wing transitioned to the RB-47E, and Det 2, 55th SRW was redesignated as Det 1, 340th BS on 15th April. The 340th BS became the 4024th BS on 1st April 1955, although the unit retained its ELINT mission. Eventually the RB-50Gs were withdrawn from service, and effective 15th June 1956 the reconnaissance presence at RAF Lakenheath relocated as Det 1, 55th SRW to RAF Mildenhall in anticipation of the operational arrival of SAC's new ELINT RB-47H.

The Jet Age

Throughout 1950, SAC's reconnaissance fleet underwent a significant and complex reorganization, with units created, redesignated, relocated, and eliminated. Moreover, SAC eagerly anticipated the arrival of the RB-47 as its primary PHOTINT collector, reducing the threat against its existing piston-powered RB-29s and RB-50s by the jet-powered MiG-15. Unfortunately, the RB-47 would not be delivered before 1952 at the earliest, so SAC 'reluctantly accepted' the North American RB-45C Tornado as a 'short-term expedient'. These were assigned to the 91st SRW at Barksdale AFB beginning in August 1950. Its operational debut was from Yokota AB, Japan, where it flew combat missions over Korea and penetration overflights of the Soviet Far East and the People's Republic of China. Experience there and tests in the US quickly revealed that the RB-45 was not the high-altitude, high-speed panacea SAC hoped for.

Operational shortfalls notwithstanding, in late 1950 the 91st SRW was alerted to prepare for the MIDWINTER deployment to RAF Manston on 10th January 1951, ostensibly to participate in the ROUNDOUT program. Along with four newly modified Boeing KB-29P boom-equipped tankers, four RB-45s arrived in England on 15th and 17th January. The deployment quickly revealed deficiencies in the new airplanes, most notably associated with air refueling. Out of eight attempts only two were successful.

There were five air refueling 'incidents' during one eight-day stretch, including one on 27th January that damaged RB-45C 48-0021 and KB-29P 44-69761 which grounded the RB-45 for nearly five months while awaiting replacement parts.

The airplanes relocated to RAF Sculthorpe on 24th February 1951 (minus 'hangar queen' 48-0021) as Det 1, 91st SRW. Efforts to fly regular profile missions (10 hours duration with one or two air refuelings) proved difficult to achieve as both the RB-45 and KB-29 experienced nagging maintenance and supply issues, prompting the deployment of additional airplanes on 8th-9th May. The loss of RB-45C 48-0026 on 15th May at RAF Sculthorpe added to the sense of disappointment. This was of considerable concern to SAC's commanders as the acquisition of radar scope photography was a top priority, and the loss of an already 'fidgety' airplane significantly reduced this capability. By the end of July Det 1 finally achieved what would be considered 'normal' operations, fulfilling its radar scope mission as well as smoothing out the air refueling process.

Acquiring this PHOTINT was one thing, delivering it to target planners was another issue altogether. SAC reasoned that because the B-45As it recently received from Tactical Air Command (TAC) could not be used for the EWP they could instead serve as 'high speed couriers.' As such, between 1st-3rd August five B-45As and six KB-29Ps deployed to RAF Sculthorpe. The usual culprits of bad weather and en route breakage combined to hamper the deployment, with the final two B-45s straggling into England on 20th August. The B-45s proved ill-suited to sustained operations, completing only one successful courier mission. At best, it was used to simulate attacking jet bombers in air defense exercises (on 18th March 1952, B-45A 47-0043 suffered a landing mishap at RAF Sculthorpe, and SAC 'abandoned' it in place – it was eventually rebuilt and transferred to USAFE, where it again crashed and was finally relegated to a base fire pit).

By the end of 1951, RB-45C missions had steadily improved with radio-silent air refueling and satisfactory PHOTINT collection in flights ranging as far afield as Italy, Spain, France, West Germany, and Belgium. In fact, these shakedown operations were a concerted effort to prepare the airplanes and crews for what would come next.

The initial deployment of SAC's RB-45Cs to the UK was fraught with technical issues, especially air refueling. 48-0031, seen here tanking from KB-29P 44-84107, was one of four RB-45s that overflew the USSR in April 1954. *Author's collection*

SAC transferred its RB-45s to TAC, and several of these ended up on base firepits. 48-0035 was one such jet, despite having flown the April 1954 overflight mission. *Author's collection*

125

'Loaners'

At the same time as the 91st SRW crews and airplanes were validating long-range PHOTINT operations and capabilities, senior USAF, SAC, and RAF officials were planning the 'ultimate' RB-45 mission. USAF Chief of Staff General Hoyt S Vandenberg, General LeMay, and their senior staffs worked directly with RAF Chief of Staff Air Chief Marshal (ACM) Sir John Slessor and his second in command, ACM Sir Ralph Cochrane to plan the RAF Special Duty Flight (SDF). Conceived and developed under the strictest secrecy, RAF crews with experience flying the high-altitude English Electric Canberra on PHOTINT missions travelled to Barksdale AFB to train in the RB-45. Under the eventual command of Squadron Leader John Crampton, the British crews (these were not exchange pilots or navigators) completed their training by 30th September 1951. After washing out one pilot, the RAF contingent returned to RAF Sculthorpe

in November. Fortunately, an RAF pilot with experience in the B-45 was found and the unit was once again fully manned.

Training continued in the UK, although 48-0041 experienced an airborne malfunction which necessitated the jettisoning of its wing-tip tanks. There were no spares in the UK, and worries about having these replaced for long-range flights permeated both RAF and SAC plans. Bad weather added to these problems. Following a January 1952 visit to Washington, however, Prime Minister Churchill finally approved Operation JU JITSU, a three-airplane deep penetration flight of the Soviet Union by RAF crews flying SAC RB-45s in RAF markings. Crampton undertook a lone preparatory mission over Berlin and East Germany during the night of 21st March. Final transfer of four RB-45s occurred on 5th April, with 48-0019, -0034, -0036, and -0042.

On the night of 17th April three RB-45s flew a northerly route ('Blue'), a central route ('Red'), and a southerly route ('Yellow'). The spare airplane went 'technical' and was not available, so it was fortunate that the three primary aircraft were fully capable. The missions were successful although not all targets were photographed. The four airplanes 'returned' to SAC and flew back to Barksdale AFB on 9th May. It appeared that the SDF would be disbanded.

A proposal by Slessor to Vandenberg in September 1952 raised the possibility of a new six-plane penetration mission, with three crews each from SAC and the RAF. The deployment

RAF crews were fully qualified in the RB-45s in America, but training continued when they returned to the UK. The JU JITSU overflight missions were more secret 'than the Mahattan Project.' Maury Seitz, author's collection

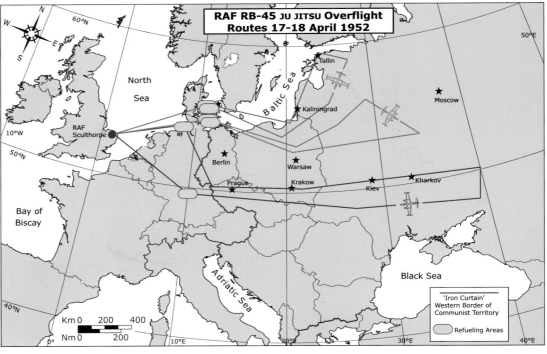

Opposite page, bottom: Each of the RB-45s required air refueling for their overflights, and earlier 91st SRW efforts smoothed the learning curve for the RAF crews. The jet-powered RB-45s needed to use flaps to fly slow enough behind the KB-29 tankers. *Maury Seitz, author's collection*

RAF RB-45 JU JITSU Overflight Routes 17-18 April 1952

Other than a red tail band and national insignia, the RAF RB-45s were completely devoid of any identifying markings. Should one be lost, the Soviets would have no trouble in claiming that the American-built airplane was to blame, irrespective of crew nationality. *Author's collection*

Plans for Operation PEPSIN, a joint SAC-RAF mission from RAF Sculthorpe, were cancelled as the US balked. The RAF pressed ahead with planning, ultimately leading to JU JITSU II. *Terry Panopalis collection*

of four 91st SRW RB-45s to RAF Sculthorpe on 21st October suggested that this plan had been approved, but with one less crew from each service. In fact, the US refused altogether and the RAF assumed sole responsibility for the operation. The proposed three-ship mission date was 13th December, with a final single-ship flight on 15th December. In any event, Churchill canceled Operation PEPSIN by 9th December and the airplanes returned to Barksdale AFB.

A third overflight was subsequently considered using the PEPSIN flight plans, which Churchill approved on 3rd March 1954. The Red, Blue, and Yellow sorties of JU JITSU II were the same as its predecessor. A single-airplane 'Black' route covered the Russian far north from Murmansk to Archangelsk. The RB-45Cs came from the 19th Tactical Reconnaissance Squadron (TRS) at Shaw AFB, SC, following their transfer in 1953 from SAC to TAC. These were 48-0031, -0035, -0037, and -0040, and the three aircraft completed their overflights of Eastern Europe on the night of 28th April. The Black route, however, was not flown by an RAF crew. Instead it would fall to a SAC RB-47E crew flying the only known SAC overflight of the USSR launched from the United Kingdom.

RAF RB-45 JU JITSU MISSION CREWS

17-18 April 1952	28-29 April 1954
Squadron Leader John Crampton (P) Flight Lieutenant Rex Sanders (N) Sergeant Bill Lindsay (CP)	Squadron Leader John Crampton (P) Flight Lieutenant Rex Sanders (N) Flight Lieutenant McAlastair Furze (CP)
Flight Lieutenant Gordon Cremer (P) Flight Sergeant Bob Anstee (N) Sergeant Don Greenslade (P)	Flight Lieutenant Gordon Cremer (P) Flight Sergeant Bob Anstee (N) Sergeant Don Greenslade (P)
Flight Lieutenant Bill Blair (P) Flight Lieutenant John Hill (N) Flight Sergeant Joe Acklam (CP)	Flight Lieutenant Bill Blair (P) Flight Lieutenant John Hill (N) Flight Sergeant Joe Acklam (CP)

P = Pilot; N = Navigator; CP = Copilot; Spare crews not identified

Project GREEN GARTER

The first RB-47 deployment to the UK took place when eight RB-47Es from the three squadrons of the 91st SRW (now at Lockbourne AFB) arrived at RAF Fairford on 8th April 1954 as part of Operation GREEN GARTER just prior to the April JU JITSU II overflights (this preceded the ROUNDOUT 26th SRW deployment described above). On 6th May 1954, six of these RB-47Es flew a formation mission to photograph the Spitsbergen Islands north of Norway. Two days later, on 8th May, another six-ship mission launched from RAF Fairford. Three continued eastward until they were approximately 100nm (185km) north of Murmansk and still in international airspace. Two airplanes turned around and returned to RAF Fairford. To the surprise and amazement of the other two crews, the third RB-47E, commanded by Major Harold R 'Hal' Austin, continued into Soviet airspace along the Black route planned for JU JITSU II.

Shortly after overflying Arkhangelsk, Austin's airplane attracted a flight of three MiGs, none of which was able to get close to the RB-47. Six more MiGs soon appeared, still below and behind Austin's airplane but closer than the first three. After some 30 minutes over the USSR a third group of six MiGs arrived, flying in two groups of three. Again, they were behind the RB-47 but were nearly at the same altitude. Aware of the RB-47's projected track, the Soviets were now launching their MiGs in advance so they would have time to climb to 40,000ft (12,192m) to intercept the RB-47. After the fifth target, a fourth group of six MiGs, this time already at 40,000ft, began firing passes at the RB-47. Mission briefers told Austin that any interceptors they *might* encounter would be lesser MiG-15s and that there were not 'significant numbers' of MiG-17 *Frescoes* in the theater – in either case both were 'highly unstable gun platforms at 40,000ft' – it was

GREEN GARTER RB-47Es and KC-97Fs

RB-47Es			
51-5270	51-5272	51-15822	51-15823
51-15826	51-15830	51-15839	51-15848

KC-97Fs			
51-0375	51-0378	51-0386	51-0387
51-0388			

patently clear that the briefers were wrong on all counts. The RB-47's copilot Captain Carl Holt managed to fire the two 20mm tail guns, although he was able to get off only a two- to three-second burst at the third MiG-17 before the guns jammed. The fourth MiG-17 made a firing pass as the RB-47 completed its run over the sixth target, at which point Austin recalls a 'whap' or bit of rough air. Unknown to the crew, they had been hit in the left main wing flap 8ft (2.4m) from the fuselage, leaving a 4in (10.2cm) hole. The shell 'exploded into the fuselage [near] the forward main wheel well and #1 main fuel tank with many shrapnel holes, the largest being 9in x 6in [23cm x 15cm] in size.' A fifth flight of six MiGs began a series of firing passes but none was able to hit the RB-47. Turning toward its eighth target the RB-47 garnered the unwanted attention of a sixth flight of six MiGs which began their efforts to down Austin's airplane as it completed its photo run and headed toward Finland. They continued attacking the RB-47 even as it entered Finnish airspace. A final group of three MiGs intercepted the RB-47 over Finland, and was close enough to 'shake hands', apparently attempting to coerce Austin to return to Soviet airspace and land (or perhaps attempt an abortive ramming of the RB-47), but to no avail. Swedish and Finnish newspapers reported 'an air battle between jet planes of unknown nationality over northern Finland,' although a US spokesman reported that 'no American planes have been in the area.'

The sole known SAC overflight of the USSR from the UK was in a 91st SRW GREEN GARTER mission flown in an RB-47E. None of the crew had any record of the tail number, much to the chagrin of aviation historians. *Courtesy Boeing*

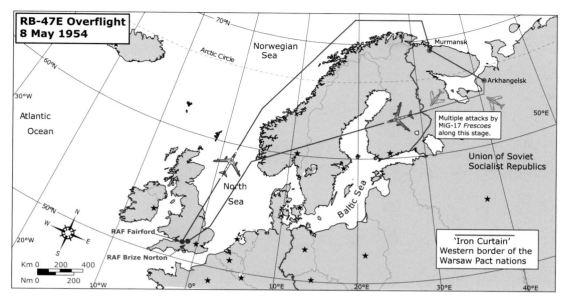

RB-47E Overflight
8 May 1954

Multiple attacks by
MiG-17 *Frescoes*
along this stage.

'Iron Curtain'
Western border of the
Warsaw Pact nations

With the MiGs behind them Austin still faced the daunting challenge of getting home. Unable to contact the spare KC-97 orbiting 50nm (93km) from Stavanger, Norway, due to what appeared to be a damaged UHF radio and now without sufficient fuel to reach RAF Fairford, Austin worried they might not reach any base in England and would be forced to bail out, losing not only the airplane but the valuable pictures they had just taken. About 150nm (278km) north of RAF Mildenhall, Austin began calling in the blind for the stand-by tanker there, and started a slow descent. The alert KC-97 there launched without permission and headed for the RB-47. In what Austin later recalled as the 'quickest and smoothest approach to refueling and boom contact I had ever made,' the RB-47 began taking fuel at only 3,000ft (914m) above the English countryside. After taking on 10,000 lb (4,536kg) of fuel, Austin called for disconnect, saluted the boomer, and headed to RAF Fairford where he landed uneventfully.

Austin's good luck in having a KC-97 tanker launch to refuel him as he neared flameout is likely the result of the earlier JU JITSU II missions. Although Austin was unaware of the role of the 91st ARS KC-97s in refueling the RB-45s some two weeks earlier, the tanker crew which 'saved' him 'guessed (or knew) where he had been and that he might be in trouble.'

In anticipation of a far less dramatic trip, 45 YRB-47Bs from the 320th BW deployed to RAF Brize Norton in June 1954. When equipped with a camera pod in the bomb bay, their mission – like that of the RB-47E – was pre-strike photography. During the latter part of July these YRB-47Bs participated in Operation DIVIDEND, the 'annual UK air defense exercise'. The airplanes also reportedly took part in 'highly classified' survey flights to Crete and Turkey, perhaps to evaluate possible candidates for post-strike recovery bases.

Some 18 RB-47Es from the 26th SRW returned to RAF Fairford on 26th-27th November 1957 for the IRON BAR exercise, a '7th Air Division training exercise which included extensive use of nuclear weapons and which would prove to be the last of its size in the UK.' In

YRB-47B deployments to the UK did not utilize the photo pallet for the bomb bay. The 1954 survey by the 320th BW physically evaluated the operational capacity of bases in Crete and Turkey rather than photographed them. *Author's collection*

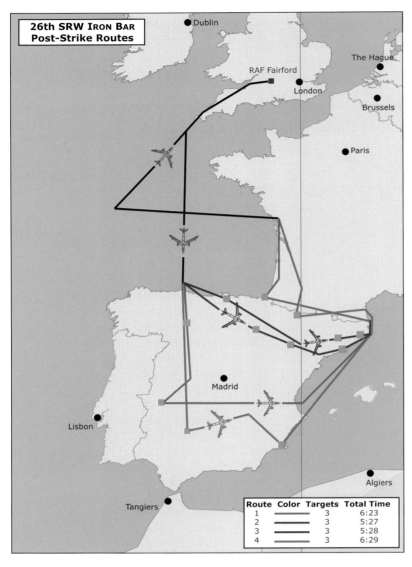

26th SRW IRON BAR
Post-Strike Routes

Route	Color	Targets	Total Time
1		3	6:23
2		3	5:27
3		3	5:28
4		3	6:29

55th SRW PROGRAM OPERATIONAL NAMES IN THE UK

Date	ELINT Operations Name	Primary ELINT Mission Name(s)
n/a	SAM SPADE	n/a
1 Jul 56	SLIP KNOT	n/a
16 Jan 57	PEP TALK	TROJAN HORSE
15 Feb 57	ROCK ISLAND	TROJAN HORSE
27 Sep 57	FREEZE OUT	TROJAN HORSE
1 Feb 58	BIG PUSH	PIED PIPER (from Det 4)
15 Dec 58	TEXAS STAR	PIED PIPER (from Det 4)
3 Jan 59	TEXAS STAR	PIED PIPER (from Det 1)
1 Jan 60	TEXAS STAR	CASTLE GATE
1 Nov 61	TEXAS STAR	BOX TOP
1 Jul 63	TEXAS STAR*	BOX TOP
1 Jan 64	OPEN DOOR*	BOX TOP
1 May 67		BURNING SKY, BRIAR PATCH, BURNING CANDY
15 Feb 68		BURNING PIPE, BUSTED JAW
17 Jan 69		BURNING PIPELINE, COBRA JAW
1 Jan 72		BURNING WIND, COMBAT SENT

*TEXAS STAR and OPEN DOOR now referred only to the deployment flights to and from each Detachment, and not the overall 55th SRW reconnaissance program

addition to the RB-47Es, IRON BAR included B-47Es from four bomb wings in England and two KC-97 tanker squadrons. Fifteen RB-47Es were slated for post-strike reconnaissance and three as weather scouts (these flew to the planned air refueling areas and relayed cloud and wind conditions back to mission planners). The first weather scout mission was flown on 28th November and the first post-strike mission took place on 30th November. Additional flights occurred in early December, after which the aircraft returned to Lockbourne AFB.

At least three RB-47Es (along with six B-47Es) remained in the UK as base 'hacks', although these lacked any reconnaissance capability.

Expanding ELINT

Throughout the 1950s and 1960s airpower grew increasingly reliant upon electronic warfare. Radars to detect and track incoming bombers, interceptors with airborne radars, plus SAMs and air-to-air missiles with radar homing all threatened SAC's bomber force and its ability to carry out its EWP mission. Understanding these highly technical systems in order to develop ECM proved essential to the success of SAC's nuclear strike role. This also resulted in a significant change in its peacetime reconnaissance capabilities. Traditional SAC PHOTINT missions using RB-29s, RB-45s, RB-50Es, RB-36s, YRB-47Bs, and RB-47Es were reduced to just peripheral U-2 sorties such as CONGO MAIDEN, while the handful of ELINT-configured RB-50Gs, RB-57Ds, and RB-36s would soon be retired. These were replaced beginning in 1956 by the RB-47H, SAC's newest reconnaissance asset. From their home base at Forbes AFB, 55th SRW RB-47Hs deployed to Operating Locations (OL) around the world, beginning with Japan and the United Kingdom. Over the next 11 years, the RB-47H would be a conspicuous visitor to bases in England and play the central and unwitting role in changing the US-UK intelligence relationship.

The original ELINT collection program from the UK was known SAM SPADE, although this changed in April 1956 with the introduction of the new RB-47H ELINT collection effort. SLIP KNOT was the initial program name for the rotational deployment of RB-47Hs from Forbes AFB to Yokota AB and RAF Mildenhall. Eighth Air Force Operational Order (OpOrd) 78-56 called for deployments to begin on 1st July 1956 (this was not the first RB-47H operational deployment overseas as four 55th SRW crews and airplanes deployed to Thule AB, Green-eyes in english skies

The arrival of the RB-47H at the 55th SRW provided a new ELINT platform, which became a regular at Det 1 in the UK, although the location of the Detachment changed over time. *USAF via William T Y'Blood*

land, during March-May 1956 for the massive HOME RUN overflights of the USSR). Two RB-47Hs departed Forbes AFB on 29th June and arrived at Det 1 at RAF Mildenhall the following day. One replacement airplane and crew would arrive at the end of each month, maintaining two on station. ELINT sorties at each of the 55th SRW detachments were given code names, beginning with Det 1 using TROJAN HORSE, Det 2 assigned RED SETTER, and Det 3 (Eielson AFB) and Det 5 (Thule AB) sharing SUN DOG.

The initial operational pace was 'busy.' Between Det 2 at Yokota AB and Det 1, RB-47Hs flew 31 sorties and 195 hours in July 1956, 186 hours in August, and 205 hours in September (official records for this period do not separate the two Dets). By 1957, Det 1 RB-47Hs averaged some 22-24 missions per quarter. More detailed records from early 1957 show that Det 1 flew six operational sorties in April, benefitting from good weather (although there was one post-mission diversion to RAF Brize Norton on 1 April) and nine TROJAN HORSE sorties in May, including one 'special' sortie of an unknown nature. Any inquiries from the British public about the RB-47H's presence at RAF Mildenhall would yield little information, as the local public affairs officers were instructed only to 'acknowledge [the] presence of SAC aircraft but unit designation, aircraft model, home station, and length of TDY [would] not be revealed.'

The detachment at RAF Mildenhall closed on 1st February 1958, and there were no subsequent RB-47 operations from the UK for most of the remaining year. From 31st October through 24th November 1958, Det 1 and Det 4 undertook 'split' operations, with one RB-47H and crew operating from RAF Brize Norton and one from Incirlik AB. The Det 4 commander was not strongly in favor of this arrangement, recommending instead 'a permanent detachment at both ends'. This dual basing continued until 3rd January 1959, with the re-establishment of a full-time detachment at RAF Brize Norton. The first airplane to arrive there was ERB-47H 53-6245 on the first deployment of the type to the UK. RB-47H 53-4289 followed on 4th January from Det 4 at Incirlik AB. The transition to this new Det generated some documentary sleight-of-hand as official records show the airplanes were, as late as 1961, at Chambley in France! Other extreme security measures applied to the 55th SRW jets included the occasional truncation of serial numbers on jets transiting England en route to Det 4 at Adana AB (later Incirlik AB). For example, 53-4286 and 53-4303 had their tail numbers reduced to '28' and '30', respectively.

During February and March 1959, RB-47H operations at RAF Brize Norton were reduced to zero given a commensurate increase in sorties from Incirlik AB. In April, part of the Det 4

During stopovers in England en route to Incirlik AB, RB-47Hs sometimes had their tail numbers modified and the wing emblem removed for security purposes. In December 1958, 53-4298 had been shortened to '29'. This appeared again on RC-135Us. *Courtesy of Angelo Romano*

RB-57Ds from the 4080th SW were rare visitors to English bases, appearing just twice at RAF Brize Norton in 1959 and 1960. *Terry Panopalis collection*

staff relocated permanently to England. Lone RB-47H 53-4306 operated in May from RAF Brize Norton under the command of Captain Willard Palm, who would return the following

PIED PIPER GYPSY **RB-57D-2 MISSIONS, FEBRUARY 1959**

Date	Aircraft	Mission	Comments
3 Feb 59	53-3968	TULSA-SKUNK	
4 Feb 59	53-3964	TULSA-DEER	
12 Feb 59	53-3964	TULSA-ANTELOPE	
14 Feb 59	53-3965	TULSA-FOX	Aborted
19 Feb 59	53-3964	TULSA-WEASEL	
22 Feb 59	53-3965	TULSA-BEAVER	
25 Feb 59	53-3964	TULSA-BEAR	
26 Feb 59	53-3968	TULSA-ERMINE	Aborted

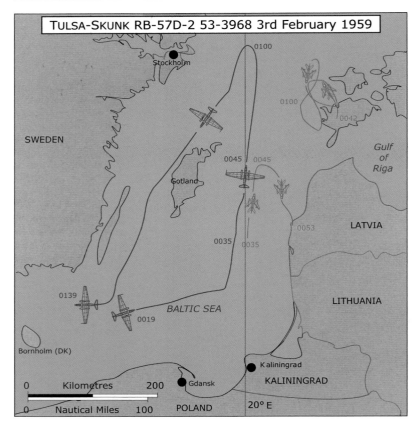

TULSA-SKUNK RB-57D-2 53-3968 3rd February 1959

June only to be lost in a tragic incident. In July 1959, Det 1 was established as a 'permanent "TDY" detachment [and] the effective date of the realignment was set as 19th August', with 'usual' complement of two RB-47Hs or one ERB-47H and one RB-47H, along with four 55th AREFS KC-97Gs. The first two airplanes assigned were ERB-47H 53-6249 and RB-47H 53-4309, and collectively flew seven operational sorties in July and seven in August.

An unusual visit to the UK included three RB-57D-2s (53-3964, -3965, and -3968) from the 4025th SRS, 4080th SW at Laughlin AFB, TX, which deployed to RAF Brize Norton for BORDERTOWN peripheral ELINT missions on 23rd January 1959. They used REFLEX ACTION B-47 call signs (*Weedpatch 38*, *58*, and *69*) and en route reporting procedures, with a single air refueling near EA Harmon AFB. The alert KC-97 at RAF Upper Heyford scrambled to refuel *Weedpatch 69* after an oxygen issue over the Atlantic forced the RB-57 to fly at a lower altitude and consume more fuel.

Once in place the RB-57s undertook a series of PIED PIPER-GYPSY missions, the first operational deployment of the System 320 SAFE (semi-automatic ferret equipment) ELINT collection system. Bad weather delayed the first of three HALF BREED orientation flights until 31st January, followed by the first operational TULSA-SKUNK sortie on 3rd February in 53-3968. By the end of the month, the three RB-57s at Det 7, 4080th SW had flown eight sorties totaling 50 hours. The unit flew seven additional operational sorties between 3rd-17th March. Missions over the Baltic Sea on the nights of 6th and 11th March prompted Soviet interception attempts but they were unable to reach the RB-57s at 62,336ft (19,000m) and 65,617ft (20,000m), respectively. A three-ship 'maximum effort' mission was scheduled for 25th March, although this was canceled due to technical issues, and the rescheduled sortie the next night was also aborted because the RB-57s 'failed to locate another flight of aircraft operating in conjunction with the same mission,' believed to be 55th SRW RB-47Hs. This capstone mission finally took place on 27th March. The RB-57Ds returned to Laughlin AFB beginning 1st April after a 'highly successful' deployment.

The same three RB-57D-2s returned to RAF Brize Norton on 22nd January 1960 as 'B-47s' *Tank 64, 66,* and *68* as part of DIP STICK. After an overnight stay they continued to Incirlik AB for a special 'low altitude ELINT' mission over the Black Sea. The Turkey deployment and its planned return proved successful in terms of ELINT collection but a disaster in terms of operational efficiency. Bad weather, technical failures, and the crash of support Fairchild C-119 53-8152 complicated the flight back to England. The RB-57Ds arrived at RAF Brize Norton on 8th March, and OL-1B, 4080th SW became operational on 10th March.

Subsequent RB-57D missions from England included one on the night of 14th March, with 53-3964 operating in conjunction with 55th SRW ERB-47H 53-6245. A series of check flights followed, with the second operational mission on 25th March using 53-3965 and the same ERB-47H. A final operational sortie took place on 29th March with 53-3968 and 53-6245. After accruing some 66 hours, the RB-57Ds returned to Laughlin AFB by 6th-7th April. Sadly, this was the end of the 4025th SRS, and all six of its RB-57D-2s were relegated to the 2704th Air Force Aircraft Storage and Disposition Group (ASDG) at Davis-Monthan AFB, AZ, on 18th-19th April.

A Significant Loss

Despite the highly visible loss of the Central Intelligence Agency's (CIA) U-2 on 1st May 1960 over the USSR, public awareness of US peripheral reconnaissance missions generally remained limited to occasional and nebulous stories in the *New York Times* about attacks on US Air Force and US Navy airplanes conducting '"electromagnetic survey data" for use in map making' or 'communications research'. Moreover, 55th SRW peripheral reconnaissance sorties continued unabated at all four primary Dets. At RAF Brize Norton, for example, RB-47H 53-4290 flew CASTLE GATE operational sorties to the Barents Sea on 7th and 15th June. The following day, 53-4281 arrived in England with the crew of Captain Willard G 'Bill' Palm (R-46) for their tour. On 22nd June, 53-4290 and its crew returned to Forbes AFB; crew R-46

flew in the accompanying KC-135 to 'observe procedures' and then returned to RAF Brize Norton. Following a local orientation flight for 'familiarization with the UK area' and a second 'shakedown sortie to operationally check all equipment' with KC-135 air refueling, Palm's crew launched on their first CASTLE GATE ELINT sortie on 1st July, accompanied by KC-135A 57-1442 from Altus AFB (also deployed to RAF Brize Norton) for refueling west of Bodø, Norway, prior to entering the 'sensitive area' east of the Kola Peninsula.

By late afternoon, the RB-47 was about half way through its mission area and approaching Holy Nose Cape, the crucial turn point which would take it away from the rapidly approaching Soviet coastline ahead to the south and instead point northeast toward Novaya Zemlya. As Palm waited for the precise time for the RB-47 to begin its left turn, copilot First Lieutenant F Bruce Olmstead was stunned to see a MiG-19 *Farmer* approximately 40ft (12m) off the right wing, unclear where it came from or how long it had been there. The *Farmer* moved to the other side of the RB-47 and opened fire, striking the RB-47's left wing and engines. Olmstead, who had started taking pictures of the MiG-19, dropped the camera and attempted to return fire using the A-5 tail gun but the *Farmer* was too close for a radar lock-on. Olmstead fired visually, expending approximately 400

One can easily imagine this as Bruce Olmstead's view moments before the *Farmer* opened fire. His RB-47H was shot down intentionally even though it was in international airspace, a Soviet 'signal' to the US just two months after the loss of a CIA U-2 over the USSR. *Colonel Johnny Drost/USAF via Geoff Hays*

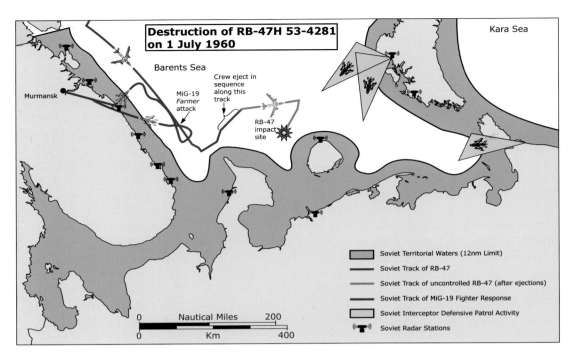

Destruction of RB-47H 53-4281 on 1 July 1960

Kara Sea

Barents Sea

Murmansk

MiG-19 *Farmer* attack

Crew eject in sequence along this track

RB-47 impact site

Nautical Miles 0 — 200

Km 0 — 400

Soviet Territorial Waters (12nm Limit)
Soviet Track of RB-47
Soviet Track of uncontrolled RB-47 (after ejections)
Soviet Track of MiG-19 Fighter Response
Soviet Interceptor Defensive Patrol Activity
Soviet Radar Stations

rounds of ammunition without success. Already in a turn to the left, the loss of thrust on those engines and damage to the left wing caused the RB-47 to enter a flat spin.

For 10 seconds Palm and Olmstead struggled to regain control, but to no avail, and Palm ordered the crew to bail out. Olmstead ejected first, breaking his back in the process. Navigator First Lieutenant John McKone ejected second, followed by Palm as the airplane continued to head northeast. No one knows if the three Ravens – Captain Eugene E 'Gene' Posa, First Lieutenant Oscar L Goforth, and First Lieutenant Dean B Phillips – tried to eject. There were no previous attempts to eject from the Raven capsule, and few Ravens believed that it would be survivable if attempted. McKone recalls seeing three parachutes in addition to his own, raising the possibility that at least one Raven did eject. Olmstead saw only two parachutes. The Soviets claimed to have recovered the body of Posa but refused to return it to the US, again suggesting that the Ravens may have attempted to eject.

McKone and Olmstead were rescued by a Russian fishing trawler and transferred to a Soviet Navy *Riga*-class frigate. They were then flown to Moscow and imprisoned in the notorious Lubyanka Prison (concurrent with CIA U-2 pilot Francis G 'Frank' Powers), and were eventually repatriated to the United States as heroes. Palm perished in the freezing waters. His body was recovered, returned to America, and on 5th August 1960 was interred in Arlington National Cemetery. The bodies of Goforth

and Phillips were not recovered. MiG-19 pilot Captain Vasilii Ambrosievitch Polyakov received the Order of the Red Banner.

The loss of 53-4281 and the diplomatic theater that followed brought considerable (and unwanted) public attention to SAC reconnaissance operations from the UK. Missions from RAF Brize Norton were immediately restricted to two flights along the East German border using RB-47H 53-4294 in conjunction with two US Navy A-3Ds during August, two RB-47H flights (TACOMA EMERALD and TACOMA SAPPHIRE) to Albania in September, and three more (WACO APOLLO, WACO APACHE, and RED SPRUCE) to Albania in October. Reconnaissance operations at RAF Brize Norton were completely suspended in November 1960 (the SHORT PUNT strip alert tanker mission was unaffected) and the RB-47s returned to Forbes AFB. The moratorium on UK reconnaissance operations did not mean an end to these missions, however, as a temporary Det 6 was established on 11th November 1960 at Wheelus AB using support personnel from RAF Brize Norton and Incirlik AB, which was undergoing runway repairs. Between 1st-16th December, RB-47H 53-4289 flew three operational sorties from Wheelus AB.

Following the loss of the RB-47H US President Dwight D Eisenhower directed the US to monitor peripheral military reconnaissance operations more closely by establishing what would become the Joint Reconnaissance Center (JRC) at the Pentagon. In addition, the British quickly imposed a prior approval requirement for all RB-47 (and later RC-135, U-2, and

SR-71) missions and their tankers from bases in England, and eventually bases 'in British territory'. By 28th July the US and UK governments had agreed that a list of all proposed missions for each month would be submitted by the 10th of the preceding month (later changed to the 15th) for approval by the British Prime Minister, with each flight requiring final sign-off 48 hours prior to departure. Delayed, canceled, or aborted missions were subject to a repeat of this process. (Missions which departed the UK and flew through the Adriatic Sea adjacent to Albania or over Greece adjacent to Bulgaria did not require British approval). After nearly a decade of essentially 'unrestricted' US reconnaissance operations from the United Kingdom, a final approval mechanism for the British leadership was at last in place.

New Procedures, New Aircraft

RB-47 missions resumed at RAF Brize Norton on 11th January 1961, and 53-4290 flew the first ops sortie (MISSION BRAD) on 13th January to the Barents Sea, the same area where Palm's aircraft had been shot down. Interestingly, this may have been a special mission for the CART

MAN program intended to 'monitor electronic impulses of the vicinity of the aerial drop zone for Russian nuclear tests.' There were five CART MAN flights accruing 32:25 hours, including MISSION BRAD, four training sorties, and two canceled operational sorties [MISSION SWIFT (Barents Sea) and MISSION SUNBEAM (Baltic Sea)]. Although the US and USSR had observed a moratorium on all nuclear tests since 31st October 1958, it appears that this mission was undertaken to determine if there were any indications of imminent tests – there were none.

Resumed flights from the UK did not last long. Likely as part of his domestic efforts associated with the release of RB-47 prisoners Olmstead and McKone, newly elected President Kennedy established a moratorium on all 'RB-47 reconnaissance flights on the periphery of the Sino-Soviet bloc.' All four Dets suspended operations on 8th February 1961, and their airplanes, crews, and Det commanders returned to Forbes AFB. During this time senior officials from the JRC, SAC, and the 55th SRW examined and revised all operational procedures, with 'the highest emphasis on continuous accuracy in navigation at all times while in the neighborhood of the Soviet Union.' In

Following the loss of the RB-47 on 1st July 1960, SAC reconnaissance operations from the UK were suspended as new procedures were developed to meet strict British control over authorization of each mission. *Author's collection*

USAFE had its own aircraft which were often confused with SAC reconnaissance assets, although they were occasional visitors to the UK. LITTLE GUY C-97G 52-2639 flew ELINT missions while assigned to the 7405th Support Squadron at Wiesbaden AB. *Gordon Macadie*

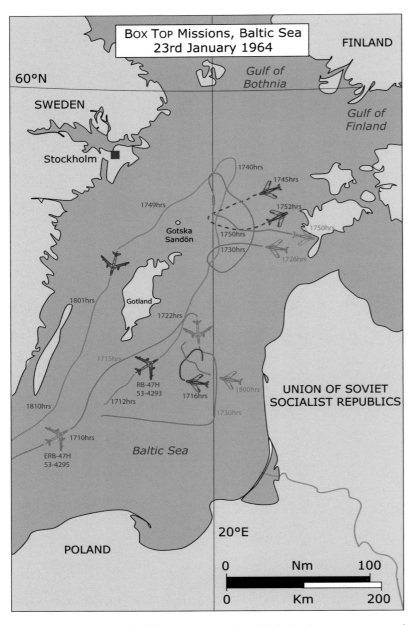

Box Top Missions, Baltic Sea
23rd January 1964

FINLAND

Gulf of
Bothnia

60°N

SWEDEN

Gulf of
Finland

Stockholm

1740hrs
1745hrs
1749hrs
1752hrs
1750hrs
Gotska
Sandön
1750hrs
1730hrs
1726hrs

1801hrs

Gotland

1722hrs

1715hrs

RB-47H
53-4293

1716hrs

1800hrs

UNION OF SOVIET
SOCIALIST REPUBLICS

1810hrs
1712hrs
1730hrs

1710hrs

ERB-47H
53-4295

Baltic Sea

20°E

POLAND

0   Nm   100

0   Km   200

BOX TOP missions to the Baltic Sea prompted multiple Soviet interceptions, not all of which were timely. The ERB-47H sortie aborted early due to loss of its Doppler radar, compelling the southward turn for the return flight to England. *via Lennart Andersson*

approving the new 'stricter procedures devised by SAC' articulated in National Security Action Memorandum 24 (NSAM 24) on 27th February, Kennedy established a 'no closer than' distance of 40nm (74km) from Soviet territory. In addition, peripheral ELINT missions were renamed from CASTLE GATE[1] (assumed to be compromised after the loss of 53-4281) to BOX TOP. Operations at RAF Brize Norton did not resume until April with ERB-47H 53-6246 flying the YELLOW COLE mission to the Baltic. Only six missions were scheduled through August.

This paucity of aircraft changed dramatically in late August 1961 with an influx of two RB-47Es, another ERB-47H, and four RB-47Ks, all related to prospective Soviet nuclear tests at Novaya Zemlya (Soviet testing resumed on 1st September). In addition to the KC-135 support tankers for the 55th SRW jets, an unusual arrival on 27th October marked the first visit to England of a reconnaissance variant of the Stratotanker. SPEED LIGHT-BRAVO JKC-135A 55-3127 flew three days later to monitor the *Tsar Bomba* 50Mt blast at Novaya Zemlya. Subsequent deployments of 59-1514 and 55-3121 as the SPEED LIGHT-DELTA and SPEED LIGHT-ECHO aircraft took place in May 1962, and again from August through October 1962. Reconnaissance activity at RAF Brize Norton decreased to almost nil with the onset of the October Cuban Missile Crisis, however, as the 55th SRW's assets were otherwise involved with missions around Cuba.

By 1963 lengthy RB-47H rotations resumed (many with the AN/ALD-4 SILVER KING ELINT pod modification). Specially configured GARLIC SALT KC-135Rs 55-3121, 59-1465, and 59-1514 from the 34th AREFS at Offutt AFB monitored Soviet nuclear tests, including the unidentified SPEED LIGHT-HAZEL mission proposed for September-October (which was canceled). In addition, JKC-135A 55-3132 visited RAF Brize Norton for the GOLDEN PHEASANT operational evaluation of the future ASD-1 automatic ELINT system for

As they neared the end of their operational lifetime, RB-47H missions from England carried the AN/ALD-4 SILVER KING ELINT pod. The system proved fickle, but when it worked the results were spectacular. *Terry Panopalis collection*

GOLDEN PHEASANT
JKC-135A 55-3132
served as the
prototype for
the AN/ASD-1
automated
ELINT collection
system planned
for the RC-135C.
It conducted
operational
evaluation
flights from RAF
Brize Norton.
*Jim Morrow
via Stephen Miller*

the forthcoming BIG TEAM RC-135C. Another 'guest' that would become quite regular was COMINT-configured KC-135A-II 60-0362, arriving at RAF Brize Norton on 24th August 1964 (it returned to Eielson AFB the next day). Assigned to the 4157th SW, this OFFICE BOY platform flew 'over the top' missions between Alaska and England. It would eventually be joined by sister aircraft 60-0356 and -0357, which were redesignated as RIVET BRASS RC-135Ds in 1965 for the COTTON CANDY mission. Det 1 relocated to RAF Upper Heyford on 21st February 1965, and once there RB-47Hs continued to mix with GARLIC SALT KC-135s and RIVET BRASS RC-135Ds.

A New Location

Despite the plan to retire the B-47E by the end of 1965, RB-47s remained as SAC's front-line ELINT collection platform pending delivery of the BIG TEAM RC-135C, and operations from RAF Upper Heyford continued at a steady pace. During the period from April-June 1965, for example, there were 22 operational sorties covering the Barents Sea and Baltic Sea, with occasional forays along the German border. The new AN/ALD-4 SILVER KING system proved troublesome, accounting for nearly all aborted or unsatisfactory missions. The GARLIC SALT airplanes were also occasional visitors. Although the August 1963 Partial Test Ban Treaty (PTBT) ended atmospheric nuclear tests, the Soviets continued underground testing at Novaya Zemlya, prompting both operational and PROUD ELTON training sorties from England.

The 55th SRW relocated from Forbes AFB to Offutt AFB on 16th August 1966, the same year that the new BIG TEAM RC-135C ELINT platform was scheduled to enter service and replace the RB-47H. Boeing delivered these RC-135Bs on time from 1964-65, but they sat as empty shells at the Glenn L Martin Company in Baltimore, MD, awaiting conversion to RC-135Cs and the installation of the ASD-1 ELINT system.

The first RC-135C (63-9792) finally reached Offutt AFB on 27th January 1967, and the first operational deployment to the UK took place on 4th May when an unidentified RC-135C departed Offutt AFB on a BURNING SKY mission to the sensitive area in Europe and then recovered at RAF Upper Heyford. Following a crew rest period, the airplane retraced its earlier route and returned to Offutt AFB. This would become the norm for most ensuing BURNING PIPE missions to and from the UK.

RC-135Ds from the 4157th continued to visit England at Det 1, 98th SW at RAF Upper

NOTE

1 CASTLE GATE was originally used from 3rd-5th May 1955 for the 55th SRW 32-ship RB-47E 'graduation' exercise to a fully operational unit. The airplanes flew PHOTINT missions over the US.

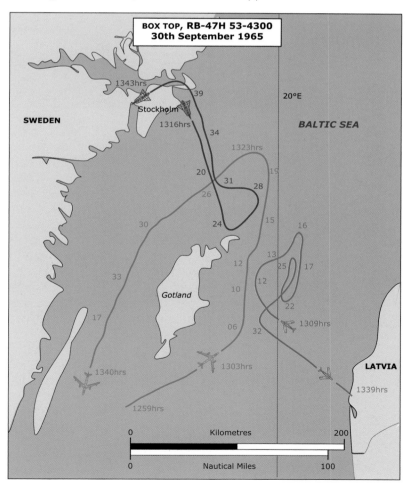

BOX TOP, RB-47H 53-4300
30th September 1965

55-3121 was a RIVET STAND/GARLIC SALT platform dedicated to reconnaissance associated with foreign nuclear tests. It is seen here in November 1966 at RAF Upper Heyford, immediately after two detonations on 27th October at Novaya Zemlya. *Author's collection*

In January 1967, the first BIG TEAM RC-135C landed at RAF Upper Heyford following a mission from Offutt AFB, returning the next day. Full-time deployments would not begin for some time. *Adrian Balch*

Heyford. The COTTON CANDY OpOrd changed in January 1967 to more regional names, including ARCTIC CANDY, BALTIC CANDY, and MEDITERRANEAN CANDY, the latter two suggesting that the RC-135Ds flew round-robin sorties from England. By May 1967, there were just two RB-47Hs in the UK. On 16th May, 53-4280 flew Mission U315, the final RB-47H sortie over the Barents Sea, and returned to Offutt AFB the following day. Two days later, on 18th May, 53-4303 flew Mission U405 to Albania and Algeria then recovering to Offutt AFB in its last reconnaissance mission from the United Kingdom. The RB-47 era in England was over.

Efforts to gather ELINT on the Soviet *Hen House* anti-ballistic missile (ABM) radars on the Kola Peninsula and in Latvia prompted the 23rd May 1967 visit to RAF Upper Heyford of BRIAR PATCH KC-135R 59-1465. It flew four missions in the Barents Sea area, but the remaining missions in the Baltic were canceled and the airplane returned to Offutt AFB. It crashed there on 20th June, and was hastily replaced by

former RIVET STAND KC-135R 55-3121. This new BRIAR PATCH jet flew similar missions from RAF Upper Heyford in February-March and April-May 1968.

CIA requirements for a dedicated Precision Parameter Measurement System (PPMS) platform led to the conversion of 55-3121 into the KC-135R RIVET JAW (this changed in December 1969 to KC-135T COBRA JAW). The COBRA JAW earned an unexpected degree of popularity when it appeared on its 9th September 1970 sortie over the Baltic Sea wearing the Ford Motor Company's Cobra Hot Wheels nose art painted by crewdog Dave Johnson. Indeed, the Soviet pilot who intercepted the airplane specifically commented on this artwork! On 10th November, two MiG-17s fired their cannons while escorting 55-3121 over the Pechora Sea. The KC-135T continued its mission and returned safely to RAF Upper Heyford, although the program was abruptly canceled.

The KC-135T was replaced by three COMBAT SENT RC-135Us beginning in 1971. One of these

In addition to the 55th SRW RC-135s that frequented English bases, the 6th SW at Eielson AFB routinely flew three jets 'over the top' from Alaska to England, primarily on COTTON CANDY COMINT missions. Originally designated as OFFICE BOY KC-135A-IIs, they became RIVET BRASS RC-135Ds. The extent of any 'round robin' missions from the UK is unclear. *Lindsay Peacock (top), Adrian Balch (upper, lower)*

Three days after this photo of 53-4280 was taken on 11th May 1967, it flew the final RB-47H mission from the UK to the Barents Sea, the penultimate mission from England. It returned to Offutt AFB on 17th May, and on 25th May went to the 'Boneyard.' *Adrian Balch*

Following the 1967 crash of 59-1465, KC-135R 55-3121 replaced it as the CIA-sponsored BRIAR PATCH aircraft. A trapeze in place of the air refueling boom was lowered in flight and a 'blivet' trailed well behind to collect sensitive signals from the Soviet *Hen House* ABM radar. *Adrian Balch collection*

Wearing the 'Cobra Hot Wheels' nose art, the lone KC-135T flew COBRA JAW missions from RAF Upper Heyford. On 17th November 1970, a Soviet MiG-17 pilot fired warning shots parallel to the airplane, but the crew continued its mission. *Author's collection*

RC-135U COMBAT SENT DEPLOYMENTS, 1972-1977

Deployment	From	To	RC-135U	Sorties Flown
Alpha	15 Jan 72	17 Apr 72	64-14847	20
Bravo	19 Jun 72	23 Sep 72	64-14849	8
Charlie	11 Nov 72	13 Dec 72	64-14847	11
Delta Phase I	5 Jan 73	23 Jan 73	64-14849	7
Range Amber I	11 Feb 73	19 Mar 73	63-9792	11
Echo	3 May 73	1 Jun 73	64-14847	11
Range Amber 2	6 Jun 73	10 Jun 73	63-9792	3
Golf	15 Apr 74	10 Jun 74	64-14847	20
Hotel	6 Aug 74	4 Oct 74	64-14847	18
Juliett	5 Mar 75	22 Apr 75	n/a	15
Kilo	2 Jun 75	24 Jul 75	64-14847	19
Lima	16 Sep 75	4 Nov 75	n/a	17
Mike	16 Mar 76	29 Jun 76	64-14847*	29
Nancy	20 Aug 76	26 Nov 76	64-14849†	29
Oscar	1 Apr 77	15 Jul 77	64-14849	29
Papa	n/a	n/a	64-14849	30

* Appeared with serials -14844 and -14848; † Appeared with serials -14850 and -14851

(63-9792) was funded by the CIA for its 'special ELINT' requirements. Global deployments were listed alphabetically, and the first of these – Alpha – reached RAF Mildenhall in January 1972 with the arrival of 64-14847. CIA deployments were identified as 'Range' missions. Subsequent rotations did not necessarily appear in alphabetical order because of concurrent or sequential trips to Kadena AB or Misawa AB, Japan. The 'U-Boats' always generated special interest among the UK spotter community, including the introduction of the bogus 'Combat Pink' reference derived from nose art of the Pink Panther cartoon character. The RC-135U was well suited to the shark-mouth it acquired while in England, and even sported false serial numbers during 1976 (64-14847 as 64-14844 and -14848; 64-14849 as -14850, and -14851). On occasion the COMBAT SENT flew missions in

Left and below:
A regular visitor to England was the RC-135U COMBAT SENT. It first arrived on 13th January 1972 (seen here) for the Alpha Deployment, surely a welcome surprise for spotters to see the initial arrival of a new variant. In later years it became quite possibly the only SAC airplane in the UK with a photogenic shark mouth. *Lindsay Peacock (upper), author's collection (lower)*

conjunction with SR-71s. On 24th October and 16th November 1977, for example, 64-14849 undertook coordinated missions with 61-7976 in the Barents Sea and Baltic Sea, respectively.

From December 1972 through January 1976, BIG SAFARI converted the BIG TEAM RC-135Cs into RIVET JOINT RC-135Vs, combining the former's ELINT capability with the retiring RC-135D's COMINT role. RC-135V 64-14848 was the first RIVET JOINT to visit the UK, with the initial mission flown on 7th January 1974. After an additional 26 sorties, the results of the new Automatic ELINT Emitter Locator System (AEELS) were discouraging. With the remaining RC-135Cs already under conversion SAC's operational ELINT capacity was significantly reduced. Indeed, the last RC-135C deployment to RAF Mildenhall ended on 6th September 1974, and RC-135D sorties began from RAF Mildenhall on 10th February 1975 to mitigate the shortfall.

These were short lived as the RC-135D was replaced beginning in March 1975 with the RC-135M in the COMINT role. The RIVET CARD RC-135Ms operated primarily from Hellenikon AB, Greece, however, leaving a substantial and lengthy gap in ELINT collection from England.

Improvements to the RIVET JOINT's ELINT system began in 1976, and RAF Mildenhall once again served as the test venue for the Improved AEELS with 17 missions flown between November 1977 and March 1978. These proved successful and the RC-135V was soon joined by RC-135Ws that had been converted from RC-135Ms. Together these flew BURNING WIND strategic SIGINT sorties from RAF Mildenhall, but were soon parsed out to meet tactical requirements. For example, on 16th February 1983 64-14843 departed England for Egypt to monitor Libyan aggression there. The majority of RIVET JOINT Middle East operations were

RC-135U 64-14849 was spuriously marked as '64-14850' both on the nose and tail during the Nancy Deployment in 1976. 64-14847 was similarly repainted during the Mike Deployment as 64-14848 while parked next to RC-135V 64-14848! *Robin Walker via Paul Crickmore*

By 22nd January 1971, the days of RC-135C and RC-135D deployments to the UK were numbered with the conversion of the BIG TEAM jets into RC-135V RIVET JOINTS, which combined the former's ELINT and the latter's COMINT missions. *Adrian Balch collection*

The first RIVET JOINT deployment took place in January 1974 (seen here) with RC-135V 64-14848. Results were disappointing, and the program was nearly canceled entirely but for the intervention of multiple generals. *Richard Vandervord*

With the termination of operations from the UK, the RC-135D's trademark J57 water-injected black exhaust on takeoff ended. All of the remaining SAC RC-135s that visited England used TF33 turbofan engines. *Lindsay Peacock*

The 55th SRW occasionally brought supplies, parts, or personnel to England using its refuelable KC-135E 59-1514. It has since been scrapped and replaced by two TC-135Ws. *Adrian Balch collection*

conducted from Hellenikon AB, however, leaving the England-based airplanes to fly peripheral sorties by 'The Fence' along the German border, missions to the Baltic Sea and Barents Sea (several of which were coordinated with SR-71 sorties), and 'over the top' flights to and from Eielson AFB. By the 1980s RIVET JOINTS were synonymous with 'The Hall,' and the number of spotters along the fence by the arrival end of runway 29 or at Pollard's Lane increased commensurately whenever 'The Wind' was in town.

The August 1990 Iraqi invasion of Kuwait prompted the deployment of RC-135V/Ws to Riyadh AB, Saudi Arabia, for Operation DESERT SHIELD. BURNING WIND missions from RAF Mildenhall decreased, but transient RIVET JOINTS as well as the 55th SRW's TC-135W trainer 62-4129 and 'hack' KC-135E 59-1514 (formerly a GARLIC SALT/RIVET STAND jet) kept the reconnaissance staff busy. The pace increased in January 1991 after

the launch of combat in Iraq and Kuwait with Operation DESERT STORM. RC-135V/Ws continued to rotate through RAF Mildenhall to and from Offutt AFB as they returned stateside for 200-hour maintenance checks, a figure reached quickly given the 15-hour missions they flew.

The success of the RIVET JOINT in combat reconnaissance made it the centerpiece in subsequent operational planning for theater commanders around the globe. Consequently, traditional BURNING WIND SIGINT missions decreased as the limited number of RC-135V/Ws constrained SAC's ability to support simultaneous strategic and tactical tasking. Flights at RAF Mildenhall other than transient deployments dropped accordingly. By the time of SAC's disestablishment in June 1992 it appeared that extensive peripheral RC-135 missions from England were a thing of the past, although they eventually resumed to a modest level under Air Combat Command.

Former RIVET CARD RC-135Ms were converted into RIVET JOINT RC-135Ws. They were identical in mission capability to the RC-135Vs. *Bob Archer*

Nearly every BURNING WIND mission from RAF Mildenhall included at least one tanker (two for longer sorties). The KC-135s waited to ensure the RC-135 became airborne before launching.
Bob Archer

It is difficult to rate a RIVET JOINT crew's priority for deployment bases, but RAF Mildenhall was certainly a top contender, followed by Okinawa and Greece, with Alaska well behind.
Author's collection

The amount of time an RC-135 was away from RAF Mildenhall was often an indicator of its mission. Shorter flights often went to the Baltic or along 'The Fence' between East and West, while longer flights typically visited the Barents Sea.
Author's collection

After the dissolution of SAC in 1992, RIVET JOINTs deployed to RAF Mildenhall wearing ACC markings, including the new OF tail code. Beginning in 2000, they acquired F108 engines, improving performance and reducing their noise footprint.
Author's collection

7 Blackbirds

On 1st May 1956 a Douglas C-124 landed at RAF Lakenheath, not looking any different than the other Globemasters that frequented US bases in England. Shortly thereafter it disgorged its shroud-covered cargo which was discreetly reassembled in a nearby hangar. The first of four Lockheed U-2s assigned to the Central Intelligence Agency (CIA) had arrived in England.

The U-2's presence in the United Kingdom has long been an admixture of its CIA missions and those of the Strategic Air Command (relevant CIA deployments to the UK merit brief consideration here to differentiate them from SAC missions). The initial deployment in 1956 of the '1st Weather Reconnaissance Squadron (Provisional)' – referred to as WRSP-1 but in actuality CIA Det A – included civilian CIA pilots, civilian Lockheed maintenance contractors, and SAC staff officers (embedded at the behest of SAC's commander General LeMay). Although the overflights planned from RAF Lakenheath were strictly a CIA operation, this blended organizational structure provided SAC with the support experience to conduct its own

INITIAL CIA U-2 DEPLOYMENT TO RAF LAKENHEATH, 1956

U-2s			
346/56-6679	347/56-6680	348/56-6681	349/56-6682

U-2 missions which, starting in October 1957, would be strictly for atmospheric sampling and specifically excluded overflights. Moreover, beginning in April 1975, SAC conducted U-2 OLIVE TREE operations from the British base at RAF Akrotiri, Cyprus, which subjected the airplanes to the same British political oversight that applied to missions flown from bases in England.

A Change of Heart

Shakedown flights of the four CIA U-2s assigned to Det A at RAF Lakenheath began on 21st May and continued intermittently throughout the month in preparation for the first planned overflight of 'denied' communist territory. Surprisingly, Prime Minister Anthony Eden balked at the idea of U-2 overflights from the UK. Previously, SAC RB-45Cs seconded to

SAC C-124 52-1018 from the 1st SSS delivers a CIA U-2 to Groom Lake, in a scene that was replicated on 1st May 1956 at RAF Lakenheath with the arrival of the first U-2 in England. Exactly four years later, the U-2 became one of the most infamous aircraft of the Cold War. *via Chris Pocock*

the RAF conducted seven overflights of the USSR and East Germany as part of the JU JITSU missions in March and April 1952 and again in April 1954, and the UK allowed a SAC RB-47E overflight of Murmansk from RAF Fairford in May 1954[1]. These were all completed during the tenure of Prime Minister Winston Churchill under whom Eden was Foreign Secretary and, according to many historians, was the *éminence grise* of the Conservative Party. Nonetheless, by 1956 Eden was deeply concerned by the failed American Project GENETRIX – where more than 500 US photoreconnaissance balloons were launched from a variety of countries (including the UK) over the USSR – and the scandalous death of Royal Navy diver Lionel

'Buster' Crabb, recruited by MI6 to investigate the Soviet cruiser *Ordzhonikidze* in Portsmouth Harbour in April. Fearing that any compromise of the U-2 overflights would lead to considerable public opprobrium and risk a potential Soviet military response against Britain, on 11th June 1956 Eden requested that Det A leave the UK, and it relocated to Wiesbaden AB, FRG. For the time being it appeared that the Dragon Lady's presence in England was over.

The 'Lakenheath U-2s' returned to the public spotlight, however, in May and June of 1960 as the British Parliament debated the 1st May U-2 Incident. Ministers were understandably worried – as Eden had feared – about Soviet retaliation against British bases should overflights be launched from there, an issue which applied equally to SAC B-47s on alert in the UK. Despite repeated questions, Her Majesty's Government stuck to the original cover story that the U-2s at RAF Lakenheath in 1956 were for only routine weather-related operations and refused further comment about their capability to conduct overflights of the USSR.

SAC's first U-2 deployment to the UK began when three silver jets (56-6681, -6712, and -6953) from the 4080th SRW at Laughlin AFB arrived at RAF Upper Heyford via Plattsburgh AFB on 19th August 1962 (the June 1959 series of planned FORTUNE FINDER II sampling missions from RAF Upper Heyford had been cancelled). This visit was widely publicized well in advance and even included the scheduled arrival date, much to the glee of British spotters. According to newspaper reports, these U-2s were intended to 'check on weather, cosmic rays, and Russian nuclear tests…round Greenland and Norway.' Most notably, they carried 'no cameras.' Given that there were multiple Soviet atmospheric tests at Novaya Zemlya from August through October, they were almost certainly flying High Altitude Sampling Program (HASP) sorties.

U-2 operations in the UK were 'active'. In addition to flying their 'scientific' missions, RAF Lightning Mk.1As from 56 and 111 Squadrons seconded to the Air Fighting Development Squadron (AFDS) at RAF Binbrook undertook missions to intercept the U-2s operating at lower-than-cruise altitudes over the Pennines and Central Scotland. From 18th October through 15th November, the Lightnings flew 19 sorties from RAF Middleton St George, and routinely acquired lock-ons of the U-2s operating at 60,000ft (11 sorties at 18,288m) and later 65,000ft (eight sorties at 19,812m) using inert Firestreak missiles. The highest altitude achieved was 77,800ft (23,713m) – well above the U-2's 70,000ft (21,336m) cruise altitude – much to the 'trepidation the U-2 pilots felt as they were intercepted with apparent ease by Britain's latest fighter.' The lessons of the intercepts were not lost on US and SAC planners, who recognized that the U-2 was now fully vulnerable not only to SAMs such as the one which shot down Frank Powers in 1960, but to increasingly lethal air-to-air missile-equipped fighters. The Lockheed/CIA OXCART program, which yielded the A-12 and SR-71, gained urgency and support.

The last reported sighting of the three SAC U-2s was of 56-6953 landing at RAF Upper Heyford on 21st October – coincidentally during the Cuban Missile Crisis – after which the U-2s returned to Laughlin AFB in November 1962.

Planning a Quick Response

A CIA U-2 from WRSP-4 (in reality CIA Det G) at the North Base of Edwards AFB, CA, hurriedly and secretly returned to RAF Upper Heyford on 29th May 1967 to monitor tensions in the Middle East as part of SCOPE SAFE. High-level discussions raised the possibility that any missions might be flown by RAF pilots assigned as part of the IDEALIST program but the British demurred. CIA planners, anticipating that some European nations might deny overflight rights from the UK, selected carrier-capable U-2G 56-6681 (Article 348) for the mission. Plans were made to relocate the U-2G from the UK to the USS Saratoga which was already in the Mediterranean Sea, but British approval to fly a mission on 2nd June from England appeared to obviate this. Washington waffled further and the presence of the U-2 leaked. Consequently, on 7th June the British requested that the lone U-2 be 'withdrawn'. A local flight took place that night, and the airplane returned to California on 9th June. Although this was strictly a CIA operation, the implications for future SAC operations were significant. American planners recognized the proximity value of RAF Akrotiri to cover the Middle East, and US policy makers understood that the U-2 could be an important 'quick-response tool' in monitoring wartime situations and cease-fire positions. In both cases, formal approval for any future missions would

Top left: XM177 was one of four Lightning Mk.1As that successfully intercepted 4080th SW U-2s operating from RAF Upper Heyford in 1962. Although the U-2s intentionally flew some 10,000ft (3,048m) below their normal cruise altitude, the Lightnings were still a real threat with similar implications for Soviet MiGs. *via Tony Buttler*

Top right: Three SAC U-2s from the 4080th SW operated from RAF Upper Heyford during mid 1962. They conducted HASP missions related to Soviet atmospheric nuclear tests at Novaya Zemlya. *Albert Gibb via Chris Pocock*

Left: U-2G 56-6681 was intended to overfly the Middle East from the USS Saratoga during the 1967 Six Day War, but plans were canceled when the airplane's presence was leaked. It ended its days as NASA N708NA. *Keith Heywood, author's collection*

The first U-2R to visit the UK was CIA 68-10331 in 1969 for SCOPE SAINT II. SAC's U-2Rs arrived later during the 1970s, such as 68-10338 seen here on 1st July 1977.
Bob Archer

Two RAF pilots overflew the USSR, including Squadron Leader Robbie Robinson, as part of Project CHALICE from 1956 through 1960. Far less well known were the eight RAF U-2R pilots seconded to Det G (later the 1130th ATTG) as part of Project IDEALIST between 1961 and 1973.
via Chris Pocock

come as much from Number 10 and Whitehall as from the White House and Foggy Bottom.

The quick-response idea continued to percolate in Washington throughout 1968, resulting in the October return of the same CIA U-2G from Det G to the UK. Following a single local flight, SCOPE SAINT I ended a week later. SCOPE SAINT II followed in April 1969, when CIA U-2R 68-10331 from Det G made a nonstop flight from California to RAF St Mawgan in 12 hours, 20 minutes. A ground incident precluded any flying from Cornwall, so RAF pilot Squadron

Leader Dick Cloke flew the airplane back to the US. During October 1969 Cloke brought another U-2R to RAF Kinloss in Scotland for SCOPE SAINT III [in mid-1969 Det G was redesignated as the euphemistic 1130th Aerospace Technical Training Group (ATTG)]. Along with fellow RAF pilot Flight Lieutenant Harry Drew, Cloke flew two missions to evaluate the new B2 version of the HR73 camera, which the RAF later purchased for their Canberra PR.9s. There were additional SCOPE SAINT deployments in October 1971 and again a year later. In both cases, a Lockheed C-141 ferried U-2R 68-10332 back to RAF St Mawgan for SCOPE SAINT IV and to RAF Wattisham for SCOPE SAINT V. These missions further demonstrated the rapid-response capability of CIA U-2Rs which offered three key advantages over SAC's U-2. The CIA airplanes could be configured with the full range of PHOTINT, ELINT, and COMINT sensors, carried appropriate defensive equipment 'to operate in a hostile environment,' and provided the US with plausible deniability in the event of a compromised mission.

A 'real-world' need for a quick response arose during the summer of 1970 when aerial battles erupted between Israel and Egypt. A cease-fire brokered by US National Security Advisor Henry A Kissinger required verification by American reconnaissance flights, and a *de facto* competition broke out between SAC and the CIA over who could send airplanes and crews the fastest. The 1130th ATTG proved ready first and even offered to have RAF pilots fly the jets from California to RAF Upper Heyford and thence to RAF Akrotiri. The British government rejected the use of its pilots so CIA pilots flew the missions instead. Both France and Italy refused overflight rights and the U-2 was forced to enter the Mediterranean Sea via the Strait of Gibraltar. The first flight over the Sinai from RAF Upper Heyford took place on 9th August, with subsequent EVEN STEVEN missions from RAF Akrotiri beginning on 11th August.

In total the CIA flew 30 missions, with the final flight on 10th November by Marty Knutson (who previously piloted two overflights of the USSR). Of these, 18 used the B-camera and 12 used the H-camera. Each flight also collected ELINT, especially of the SA-3 *Goa* SAM. The two U-2s returned to RAF Upper Heyford and were flown home on 14th December by RAF pilots Cloke and Drew.

Technology Evaluation

Aerial losses to SAMs in Southeast Asia (SEA) prompted the Air Force to evaluate programs to locate active SAM sites and then relay these data to strike aircraft. One project, known as PAVE ONYX, included the Advanced Location Strike System (ALSS) – approved on 5th May 1972 – which used the time of arrival of radar pulses from the SAM's radar to triangulate its position. Three U-2s equipped with E- and F-band sensors would triangulate the SA-2's *Fan Song* radar to pinpoint the SAM's location within 30ft (10m). This location would then be relayed to awaiting fighters to attack and destroy the site. The Air Force expected ALSS to be fully operational by January 1973. Although this was a tactical program, testing fell to SAC as it was the only operational military user of the U-2, and because SAC U-2s would fly the combat missions in SEA once ALSS was in service. Consequently, six U-2Cs in flyable storage plus one U-2C trainer were selected for ALSS testbeds under the name SENIOR BALL. Tests began at Davis-Monthan AFB in early 1973 with mixed results, delaying the planned combat deployment of the ALSS U-2s.

USAFE also expressed interest in ALSS to meet operational requirements for any war in Europe. With the end of direct US involvement in the Vietnam war, the Air Force shifted the ALSS tests to Europe. During 1973, SAC evaluated both RAF Mildenhall and RAF Wethersfield as the prospective U-2C ALSS test base. The U-2s would have disrupted the busy KC-135 and RC-135 operations at RAF Mildenhall, so SAC elected to use RAF Wethersfield. Six U-2Cs – sporting a two-tone grey scheme – began deploying there on 24th April 1975. The overall name for this program was CONSTANT TREAT, while the U-2 mission name was OLYMPIC JUMP.

OLYMPIC JUMP **ALSS U-2s**

ALSS U-2Cs			ALSS U-2CT
56-6680	56-6701	56-6714	56-6692†
56-6700*	56-6707	56-6716	

* crashed 29 May 75; † did not deploy to the UK

Between 15th May - 8th July 1975, U-2Cs flew 18 OLYMPIC JUMP missions. Each mission lasted some seven hours (with 4.7 hours collecting ELINT) and flew adjacent to the 20-30nm (37-56km) buffer zone between the FRG and the GDR from the North Sea to Switzerland. Data were relayed to the ground station at Sembach AB, FRG. While the overall mission effectiveness of the U-2Cs was 93%, weaknesses in the remaining portions of the overall system lowered this figure to 76%. Targeting accuracy was a disappointing 75-100ft (23-30m), substantially worse than the predicted (and desired) 30ft. Moreover, on 29th May 1975, U-2C 56-6700 crashed near Winterberg, FRG. With these unhappy results and loss of an airplane all U-2Cs returned to the US by 18th July 1975.

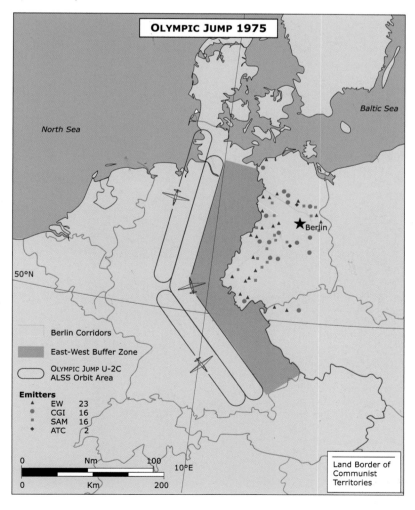

OLYMPIC JUMP 1975

Baltic Sea

North Sea

★ Berlin

50°N

Berlin Corridors

East-West Buffer Zone

OLYMPIC JUMP U-2C ALSS Orbit Area

Emitters
▲ EW 23
● CGI 16
■ SAM 16
◆ ATC 2

0   Nm   100
0   Km   200

10°E

Land Border of Communist Territories

149

After experiencing flight control problems while at altitude over West Germany, U-2 56-6700 entered 'Mach tuck,' forcing pilot Captain Terry Rendleman to eject safely. *Richard Vandervord*

Six U-2Cs were sent to the UK to evaluate the ALSS designed to pinpoint and target SAM sites during 1972. A seventh two-seater did not deploy to England. *Bob Archer*

While deployed to RAF Wethersfield, the OLYMPIC JUMP U-2Cs wore a distinctive two-tone grey color scheme. The bulge beneath the Q-bay covers the additional ALSS equipment. *Lindsay Peacock*

Rear view of 56-6714 reveals the large single flaps and the 'sugar scoop' beneath the exhaust to mitigate infra-red missile detonations. Despite the plan for ALSS, the U-2 was ill-suited for tactical combat operations. *Terry Panopalis collection*

Overall the ALSS program met with mixed success. Systems effectiveness was less than desired. Nonetheless, the program eventually led to the TR-1. *Author's collection*

Although SAC's U-2 HASP ended in September 1968, by 1972 US officials anticipated the resumption of Soviet atmospheric atomic tests as well as continued tests by France and the PRC. Increasing costs and decreasing reliability of Military Airlift Command's (MAC) General Dynamics WB-57 raised the possibility that the sampling mission should return to SAC with its new U-2Rs. Senior commanders considered this new OLYMPIC RACE mission to have the 'highest national reconnaissance priority,' usurping airplanes and personnel from combat reconnaissance missions in Southeast Asia. The plan was for three U-2Rs to be based at Osan AB, Republic of Korea, with additional airplanes deployed to Eielson AFB and 'either Spain or the United Kingdom.' Should there not be sufficient U-2Rs available, two U-2Cs would be configured with sampling gear. Eventually, OLYMPIC RACE was assigned to Osan AB and Torrejón AB bypassing the UK altogether.

Expanding UK Operations

Between 7th-23rd September 1976, SAC SENIOR BOOK-configured U-2R 68-10336 returned to RAF Mildenhall to join an SR-71 and RC-135s in support of the NATO COLD FIRE '76 and TEAMWORK '76 exercises. Assigned to Det 1, 306th SW, it flew a combined total of 30 missions over the three-week period. Results were impressive, prompting calls for 'a permanent U-2R detachment in Europe.' In response, between June and October 1977, SAC sent a single U-2R to 'collect a reliable and timely COMINT product in the dense signal environment'. The first of 34 OLYMPIC FLAME COMINT missions took place on 10th June. On occasion the U-2 operated in conjunction with US Army Beechcraft RC-12 Guardrail aircraft. Once again, the results were appealing to USAFE commanders, who continued to press for a dedicated U-2 unit.

The establishment of Det 4, 9th SRW at RAF Mildenhall on 1st April 1979 provided a base of operations for a single regular U-2R OLYMPIC TORCH COMINT mission from the UK. Data were downloaded to Electronic Security Command (ESC) ground site Metro Tango near Hahn AB, FRG. The airplane could also collect PHOTINT when requested, but its primary task remained theater COMINT unhampered by the curvature of the earth. The first OLYMPIC TORCH sortie took place over the FRG on 2nd April 1979 and the first PHOTINT-only mission followed on 18th May 1979. Each nine-hour mission used only a single track with seven hours on station.

During June-July 1979, SENIOR RUBY configured U-2R 68-10339 deployed to RAF Mildenhall for evaluation flights. The airplane flew three shakedown missions followed by 16 assessment flights between 19th June through 24th July. From 3rd-7th July the airplane flew one sortie daily for five days, demonstrating surge capability. Overall these initial flights from RAF Mildenhall proved highly valuable, accruing 80 sorties in 1979 and 111 in 1980. The OLYMPIC TORCH U-2R initially carried the SENIOR BOOK sensor package, but this was replaced on 8th January 1980 with SENIOR RUBY – the Remote Tactical Airborne SIGINT System (RTASS and later known as SENIOR GLASS) – and the SENIOR SPEAR system that allowed for simultaneous ELINT and COMINT collection. This system is believed to have been used during sorties associated with the Polish labor crisis during 1980-81. These flights averaged nine per month and continued until 1983 with the arrival of the Lockheed TR-1.

During the spring and late summer of 1980, SAC's U-2R flew 26 special missions monitoring Soviet ships and to participate in a NATO exercise. Between 31st March through 30th April they flew 16 OLYMPIC FIRE I missions to collect SIGINT from Soviet vessels. Each mission lasted an average of 10.9 hours although only four

STRATEGIC AIR COMMAND IN THE UK

SAC's U-2Rs appeared in a variety of configurations associated with ELINT and COMINT collection. 68-10339 was the testbed for the SENIOR RUBY ELINT system as part of OLYMPIC TORCH from RAF Mildenhall.
Steve Donald via Bob Archer

U-2R operations at RAF Mildenhall ended with the departure of 68-10337 in 1983, following the arrival of SAC's TR-1As at RAF Alconbury. Ground handling for both types utilized a special trolley with an appropriately attired crewman to balance the wings.
Paul Bennett via Bob Archer

hours were spent on station due to the lengthy transit time from RAF Mildenhall. Overall the U-2s accrued 174.6 hours, with 54.2 hours of intelligence downlinked to the USS *Harlan County* for analysis. During September there were 10 OLYMPIC FIRE II flights to the North Atlantic west of the UK, over the Norwegian Sea north of Scotland, and to the Norwegian Sea near northern Norway. The flights totaled 73.3 hours and collected 'Blue' (or friendly) COMINT, with 39.7 hours of downlink to the USS *Nimitz*.

SAC SR-71 and U-2 search-and-rescue (SAR) operations were known as BUSY PLAYMATE. On 23rd November 1980, Italy suffered a significant earthquake that killed at least 2,500 persons and caused damage over more than 10,000 square miles (26,000 km²). The Italian government requested high-altitude photography to assess the impact. Because an SR-71 would produce a sonic boom that risked collapsing already damaged buildings, SAC sent a U-2R on a seven-hour mission on 10th December, producing 'useful' results.

Det 4's U-2 operations ended on 22nd February 1983 when U-2R 68-10337 departed RAF Mildenhall for Beale AFB, shortly after

the arrival of the 17th RW's TR-1As at RAF Alconbury.

SAC Operations from Cyprus

Following the initial GIANT REACH SR-71 missions over the Middle East during the 1973 October War, senior US officials sought to provide an ongoing aerial reconnaissance presence to monitor and verify the cease fire agreement. The operational cost and the decreased SAM threat obviated the need to continue with SR-71 overflights, and SAC's U-2s operating from Cyprus were an ideal replacement. Plans had existed as early as 15th September 1971 for OLIVE FARM missions from Cyprus. In addition, US reconnaissance aircraft had British permission to use RAF Akrotiri as an emergency divert base; by the end of 1973 there had been only two such diversions over the previous 12 years. Using the base on Cyprus as the *origin* of US reconnaissance flights, however, was a different matter.

SAC considered the OLIVE FARM plan as the basis for a 1973 proposal to do so, although with sufficient variations to warrant a change

152

in the operation's name to OLIVE HARVEST. Missions would be flown every 10-14 days with the departure at sunrise on a Saturday or Sunday to minimize disruptions to the airfield while maintaining a 'low profile'. Britain was especially keen to minimize 'overflight of Cyprus to lessen the likelihood of Cypriot left-wing elements alleging espionage', necessitating as little flight time over the island as possible. Collection results would be shared with the Egyptians, Syrians, and Israelis. Because these flights were undertaken with the approval of the overflown countries, they were not considered PARPRO sorties and were not subject to those operational constraints.

There were immediate obstacles, however, including negotiations with Britain for basing at RAF Akrotiri and a shortage of airplanes (at the time SAC had only seven U-2Rs spread across multiple global missions). Pending SAC's acquisition of additional airplanes, the Sinai overflight missions were initially undertaken by the CIA's 1130th ATTG, which was in place by 22nd April 1974. The first CIA mission was flown on 12th May 1974 in U-2R 68-10333 along track J-001 adjacent to the Suez Canal (track J-006 was over the Golan Heights), with a '100% effective' coverage. The second (and final) CIA mission took place on 3rd June. SAC's 100th SRW from Davis-Monthan AFB took over the OLIVE HARVEST mission after receiving four additional U-2Rs beginning in August 1974, and RAF Akrotiri was designated as OL-OH (for OLIVE HARVEST)

These missions were complicated by political constraints on the routes which did not necessarily account for the flight characteristics of the U-2, particularly over the Golan Heights. Pilots flew by dead reckoning and the terrain of the Golan proved difficult for precise positioning. During a mission on 6th December

1974, for example, winds aloft were higher than predicted and the U-2 drifted 7nm (13km) off course over Syria. Installation of the Litton LN-33 inertial navigation system (INS) eliminated these errors.

The pace of SAC OLIVE HARVEST sorties increased the following year, with 50 flights. Missions lasted two hours for Golan (approximately three per month) and four hours for Sinai (approximately five per month), and up to five hours to cover both. Despite the loss of U-2R 68-10330 which crashed on takeoff from RAF Akrotiri on 7th December 1977, OLIVE HARVEST U-2Rs flew 189 missions over the following three years; 67 in 1978, 57 in 1979, and 65 in 1980. In addition, SENIOR LOOK U-2R PARPRO missions were proposed from RAF Akrotiri but this was abandoned to avoid irritating Egypt, Syria, and Israel (SENIOR LOOK missions had been flown previously from the joint British-American base at Diego Garcia, with the first of six flights on 19th April 1975 to monitor 'Soviet intentions in the Indian Ocean and the Gulf of Aden').

There were considerable changes to OL-OH in 1980, beginning with four new tracks: Sinai-Israel-Golan Heights (J-023) starting on 3rd June, Sinai-Israel (J-018) on 10th June, Golan Heights-Israel (J-007) on 4th August, and Golan Heights-Israel-Sinai (J-022) on 4th September. Organizationally OL-OH became Det 3, 9th SRW on 1st September 1980, resolving several manpower issues for the Det 3 staff. In addition to the OLIVE HARVEST sorties, a U-2R flew a single 8.5-hour SENIOR LOOK mission to Yemen on 27th January, expanding the scope of operations beyond those associated with the Arab-Israeli dispute.

In April 2014 OLIVE HARVEST celebrated its 40th anniversary on 'Fantasy Island' with the tongue-in-cheek slogan 'Still Not Here After 40 years.'

OLIVE HARVEST peacekeeping missions from RAF Akrotiri were initially constrained by a shortage of U-2Rs in SAC, and some airplanes operated from both Cyprus as well as the UK on other missions. *Bob Archer*

Unlike the OLIVE HARVEST *sorties from Cyprus which provided PHOTINT to Egypt, Syria, and Israel to verify post-war agreements,* OLIVE TREE *COMINT missions were PARPRO sorties and subject to British approval.*
Lindsay Peacock

Expanding to COMINT

The operational success of the OLIVE HARVEST PHOTINT missions from Cyprus prompted US intelligence officials to explore options for other missions. On 19th November 1974 the US requested permission to deploy a 'specially configured U-2 aircraft' to RAF Akrotiri pending endorsement in the US by the 40 Committee (which authorized important intelligence operations). Formal request for the SENIOR STRETCH COMINT mission followed on 17th January 1975, seeking 10 evaluation flights over a 90-day period. These missions would 'improve US intelligence in the area generally but more importantly...establish a contingency capability in the event that a renewed crisis in the Middle East put an end to their more normal photo and SIGINT operations.' The U-2 'would transmit its collected material in flight back to a collecting center [on Cyprus] from whence it would be beamed direct to America.' The British were 'strongly in favor' of the proposal, noting that the results would be shared with the UK under the UK-USA SIGINT agreement, and that the operation would be an 'interesting experiment which could have a bearing on our own future dependence on [Cyprus] for SIGINT.'

British approval followed promptly and the mission name changed to OLIVE TREE. The first flight took place on 15th April 1975. There would be 8-10 flights planned each month with a nine-hour duration and seven hours on station using three different tracks (these were consolidated into a single route on 9th June 1980). Unlike the OLIVE HARVEST flights which were acceded to in advance by the Egyptians, Syrians, and Israelis (and were therefore not considered PARPRO missions), OLIVE TREE sorties operated under strict reconnaissance rules. The mission track was at least 50nm (93km) from each coast over international waters and required British approval 48 hours before launch for each flight.

Interestingly, the OLIVE TREE flights had their 24-channel SENIOR SPEAR COMINT receivers controlled by National Security Agency (NSA) 'analysts' (read 'linguists') at Ft Meade, MD. According to a SAC history, this 'revolutionary' OLIVE TREE collection 'was relayed to a Defense Systems Communications Satellite (DSCS)' in orbit 22,300 miles (35,888km) above the Atlantic Ocean. It was then 'passed to the Defense Communications Agency (DCA) TSC-54 satellite terminal at Ft Dietrich, MD,' and then via land line to NSA analysts at Ft Meade.

Despite the 'low profile' by U-2 personnel to mask the OLIVE TREE COMINT mission as a 'benign' OLIVE HARVEST sortie, the flight route and the lengthy on-station time betrayed their true purpose. As a British memorandum recounted, the 'Russians and Israelis have spotted what is going on but..., for their own different reasons, they are not likely to make capital out of it; even if they did, the allegation is deniable.' OLIVE TREE sorties stabilized at approximately one every three days, with 96 in 1978, 113 in 1979, and 106 in 1980. Ill fortune struck on 24th April 1980 when U-2R 68-10333 crashed on takeoff from RAF Akrotiri due to hydraulic failure while on an OLIVE TREE flight (it was later repaired). U-2R 68-10332 replaced the out-of-commission airplane, but it required nearly a month to configure it to the SENIOR SPEAR configuration, so no missions took place during May 1980.

As late as 1990 the British government was still ambiguous about OLIVE TREE missions. In a 15th June 1990 question to Parliament about RAF Akrotiri and U-2 operations there, Sir Archie Hamilton replied, 'The USAF U-2 aircraft has been permanently stationed at RAF Akrotiri since 1974 in support of middle east peacekeeping arrangements. It operates with the knowledge of all Governments directly involved.' While this was certainly true of OLIVE HARVEST peacekeeping missions monitoring Israel-Egypt-Syrian activity, it was not true of the concurrent OLIVE TREE COMINT sorties.

Tactical Reconnaissance

After a lengthy and convoluted series of proposals, evaluations, and counter proposals, the Air
Force settled on a newly built variant of the U-2R
to provide tactical battlefield intelligence to theater commanders. From July 1981 through May
1989 the Air Force expected to receive 25 Lockheed TR-1As (in lieu of the 90 General Dynamics
RF-111Ds originally proposed and later the COM-
PASS COPE unmanned aerial vehicle), although this
number increased to 35 during mid-1979. In an
effort to minimize budgetary and congressional
'interference' in the acquisition of the new airplanes they were designated as TR-1s (originally
SAC suggested it be redesignated as the U-2S
but this was rejected). The TR-1 was similar to
the U-2Rs in its SENIOR SPEAR COMINT configuration, but it would also carry a Hughes Aircraft
Advanced Synthetic Aperture Radar System II
(ASARS II) radar under development [this would
become the Precision Location Strike System
(PLSS), derived from the ALSS program]. Actual
differences between the TR-1 and U-2R were
modest, with a 'commonality factor of 99%,'
as only the TR-1 was configured with the PLSS
wiring in the nose, and only the U-2R could be
configured for aerial sampling. Notably the TR-1
had a 'better urine collection system' – installed
at the request of pilots – as well as a VHF radio.

According to the 1978-1980 SAC Reconnaissance History, by using its air-to-ground data
link, a fully operational TR-1 would 'provide
European combatant commanders with broad-
area, near-real time intelligence that would
enable troops, air strike forces, and their supporting control structures to react more readily
to time-sensitive targets' while operating 'well
behind the forward edge of the battle area
[FEBA] in all types of weather and light conditions and to revisit a given target several times

in the course of a single mission.' Although
the TR-1 was not planned to collect PHOTINT,
it could do so if additional cameras were purchased at a later date. Once the TR-1 became
operational, SAC's European U-2R OLYMPIC TORCH
mission would be terminated.

Ownership and basing of the TR-1 proved
highly contentious. When considering its mission, USAFE argued that the TR-1 was a tactical
aircraft, as did the commander of the Pacific Air
Forces who hoped to acquire TR-1s for use in his
theater. SAC objected, arguing that it had operated the U-2 since 1957 and – since 1974 – was
the AF single manager for U-2 operations. The
Air Staff at the Pentagon agreed, and on 30th
September 1978, SAC became the owner of the
TR-1 while mission tasking came from USAFE.

Only bases in West Germany and the UK
were considered, but the FRG was rejected
early in the decision process to keep the TR-1
far away from any potential ground combat.
UK choices included RAF Alconbury, RAF

TR-1A 80-1099
appears here with
the ASARS nose
and radar imaging
super pods. By
1985 the airplane
had evolved well
beyond the 1975
ALSS program
evaluated by SAC
U-2Cs.
Lindsay Peacock

Where to base
the new TR-1
proved somewhat
contentious,
especially given
the unwieldly
ground footprint
and the airplane's
vulnerability
to crosswinds.
Eventually RAF
Alconbury was
chosen. *Bob Archer*

80-1068 was the first TR-1 to arrive in the UK on 12th February 1983. The absence of fully established ground facilities complicated early operations, and there were only three TR-1s in use through 1985. *Richard Vandervord*

Greenham Common, RAF Sculthorpe, and RAF Wethersfield. Of these, RAF Alconbury was the least crowded, could easily support additional personnel, and was large enough to obviate additional land acquisition. RAF Wethersfield had supported the ALSS evaluation, however, and SAC was not ready to reject it out of hand. RAF Alconbury had a 9,000ft (2,743m) runway with only light crosswinds under normal conditions, and had the best family housing of any UK base (plus adequate off-base housing). Conversely, RAF Wethersfield had 'deteriorating' infrastructure dating from the 1940s and 1950s and was close to Stansted Airport, then under consideration as London's 'third airport,' complicating airspace management issues for the 'delicate' TR-1. SAC recommended RAF Alconbury, and USAF accepted this on 10th October 1979. The British, however, did not approve this until 22nd September 1980 out of concerns that 'left wing politicians might draw misleading parallels between the TR-1 and the U-2.' Moreover, the US was negotiating rights to place its ground-launched cruise missile

(GLCM) in the UK, the subject of considerable hostility among many British politicians and the public. Prime Minister Margaret Thatcher considered the TR-1 and GLCM basing issues as 'inseparable,' finally deciding to announce the GLCM assignment to RAF Molesworth amid considerable public clamor, followed by the surprisingly ignored announcement of the TR-1 basing at RAF Alconbury, although with a 20-airplane peacetime maximum.

The TR-1s would be assigned to the 95th Reconnaissance Squadron (RS), 17th Reconnaissance Wing (RW) at RAF Alconbury beginning in October 1982, although only 18 were eventually located there due to limits of hangarage. The remaining 15 TR-1As and two TR-1B trainers would be assigned to the 9th SRW at Beale AFB for training and contingency operations. Delays in the ASARS II program resulted in the deployment of the first of five TR-1s (80-1068) to RAF Alconbury on 12th February 1983 equipped with the SENIOR SPEAR COMINT package, but with the SENIOR RUBY system in lieu of the ASARS II as part of the overall CREEK SPECTRE program. The

Seen at RAF Alconbury less than a month after its initial arrival in the UK in March 1989 is SENIOR SPAN TR-1 80-1070. The dorsal fairing housed a narrowband satellite link optimized for ELINT and COMINT. *Bob Archer*

anticipated light crosswinds at RAF Alconbury failed to materialize early in the TR-1 deployment so the first three operational sorties were compelled to divert to RAF Mildenhall.

General TR-1 operations included training flights and a daily CREEK SPECTRE sortie (or two), with the latter increasing in frequency to coincide with Warsaw Pact maneuvers each April and September. During the second quarter of 1984, for example, TR-1s completed 43 CREEK SPECTRE flights, three SENIOR LOOK PHOTINT sorties, 10 'combat collection capability development' sorties, three CENTRAL ENTERPRISE missions, and 86 low-altitude training flights. By March 1985 there were six TR-1s in England, now with the much-delayed ASARS-II, which flew its first sortie on 9th July 1985. Perhaps the most conspicuous TR-1 configuration saw the addition of a satellite link on top of the fuselage. The first such SENIOR SPAN TR-1 is believed to be 80-1070 during March 1989.

According to a 17th RW history, a TR-1 may have participated in some fashion in the 15th April 1986 EL DORADO CANYON strikes. Spotter records suggest that two TR-1s departed RAF Alconbury to Ramstein AB (or beyond) immediately prior to the strike. None of these reports have been independently verified.

Three TR-1s crashed or were damaged at RAF Alconbury, although all three were repaired and returned to service (80-1069 October 1983; 80-1084 9th December 1987; and 80-1078 24th April 1990).

Following the August 1990 Iraqi invasion of Kuwait, two TR-1s were deployed to OL-CH (referred to as 'camel hump') at Taif AB, Saudi Arabia. Eventually four TR-1s were assigned to OL-CH, as were five U-2Rs.

The 17th RW was inactivated in June 1991 and the 95th SRS was reassigned to the 9th SRW at Beale AFB while the TR-1s remained at RAF Alconbury. During October 1991 the TR-1s were redesignated as U-2Rs.

The Habu in England

Unlike the 1967 Six-Day War in the Middle East, the 1973 October War caught Israel flat footed, if not downright surprised. Although Israeli intelligence knew of Egyptian and Syrian war plans, the Israelis incorrectly concluded that the Arab nations were not ready to start a war. Consequently, Israeli mobilization began just hours before Egyptian forces crossed the Suez Canal on 6th October and attacked the Israeli Bar Lev line protecting Sinai, followed by Syrian attacks in the Golan Heights. Despite early gains by Arab forces, within 10 days the Israelis had reversed the situation with armored forces crossing the Suez into Egypt. The precarious Israeli position in the Golan was solidified by 9th October and two days later Israeli forces began an assault on Syrian forces there, ultimately reaching a point from which they could shell Damascus. Both sides benefitted from massive airlifts of supplies and (in the case of Israel) replacement F-4 Phantoms and Douglas A-4 Skyhawks from American inventories. A cease fire began on 22nd October with the Arabs defeated militarily but emboldened politically by their early successes.

Israeli intelligence was not alone in being blindsided by the Arab attacks. US intelligence agencies also failed to predict the onset of the war, and remained hampered in acquiring timely information about the rapidly evolving battlefield situation. Satellites were not in a position to gather timely PHOTINT or ELINT, so US intelligence agencies turned to SAC's fleet of SR-71s to overfly the Middle East to collect PHOTINT. Basing and overflights of the Blackbird, however, proved to be contentious.

The SR-71 was home-based at Beale AFB and had previously deployed overseas only to Kadena AB, Okinawa, in support of US combat operations in Southeast Asia. During July 1969 SAC began informal negotiations to base

Beginning in 1968, the SR-71's operational deployments were exclusively to Kadena AB, Okinawa, in support of the war in SEA. In spite of GIANT REACH plans to send the SR-71 to Europe, the Blackbird would not make its first visit there until 1974. *Toshiyuki Toda via Stephen Miller*

SR-71s in the United Kingdom to cover potential targets in Eastern Europe and the Middle East. There was a competing proposal within SAC to operate the SR-71 from Torrejón AB, but the Spanish government prohibited 'overt reconnaissance missions' from any Iberian base. Consequently, SAC moved ahead with plans to establish an SR-71 detachment in the UK. By 1970 most of the details had been resolved, including the issue of noise (SAC convinced the British that the SR-71 was no louder than a KC-135!). The following year SAC allocated $50,000 for 'concrete apron work' adjacent to what would become the SR-71 hangar at RAF Mildenhall. GIANT REACH was the name given to SAC's preplanned '…contingency operation to collect imagery and/or ELINT from the Eastern Mediterranean and the Communist nations of Eastern Europe.' Plans called for maintenance crews and support equipment to deploy to RAF Mildenhall for 30 days, with one SR-71 to launch from its home base at Beale AFB, fly its mission to the Middle East or Eastern Europe, and then recover to the UK. Three KC-135Qs would proceed to RAF Mildenhall, while five would deploy to Incirlik AB to refuel the SR-71 on any of seven air refueling tracks. Six to eight SR-71 round-robin sorties from RAF Mildenhall would be scheduled during each 30-day deployment. Intelligence processing would be provided by the 497th Reconnaissance Technical Group (RTG) at Schierstein, FRG, for PHOTINT and by the 9th Reconnaissance Technical Squadron (RTS) at Beale AFB for ELINT and high-resolution radar (HRR) analysis.

Despite these preparatory efforts, plans in October 1973 to launch the SR-71 from Beale AFB, overfly the battlefields in the Middle East, and recover into RAF Mildenhall were scuppered, and senior US officials debated basing the SR-71 in Greece or Iran. In the 2016 edition of *Lockheed Blackbird: Beyond the Secret*

Missions, author Paul Crickmore quotes Colonel Pat Halloran (who flew both the U-2 and the SR-71 before retiring as a Major General) who recalled that upon landing in a KC-135Q at RAF Mildenhall to set up shop for the detachment, 'I was informed that the British government had had second thoughts and denied us authority to operate from the UK.' British Prime Minister Edward Heath's government reportedly opted instead to guarantee unfettered oil supplies by not offending its Arab producers. Similarly, Turkey rejected plans to refuel SR-71s from KC-135Qs deployed to Incirlik AB. Indeed, all but two North Atlantic Treaty Organization (NATO) nations refused basing, transit, or overflight rights for SR-71 missions (or their tankers) out of fear of a potential oil embargo imposed by the predominantly Arab Organization of Petroleum Exporting Countries (OPEC) Despite kowtowing to OPEC, the UK joined the Netherlands, the US, Canada, Japan, and Portugal as victims of an oil embargo that lasted through March 1974.

Declassified documents show the claim of British refusal to allow the SR-71 missions to operate from RAF Mildenhall was not altogether accurate. On 8th November 1974 Foreign Secretary James Callaghan wrote to Prime Minister Harold Wilson about US reconnaissance flights over the Middle East. The Americans, he said, 'approached us in October 1973 with a similar request to use their facilities at Mildenhall…[to which Prime Minister Edward] Heath agreed, but asked for assurances, which the Americans gave [that]: a) the President [Richard M Nixon] himself personally approved the flights; b)… the flights and their produce would not be communicated to anyone except [Britain]; [and] c) … the US government were satisfied on each occasion that there was an urgent and important reason for the flight and that the risks involved were minimal.' Callaghan

SAC preferred to fly its 1973 GIANT REACH missions to the Middle East from England, but political confusion forced the SR-71s to operate from US bases instead. 61-7964 flew two of these sorties.
Adrian Balch

SR-71 TRANS-ATLANTIC SPEED RECORDS, 1974

Route and crew	Time	Average speed	Distance
New York to London, 1st September Major James V Sullivan (Pilot) Major Noel F Widdifield (RSO)	1hr 54m 56.4s	1,810.9mph (2,914.4km/h)	3,033nm (5,617km)
London to Los Angeles, 13th September Captain Harold B Adams (Pilot) Major William C Machorek, Jr (RSO)	3hr 47m 39s	1,487.1mph (2,393.2km/h)	4,905nm (9,084km)

noted that these were the same assurances in the 1971 agreement for SR-71 basing in the UK. In fact, according to Callaghan's 'Top Secret' minute, it was 'the Americans [who] called off the flights, because of what they thought was "the obvious deep concern in London" and that newly confirmed US Secretary of State Henry Kissinger 'felt that the United States could not use Mildenhall because [the US-UK] agreement [to do so in October 1973] had been given "so grudgingly and reluctantly", although this was not in fact the case.' This was reinforced in a 'Top Secret UK Eyes' 16th November 1973 letter to Sir Alec Douglas-Home, the Secretary of State for Foreign and Commonwealth Affairs. Summarizing a meeting with US Secretary of Defense James R Schlesinger regarding the SR-71 missions, British Ambassador to the United States Rowland Baring noted that the UK had 'gone out of our way to agree to the US request' but the UK was not willing to share 'material derived from the flights … [with]…Israel' due to the British 'policy of strict neutrality.' This was 'assurance b' which Callaghan mentioned in his letter a week earlier. In light of this reservation 'Schlesinger let the matter drop.' No doubt this sharing issue was what Kissinger viewed as Britain's 'grudging reluctance' to approve the missions from RAF Mildenhall.

Nine GIANT REACH SR-71 missions were instead flown from Griffiss AFB, NY, (four flights) and Seymour-Johnson AFB, NC, (five flights – including two BUSY PILOT 'post-war' missions in 1974) beginning on 13th October with the last flight on 25th January 1974. Each flight cost $500,000, required five or six air refuelings with up to 16 KC-135Q tankers and a total of 230,000 gallons of fuel, and covered some 12,000nm (22,224km). These GIANT REACH sorties provided both battlefield intelligence as well as post-war baseline data for peacekeeping purposes, although their importance was later exaggerated in the British House of Commons. During a debate on Royal Air Force procurements held on 2nd February 1984, Minister of State for Defence Procurement Geoffrey Pattie told the assembled delegates that 'During the

1973 Arab-Israeli conflict valuable information was obtained from the United States SR-71 Blackbird. That information probably changed the course of history by locating missiles, which might have been used in that conflict. President Nixon told the Soviet Government that they must be pulled back because they were endangering world peace.' The inaccuracy of preserving 'world peace' aside, the practicality of continuing trans-Atlantic SR-71 missions proved unreasonable. This led to two concerted reconnaissance efforts inextricably linked to SAC's association with the United Kingdom: the establishment of U-2 OLIVE HARVEST and OLIVE TREE missions from the British base at RAF Akrotiri (as well as other U-2 operations from England and Cyprus, described above), and the resumption of efforts to establish a long-term SR-71 detachment at RAF Mildenhall.

Farnborough

During 1974, the Society of British Aerospace Companies (SBAC) requested that an SR-71 attend the biannual airshow at RAE Farnborough held from 1st-8th September. Somewhat surprisingly, SAC agreed as the political and diplomatic stars aligned for a visit. Earlier proposals for record-setting flights from San Francisco to New York or New York to London (or Paris) in 1969 and New York to Paris in 1971 had been rejected as too costly and because of the diplomatic issues associated with European overflight permissions. On 1st September 1974, SR-71A 61-7972 set a speed record from New York to London (landing at RAE Farnborough) in a positioning mission known as GLOWING HEAT (this name was used for all subsequent deployment/redeployment missions). The airplane relocated from RAE Farnborough to RAF Mildenhall on 8th September. Following an aborted attempt on 12th September the same airplane set a speed record the next day from London to Los Angeles during the L A HIGHWAY return mission.

In the aftermath of the public relations success of the SR-71's visit to the UK (pro-Labour newspaper *The Sun* called the flights 'aston-

SR-71 DEPLOYMENTS TO THE UNITED KINGDOM

From	To	Aircraft	Comments
1 Sep 74	13 Sep 74	61-7972	Record-setting Farnborough flights
20 Apr 76	30 Apr 76	61-7972	
6 Sep 76	18 Sep 76	61-7962	
7 Jan 77	17 Jan 77	61-7958	1st PARPRO mission from RAF Mildenhall
16 May 77	31 May 77	61-7958	1st RC-135V coordinated mission
24 Oct 77	16 Nov 77	61-7976	2 RC-135U coordinated missions
24 Apr 78	12 May 78	61-7964	
16 Oct 78	2 Nov 78	61-7964	
12 Mar 79	28 Mar 79	61-7972	Yemen mission
17 Apr 79	2 May 79	61-7979	
18 Oct 79	13 Nov 79	61-7976	
9 Apr 80	9 May 80	61-7976	
13 Sep 80	2 Nov 80	61-7972	
12 Dec 80	7 Mar 81	61-7964	
6 Mar 81	5 May 81	61-7972	
12 Aug 81	6 Nov 81	61-7964	Bodø divert 12 Aug 81
16 Dec 81	21 Dec 81	61-7958	Poland missions
5 Jan 82	27 Apr 82	61-7980	
20 Apr 82	13 Dec 82	61-7974	Bodø divert 7 May 82
18 Dec 82	6 Jul 83	61-7972	
23 Dec 82	2 Feb 83	61-7971	
7 Mar 83	6 Sep 83	61-7980	Defaced at RAF Greenham Common
9 Jul 83	30 Jul 83	61-7955	As 61-7962 for ASARS tests
2 Aug 83	7 Jul 84	61-7974	
9 Sep 83	12 Jun 84	61-7958	
14 Jun 84	Jul 85	61-7979	Lebanon mission
Jul 84	16 Oct 84	61-7975	
19 Oct 84	Oct 85	61-7962	
19 Jul 85	29 Oct 86	61-7980	EL DORADO CANYON
29 Oct 85	29 Jan 87	61-7960	EL DORADO CANYON
1 Nov 86	22 Jul 87	61-7973	
5 Feb 87	Mar 88	61-7964	
27 Jul 87	3 Oct 88	61-7980	Bodø divert 20 Oct 87
13 Mar 88	28 Feb 89	61-7971	
5 Oct 88	18 Jan 90	61-7964	Final operational mission to Barents Sea
2 Mar 89	19 Jan 90	61-7967	Final redeployer to Beale AFB

Right and below: SR-71A 61-7972 was the star attraction at the 1974 Farnborough air show after setting the world speed and time record for a New York to London flight. It set the London to Los Angeles record on its return flight to the US. '972 made five more trips to the UK, joining '964 for the most deployments. *Adrian Balch*

ishing' and noted that the eastbound flight was 'quicker than it took thousands of air passengers to reach Heathrow Airport from Central London') the time seemed propitious to reconsider the moribund proposal to establish a permanent SR-71 detachment in the UK to meet NATO reconnaissance requirements. SAC prudently recommended a more tentative approach, with twice yearly 'training deployments' that would 'test support facilities under actual SR-71 operating conditions.' Moreover, the visits would 'acquaint Englishmen…with the striking appearance of the supersonic aircraft' as well as 'familiarize British air traffic controllers…with the unique high-altitude and high airspeed control procedures' associated with the SR-71. To 'sweeten the pot' for British approval for the visits – which had already been given but remained unimplemented – Kissinger 'informed Her Majesty's Government that the United States would of course be prepared to

SAC opted for a phased introduction of the SR-71 to British bases to orient air traffic controllers with its unique operations. SAC also undertook a sizeable public relations effort to familiarize Britons with the SR-71's unique appearance and noise (no louder than a KC-135!).
Bob Archer

During 1976, 61-7962 took part in the NATO COLD FIRE exercise, and on 7th September flew the first operational sortie from the UK to the Barents Sea (although SAC did not consider this a PARPRO sortie!).
Lindsay Peacock

share with the British information produced by SR-71 missions.' The offer worked.

The first 'training deployment' began with SR-71 61-7972 departing Beale AFB on 20th April 1976 for RAF Mildenhall. Two KC-135Qs carried 65 personnel as well as '7,600 square feet' (706 square meters) of support equipment. On 23rd April, 61-7972 flew the first round-robin sortie from a European base. Additional training missions were flown along three different tracks previously approved by the British. The second training deployment began on 2nd September 1976 when SR-71 61-7962 departed Beale AFB but aborted into Goose AB following an in-flight engine failure. It finally reached RAF Mildenhall on 6th September. From 7th-10th September 1976, the SR-71 joined SAC RC-135 RIVET JOINTs and U-2Rs in support of COLD FIRE '76 in West Germany, and from 10th-23rd September in support of TEAMWORK '76 for NATO nations bordering the North Sea.

A Barents Sea mission on 7th September was the first SR-71 'operational' sortie from England (this was *not*, however, according to the 1977 SAC Reconnaissance History, a PARPRO mission, a subtle but important distinction).

Overall the SR-71 flew six sorties during a 16-day period. Although its participation in these operations was deemed 'beneficial', it suffered from bureaucratic delays in acquiring overflights rights and inadequate billeting at RAF Mildenhall, forcing maintenance personnel to reside at RAF Wethersfield, some 80 minutes away. Moreover, higher than planned atmospheric temperatures increased the SR-71's fuel consumption during the April deployment, forcing an aerial abort to each planned mission. More importantly, although the 1976 agreement allowed the possibility of future training deployments, these would still be authorized only on a case-by-case basis rather than any blanket approval.

161

Seen here at RAF Mildenhall on 29th May 1977, 61-7958 flew the first and second official PARPRO sorties from the UK that month. It covered the Norwegian Sea and later 'the Fence' between the two Germanys. *Adrian Balch*

Warsaw Pact, B-52s, and CINCSAC

Beginning in 1976 SAC developed operational plans to support NATO using conventional bombing in containing Soviet and Warsaw Pact forces should they invade Western Europe. To meet the pre-strike targeting and bomb damage assessment (BDA) requirements of this prospective bomber force, SAC needed both the SR-71 and U-2 for PHOTINT and SIGINT collection. Moreover, the Warsaw Pact 'wargame' that began on 31st December 1976 was, as

THE SR-71 MOBILE PROCESSING CENTER

'Each of the two Mobile Processing Centers (MPC) owned by SAC in 1977 consisted of 24 trailer-like vans, each measuring 8ft x 8ft x 40ft (2.4m x 2.4m x 12m) [as well as 290,000 lb (131,542kg) of support equipment]. Collectively they contained all the equipment needed to process the raw intelligence data collected by the [SR-71's] cameras, high-resolution radar [HRR], and for giving a preliminary readout of its electromagnetic reconnaissance (EMR) ELINT sensors.

'…Each MPC could be deployed overseas in various tailored packages, or combinations of vans, to support various levels and types of reconnaissance operations. The complete 24-van package when fully operational was designed to support one SR-71 mission per day. About 60 officers, airmen, and civilians were needed to operate a complete MPC. They could have photography and HRR imagery available for scrutiny within four hours after the SR-71 landed, although processing time was proportionate to the amount of film collected. For a typical mission it took MPC technicians about three hours from the time the aircraft returned to its forward operating base to have high-interest ELINT signals ready for first-stage analysis.'

History of SAC Reconnaissance Operations, 1 January – 31 December 1977, Historical Study #171, Office of the Historian, Strategic Air Command, Offutt AFB, NE, 22nd March 1979, 77.

CINCUSAFE General Richard Ellis described, 'far more complex and intensive' than any NATO exercises, and had a 'coordinated and extensive use of airborne command posts… [simulating] at all levels the ability to control forces when required, particularly during/after global nuclear exchange.' Again, Ellis was 'most desirous' that SR-71s and U-2s deploy regularly to the UK 'at levels the [CINCSAC] deemed appropriate' beginning in 'early 1977.'

Training deployments to RAF Mildenhall continued, beginning on 7th January 1977 to coincide with the inauguration of new US President James E 'Jimmy' Carter and to reaffirm the US commitment to its NATO partners. SR-71 61-7958 flew two sorties over the North Sea and the Norwegian Sea prior to its return to Beale AFB, including the first SR-71 PARPRO mission from RAF Mildenhall. At the end of this successful deployment, SAC proposed the 'first-ever operational deployment to Europe' during mid-May. SR-71 61-7958 returned on 16th May, by which time a second Mobile Processing Center (MPC) had been declared operational at RAF Mildenhall (although without the capability to process ELINT tapes; the only two centers that could do this were at Beale AFB and Kadena AB). During this trip to the UK 61-7958 flew a training sortie on 18th May, and on 20th May flew a coordinated mission with a 55th SRW RC-135 RIVET JOINT to the Barents Sea. The SR-71 completed its two successful passes in just 45 minutes, collecting intelligence not only on the submarine bases scattered across Murmansk Oblast but also on newly deployed SA-5 *Gammon* SAMs in the region. A second PARPRO sortie took place on 24th May 1977 over West Germany. Both collected ELINT as well as HRR imagery.

SR-71 61-7976 arrived for a second deployment held from 24th October through 16th November. The deployment flight from Beale AFB on 24th October was itself an operational

Left and below: The SR-71 often flew coordinated missions with other recon assets, acting as the 'stimulator' while other collectors recorded hostile reactions. During October and November 1977, 61-7976 flew two such missions with RC-135U 64-14849. *Toshiyuki Toda via Stephen Miller (top), Bob Archer (bottom)*

PARPRO mission, validating the GIANT REACH conceptual planning of an 'ops sortie' launched from Beale AFB and recovering at RAF Mildenhall (the flight was planned for 20th October, but bad weather at Thule AB – an emergency divert field – delayed the flight until 24th October). In this case it was a coordinated mission with RC-135U 64-14849 to the Barents Sea. Throughout October and November, the SR-71 flew a total of eight PARPRO 'single pass' sorties 'along the fence' – the border between West and East Germany. Over time other coordinated missions with SR-71s included those with the RAF's 51 Squadron's British Aerospace Nimrod R.1 ELINT platforms, as well as West German Bundesmarine Breguet Br.1150 Atlantics. The SR-71 acted as the 'provocateur' while the other assets were in position to collect SIGINT. The SR-71/RC-135U pair flew another mission together on 16th November, this time over the Baltic. The RC-135U returned to the UK while the SR-71 joined track X-027 parallel to the East German-Czechoslovakian border before returning nonstop to Beale AFB. This homeward flight lasted six hours, 11 minutes, making it the longest sortie of 1977.

Naval Requirements

By early 1978 there were nearly 100 nuclear submarines (including ballistic missile 'boomers') in the Soviet Union's Northern Fleet headquartered at Severomorsk. The majority of these were based throughout Murmansk in the 'Kola Gulf region', kept ice free year-round by warm Gulf Stream waters that allowed the subs unimpeded access from their ports to their launching areas in the Barents and Norwegian Seas. During May 1978, Chief of Naval Operations (CNO) Admiral James L Holloway, III, asked the US Defense Intelligence Agency (DIA) to approve his request for seven SR-71 reconnaissance missions over the Barents Sea each month to monitor Northern Fleet operations. SAC demurred, saying it did not have enough SR-71s to meet this tasking. There were only eight operational SR-71s authorized (more were built but were in storage) and these were spread thinly to meet Western Pacific operations, SIOP requirements, contingency operations, the Strategic Projection Force (SPF), two or three annual deployments to the UK, and training at Beale AFB. In addition, cloudy winter

The US Navy was rightly concerned about Soviet ballistic missile submarines operating in the Norwegian Sea that could strike the US, requiring constant updates to the status of all naval operations in the Murmansk region of the Barents Sea.

SR-71 departures were always impressive, especially at dusk when the afterburners were visible. Each launch was accompanied by one or two KC-135Q tankers, often using water injection for added thrust but rattling the windows of nearby homes. Seen here are 61-7971 and 58-0129. *Bob Archer (top), Lindsay Peacock (bottom)*

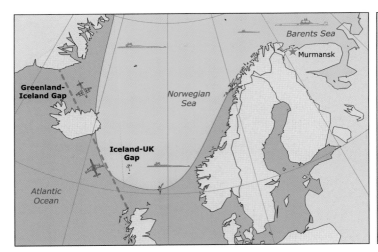

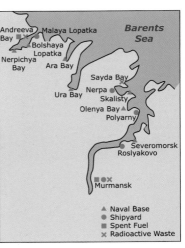

weather conditions in the Barents region were not conducive to PHOTINT collection. Holloway's request, while declined, did serve to prod SAC into moving forward with additional efforts for a permanent SR-71 'bed down' at RAF Mildenhall, pending approval of the British government. To meet the CNO's intelligence needs required two crucial changes: a different operational approach to overcome the weather issue, and a budgetary and logistical solution to resolve the shortfall of SR-71s in SAC's inventory.

Instead of PHOTINT, SAC elected to use the SR-71's HRR capability to gather Radar Intelligence (RADINT), peering through the cloud

cover prevalent in the winter months. Beginning in the Spring of 1979, SAC agreed to collect RADINT on 'two to four' PARPRO sorties via RAF Mildenhall [in addition, SAC flew three unique RADINT missions (one in 1979, two in 1980) from Beale AFB to the Barents Sea and back to Beale AFB]. Round-robin missions from RAF Mildenhall on behalf of CNO requirements also included sorties to the Baltic Sea that then flew onward to the Barents Sea. These extended sorties each lasted approximately seven hours and required four air refuelings from KC-135Qs also deployed to RAF Mildenhall.

Having suitable sensors in the SR-71 to mitigate the bad weather over the Barents was one thing, but having the requisite number of SR-71s to fly all the missions for which they were tasked was another matter altogether. Although there were sufficient SR-71s in storage to meet the demand of adding one dedicated for RAF Mildenhall (which was an existing storage facility for the airplane's JP-7 fuel), the cost of operating the SR-71 was considerable and SAC did not want to be stuck with the entire bill to meet a US Navy intelligence requirement. Any decision to add a full-time detachment in England would necessitate Congressional funding and considerable Department of Defense (DoD) budget wrangling. Moreover, although Britain had approved brief deployments to England, it was not clear if the UK government would tolerate the 'political sensitivities' associated with permanent basing.

Support for the SR-71 base, however, came from an unplanned source: Supreme Headquarters Allied Forces Europe (SHAFE), which argued that the SR-71 could 'overcome many of the reconnaissance deficiencies then existing in Europe, and [which] would remain until the TR-1 became fully operational in the late 1980s.' It would also add to the HRR database in Europe. Air Force Chief of Staff General Lew

The US Navy wanted better coverage of Soviet naval activity in the Barents Sea, an ideal mission from the UK. SAC, however, did not want to pay for the missions, warned that there were insufficient airplanes in the operational inventory, and argued that the SR-71's cameras were ineffective in bad weather. These protestations led to two more active SR-71s and improved HRR sensors. *Adrian Balch.*

Allen, Jr, (previously the Director of NSA) agreed that a permanent SR-71 detachment in the UK was essential and supported the addition of not one but two SR-71s to the eight already in the operational inventory to meet this need. Budgetary constraints and the emphasis by the Carter administration on cutting defense spending, however, precluded this through late 1980. SAC, sensitive to the November 1980 presidential election of Ronald W Reagan (who favored a far more hardline stance against the USSR than did Carter), optimistically eyed FY82 as an initial operational date.

Ongoing Deployments

Pending any official decision on permanent basing in the UK, SR-71 'training' (or perhaps 'operational test and evaluation') deployments to England continued through the late 1970s with two in 1978, three in 1979, and three in 1980. Of these, six coincided with the annual Spring and Fall Warsaw Pact maneuvers, with each outbound and return flight from Beale AFB functioning as a PARPRO mission. In addition, during this three-year period there were some 29 round-robin missions from England. On 31st March 1979, Det 4, 9th SRW was established at RAF Mildenhall, providing operational support for *visiting* U-2s and SR-71s. A *permanent* base in the UK, however, remained elusive.

Additional special missions from RAF Mildenhall continued. For example, Saudi Arabia was concerned about the growing militarism of communist South Yemen which had received military aid from the Soviet Union and the PRC. On 24th February 1979 the Yemen Arab Republic (North Yemen) invaded the People's Democratic Republic of Yemen (South Yemen). A cease fire was established on 2nd March but fighting continued. On 12th March the JCS

directed that an SR-71 deploy to RAF Mildenhall in preparation for a Yemen mission, although this was a month early for the planned deployment to England to cover the Spring Warsaw Pact maneuvers.

The 10+ hour Yemen mission from RAF Mildenhall took place on 21st March in SR-71 61-7972, covering 6,000 miles (9,656km) and required six air refuelings. In a move reminiscent of the 1973 October War sorties, France, Turkey, and Israel all declined overflight permission and tanker basing rights for the SR-71. In a display of NATO comity, however, Italy did allow the SR-71 to be air refueled over Sicily. KC-135Qs from RAF Mildenhall covered the initial and final refueling, while those deployed to the 306th SW at Zaragoza AB provided the second and fifth refueling. In an interesting twist, KC-135As (*not* KC-135Qs) detached to Cairo IAP covered the two middle refuelings over Egypt and the Red Sea. Results of the SR-71 mission were hampered by 45% cloud cover, and analysts consider the PHOTINT collected to be only 'fair'. Despite this, no military activity was observed at any of the 24 primary targets, and the PHOTINT verified that South Yemen had indeed withdrawn its forces from contested areas.

Among the more 'out-of-the-ordinary' SR-71 sorties from RAF Mildenhall were the 12th August 1981 flight in 61-7964, the first of three SR-71s to divert into Bodø, Norway, with mechanical problems. A second diversion took place on 7th May 1982 in 61-7974, with a third diversion occurring on 20th October 1987 in 61-7980.

Economic turmoil and evolving labor unrest in Poland beginning in late 1980 and continuing through the year raised the possibility of a collapsed Polish communist government. In prior occasions where the pro-Soviet governments

Right and below:
Three SR-71s diverted into Bodø, Norway, following in-flight emergencies, necessitating time-consuming repairs prior to their return trip to RAF Mildenhall. The first of these was 61-7964, aptly nicknamed *Bodonian Express* written in chalk on the vertical stabilizer. 61-7974 and 61-7980 both followed suit.
Bob Archer (top), Adrian Balch (bottom)

of Hungary (1956) and Czechoslovakia (1968) were at risk of falling, the USSR and its Warsaw Pact allies intervened militarily. Western fears of a similar intervention – led by Polish neighbors East Germany, Czechoslovakia, and the USSR – were fueled by the 8th December 1980 call-up of military reservists for the planned *Soyuz*-80 Warsaw Pact exercise, seen as a pretext for mil-

itary action against Polish labor unions and an increasingly anti-Soviet public. The wargames took place but there was no invasion.

Civil strife continued throughout 1981, including the imposition of martial law. Western concerns of an invasion remained, especially within the new Reagan administration. Following its divert into Bodø on 12th August

Wearing a 'For Sale' sign following its recent divert to Bodø, 61-7964 flew Baltic missions to assess the potential for a Warsaw Pact invasion of Poland in late 1981. It was replaced by 61-7958.
Bob Archer

Spotters dutifully noted the arrival of SR-71 '61-7962' in July 1983. In fact, this was Palmdale's test bird 61-7955 conducting an evaluation of the ASARS. In August, when this image was taken, it had regained its standard serial and Skunk Works logo. *Don McGarry via Stephen Miller*

1981, 61-7964 repositioned to RAF Mildenhall on 16th August, from where it undertook Baltic missions (no doubt monitoring the situation in Poland) until its return to Beale AFB on 16th November 1981. December again seemed a likely time for Soviet intervention given planned maneuvers, so two SR-71 missions were flown to monitor the situation. On 16th December, 61-7958 diverted into RAF Mildenhall during a planned round-robin Poland mission from Beale AFB. Two days later 61-7958 flew a Baltic sortie to monitor the events in Poland, followed by another mission on 21st December through both the Baltic and the Barents prior to returning non-stop to Beale AFB. One final Poland mission took place on 5th January 1982 when 61-7980 flew to the Baltic from Beale AFB and recovered at RAF Mildenhall. None of the intelligence collected suggested an imminent invasion.

A Permanent Presence

By early 1982 formal recognition of a permanent detachment remained elusive. During a Parliamentary debate on 5th April the government confirmed that it intended to approve the presence of two SR-71s at RAF Mildenhall. It took nearly a year, however, to bring this to fruition. On 18th December 1982, 61-7972 arrived at RAF Mildenhall, followed five days later by 61-7971 on 23rd December. Although two were approved, there were periods when just a single Blackbird was in residence. The 9th July 1983 arrival of SR-71 '61-7962' appeared to increase the number back to two. Unbeknown to the retinue of British spotters, this was in fact 61-7955 configured for the operational evaluation of the Loral ASARS. The final ASARS mission was on 30th July when 61-7955 returned to the United States. It was replaced on 2nd August by 61-7974.

61-7980 arrives on 21st July 1983 at RAF Greenham Common for its annual airshow. Four days later, protestors splashed it with red paint. After an all-night cleaning session, its early morning departure left an audible impression on those responsible. *Adrian Balch*

The SR-71 gained a measure of unwanted notoriety on 22nd July 1983 while 61-7980 was in a static display at RAF Greenham Common. A group of protesters opposed to a variety of policies – notably the Reagan administration's plan to station GLCMs at the base – sprayed the airplane with red paint at 2:30AM on 25th July. After a laborious cleaning session, pilot Major Jim Jiggens (a former US Air Force Thunderbirds display team pilot) took off, made a very low pass – supposedly just 100ft (30m) – above the encamped protesters at 7:00AM, lit both afterburners, and then commenced an abrupt climb leaving a wake-up call the protesters were unlikely to forget.

At long last a permanent UK base was approved on 5th April 1984 when Thatcher formally announced that SR-71s would be located at RAF Mildenhall. SR-71s were given 'blanket' permission to fly missions from the UK, although 'certain sorties' would still necessitate authorization from the Ministry of Defence, with especially sensitive missions requiring approval by the Prime Minister.

One such 'high profile' mission was the flight by 61-7979 to Lebanon. The general collapse by 1982 of the centralized government of Lebanon led to multiple factions fighting for control as well as undertaking terrorist raids against Israel. The 6th June 1982 Israeli *Peace for Galilee* operation prompted the Israeli occupation of portions of Lebanon and Beirut and resulted in extensive sectarian conflict. American peacekeeping efforts there suffered a visible setback with the 18th April 1983 bombing of the US Embassy and the 23rd October 1983 suicide attack on a military barracks, killing 241 Marines. Following the US withdrawal in early 1984, American leaders were concerned about reports of Iranian support of terrorist organizations leading to a 27th July 1984 SR-71 mission (again via the Straits of Gibraltar thanks to yet another French refusal of overflight permission).

Perhaps the most well-known missions from RAF Mildenhall were the BDA sorties in support of the US strikes on Libya during EL DORADO CANYON. Detachment 4 launched two SR-71 BDA sorties on 15th April. The primary jet (61-7980)

Following the 1986 EL DORADO CANYON attack on Libya, SR-71 61-7980 served as the primary BDA aircraft on the first post-strike mission. Additional sorties followed, reaffirming a capability that many argued had been prematurely retired prior to DESERT STORM five years later. *Adrian Balch*

On 18th January 1990, 61-7964 departed RAF Mildenhall, flew a mission to the Barents Sea, and recovered at Beale AFB. This was the final SR-71 reconnaissance mission from the UK, totaling just over 900 sorties. *Lindsay Peacock*

With the closure of Det 4, 9th SRW at RAF Mildenhall in January 1990, there would be no more parades of maintenance and support vehicles following each SR-71 to the hammerhead for departure. 61-7967 was the final jet to leave England for the US, seen here in better days. Gloomy weather on 19th January added to the sense among the crowds of spotters eager to glimpse '967's departure that something great and important had come to an inauspicious end. *Bob Archer (top, middle), Lindsay Peacock (bottom)*

completed the highest-altitude air refueling of an SR-71 from KC-10 83-0075 at 31,500ft (9,449m). SR-71 61-7960 was the airborne spare which returned to RAF Mildenhall after reaching the pre-arranged abort point west of Gibraltar once the primary crew reported that it could complete the mission. Bad weather hampered intelligence collection, so a second mission took place on 16th April with 61-7960 as primary and 61-7980 as backup. A third mission followed the next day, with the primary and backup aircraft reversed. Additional sorties over Libya took place on 27th, 28th, and 30th August.

Finale

Less than six years after Det 4 was approved as a permanent base for SR-71s in the UK, and a little more than 15 years after its first visit, the SR-71's presence in the UK came to an end. Despite the value to the CNO of continued Barents Sea missions, the US Navy was unwilling to pay for the expensive operations (especially in light of improvements to RADINT satellite capability), and SAC was equally unwilling to pay for an asset it considered unnecessary to meet its own requirements. Not surprisingly the last operational sortie from RAF Mildenhall was on 18th January 1990 when 61-7964 flew to the Barents Sea and then home to Beale AFB. The following day 61-7967 flew back directly to Beale AFB.

During its 15-year presence, 61-7972 and 61-7964 visited the UK the most number of times (six apiece), beginning with the record-setting flights in 1974. SR-71 61-7962, which visited twice, is now in residence at the Imperial War Museum Duxford on display at the American Air Museum building. The total number of SR-71 missions from England is unclear, as no official source has been declassified. Using estimates based on the total number of SR-71 operational missions (3,551) minus those flown from Kadena AB (2,538) as well as missions flown over other areas of interest, a rough total of 919 missions originated in the UK.

***

The end of SAC in June 1992 did not mean the end of reconnaissance operations from the UK. SAC's RC-135's still visited RAF Mildenhall although wearing an OF tail code and with their SAC emblem replaced by that of Air Combat Command. Several RC-135s became new visitors to England, notably the RC-135S COBRA BALL to monitor boost phase launches of Russian ballistic missiles launched from the Kara Sea or Plesetsk. OC-135Bs from the OPEN SKIES

program passed through RAF Mildenhall as its obligatory western Euro-Asian terminus for sanctioned overflights of any of the regional treaty signatories. The CONSTANT PHOENIX sampler WC-135W and WC-135C replaced the MAC WC-135Bs that 'sniffed' the air searching for isotopes indicative of nuclear weapons production and testing. By 2000 even the 'sound of freedom' around RAF Mildenhall was substantially quieter with the re-engining of the RC-135 fleet with F108 engines replacing their shrill TF33s and the elimination of KC-135A 'steam jet' and KC-135E tankers that converted jet fuel to noise. With the disestablishment of SAC in June 1992 the TR-1s fell under the operational authority of ACC, and in September 1993 the airplanes relocated to Beale AFB.

By 2006 the Royal Air Force's primary ELINT platform – the Nimrod R.1 from 51 Squadron at RAF Waddington – was nearing the end of its operational lifetime and was replaced in 2013 with the first of the RAF's own Airseeker RIVET JOINTS. Some 20 years after SAC's disestablishment, there were proposals to move the USAF RC-135 operations in England from RAF Mildenhall to RAF Waddington in a potential reconnaissance 'super base'. The inadequate length of the runway there prohibited maximum-weight takeoffs so the American airplanes were instead slated for reassignment to RAF Fairford.

The most notable change to RC-135 operations from the UK involved its mission. For decades SAC reconnaissance flights – RB-50s, RB-36s, or RB-47s – flew PARPRO missions along the borders of the Soviet Union and Warsaw Pact nations. Following the RC-135's operational success in combat reconnaissance sorties during DESERT STORM they increasingly were assigned to tactical theater missions. Traditional BURNING WIND missions dwindled as the post-Cold War 'peace dividend' and Russian comity with the West increased. Moreover, RC-135s were increasingly assigned to US and NATO combat or peacekeeping missions in the Balkans and Southwest Asia. New RC-135s were converted, but there were still insufficient numbers of RIVET JOINTS to gather routine ELINT and COMINT that could otherwise be collected by overhead means – satellites. With a revanchist Russia overseeing irregular low-intensity conflict in the Ukraine, as well as the increased militarization of the Russian enclave on the Baltic in Kaliningrad, US reconnaissance operations in the 2010s and onward once again restored the frequency of peacetime SIGINT missions from England, although not necessarily to levels comparable to those sustained during the Cold War.

8 Overlooked and Over Here

Strategic Air Command was synonymous with its heavy bombers, their supporting tankers, and its reconnaissance assets, but was not an exclusive club of 'strategic' aircraft. SAC operated its own fleet of fighters, heavy transports, air rescue assets, and even medium-range ballistic missiles from bases in the United Kingdom, all of which either provided direct support for SAC's bombing mission or added to its offensive capability.

Beginning with its inception on 21st March 1946, SAC controlled a small number of fighter units, a vestige of Second World War requirements to escort long-range bombers. Beginning with Republic P-47 Thunderbolts, North American P-51 Mustangs, and F-82 Twin Mustangs, SAC's commanders understood by 1950 that these airplanes lacked the operational range and altitude to support B-29, B-50, and B-36 missions, let alone the forthcoming jet-powered B-47. Consequently, SAC acquired some 82 North American F-86 Sabres, 126 Lockheed P-80 Shooting Stars, and more than 550 F-84 Thunderjets to meet these needs.

During SAC's early years, existing war plans called for B-29s and B-50s – along with SAC's indigenous fighter force – to deploy to overseas bases in friendly countries as preparations for war were underway. Once war broke out SAC fighters (and those of USAFE) would escort the bombers from their overseas bases to their targets. SAC fighters also had a secondary mission to 'destroy hostile air forces on the ground or in area defense' by traditional 'fighter-bomber sorties in cooperation with friendly ground forces.' This was part of SAC's ROMEO commitment – the 'retardation' of a Soviet attack against Western Europe.

This escort role was organizationally recognized on 1st February 1950 when SAC redesignated its 27th Fighter Wing (FW) at Bergstrom AFB, TX, as the 27th Fighter Escort Wing (FEW). In addition, SAC's fighters were tasked to protect overseas bases from aerial attack by hostile forces. Three active duty fighter wings and four ANG wings were assigned to SAC between 1st July 1950 and 24th January 1953. One active duty unit – the 31st Fighter Bomber Wing (FBW) at Turner AFB, GA – was redesignated as the 31st FEW, while the 12th FEW at Bergstrom AFB and 508th FEW at Turner AFB were both activated. None of the four ANG units were redesignated as FEWs.

SAC's escort mission evolved as a consequence of improvements in escort capability, ending with the proposed McDonnell F-101

SAC established its own fighter force to escort its bombers as they neared hostile territory. Many of these units, like the 12th SFW at Bergstrom AFB, ended up flying F-84Fs, and most visited the UK at least once. *Terry Panopalis collection*

Voodoo. Plans to use the supersonic F-101A as a fighter escort meant that it could precede bombers on their EWP routes and destroy waiting hostile interceptors, egress hostile airspace to be air refueled, and then resume escort duties for the subsonic bombers, doubling their escort value. Declassified plans do not show how the F-101s would rearm in flight! Delays in F-101 deliveries until May 1957 meant that the Voodoo was only in the SAC inventory for less than two months as SAC's fighter operations ended on 1st July 1957. As a consequence, the F-101 did not deploy with SAC units to the UK, although it was destined to see service with USAFE's 81st TFW at RAF Bentwaters and RAF Woodbridge.

Moreover, as atomic weapons decreased in size and weight, the primary mission for SAC's fighters changed by 1953 from strictly escort duties to atomic delivery, increasing the number of SAC aircraft – specifically F-84s – that could strike Soviet and 'Red Chinese' targets from forward bases in Europe and Asia.

Across the Pond

The first deployment of SAC fighters to bases outside of the continental United States took place on 18th December 1946 when 28 P-51Hs from the 62nd Fighter Squadron (FS), 56th FW departed Selfridge Army Air Field (AAF), MI. They arrived at Ladd Field, AK, on 28th December, where they remained until April 1947. Additional deployments to Alaska continued, but these all followed overland routes. During 1948 SAC planners sought to 'provide training in overwater flying and long-range navigation' with flights to Ramey AFB, Kindley AFB, and Vernam AFB, Jamaica. These were undertaken in P-80s from the 4th FW and the

56th FW from Andrews AFB, MD, and Selfridge AFB, respectively, during May and June 1948, followed by 55 F-82s from the 27th FW flying from Kearney AFB, NE, to Howard AFB, Panama, and back in February 1949.

These lengthy overwater flights proved successful, so SAC prepared to send its first fighter detachment to the United Kingdom. The goal of this deployment was threefold: 'to determine the feasibility of ferrying jet-propelled combat aircraft over [the] North Atlantic, to study logistical and operational problems involved in such a maneuver, and to perform limited training in [the] European theater.' There were two routes, both of which were used by Air Transport Command (ATC) during the Second World War for ferry purposes. The northern route ran between Maine and England via Goose AB, Narsarssuak (Bluie West One – BW-1) Greenland, Iceland, and Prestwick. The southern route was between Georgia and Nouasseur AB via Kindley AFB and Lajes Field and then to the UK. Over time the northern route became the primary route for SAC fighters, especially as aerial refueling became available.

The first trans-Atlantic crossing of SAC fighters was FOX ABLE ONE (**F**ighter, **A**tlantic, #1) undertaken by the 56th FW. The flight began on 14th July 1948 with 16 recently acquired F-80s, four Douglas C-47s carrying parts and personnel, two Boeing B-17s for air-sea rescue, and a lone B-29 as the weather scout and 'pace airplane.' Following stops at Dow AFB, ME, Goose AB, BW-1, Keflavik AP, and RAF Stornoway, they finally reached RAF Bovingdon on 20th July without incident. After a brief stay in England, the 56th FW continued to Fürstenfeldbruck AB, arriving on 25th July. FOX ABLE TWO followed on 9th June 1949, routing via RAF Kinloss to RAF Manston with 12 F-80Bs (one was damaged at BW-1) and 4 Lockheed T-33s from the 56th FW. The eastbound transit took 16 days.

The success of FOX ABLE ONE and FOX ABLE TWO prompted plans for the deployment of fighters from Continental Air Command (ConAC) units to Europe. SAC coordinated each deployment with ConAC while MATS provided rescue aircraft, weather support, and en route navigational guidance. The first of these was FOX ABLE THREE, which ferried 180 F-84Es to the 36th Fighter FBW at Fürstenfeldbruck AB and the 86th FBW at Neubiberg AB. Oddly enough, the plan was for SAC's 27th FEW at Bergstrom AFB – which was in the process of converting from F-82s to F-84s – to fly the airplanes from the US to the FRG. The mission was slated for May 1950 and included fuel stops at Turner

SAC FIGHTER DEPLOYMENTS TO THE UK

Year	Unit*	Period	Aircraft	Deployment
1948	56th	14 July	F-80	FOX ABLE ONE
1949	56th	9 June	F-80	FOX ABLE TWO
1950	27th	15 Sep/15 Oct	F-84E	FOX ABLE THREE
	31st	26 Dec-50-27 Jul 51	F-84E	FOX ABLE TEN
1951	12th	18 Jul 22 Dec	F-84E†	
	123rd ANG	22 Dec-10 Jul 52	F-84E†	
1952				
1953	31st	22-31 Aug	F-84G	LONGSTRIDE
	508th	20 Aug-9 Sep	F-84G	LONGSTRIDE
1954	508th	5-22 Oct	F-84G	
1955	27th	9 May-17 Aug	F-84F‡	
	31st	Aug	F-84F (canceled)	

* Unit designations changed over time;
† Airplanes were already deployed by the 31st SFW in 1950;
‡ Unit transitioned from F-84Gs to F-84Fs on 18 Jun 54

OVERLOOKED AND OVER HERE

FOX ABLE EIGHT routed the 20th FBW via Prestwick prior to their return to Shaw AFB. SAC understood the need to provide non-stop deployments via aerial refueling to support its EWP. *Gordon Macadie*

AFB, Otis AFB, MA, Goose AB, BW-1, Keflavik, RAF Lakenheath or RAF Sculthorpe, and then onward to West Germany. Production delays resulted in this deployment being rescheduled to September.

By the end of January 1950, Republic Aviation had delivered only 80 F-84Es to the 27th FEW. This shortage plus further production problems resulted in the postponement of the trans-Atlantic flight. This allowed the out-of-sequence FOX ABLE SIX deployment to take place on 20th July 1950, relocating 69 ConAC F-84Ds of the 20th FBW from Shaw AFB, SC, to RAF Manston for their TDY overseas. Although it would be a USAFE asset, part of the Wing's UK mission was to provide escort for SAC bombers.

FOX ABLE SIX was split into two sections; the first had 37 F-84s and the second had the remaining 32 airplanes. Awful weather caused en route delays, and the loss on 25th July of F-84D 48-0726 and its pilot between BW-1 and Keflavik highlighted the risks involved. The bulk of the 20th FBW arrived at RAF Manston

via RAF Kinloss on 26th July, with the stragglers finally reaching England two days later. The 20th FBW returned to Shaw AFB via Prestwick beginning 1st December 1950 as FOX ABLE EIGHT. The unit permanently relocated to RAF Wethersfield and RAF Woodbridge on 31st May 1952, continuing its partial commitment to the SAC escort mission.

Lessons learned from FOX ABLE SIX prompted helpful changes to the still-pending FOX ABLE THREE. Most notable among these was the use of 230gal (871 liters) drop tanks instead of the smaller 185gal (700 liters) tank. This eliminated one refueling stop, with McGuire AFB, NJ, replacing both Turner AFB and Otis AFB. By 1st August 1950 the 27th FEW had some 93 F-84Es on hand with another 120 planned to arrive at Bergstrom AFB from the Republic Factory on Long Island, NY, by the end of the month. This further moved the departure date for the first tranche of 90 F-84s to 15th September. Flights of eight departed Bergstrom AFB at 10-minute intervals. Minor maintenance issues

For FOX ABLE THREE, the 27th FEW used larger 230 gal drop tanks for their Atlantic crossing, departing Bergstrom AFB on 15th September 1950 en route to Fürstenfeldbruck AB. *Jim Webb collection*

kept several of the F-84s grounded but nearly all reached Goose AB to remain overnight (RON). Bad weather at BW-1 on 16th September delayed the departure until midday, and 89 F-84s reached BW-1 without incident. Of these, 42 were promptly refueled and departed for Keflavik where they spent the night. They were joined the following day by the 47 jets from BW-1, and all 89 then departed for RAF Manston to RON. The flight continued on 18th September from RAF Manston to Fürstenfeldbruck AB, with the final jets arriving the next day.

The second tranche of 92 F-84Es departed Bergstrom AFB on 18th October 1950, but their crossing was far more problematic. Two airplanes lost their canopies in flight, although these were repaired and quickly rejoined the main group. Bad weather at Goose AB prevented the group's onward movement from McGuire AFB where they had stopped for fuel. Excessive oil consumption dictated an overnight engine change in 14 of the airplanes. The following day the 86 flyable jets departed for Goose AB but were forced to turn back due to bad weather, diverting to Otis AFB where they remained for four days. All 92 jets finally left for Goose AB on 21st October. F-84E 49-2252 was lost in a successful wheels-up landing at Havre-St Pierre, Quebec, following engine failure. The next day the remaining 91 F-84s reached BW-1, where they were again grounded by inclement weather. They eventually arrived at Neubiberg AB on 26th October. SAC's 27th FEW received the prestigious Mackay Trophy for this undertaking.

'Little Friends'

Although FOX ABLE ONE and TWO both involved SAC F-80s, their final destination was West Germany rather than the UK. Moreover, even though SAC pilots flew the airplanes in FOX ABLE THREE, this was a delivery flight for USAFE. SAC had yet to send any of its organic fighter units to England. Following the 1st July 1950 transfer of the 31st FEW from ConAC to SAC, this unit became the first SAC fighter wing to relocate specifically to England and benefitted from the operational expertise acquired during the previous transatlantic movements.

Ongoing engine problems with the F-84E delayed the planned departure date of from the Summer of 1950 to 15th December 1950, when SAC deployed 74 F-84Es and four T-33s from Turner AFB to RAF Manston as part of FOX ABLE TEN. As with previous deployments, bad weather and misfortune affected the move,

which did not begin until 26th December. T-33A 49-0945 from the 307th Fighter Escort Squadron (FES), 31st FEW, was destroyed in a ground incident at Narsarssuak on 31st December 1950. By 6th January 1951 all of the F-84Es and two of the T-33s had arrived in England. Once in place at RAF Manston, additional losses included T-33A 49-0946 southwest of RAF Manston on 18th January 1951, F-84E 49-2105 on 24th January 1951 northeast of RAF Manston, F-84E 49-2079 on 21st June at RAF Manston, and F-84E 49-2055 on 26th June northeast of Dover.

While in England the 31st FEW practiced the bomber escort procedures they would use during wartime. One representative mission took place from 5th to 9th July, when an unspecified number of F-84Es flew to bases in Norway (believed to be Sola AB and Gardermoen AB). Once there, they refueled, launched, and proceeded to a pre-arranged rendezvous point, met B-50s from the 2nd BW, and escorted them to within 50 miles (80km) of their simulated target.

Beginning 18th July 1951, pilots and maintenance personnel from the 12th FEW at Bergstrom AFB, under the command of Colonel Cy Wilson, took over the 31st FEW's aircraft and supporting equipment in situ as 31st FEW personnel returned to Turner AFB. Significant problems with the F-84's J35-A-17 engine, as well as the overseas supply chain of parts for it and other components, crippled the unit's operational readiness. For four months the 12th FEW readiness level remained below 40%, and for the last two months of its deployment was less than 20% (during November 1951 it was an appalling 8%). If SAC went to war at this time it would be hard pressed to have sufficient escorts. In addition to poor supply and reliability issues, the 12th FEW lost 560th FES F-84E 49-2346 on 25th August some 3.5 miles southeast of Varde, Denmark, the first of a string of crashes. F-84E 49-2034 from the 560th FES was lost on 29th August 1951 when it struck 49th BS, 2nd BW B-50D 48-0066 on the ground at RAF Mildenhall and crashed into a nearby street (B-50D 48-0071 was also damaged). In addition, 560th FES F-84E 49-2088 flew into the sea on 13th September off North Foreland, F-84E 49-2368 from the 559th FES crashed on takeoff on 18th September from Neubiberg AB, and 560th FES F-84E 51-0644 was lost on 13th October during a takeoff accident at Wheelus AB. As a result of this spate of bad luck, the Wing was grounded in October 1951, with only limited flying after that. At the time of the grounding some 17 of the wing's airplanes were deployed to Wheelus AB, Libya, but these promptly returned to RAF Manston.

The 12th FEW continued SAC escort mission training through 22nd December 1951 when its personnel returned to Bergstrom AFB and the F-84s were handed over *in situ* to the 123rd FBW of the Kentucky ANG during that unit's federal activation. Its mission was the same as that of the 31st FEW – to escort SAC bombers. The 123rd FBW had previously flown F-51Ds and much of its time at RAF Manston was spent qualifying pilots in the F-84E. Not surprisingly, there were multiple training incidents as the F-51 pilots transitioned to jets, with the loss of six F-84Es: 49-2053 from the 167th FBS crashed on 4th December 1951 at Vlandern, Luxembourg, 49-2057 of the 167th FBS was lost on 12th March 1952 during a landing accident at RAF Manston, 49-2327 from the 156th FBS suffered an explosion in the cockpit on 21st March and crashed on approach to RAF Manston, 49-2044 from the 167th FBS crashed on 27th March near Canterbury, England, 49-2111 of the 165th FBS crashed into houses on 27th April after departing RAF Manston, with the final loss occurring on 14th May when 49-2074 from the 156th flew into the sea during approach to RAF Manston.

Despite these losses the 123rd FBW was nearly combat ready by March 1952. This was short-lived as the Wing was released from federal duty on 10th July 1952 and its personnel returned to their ANG role in Kentucky. The airplanes were subsequently turned over to the newly activated 406th FBW, which continued in the escort role but under the auspices of USAFE's 3rd Air Force which oversaw US tactical air operations in Europe, rather than SAC.

There were no new movements to the UK during 1952.

Operation LONGSTRIDE

Previous SAC fighter deployments to the UK were essentially 'island hopping' affairs, with jets stopping en route for fuel and repairs or for bad weather that precluded continuing along the route. As with its bomber force, SAC planners understood the need to relocate its fighters without the limits imposed by these interim stops. With the increased reliability of air refueling it became apparent that SAC fighters could fly nonstop from home bases in the US to forward locations in the UK and North Africa. To that end, during 1950 SAC and Air Materiel Command (AMC) suggested a feasibility mission from London to Limestone AFB (which eventually became RAF Manston to Mitchel Field, NY) with air refueling in lieu of the standard 'pit stops'. Westbound flights routinely faced significant headwinds and were

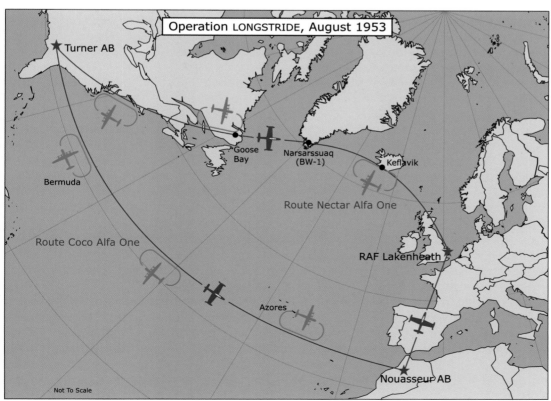

OPERATION LONGSTRIDE **F-84GS**

508th SFW	Direct to RAF Lakenheath			
52-3211	52-3244	52-3245	52-3246	52-3249
52-3250	52-3252	52-3255*	52-3256	52-3260
52-3262	52-3266	52-3271	52-3273	52-3274
52-3275	52-3304*	52-3309*	52-3322	52-3324

31st SFW	Via Nouasseur AB			
52-3293	52-3307	52-3308	52-3311	52-3323
52-3325	52-3326	52-3327		

* Diverted into Keflavik AP en route

consequently longer than the eastbound flight, so this proved a natural choice to evaluate this capability. Planned in advance of the much-delayed mass deployment of the 27th FEW from Bergstrom AFB, FOX ABLE FOUR took place on 22nd September 1950 using a pair of F-84Es from the 2750th Air Base Wing (ABW) at Wright-Patterson AFB, OH, and SAC KB-29Ms. Only one of the F-84s – flown by Colonel David C Schilling (commander of the FOX ABLE ONE deployment in 1948) – completed the 3,300 mile (5,311km), 10-hour trip, although he was obliged to land at Limestone AFB rather than Mitchel Field due to strong headwinds. Technical issues prevented the second airplane from receiving fuel at the halfway point, so the pilot of F-84E 49-2086 – a Lieutenant Colonel Ritchie – bailed out and was rescued. Given the loss of an airplane, FOX ABLE FOUR certainly seemed a disappointment. Both SAC and AMC, however, concluded that it successfully demonstrated that fighters could be air refueled on transoceanic flights. Moreover, the recovery of the downed pilot just 19 miles (31km) from Goose AB validated the careful rescue planning undertaken by SAC and MATS.

Translating FOX ABLE FOUR into reality over the Atlantic proved difficult as the ongoing war in Korea monopolized many of SAC's tactical refueling assets and refuelable fighters. Initially, SAC fighters bound for combat in Korea were embarked onto US Navy escort carriers at San Diego, CA, and then shipped to Yokosuka, Japan. From 4-16th July 1952, however, the 31st FEW undertook FOX PETER ONE (**F**ighter, **P**acific, #1), the first trans-Pacific fighter deployment using air refueling. The airplanes were refueled in flight from Turner AFB to Travis AFB, and again from Travis AFB to Hickam AFB, HI. They subsequently 'island hopped' to Midway, Wake, Eniwetok, Guam, and Iwo Jima to reach Japan. Beginning 3rd October 1952, FOX PETER TWO saw the 27th FEW fly from Bergstrom AFB to Travis AFB and then to Hickam AFB using air

refueling. The airplanes next flew to Midway, refueled on the ground, and then flew nonstop to Misawa AB, Japan, again with air refueling. This final leg of 2,575 miles (4,144km) set the record for the longest overwater refueling flight in single-engine jets.

With the success of the FOX PETER initiatives, SAC applied the lessons learned to the relocation of its fighter assets to England. This led to Operation LONGSTRIDE, the 20th August 1953 deployment of F-84Gs assigned to the 31st Strategic Fighter Wing (SFW – it had been redesignated from a Strategic Escort Wing on 20th January 1953) and the 508th SFW from Turner AFB to Nouasseur AB and RAF Lakenheath, respectively. Eight F-84Gs from the 31st SFW, again led by Colonel Schilling, were refueled along the Central Atlantic route (Coco Alfa One) by KC-97s from the 26th and 305th AREFS, reaching Nouasseur AB after a flight lasting 10 hours, 20 minutes (sadly, Schilling died on 14th August 1956 in an automobile accident at Eriswell, Suffolk).

Twenty F-84Gs from the 508th SFW, led by Colonel Thayer S Olds and Colonel Cy Wilson, took the North Atlantic route (Nectar Alfa One), and were refueled over Boston, MA, by five KB-29Ps from the 100th AREFS, followed by a second refueling from eight KC-97s from the 26th AREFS some 100 miles east of Cape Harrison, Labrador. Six KC-97s on temporary duty with the 7th AD provided the third air refueling, but three F-84s could not take fuel and diverted to Keflavik. Some 11 hours, 20 minutes later the 17 remaining F-84s landed at RAF Lakenheath.

The 31st SFW flew from Nouasseur AB to RAF Lakenheath on 22nd August for maintenance prior to their return to the United States along the Northern Route. These eight F-84s departed England on 31st August and stopped at Keflavik AB. They left the next day with a single refueling by four KB-29Ps from the 100th AREFS over BW-1, continuing to Limestone AFB. Redeployment of the 508th SFW proved more troublesome. All 20 F-84s departed RAF Lakenheath on 9th September but were forced to land at Prestwick due to higher than planned headwinds. They left Iceland the following day reaching Goose AB, and finally arrived at Turner AFB on 12th September.

According to the 7th AD history, flight commander Colonel Wilson declared that LONGSTRIDE 'proved that "non-stop deployment of fighter wings utilizing in-flight refueling is extremely practical, safe, and provides a rapid means of deploying fighter aircraft with a minimum of

The return portion of the 31st FEW during LONGSTRIDE would have appeared similar to this 307th AREFS KB-29P refueling a 12th FEW F-84G. *Jim Webb collection*

delay and losses resulting from weather and en route stops." Its success, he added, "clearly demonstrated the ability of jet fighter aircraft to deploy anywhere needed in a very short period of time".' As with FOX ABLE TEN, Operation LONGSTRIDE earned the Mackay Trophy for 1953.

Atomic Fighter Bombers

In an interesting historical omission, SAC's quasi-official history *SAC Fighter Planes and Their Operations* does not describe the next SAC fighter movement to the UK, and only lists it cryptically in a table without explanation. The 7th AD history 'SAC Operations in the United Kingdom, 1948-1956,' however, provides a brief glimpse of this significant deployment. From 5th-22nd October 1954, 24 F-84Gs from the 508th SFW, under the leadership of LONGSTRIDE commander Colonel Wilson, flew from Turner AFB to RAF Sturgate along the Central Atlantic route with stops at Kindley AFB and Lajes Field. The unit practiced escort operations from Sola AB and Gardemoen AB, as well as Nouasseur AB.

The 508th SFW also trained for its new atomic strike mission. The F-84 was configured to carry the Mk 7 fission (atomic) bomb. It weighed some 1,600 lb (726kg) and had a variable yield of between 8-61kt (kilotons). This role as an atomic bomber required the development of pioneering tactics and qualification of pilots and ground crews. Initially, the Air Research and Development Command (ARDC) recommended the Low Altitude Bombing System (LABS – also known as 'Pathfinder Delivery') which was then under development for the B-47, while SAC evaluated a derivative of the Pathfinder method known as the Vertical Angle Release

(VAR). In the VAR delivery, the F-84 approached the target at 600ft (183m) above ground level (AGL) and 500mph. At 5,600ft (1,707m) from the target, the airplane began a 3.5g climb to arrive at 90° pitch angle at 5,100ft (1,554m) AGL directly above the target. It then released the atomic bomb in a vertical trajectory. The bomb was forecast to stall at 9,000ft (2,743m) above the target and then fall straight down and detonate. The F-84 would continue in a modified half Cuban eight and egress the area at a lateral distance of 25,000ft (7,620m) from ground zero. Two key weaknesses in the VAR solution were the need for absolute precision in beginning the loop (not substantially different from the Pathfinder approach), and the F-84 was directly above the target and vulnerable to anti-aircraft artillery (AAA) fire throughout the critical phases of the maneuver. SAC opted for the VAR technique because it 'provided a

A KC-97 from RAF Mildenhall refuels a USAFE F-84G from the 77th FBS, 20th FBW in 1954. Along with SAC's 508th FBW which deployed to England in October, these F-84Gs had an atomic strike mission rather than a fighter escort role. *Jim Webb collection*

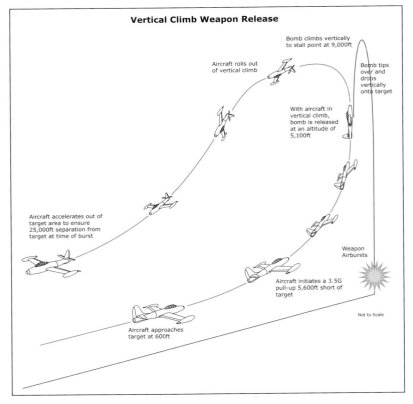

Vertical Climb Weapon Release

Bomb climbs vertically to stall point at 9,000ft

Aircraft rolls out of vertical climb

Bomb tips over and drops vertically onto target

With aircraft in vertical climb, bomb is released at an altitude of 5,100ft

Aircraft accelerates out of target area to ensure 25,000ft separation from target at time of burst

Weapon Airbursts

Aircraft initiates a 3.5G pull-up 5,600ft short of target

Not to Scale

Aircraft approaches target at 600ft

direct, simple, and flexible' method of delivering atomic bombs. The Pathfinder method would be used as a secondary tactic.

Despite this extensive testing, modification of aircraft, and crew training, no SAC fighter unit ever *possessed* nuclear weapons. During the mid 1950s, the Mk 7s were stored at RAF Wethersfield and RAF Woodbridge with the understanding that they would be relocated to RAF Manston or RAF Sturgate as the need arose and only *after* SAC's F-84s had arrived in England. Another storage facility was added at

RAF Lakenheath until SAC finally suspended its fighter-bomber commitment on 1st July 1957.

The 508th SFW flew back to Turner AFB on 22nd October, where they converted from F-84Gs to F-84Fs.

SAC deployments to the UK resumed in 1955 but were fraught with cancellations. Under the command of Colonel Richard N Ellis (not the later CINCSAC General Richard *H* Nellis), the 27th SFW flew 75 F-84Fs from Bergstrom AFB to RAF Sturgate on 2nd May 1955. Six flights (five with 12 F-84s and one with 15 F-84s) were refueled during Operation SNEAK PLAY over Lockbourne AFB en route to Goose AB, but only 35 out of 48 F-84s actually reached Goose AB with the remainder diverting elsewhere (including three to Limestone AFB). A second wave of 27 left Bergstrom AFB on 3rd May with 25 arriving at Goose AB. Some 48 F-84s departed Goose AB on 4th May. Of these, 43 finally reached RAF Sturgate with five diverting to Keflavik due to in-flight refueling problems. By 9th May all 75 F-84s had arrived safely at RAF Sturgate. Unfortunately, 310th AREFS KC-97G 53-0110 was lost 90 miles southwest of Iceland.

Operations from RAF Sturgate were significantly different than those of FOX ABLE TEN at RAF Manston four years earlier. Most notably, the operational readiness levels were much improved. The airplane readiness rate never dropped below 75%, with the Aircraft Out of Commission for Parts (AOCP) rate a tiny 1.96%, reflecting the greater emphasis on the supply chain. Indeed, most critical parts were now being airlifted as 'priority' items. In addition, the 27th SFW spent the majority of its time while deployed practicing its role as an 'atomic fighter-bomber unit.' Between 18-20th July,

The 27th SFW made the final SAC fighter deployment to England during the summer of 1955. Deteriorating runway conditions at RAF Sturgate precluded the planned movement of the 31st SFW later that year. *Terry Panopalis collection*

the 27th SFW underwent its USCM evaluation. It flew eight simulated strikes each day against targets in France. These training missions were not without embarrassment. On 6th July F-84F 52-6544 from the 522nd SFS accidentally dropped a clip of Mk 23 mod 1 practice bombs near Rampton, Nottingham. In addition, four airplanes suffered Category 3 damage that warranted extensive repair at Farmingdale: 52-6637 of the 522nd SFS on 25th June 1955 at RAF Sturgate, followed by three F-84Fs which all experienced landing incidents at RAF Sturgate on 29th June (51-9386 of the 522nd SFS, as well as 51-17070 and 52-6524 of the 524th SFS). Of these, F-84F 51-17070 was relegated to the 3928th Air Base Group (ABG) for maintenance on 5th August but was deemed beyond repair and finally stricken off charge on 19th March 1956, and 51-9386 was scrapped at Farmingdale.

The 27th SFW's return trip from England proved a bit more spectacular than normal. Commanders from the 27th SFW proposed that the entire wing fly nonstop back to Bergstrom AFB, but SAC Headquarters rejected this plan as too risky. Instead, SAC approved an alternate plan of 12 F-84s flying back to Texas with aerial refueling over Keflavik, Goose AB, and Binghamton, NY. The 12 airplanes departed RAF Sturgate on 17th August 1955 and arrived at Bergstrom AFB after a flight lasting 10 hours, 43 minutes. The remaining F-84s routed through Iceland and Labrador, with 51-9392 lost when it crashed while landing at Bergstrom AFB on 19th August.

SAC had originally planned to replace the 27th SFW in the UK with the 506th SFW, but the nagging problems with the J35 engine precluded the 506th SFW's participation. Instead SAC selected the experienced 31st SFW for yet another transoceanic flight, but runway 'deterioration and repairs' at RAF Sturgate and Keflavik forced SAC to cancel the August 1955 deployment entirely. This proved to be the end of SAC fighter deployments to England, although they continued across the Pacific Ocean to the Far East. Beginning 1st July 1958 SAC briefly resumed fighter operations for base defense in Europe with Convair F-102s from the 497th Fighter Interceptor Squadron (FIS) and the 431st FIS at Torrejón AB and Zaragoza AB, Spain, respectively. Other than occasional visits of one or two airplanes from these units to English bases, there were no more SAC fighters in the United Kingdom, and all SAC fighter assets in Europe were reassigned to USAFE on 1st July 1960.

'LeMay Airlines'

SAC's reputation for heavy bombers did not exclude its own fleet of heavy transports. In the event of general war with the Soviet Union during the early 1950s most of SAC's bomber force would pack up and deploy overseas to allow its B-29s, B-47s, and B-50s to reach their targets from bases in England, North Africa, Alaska, and Guam. Although B-36s could reach their targets within the USSR after flying direct from US bases within the ZI, they would still need to recover overseas and prepare for subsequent attacks, requiring support personnel and equipment to be transshipped across the Atlantic or Pacific. Moreover, most assumptions of general war expected a simultaneous (or impending) Soviet ground invasion of Western Europe, requiring the rapid mobilization and deployment of US Army units from the ZI to staging bases in West Germany and elsewhere. Based on his experience in the Pacific during the Second World War where theater commanders were unable to meet the demand for incendiary bombs for his B-29 force, LeMay understood that the recently constituted MATS could not support both missions simultaneously, especially at the intensive level he required.

One of LeMay's lesser-known but underappreciated initiatives was the establishment of a dedicated transport component within Strategic Air Command. These were more than 'trash hauling' units or very important person (VIP) taxi services. Heavy transports such as Douglas C-54s and C-124s as well as C-97s carried replacement engines, repair tools and 'fly away kits', maintenance personnel, fuel trucks and other support vehicles, Thor missiles, and – most notably – atomic weapons for bomber units deploying or returning from overseas. In effect, this was 'LeMay Airlines.'

The low reliability of the F-84F's J35 engine raised doubts about the wisdom of flying it across the Atlantic and back. In turn, this undermined the fighter protection for SAC's B-47s in the UK. All this would change with the advent of REFLEX ACTION. *Terry Panopalis collection*

SAC STRATEGIC SUPPORT SQUADRON

Unit	Base	From	To
1st ATU	Roswell AAF	30 Jul 46	22 Sep 47
	Fort Worth AAF	22 Sep 47	13 Jan 48
	Griffiss AFB*	13 Jan 48	29 Jan 48
	Carswell AFB	29 Jan 48	31 May 48
1st SSU	Carswell AFB	1 Jun 48	13 Dec 48
	Biggs AFB	14 Dec 48	14 Jan 49
1st SSS	Biggs AFB	14 Jan 49	15 Jan 59
2nd SSS	Biggs AFB	14 Jan 49	18 Apr 50
	Walker AFB	18 Apr 50	16 May 51
	Castle AFB	16 May 51	1 Sep 56
	Pinecastle AFB	1 Sep 56	7 May 58
	McCoy AFB	7 May 58	15 Jun 61
3rd SSS	Hunter AFB	16 Nov 50	5 Jan 53
	Barksdale AFB	5 Jan 53	15 Jun 61
4th SSS	Ellsworth AFB	18 Feb 53	15 Jun 57
	Dyess AFB	15 Jun 57	13 Mar 61

* Ft Worth AAF was briefly named Griffiss AFB; name transferred to Rome Air Depot, NY

AAF = Army Airfield; AFB = Air Force Base; ATU = Air Transport Unit; SSU = Strategic Support Unit; SSS = Strategic Support Squadron; TCS = Troop Carrier Squadron

SAC STRATEGIC SUPPORT SQUADRON C-97s

Aircraft Type	Serial	From	To
YC-97	45-59588	11 Aug 48	2 Sep 50
YC-97	45-59589	25 Aug 48	11 May 50
YC-97	45-59590	14 Feb 49	17 May 50
YC-97A	45-59594	27 Jan 49	3 Mar 49
YC-97A	45-59595	24 Apr 49	19 Jul 50
C-97A	48-0401	30 Dec 49	1 May 51
C-97A	48-0402	13 Mar 50	20 May 51
C-97A	48-0403	13 Mar 50	16 Dec 50
C-97A	48-0404	13 Mar 50	21 May 51
C-97A	48-0405	12 Apr 50	20 May 51
C-97A	48-0406	11 Apr 50	10 May 51
C-97A	48-0407	21 Apr 50	20 May 51
C-97A	48-0408	21 Apr 50	20 May 51
C-97A	48-0409	4 May 50	20 May 51
C-97A	48-0410	4 May 50	30 Apr 51
C-97A	48-0411	21 Apr 50	20 May 51
C-97A	48-0412	21 Apr 50	10 May 51

SAC's strategic transport units trace their origins to a support unit dedicated to the 509th Composite Group's (CG) atomic bomb-configured B-29s. The 320th Troop Carrier Squadron (TCS) – known as 'Green Hornet Airlines' – was activated at Wendover AFB, UT, on 17th December 1944. Its C-54s provided high-priority transport for wing and scientific personnel, particularly once the unit deployed to Tinian. Following the end of the Second World War, the 509th CG relocated to Roswell AFB and the 320th TCS supported the March 1946 atomic tests at Bikini Atoll as part of Operation CROSSROADS. The 320th TCS was subsequently inactivated and replaced by the 1st Air Transport Unit (ATU) on 30th July 1946. The 1st ATU carried aircraft parts for the 509th CG's SADDLETREE-configured B-29s (formerly SILVERPLATE) deployed to West Germany during November and December 1946, but no weapons or components were transferred.

Post-war Army Air Force (AAF) commanders argued that the C-54Ds were ill-suited to carry 'special weapons' to overseas bases (the ill-fated USS *Indianapolis* brought the 'Little Boy' core to Tinian, but a 320th TCS C-54 delivered the 'Fat Man' core). As a result, during 1945 the AAF established Project CHICKENPOX to provide a dedicated air mobility platform to carry atomic weapons from their storage depots in the ZI to domestic bases (CASH BOX missions) and foreign bases, and then to assemble them for B-29 combat units. This eliminated the need for expensive facilities duplicated at each base. CHICKENPOX called for uniquely configured C-97s to replace the C-54s assigned to the 1st ATU.

Specialized kits were developed in 1947 for the C-97s to carry the Mark IV and Mark VI atom bombs and then assemble them in arctic, tropic, and desert locales. The 1952 'History of Project CHICKENPOX' reported that the first C-97 was delivered on 28th October 1947 after the

Former CHICKENPOX YC-97 45-59588 and a C-54, now part of the 1st SSS, at Goose AB in 1949. Aside from its convenient location between the CONUS and England, Goose AB was a storage facility for US atomic weapons. *Gene Van Houten photo, author's collection*

Seen here in 1960 as one of SAC's VC-54Ds, 42-72529 was one of the original nuclear weapons carriers, even predating the founding of SAC in March 1946. *Terry Panopalis collection*

SAC STRATEGIC SUPPORT C-54s

Serial	320th TCS*	1st ATU	1st SSU	1st SSS	2nd SSS	Left SAC	Comments
42-72460		14 Apr 47	16 Dec 48			31 May 48	Crashed Resolute Bay, NWT
42-72469				23 Nov 49	5 Dec 49	26 Jan 50	Missing over Yukon Territory
42-72473				14 Jan 49	30 Mar 50	6 Sep 50	To AMC then to 8th AF, Carswell AFB
42-72523				23 Nov 49	2 Dec 49	11 Nov 50	
42-72529	20 Feb 46	13 Nov 46	16 Dec 48	14 Jan 49	18 Apr 50	15 May 50	To 3902nd ABG Offutt AFB
42-72535		3 Nov 46				11 Dec 46	
42-72573	28 Feb 46					30 Mar 47	
42-72586		7 Jul 48				10 Aug 48	
42-72594	2 May 45	13 Nov 46	16 Dec 48	14 Jan 49		27 Jan 50	To 3902nd ABG Offutt AFB
42-72605	9 May 45	13 Nov 46	16 Dec 48	14 Jan 49	18 Apr 50	21 Jun 50	To AMC then to 8th AF, Carswell AFB
42-72608	30 Jan 46					9 Jun 47	
42-72609	31 Jan 46					1 Feb 46	Immediate transfer to AMC
42-72611		14 Apr 47	16 Dec 48	14 Jan 49	21 Mar 49	10 May 51	
42-72612		3 Nov 46				11 Dec 46	
42-72613		3 Nov 46				31 Dec 46	
42-72616	30 Jan 46					2 Jun 47	
42-72626	31 Jan 46					15 May 46	
42-72627	1 Feb 46					30 Nov 46	
42-72642		3 Nov 46				11 Dec 46	
42-72649	30 Jan 46			23 Nov 49	2 Dec 49	16 Jun 50	To AMC 5 May 46; returned to 1st SSS; to 8th AF, Carswell AFB
42-72650	28 Feb 46	13 Nov 46	16 Dec 48	14 Jan 49	20 May 49	27 Sep 50	To 22nd BW, March AFB
42-72655		3 Nov 46				5 May 47	
42-72656	28 Jan 46					7 May 47	
42-72662		3 Nov 46				20 Mar 47	
42-72668				23 Nov 49	5 Dec 49	30 Oct 50	
42-72682	28 Feb 46					8 Jun 47	
42-72691	1 Feb 46	13 Nov 46	16 Dec 48	14 Jan 49		16 May 50	To 2nd AF, Barksdale AFB
42-72704	1 Feb 46					27 Mar 47	
42-72708		3 Nov 46				25 Dec 46	
42-72710				23 Nov 49	5 Dec 49	4 Dec 50	
42-72711	2 Feb 46					7 Aug 46	
42-72720						6 May 47	
42-72721				23 Nov 49	2 Dec 49	22 Feb 51	To 3902nd ABG Offutt AFB
42-72725		13 Apr 47	16 Dec 48	14 Jan 49		10 May 50	To 22nd BW, March AFB
42-72758		14 Apr 47	16 Dec 48	14 Jan 49	21 Mar 49	14 Sep 50	To 8th AF, Carswell AFB
42-72760		14 Apr 47	16 Dec 48	14 Jan 49	26 May 50	20 Sep 50	To 3902nd ABG Offutt AFB
43-17201				23 Nov 49	8 Dec 49	16 Oct 50	To 22nd BW, March AFB

* All 320th TCS C-54s supported Operation CROSSROADS except 42-72609; AMC = Air Materiel Command

1st ATU had relocated to Fort Worth AAF, TX. Aircraft records, however, show that YC-97 45-59588 was the first airplane assigned to the 1st Strategic Support Unit (SSU) nearly a year later on 11th August 1948. The CHICKENPOX history adds that four additional YC-97s and a lone YC-97A were handed over in 1948, and the XC-97 prototype (43-27470) became the CHICKENPOX ground trainer. Again, conflicting aircraft records show that a total of two YC-97s were assigned in 1948, one YC-97, two YC-97As, and one C-97A in 1949, and 11 C-97s in 1950. The disparity in dates may refer to when the airplanes were assigned and not when they were fully configured and operational.

The 1st ATU underwent two unit redesignations to become the 1st Strategic Support Squadron (SSS), and by the end of 1948 had been reassigned to Biggs AFB along with the 2nd SSS, which was activated on 14th January 1949. Operationally the 1st SSS and 2nd SSS were interchangeable and considered to function as one unit, although for administrative purposes they were two separate entities. Despite this organizational sleight of hand, the CHICKENPOX C-97s were assigned only to the 1st SSS, although both units continued to operate C-54s.

By August 1949 CHICKENPOX had been canceled due to the excessive time required for each C-97 to be operationally ready at its deployed base, as well as the projected shortfall of available airplanes. For example, the December 1949 history of the 1st SSS notes that only one of four fully configured C-97As slated for delivery to the 1st SSS would actually reach the unit that month. Moreover, the handful of C-97s planned for CHICKENPOX could not possibly meet the transport and assembly requirements of SAC's 300+ B-29s and B-50s, let alone the forthcoming B-36s. Ultimately, however, the main reason for the program's cancelation – according to the CHICKENPOX history – was the 'indefensible waste of resources [as] a nonessential luxury for handling the Mk VI, particularly when airborne insertion [of the atomic pit] becomes a reality, predicted for the not too distant future.'

Although C-97s and C-54s were occasional visitors to the UK through 1950, their days as

SAC STRATEGIC SUPPORT SQUADRON (SSS) C-124s

Serial	1st SSS	2nd SSS	3rd SSS	4th SSS	Left SAC	Comments
49-0235		18 Jul 50			3 Apr 61	
49-0236		1 Sep 50			1 May 61	
49-0237	26 Jan 52				3 Feb 52	2nd SSS 5 Sep 50-20 Jul 51, then to 28th SRW, then to 1st SSS
49-0238		21 Aug 50			28 Apr 61	
49-0240		31 Aug 50			16 May 61	
49-0241		5 Sep 50			1 Jun 61	
49-0242		14 Sep 50			1 Jun 61	
49-0243		21 Sep 50			3 May 61	
49-0244		3 Oct 50			23 Mar 51	Disappeared over Atlantic; Loss of BGEN Cullen
49-0245		3 Oct 50			3 Jun 61	
49-0246		3 Oct 50			3 Apr 61	
49-0247		22 Sep 50	22 Dec 50		1 May 61	
49-0248		25 Oct 50	22 Dec 50		10 May 61	Loaned from 3rd SSS to 4th SSS 14 Jan 14 Feb 60
49-0249		6 Nov 50	22 Dec 50		7 Apr 61	
49-0250		14 Nov 50	22 Dec 50		1 Jun 61	
49-0253			14 Nov 50		2 Dec 52	Returned to 1st SSS 28 Aug 57, then to 3rd SSS 10 Jan 59, out of SAC 7 Apr 61
49-0254			22 Dec 50		6 Jul 59	BROKEN ARROW crash on takeoff at Barksdale AFB; two weapons destroyed
49-0255			22 Dec 50		11 May 61	
49-0256			8 Feb 55		16 May 61	
49-0257	18 Jan 51	26 Jan 54			3 Apr 61	
49-0258			31 Jan 51		7 Apr 61	Preserved; Dover AFB, DE
49-0259			31 Jan 51		2 Jun 61	
50-0083			19 Feb 51		29 May 51	
50-0084			23 Feb 51		5 Jun 61	
50-0085			7 Mar 51		23 May 61	
50-0086	8 Mar 51		8 Mar 54		7 Apr 61	
50-0087	8 Mar 51		10 Jan 59		17 May 61	
50-0088	14 Mar 51				27 Jan 57	Ditched after takeoff at Elmendorf AFB, AK
50-0089	16 Mar 51		10 Jan 59		22 May 61	
50-0090		31 Mar 51			1 Jun 61	

SAC's special weapons support platforms were numbered, as SAC acquired a total of 60 newly built C-124A Globemaster IIs (and later C-124Cs) as replacements. On 18th July 1950 the 2nd SSS received SAC's first C-124A (49-0235 nicknamed *Apache Chieftain*) concurrent with the unit's relocation to Walker AFB. It retained its C-54s until 1951. The 1st SSS acquired its first C-124 on 18th January 1951 (49-0257) while at Biggs AFB, retiring its C-97s afterward. The 3rd SSS was established on 16th November 1950 at Hunter AFB, two days after receiving its first C-124 (49-0253) and relocated to Barksdale AFB on 5th January 1953. The 4th SSS was activated on 18th February 1953 at Ellsworth AFB (although it did not receive its first three airplanes until 14th August), and was reassigned to Dyess AFB, TX, on 15th June 1957.

Operational deployments of C-124s to the United Kingdom have not been easily tracked, although their use in carrying cargo, personnel, and weapons was routine. Strategic Support unit histories remain classified due to their association with atomic weapons. A few spot-

ter reports – notwithstanding Korean War censorship – have helped correlate a few trips with combat unit deployments. Some British sources refer to the C-124s which carried atomic weapons as American 'Service Aircraft', which was a euphemism that masked their sensitive cargo. Indeed, during a House of Commons debate on 30th May 1960, the issue arose of how these Service Aircraft filed a flight plan (and who in the UK approved it). In fact, the flights were treated no differently than other SAC flight plans into the UK.

The first known visit of a SAC Support Squadron came during July 1948 when 1st SSS C-54s and C-97s participated in the initial deployment of B-29s to the UK, beginning on 17th July with the 307th BG to RAF Marham and on 18th July with the 28th BG to RAF Scampton. These did not carry any atomic weapons and instead brought parts such as spare engines and tools. SAC atomic weapons first reached the UK during the July 1950 buildup in response to the war in Korea, although there is disagreement over how they all arrived. B-50s from the

Serial	1st SSS	2nd SSS	3rd SSS	4th SSS	Left SAC	Comments
50-0091	29 Mar 51	13 Jan 59			15 May 61	
50-0092	6 Apr 51				3 Mar 53	
50-0093		14 Apr 51			1 Jun 61	
50-0094	23 Apr 51		9 Jan 59		5 May 61	
50-0095	7 May 51	12 Jan 59			23 May 61	
50-0096	7 May 51	12 Jan 59			5 Jun 61	
50-0097	7 May 51				6 Sep 55	Crashed on takeoff, Kirtland AFB, NM
50-0098	21 May 51	18 Dec 58			6 Jun 61	
50-0111			20 Jul 51		9 May 52	
51-0073			6 Mar 53		30 Mar 55	
51-0115			6 Jun 52		30 Mar 55	
51-0148	25 Sep 52				3 Oct 52	
52-0973	11 Aug 53			19 Dec 58	10 Feb 61	
52-0974				14 Aug 53	11 Jan 61	
52-0975				14 Aug 53	13 Jan 61	
52-0976				14 Aug 53	12 Jan 61	
52-0977				20 Aug 53	10 Feb 61	
52-0978				20 Aug 53	9 Feb 61	
52-0979				24 Aug 53	10 Jan 61	
52-0984				10 Sep 53	8 Feb 61	
52-0985				18 Sep 53	13 Jan 61	
52-0986				18 Sep 53	11 Jan 61	
52-0987				15 Sep 53	8 Feb 61	
52-0988				23 Sep 53	8 Feb 61	
52-0989				23 Sep 53	10 Feb 61	
52-1016				22 Dec 53	12 Jan 61	
52-1018	7 Jan 54			13 Jan 59	3 Jan 61	
52-1019	7 Jan 54			13 Jan 59	8 Feb 61	
52-1020	4 Jan 54			14 Jan 59	3 Jan 61	
52-1021	4 Jan 54				31 Aug 57	Crashed on approach to Biggs AFB, TX

C-124A 49-0241 sports the green wings of the 2nd SSS. SAC was eager to publicize the Globemaster's cargo and transport role to emphasize the command's global mobility, but kept its atomic weapons mission a tight secret.
Author's collection

C-124 50-0087 spent a decade with the 1st and 3rd SSS, making regular trips to the UK. It returned to RAF Mildenhall while assigned to the 442nd Military Airlift Wing in April 1968.
Lindsay Peacock

In addition to overseas delivery and retrieval of SAC's atomic weapons, its C-124s also flew similar CASH BOX missions to CONUS bases. In any case, its slow 200 knot (370 km/h) cruise speed made for long flights.
Kent Kistler via Stephen Miller

The deployment of SAC bomb wings to the UK after 1950 typically involved 3 C-124s, as well as MATS transports pending the 1954 final delivery of SAC's full complement of C-124s.
Terry Panopalis collection

LeMay understood the complex logistics of relocating entire bomber wings to England, and the C-124's primary mission was transport of aircraft parts, personnel, and even fuel trucks.
Photo P16919 courtesy Boeing

97th BG and 93rd BG each brought their own Mark VIs, but the SADDLETREE/GEM 301st BG B-29s at RAF Lakenheath and RAF Sculthorpe since May 1950 had its atomic weapons shipped via SAC's *Globemasters*. This arrival date, however, remains uncertain. Kenneth Werrell's *Who Fears? 301st in War and Peace, 1942-1979* includes an undated eyewitness report of Mark IVs being unloaded from a C-124 at RAF Lakenheath. The first SAC C-124 (49-0235) was delivered to the 2nd SSS on 18th July 1950 with the second on 21st August, so any C-124 visits would almost certainly have occurred after mid-July.

Additional records of SAC's C-124 visiting England show that three C-124s (49-0236, 49-0237, and 49-0244) from the 2nd SSS arrived at RAF Lakenheath during the November 1950 deployment of 7th BW B-36s from

Carswell AFB. There is no indication of what their cargo might have been.

Four 1st SSS C-124s (50-0086, 50-0087, 50-0088, and 50-0089) were noted at RAF Brize Norton circa 27th June 1952 concurrent with the deployment of 11th BW B-36s, also from Carswell AFB. Sometime during the first half of 1953 C-124's from the 1st SSS and 2nd SSS transferred atomic bombs from England back to the United States, although further details of this movement remain classified.

Later C-124 visits included the February 1957 OPEN FENCE bomber stream mission for the 303rd BW B-47s from Davis-Monthan AFB, and the ROUGH GAME USCM for the 40th BW on 12th February 1958. The 4th SSS assisted with the additional February 1958 movements of the 100th BW B-47s from Pease AFB, to RAF Brize Norton in the middle of its 29th December 1957 to 1st

For all its utility, the C-124 suffered from considerable maintenance problems which claimed 5 of SAC's 59 Globemasters, including the loss of the 7th AD commander and his staff in 1951. *Gordon Macadie*

Despite its capacity, the C-124 was very slow, making trans-Atlantic trips long and tedious. They also had a reputation for engine problems, making the flights even more nerve-wracking. 49-0255, seen here in 1955, spent its entire SAC career with the 3rd SSS. *Brian Baldwin*

When the weather was good, England proved to be an idyllic location for SAC crews. Going home, as this C-124 prepares to do, had its own charm, especially after a three-month deployment away from family and friends. *Mike Hooks via Nick Stroud/TAH*

Using a heavy crane to replace an R4360 engine reflects the challenges of overseas deployments. In the absence of the extensive infrastructure at CONUS bases, crews often had to improvise. *Terry Panopalis collection*

April 1958 deployment there. The 4th SSS also supported the USCM ROUGH GAME and TALL BOY that same month for the 2nd ADS, 3918th ABG at RAF Upper Heyford and again for the 3913th ABG at RAF Mildenhall. In these latter two cases, unit histories record that ground units practiced unloading and loading 'special weapons' from the C-124s. An unspecified number of 1st SSS C-124s returned to RAF Brize Norton during April 1958 to support B-52Ds from the 92nd BW at Fairchild AFB participating in the RAF Bombing Competition. A severe windstorm at Dyess AFB damaged all of the 4th SSS aircraft there, but they were sufficiently back in service by June 1958 to participate in Operation BELL HOP to the UK. During January 1959, C-124s provided logistical support for the 6th BW APPLE CART deployment, and the 3rd SSS assisted the 16-19th June DREAMY RIVER movement for the 92nd BW.

The four SAC C-124 squadrons were supplemented by three Logistics Support Squadrons (LSS) assigned to AMC. These comprised the 7th LSS at Robins AFB, GA, the 19th LSS at Kelly AFB, TX, and the 28th LSS at Hill AFB, UT, all of which were Air Materiel Area (AMA) bases (eg, Warner Robins AMA or WRAMA). On 6th February 1955, these squadrons were reassigned without a change in station to the 3079th Aviation Depot Wing (ADW) at Wright-Patterson AFB. Their mission was the same as the SAC C-124s – to transport nuclear weapons, although they were not reserved exclusively for SAC operations. For example, the 28th LSS were part of the 1962 DOMINIC nuclear tests in the South Pacific, and they transported tactical nuclear weapons to USAFE and Pacific Air Force (PACAF) bases. By 1958, SAC ceased to carry its own atomic weapons for each overseas REFLEX deployment, and the LSS units rotated the

The days of SAC C-124s carrying atomic weapons were numbered, as Logistics Squadrons took over the role of nuclear courier aircraft. *Mike Hooks via Nick Stroud/TAH*

Top and below: Beginning in 1950, SAC had at least 3 VC-97Ds for VIP operations based at Offutt AFB. They were still in use when seen at RAF Greenham Common on 31st August 1962 (top) and 15th April 1961 (bottom) at Prestwick. CINCSAC General Power eventually acquired KC-135A 57-2589, which made its first trip to the UK on 26th May 1961 to RAF Brize Norton. *Brian Baldwin (upper), Adrian Balch collection (middle), Jim Webb collection (lower)*

When this photo was taken of C-97E 53-0197 at Goose AB in August 1964, SAC's bomber deployments to the UK were nearing an end and KC-135s had become the SAC transport of choice. *Adrian Balch collection*

stockpile of nuclear weapons in the UK that were uploaded into newly arrived B-47s that were placed on alert.

In addition to the four SSS units, beginning in 1950 the 3902nd Air Base Group (ABG) at Offutt AFB acquired three VC-97Ds (49-2593, 49-2594, and 49-2595), at least four C-54Ds (42-72529, 42-72594, 42-72721, and 42-72760), and a C-54G (45-0546) for personnel movements, including overseas trips to the UK.

Air Rescue Services

LeMay's vision extended beyond the need for an indigenous airlift fleet to support SAC's operational requirements. In the event of general war with the USSR, few SAC bomber crewmembers believed they would survive their strike mission and land at a recovery base to reconstitute for second- or third-wave attacks. Even fewer were under the illusion that, if shot down while on their mission, they could be rescued. Despite the odds stacked heavily against any successful rescue, LeMay championed the need to train his crews to survive under any conditions while awaiting recovery. SAC created the Aircrew Recovery Program to educate crews in basic survival and evasion skills such as map-and-compass navigation on all terrain as well as gathering food and preparing shelter. In addition, SAC crewmembers were subject to the 'torture course' which taught techniques to 'survive' interrogation as well as how to escape. One radical program even required SAC crews to learn basic Russian to use while evading capture in the Soviet Union after nuking nearby facilities. This was wisely canceled after it took up too much time needed for operational training and was unlikely to be successful, especially as not everyone in the USSR spoke Russian.

On 16th December 1949, SAC established the 3904th Training Squadron (TS) at Ft Carson, CO, to provide basic survival training. This expanded on 21st October 1950, becoming the 3904th Composite Wing (CW) to include the 3904th TS and the 8th Air Rescue Squadron (ARS). These moved to Stead AFB, NV, on 1st September 1951 and included the newly formed US Air Force Survival School. The 3904th CW transferred to Air Training Command (ATC) on 1st September 1954 and was redesignated as the 3635th Combat Crew Training Wing (CCTW), and MATS acquired the air rescue mission. The flying component of the 3904th CW was redesignated the 8th Air Rescue Group (ARG) and reassigned to MATS with

two Air Rescue Squadrons each at Stead AFB, NV, (61st and 62nd ARS), and Norton AFB, CA, (63rd and 64th ARS). The survival school relocated in 1966 to Fairchild AFB, WA.

Initially, the school included a few C-119s but this changed to SC-47s. These were configured with extra fuel tanks for greater endurance and range. Additional radios monitored rescue frequencies used by downed crewmen. The SC-47s could also be fitted with rocket-assisted takeoff (RATO) for short-field performance, as well as skis. These deployed on a TDY basis to RAF Lakenheath and RAF Mildenhall during 1952 in support of 7th AD operations, followed by another deployment in 1953 to RAF Upper Heyford, known as MEADOW LARK. During November 1954, the 14th ARG relocated from Norton AFB to RAF High Wycombe where it served to coordinate rescue operations with SAC's 7th AD. By 1957, budget cuts led to the disestablishment of the 14th ARG and its duties were reassigned to Ramstein AB, FRG. This also resulted in the end of dedicated SC-47 operations in support of SAC's Aircrew Recovery Program.

Operations in the UK

Rescue support for SAC after 1954 took place from three primary UK bases: RAF East Kirkby, RAF Greenham Common, and RAF Sturgate, although the SC-47s were noted at other locations, especially during runway repairs.

RAF East Kirkby – The first MATS rescue deployment began when 15 SC-47s from the 63rd ARS departed from Norton AFB on 1st January 1955 en route to EA Harmon AFB. Bad weather and ground mishaps delayed their departure and the SC-47s finally straggled in beginning 11th January. The final three arrived at RAF East Kirkby on 24th January. Records show they took part in exercises known as QUICK STEP and PEA PATCH prior to the end of their deployment on 22nd March when they returned to Norton AFB.

In 1957 SAC ended its internal rescue mission, but a number of its SC-47s remained in use as base 'hacks'. *N Wayne Schultze via Stephen Miller*

189

USAFE eventually acquired the air rescue mission from SAC, which involved considerable liaison between command elements on the continent and bases in England. VC-47A 42-93817 from the 7167th ATS at Rhein-Main AB routinely shuttled officials to negotiate this transfer.
Brian Baldwin

SAC C-47A 42-23775 was assigned to the 62nd ARS when visiting RAF Greenham Common sometime during October-December 1955. SAC took its rescue commitment very seriously, although few crewmembers believed that anyone would survive a nuclear first strike.
Brian Baldwin

These were replaced by eight SC-47As and seven SC-47Ds from the 63rd ARS at Stead AFB, arriving on 5th April 1955. Known operations include SPRING CORN and MAIN ROAD. The airplanes returned to Stead AFB beginning 22nd June. A final deployment to RAF East Kirkby started on 1st July when seven SC-47As and eight SC-47Ds from the 64th ARS departed Norton AFB and arrived in the UK. While in England the unit took part in STRIKE OUT (29th July through 4th August) and LOW GEAR (19th-26th August). The squadron headed back to California on 22nd September, and this proved to be the last of planned rescue deployments to RAF East Kirkby.

SAC ARS BASES IN THE UNITED KINGDOM

Base	From	To	Unit	Comments
RAF Lakenheath	12 Aug 52	7 Sep 52	3904th CW	to RAF Mildenhall
RAF Mildenhall	11 Aug 52	17 Oct 52	3904th CW	
RAF Upper Heyford	5 Jul 53	9 Sep 53	3904th CW	Additional SC-47As at Wheelus AB from 4 Jul 53-5 Sep 53
RAF East Kirkby	3 Jan 55	27 Mar 55	63rd ARS	
	4 Apr 55	28 Jun 55	61st ARS	
	4 Jul 55	22 Sep 55	64th ARS	
	56		62nd ARS	
	1 Apr 57		61st ARS	
RAF Greenham Common	28 Sep 55	16 Dec 55	62nd ARS	
	15 Dec 55		61st ARS	
	56		61st ARS	JUMPING BUG, WALKING CANE
RAF Fairford	56		63rd ARS	At RAF Sturgate due to repairs
RAF Sturgate	56		63rd ARS	DUFFEL BAG
	1 Apr 57		61st ARS	TDY to Wheelus AB May-June 57
RAF Stansted	1 Apr 57	Jun 57	63rd ARS	

RAF Greenham Common – The first rotation following the cessation of rescue operations from RAF East Kirkby was that of the 62nd ARS from Stead AFB to RAF Greenham Common beginning 24th September 1955, with 10 SC-47As and four SC-47Ds arriving there by 28th September. Unfortunately, SC-47D 43-16145 ran out of fuel near Burns, WY, and crashed with loss of the crew. Known operations include TEST MATCH (14th-20th October), and HIGH TIME (23rd-27th November). Three of the 62nd ARS SC-47s returned to the US when the deployment ended on 16th December, while the remaining airplanes were supplemented by 10 SC-47As and two SC-47Ds from the 61st ARS at Stead AFB, which had arrived at RAF Greenham Common by 13th January 1956. While in the UK the SC-47s took part in JUMPING BUG (15th-21st February) and WALKING CANE (1st-4th March). The deployment ended and the 61st ARS airplanes left England on 27th March.

The planned April 1956 rotation of the 63rd ARS from Norton AFB to RAF Greenham Common was cancelled.

RAF Sturgate – The aborted 63rd ARS rotation to RAF Greenham Common finally reached the UK on 1st September 1956 when just six SC-47Ds arrived at RAF Sturgate. During this brief (30 days) deployment, the squadron participated in DUFFLE BAG (21st September-3rd October). The 63rd ARS returned to Norton AFB on 15th October 1956. Yet another planned deployment to the UK was cancelled when SC-47s from the 62nd ARS suffered from wing-tank problems. The 63rd ARS visit was the last SC-47 deployment to the UK.

SAC's 'Unmanned Bombers'

By the late 1950s, SAC was becoming increasingly invested in ballistic missiles as potential adjunct delivery vehicles in its nuclear armada. Long-range ICBMs were as yet not sufficiently mature to incorporate wholesale into SAC's alert force, but intermediate range ballistic missiles (IRBM), such as the US Army's Chrysler PGM-19 Jupiter and the US Air Force's Douglas PGM-17 Thor were ready for initial service. Given that their range was limited to some 1,500nm (2,778km), bases in Europe and elsewhere around the periphery of the USSR were essential to achieve their targeting commitments.

Proposals to base SAC missiles in the UK were first articulated in 1951, when AMC declared that the yet-to-be-declared operational B-47 would carry the air-to-surface Bell GAM-63 Rascal stand-off missile, and its first overseas deployment would be to RAF Greenham Common in early 1956. Similarly, by 1953 efforts were underway to base a squadron of Northrop SM-62 Snark surface-to-surface cruise missiles at RAF Lakenheath. Pilotless Bomb Squadrons (PBS) would oversee Snark operations and prepare the Rascals for mating with specially configured DB-47Bs transient from the 445th BS, 321st BW at Pinecastle AFB. In both cases, wiser heads prevailed and plans to relocate these ineffective weapons were cancelled.

Placing IRBMs in England, however, was first broached during a July 1956 visit to London by US Secretary of the Air Force Donald A Quarles, with both the Thor and Jupiter under consideration. Quarles preferred the use of existing American bases to host eight squadrons with 15 missiles each. Initial proposals had favored a single US base, but this increased the IRBM's vulnerability to attack. Subsequent recommendations expanded the basing option to include British bases with operational control of the missiles by either the Royal Air Force or British Army forces. In exchange for basing rights, the US planned to offer the RAF the Convair F-106 Delta Dart to replace the Gloster Javelin (the RAF preferred the Canadian Avro CF-105 Arrow).

Although the British declined the F-106 offer, they nonetheless decided to move ahead with an IRBM operated by the RAF. Initial operational capability was anticipated by October 1958, with all 60 missiles (plus spares) delivered by July 1959. The issue of which missile – Thor or Jupiter – remained unresolved. On 24th February 1958, an official announcement in Parliament revealed that the UK had decided on a missile, but did not actually specify the Thor in the statement. Records show that 'the missiles [would] be manned and operated by personnel from the Royal Air Force. The Agreement provides that the missiles shall not be launched except by joint positive decision of both Governments.' The announcement was equally vague about where the IRBMs would be based, saying only that they would be 'generally located' in Yorkshire, Lincolnshire, and East Anglia. Finally, there was no mention of the 5-year time frame for the agreement.

Debate soon arose over projected sites, with the central issues being the number of primary bases, dispersed bases, and ownership – RAF or USAF (which in the case of nuclear-armed ballistic missiles meant SAC). The original four bases, each with 15 missiles, included RAF Feltwell/RAF Methwold, RAF Hemswell, RAF Driffield,

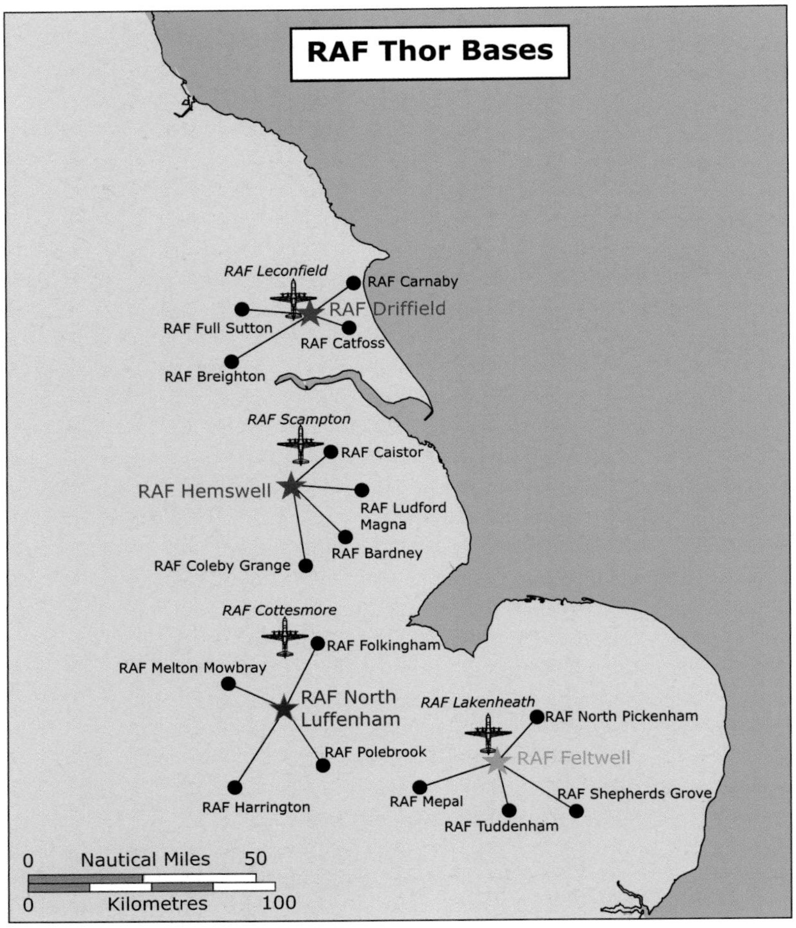

RAF THOR UNITS

Site	SM Sqn	From	To
Feltwell (Primary)	77 Sqn	1 Sep 58	10 Jul 63
Shepherds Grove	82 Sqn	22 Jul 59	10 Jul 63
Tuddenham	107 Sqn	22 Jul 59	10 Jul 63
Mepal	113 Sqn	22 Jul 59	10 Jul 63
North Pickenham	220 Sqn	22 Jun 59	10 Jul 63
Airhead: RAF Lakenheath			
Hemswell (Primary)	97 Sqn	1 Dec 58	24 May 63
Caistor	269 Sqn	22 Jul 59	24 May 63
Ludford Magna	104 Sqn	22 Jul 59	24 May 63
Coleby Grange	142 Sqn	22 Jul 59	24 May 63
Bardney	106 Sqn	22 Jul 59	24 May 63
Airhead: RAF Scampton			
Driffield (Primary)	98 Sqn	1 Aug 59	18 Apr 63
Full Sutton	102 Sqn	1 Aug 59	27 Apr 63
Carnaby	150 Sqn	1 Aug 59	9 Apr 63
Catfoss	226 Sqn	1 Aug 59	9 Mar 63
Breighton	240 Sqn	1 Aug 59	8 Jan 63
Airhead: RAF Leconfield			
North Luffenham (Primary)	144 Sqn	1 Dec 59	23 Aug 63
Polebrook	130 Sqn	1 Dec 59	23 Aug 63
Folkingham	223 Sqn	1 Dec 59	23 Aug 63
Harrington	218 Sqn	1 Dec 59	23 Aug 63
Melton Mowbray	254 Sqn	1 Dec 59	23 Aug 63
Airhead: RAF Cottesmore			

SM = Strategic Missile

and RAF Stradishall. The latter site was replaced by RAF North Luffenham in the final order of battle. The RAF preferred a more dispersed arrangement, however, with each base housing three missiles. For example, in addition to the three Thors at RAF Feltwell, that unit would oversee three missiles each at RAF Shepherds Grove, RAF Tuddenham, RAF Mepal, and RAF North Pickenham.

The final order of battle included four RAF Bomber Command wings to operate and command its own Thors, as well as to exer-

Each Thor site had three IRBMs. In this image of RAF Feltwell, the central Thor has been raised while the other two remain under their retractable cover. This distribution supposedly provided a measure of protection, but would have been doubtful from a nuclear attack. *John Boyes collection*

cise command responsibility for four attached squadrons. Each outlying squadron was between 12-30 miles (19-48km) straight-line distance from the main base. This complicated Soviet targeting (assuming 20 Soviet warheads would be needed to destroy all the Thors on the ground) as well as minimized their vulnerability to sabotage not only from Soviet agents but from domestic threats such as the Irish Republican Army (IRA)!

The US would pay for hardware, facilities, and training of both US and RAF personnel, while the RAF would pay for base construction, maintenance, and operational costs of personnel. On 27th March 1958, the RAF gave the Thor program the code name Project EMILY. Interestingly, while the US planned to deploy its IRBMs to Europe, in 1959 the Soviet Union deployed SS-3 *Shyster* medium range ballistic missiles (MRBM) to two locations in the GDR, keeping this secret even from the East Germans. They were removed the same year.

Initial Deployment

The first Thor to arrive was missile 139 (the second production example), which was airlifted into RAF Lakenheath by a C-124 on 29th August 1958. Subsequent missiles for RAF North Luffenham, RAF Driffield, and RAF Hemswell were flown directly to the airheads for those bases, after which the runways were closed out of fear of an airplane crash in close proximity to the Thors. Arrivals at RAF Driffield, for example, took place from 3rd April through 3rd November 1959. Thor was declared operational on 1st November 1959, with the five-year agreement ending on 31st October 1964.

Technically, the Thor was quite modest. Its range was between 300-1,500nm (556-2,778km) with an expected accuracy of 50% of warheads hitting within 10,560ft (3,219m) of the aim point. It weighed 110,000lb (49,895kg), of which 98,500lb (44,679kg) was fuel and oxidizer. The engine had a maximum burn time of 156 seconds, although this could be reduced for targets at closer ranges.

It was not altogether clear if the Thor represented much of a meaningful strike capability for the RAF. According to rigorous research by John Boyes, Thor held only 46 cities at risk (35% of desired coverage) and only 10 (50%) of the 'most desired targets' at a range of 1,400nm (2,593km), just short of Moscow. Senior Bomber Command officials were suspicious of the Thor's value, an opinion held by their American counterparts in SAC. Their ini-

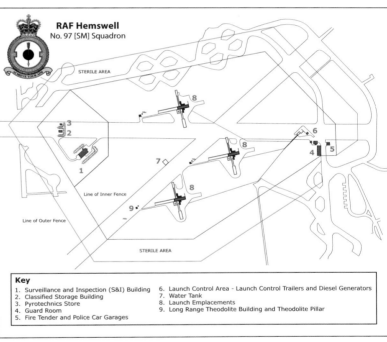

Key
1. Surveillance and Inspection (S&I) Building
2. Classified Storage Building
3. Pyrotechnics Store
4. Guard Room
5. Fire Tender and Police Car Garages
6. Launch Control Area - Launch Control Trailers and Diesel Generators
7. Water Tank
8. Launch Emplacements
9. Long Range Theodolite Building and Theodolite Pillar

tial worries about the Thor's reliability were due to launch failures in the US, where only 10 of 25 early launches (including both US and RAF missiles) were successful. These concerns were eventually assuaged. Between 16th April 1959 and 18th June 1962, for example, there were 21 Thor launches by RAF crews from Vandenberg AFB, CA, with only two failures.

The SAC Component

The SAC contribution to the RAF Thor mission was the 705th Strategic Missile Wing (SMW), which was established on 20th February 1957 at RAF Lakenheath, but which later relocated

Top: The arrival of a Thor at one of the four support airfields was always a high-security event (note guard dog!). In this case, the final Thor – *sans* warhead – arrives by C-124 at RAF North Luffenham on 10th March 1960. *John Boyes collection*

Although the Thor was nominally under the control of RAF personnel, its W-49 warhead was the exclusive domain of SAC personnel. On the whole, the Thor was of questionable military value, and its dual-command structure resulted in enough ambiguity to raise doubts about who could – or could not – authorize its launch. *John Boyes collection*

to South Ruislip. Publicly the British said there would be no US involvement in the routine Thor operations, only RAF personnel. As Boyes notes, 'USAF participation extended only to technical assistance and the provision of equipment.' The operative word in the British public relations campaign to reassure the public was 'routine', as SAC had a very specific role in Thor operations both on alert and in the event of war which was not widely discussed.

The W-49 thermonuclear warhead (with a yield of 1.44Mt) remained under strict American control. The re-entry vehicle (RV), which included the warhead, was loaded onto each RAF Thor exclusively by SAC personnel from the 99th Munitions Maintenance Squadron (MMS), and an American officer set the war-

head burst height (either ground or airburst from 3,000-10,000ft ±1,000ft [914-3,048m (±305m)]. Moreover, launch authority was a 'joint decision in light of the circumstances at the time and having regard to the two Governments' obligations under Article 5 of the North Atlantic Treaty. Initially, the plan was to keep all of the warheads at RAF Lakenheath and then deliver them to individual sites during times of increased tension. However, this would require some 52 hours to accomplish, well in excess of the 24-hour limit set by SAC and the RAF.

This dual control of 'special weapons' was not unique to the Thor program. Under 'Project E', the US loaned nuclear weapons to the UK pending sufficient production of British 'Yellow Sun' weapons. Project E weapons were under absolute US control until released to the RAF. Even so, SACEUR controlled Project E bombs that went to the English Electric Canberra Light Bomber Force while the Pentagon controlled those destined for the V-bombers (Valiant, Vulcan, and Victor) with operational orders issued from SAC Headquarters via 7th AD.

Operational manning of the Thor sites was straightforward. In addition to the missile maintenance crew and ground support personnel (ranging from fuel specialist to cook to dog handler), all of whom were RAF, there was a station commander (an RAF officer), five RAF Launch Control Officers (LCO), and five SAC Authentication Officers (AO). The LCO had a key that would initiate the launch sequence, while the AO had a separate key that would arm the warhead. The instructions were unequivocal in stipulating the independent but controlling SAC role for a Thor launch:

'One USAF [SAC] representative will be on duty in each squadron launch control station at all times after each squadron becomes capable of launching a weapon operationally. He will be in addition to the normal RAF launch crew. The USAF representative's duty will be to receive the *US authentication launch order through US channels of communication*. If the countdown has been started and the RAF authentication order has been received and the *USAF authentication order has not been received*, the USAF representative will, by use of a keying mechanism, introduce a tactical hold of the missile countdown. This tactical hold *will be released by the USAF representative upon receipt of the US authentication order*' [emphasis added].

A variety of technical issues effectively bypassed this two-man decision-making policy. On one occasion, a screwdriver sufficed for the AO key! These issues were common across

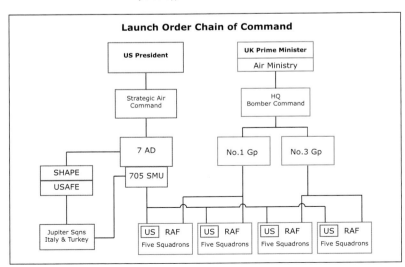

Launch Order Chain of Command

all of SAC's missile units at the time, and were eventually addressed to make the process more secure and reliable.

Thor units participated in the annual RAF exercise MAYSHOT, as well as other exercises including RESPOND, REDOUBLE, RECLAIM, and NIGHT-CHECK. In these cases, the missiles were read-ied to the 'launch minus 15 minutes' stage and were without warheads. Just as with SAC and RAF flying units, Thor sites experienced their share of mishaps. For example, on7th December 1960 a liquid oxygen (LOX) spill at RAF Ludford Magna raised the specter of a massive explosion of an unarmed missile, but the LOX dissipated without incident. On 22nd August 1962, North American F-100D 55-2784 assigned to the 48th Tactical Fighter Wing (TFW) at RAF Lakenheath crashed close to the Thor site at RAF Shepherds Grove, a near-disaster not totally mitigated by the closure of nearby airfields!

A Credible Ending

On 1st May 1962, US Secretary of Defense Robert McNamara told UK Minister of Aviation Peter Thorneycroft that the US would not extend the Thor agreement past the end of October 1964. SAC's Atlas, Titan, and solid-fueled Minuteman ICBMs had rendered Thor obsolete. Discussions within the UK's Ministry of Defense to extend the Thor's RAF service, such as improvements to its range, offered the added benefit of complicating Soviet targeting, but these were considered ineffectual compared to the £5 million per annum outlay required.

The RAF/SAC Thor IRBMs were only once ever 'at the precipice' for launch against Soviet targets. On 27th October 1962, during the height of the Cuban Missile Crisis, Air Officer Commanding-in-Chief Bomber Command Air Marshal Sir Kenneth B B 'Bing' Cross ordered UK Alert Condition 3, with the Thors at Readiness State One-Five (15 minutes to launch). All but one of the 60 missiles were ready to launch, eventually joined by the final Thor. Of these, the RAF believed that 90% (54 missiles) could have been successfully launched should the order have been given. SAC AOs were on a higher state of alert compared to RAF personnel. The AOs wore their launch keys around their necks rather than leaving them in the safe and guzzled coffee at their launch stations, while RAF personnel attended Halloween parties and one RAF station commander even took leave. Bomber Command reverted

to Alert Condition 4 on 5th November, but SAC remained at Defense Condition (DEFCON) 2 for another 10 days, creating an 'imbalance of urgency' between RAF LCOs and SAC AOs.

Despite its successful readiness during the October crisis, the days of the Thor were circumscribed. As one RAF commander dourly noted, 'I should have thought that after five years the Thor would be so much of a dead duck in an operational sense that we would want to get rid of it.' On 1st December 1962, Thor #43 was removed from LE40 at RAF Breighton and made safe for the return flight to the US. The final missile left England on 27th September 1963. Some 50 years later many of the sites have been transformed for agricultural or industrial use, including a gravel pit and a pig farm. In summarizing the role of the Thor in defense of the UK, John Boyes considered it a 'political expedient rather than a military requirement'. As SAC's only foray into ballistic missiles based in the UK, it was a little-known footnote amid the many chapters of bombers, tankers, and spyplanes.

Given their complexity and the relative new technology associated with ballistic missiles, Thor sites were susceptible to more than a few mishaps. Fortunately, these did not lead to any explosions, especially once configured with their atomic warheads. *John Boyes collection*

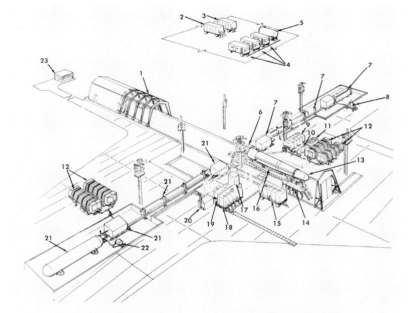

1. PANELIZED PREFABRICATED BUILDING SHU-2/E
2. TRAILER-MOUNTED POWER SWITCHBOARD JEU-2/M
3. TRAILER-MOUNTED LAUNCHING CONTROL GROUP A/M24A-2
4. TRAILER-MOUNTED DIESEL ENGINE GENERATOR SET AF/M32A-12*†
5. DIESEL FUEL STORAGE TANK TMU-5/E*
6. BALLISTIC MISSILE ERECTING-LAUNCHING MOUNT MTU-1A/E
7. FUEL PIPELINE OUTFIT GSU-6/E AND FUEL STORAGE TANK TMU-4/E
8. TRAILER-MOUNTED FUEL FILTER UNIT GSU-7M†
9. TRAILER-MOUNTED HYDRO-PNEUMATIC SYSTEMS CONTROLLER AF/M46A-1
10. HIGH PRESSURE GAS STORAGE TANK TMU-6/E*
11. POWER-DRIVEN RECIPROCATING COMPRESSOR A/M32A-27*†
12. COMPRESSED GAS CYLINDER SEMITRAILER AF/M32A-17 TYPICAL (2 PLACES)*†
13. SM-75 MISSILE*
14. SHORT RANGE AZIMUTH ALIGNMENT ELECTROTHEODOLITE AN/GVQ-3
15. TRAILER-MOUNTED BALLISTIC MISSILE SYSTEM CHECKOUT STATION TTU-92/M*
16. BALLISTIC MISSILE ERECTING-TRANSPORTING BOOM GSU-33/E, AND REAR DOLLY GSU-32/M
17. TRAILER-MOUNTED AIR CONDITIONER AF/M32C-1*
18. TRAILER-MOUNTED MISSILE LAUNCHING COUNTDOWN GROUP A/M24A-1A
19. HYDRAULIC PUMPING UNIT PMU-14/E
20. SKID-MOUNTED POWER SWITCHBOARD JEU-1/E
21. LIQUID OXYGEN PIPELINE OUTFIT GSU-5/E
22. TRAILER-MOUNTED VACUUM PUMP PMU-1/M†
23. LONG RANGE AZIMUTH ALIGNMENT ELECTROTHEODOLITE AN/GVQ-4

*THIS EQUIPMENT LOCATED AT THE LAUNCH EMPLACEMENT AND RIM BUILDING

†INSPECTION REQUIREMENTS ON THIS EQUIPMENT DO NOT APPEAR IN THE INSPECTION REQUIREMENTS MANUAL

Thor Work Area Diagram

Epilogue
It's All About the Bombers

As the sun was setting in the western Louisiana sky on Thursday, 14th March, B-52H 60-0024 accelerated down Runway 33 at Barksdale AFB, took off, and headed northeast toward Canada. Inside, the crew was busy with navigation, reviewing the route and mission plan, and focusing on staying awake for the long flight ahead. In a little under 10 hours they approached the coast of Kaliningrad, which for years was the only truly Soviet territory bordering the Baltic Sea other than the narrowly constrained port at Leningrad. Some 60nm (111km) away from entering the airspace over Kaliningrad, the crew simulated the launch of their nuclear-armed weapons, then turned back toward England to land at RAF Fairford at 1330Z, just in time for lunch.

Although these missions have gone on since the days of Strategic Air Command's B-36s and B-47s, this Air Combat Command sortie took place in 2019, nearly 30 years after the demise of SAC and the collapse of the Soviet Union. Instead, 60-0024's simulated target was in the Russian Federation, successor to the USSR. Just as with the earlier SAC missions, its flight was intended as a clear message to Russian civilian and military leaders that the United States had the ready capability to strike targets that would cripple Russian defenses as well as eliminate

any threat to America or its allies. Irrespective of whether they were hosting bombers assigned to SAC or ACC, bases in the United Kingdom have for decades been essential to the success of these flights and their political messaging. Once again, British domestic and foreign policy was nestled squarely within the American fold, linked inextricably to the vagaries of Russo-American relations. After 30 years, little has changed.

***

SAC's presence in the United Kingdom from 1946 through 1992 was always 'about the bombers,' its ability to strike the Soviet Union and its Warsaw Pact allies in sufficient time to thwart a successful strike against the United States, or failing that, to destroy the ability of the USSR to exist as an industrialized nation in a post-nuclear-holocaust world. Basing B-29s, B-50s, and B-47s in England meant that SAC's strike force could reach Soviet targets and then, in theory, return to refuel and rearm for additional attacks. This capability raised critical questions for British leaders, most importantly who would authorize the expenditure of nuclear weapons from English soil. Moreover, it highlighted the vulnerability of the British public to Soviet pre-emptive and retaliatory strikes against SAC bases. For many Cold War critics in

both America and Britain, there was no security benefit to Britain associated with these bases, only risk. The expense of deploying SAC air-craft to and from England, as well as the fixed costs of each base, added to the complexity of SAC's presence in Blighty. For Congress this was money well spent while for Parliament it was money happily received. For the taxpaying (and eventually war-weary) American and the Briton living amid the din of constant airplane operations and the impact of more than a few crashes, however, SAC bomber operations in the UK were of doubtful economic sense. Finally, with the advent of IRBMs and ICBMs, the stra-tegic and economic value of forward bases in England and elsewhere deteriorated to virtually nil. An IRBM launched from East Germany or even the USSR could destroy REFLEX alert bases well before the specified launch time of the first B-47, let alone the remaining five or eight jets at one-minute intervals. Eventually, even conven-tional bomber operations from the UK, such as those from RAF Fairford during Operation DESERT STORM, were of limited utility given the distances involved in reaching their target areas.

Similarly, SAC's tanker force in the UK evolved from pre-positioned KB-29 and KC-97 tankers dedicated to refueling B-29s, B-50s, and B-47s en route from British bases to their targets in the USSR, to KC-97 tankers intended to refuel B-47s returning from their attacks in the Soviet Union, to KC-135 and KC-10 tankers devoted almost exclusively to theater support of USAFE, RAF, and NATO tactical aircraft and cargo air-craft flying between the US and bases in the Middle East or Southwest Asia.

Locating exactly where atomic- and con-ventionally armed B-29s, B-50s, B-36s, B-47s, B-58s, and B-52s would deliver their weap-ons fell, in part, to SAC's dedicated strategic aerial reconnaissance force operating from English bases. As with SAC's bomber fleet, the presence of these mysterious 'spy flights' that 'needlessly provoked' an 'otherwise friendly' USSR risked a Soviet pre-emptive nuclear strike against British bases, no doubt killing thou-sands of Britons living nearby. The U-2 fiasco in May 1960 and the loss of an RB-47H two months later led to greater, if not decisive, Brit-ish political control over these flights, but not their elimination. Indeed, although the RAF had its own aerial collection capability, intelligence acquired from SAC's RB-50s, RB-47s, RC-135s, U-2s, and SR-71s found its way to British agen-cies, along with Commonwealth nations as part of the Five Eyes intelligence-sharing agreement.

In all of these cases, the United States and

Below: Arguably the RC-135 and the SR-71 were the most significant SAC recce assets operating from the UK. RC-135 variants have departed there on missions for more than 50 years, and the SR-71 (often in collaboration with RC-135s) conducted missions of the highest national priority while captivating Britons with its mystique. *Richard Vandervord (upper), Bob Archer (lower)*

Great Britain developed a satisfactory 'working arrangement' that allowed SAC to achieve its needed measure of latitude in bomber, tanker, and reconnaissance operations while ensuring that Britain retained its sovereignty and control over foreign military and intelligence operations from its native soil. For Strategic Air Command, operations from the United Kingdom were an integral part of its successful evolution from that of a "hollow force' in the late 1940s to what many have argued was the single most powerful military organization in history.

Appendix I
SAC Bases in the UK

One of the most contentious issues in the history of Strategic Air Command's presence in the United Kingdom was the matter of basing. American and British politicians, military officials, and even the public were deeply invested in identifying potential venues, paying for land acquisition, infrastructure repairs and new construction, sharing of ramp space for bilateral operations, air and ground defense of each facility, and cultivating local support and quelling opposition.

Curiously, between the time of the first SAC B-29 visit to the UK in 1946 and the dissolution of SAC in 1992, there were no US Air Force bases in England. Bitburg AB in West Germany

SAC's U-3B 60-6048 was home-based at RAF Northolt in support of Headquarters missions from RAF South Ruislip. It is seen here at RAF Booker, and at Prestwick with the addition of the SAC Milky Way and shield. *Ken Elliott via Steve Bond (upper), Gordon Macadie (lower)*

or Yokota AB in Japan, for example, reflect direct American 'ownership' of US air bases abroad. In the UK, however, US Air Force units – and specifically those from SAC – were tenants at established RAF bases. The challenge was defining 'tenant', as SAC unit commanders often were responsible for operations while RAF officers were responsible for managing the base itself. Moreover, until the establishment of the 17th RW at RAF Alconbury in October 1982, there were no SAC combat wings *assigned* to the UK, as SAC operations there were under the aegis of air base groups (ABG), all reporting to a single SAC authority in Europe such as the 7th AD at RAF South Ruislip or RAF High Wycombe. Most of the ABGs had an assigned 'hack' aircraft such as C-47s, a Cessna U-3B 'Blue Canoe', and even a few B-47s for the unit staff to travel to meetings or carry parts and personnel to repair aircraft that diverted elsewhere. These bounced around as units were inactivated and reactivated, but (except in the most extreme cases) lacked an operational mission.

Tracing the history of SAC operational venues in the UK is an exercise of near-Byzantine complexity. There were primary peace-time bases, emergency war-time bases, post-strike recovery bases, and even bases that existed on paper but were never used, all of which changed their mission tasking on multiple occasions. Some SAC bases hosted just bombers, others just tankers or fighters. By the end of SAC's tenure in England, RAF Mildenhall, for example, had become synonymous with the European Tanker Task Force and US strategic aerial reconnaissance operations involving SR-71s and RC-135s. During portions of SAC's early years in the UK, however, RAF Mildenhall was considered just a 'second tier' post-strike base.

Evolution

The first SAC bombers to visit the UK arrived on 9th June 1947, and included nine B-29s from the 340th BS, 97th BG, which was then

SAC IN THE UK COMMANDERS

From	To	Unit	Commander	Location	Comments
2 Jul 48	15 Jul 48	B-29 Task Force Command	n/a	RAF Marham	
16 Jul 48	22 Aug 48	3rd Air Division (Provisional)	Col Stanley T Wray	RAF Marham	Retired as a MGEN
23 Aug 48	7 Sep 48	3rd Air Division	MGEN Leon W Johnson	RAF Marham	Medal of Honor for Ploesti Raid, retired as GEN
8 Sep 48	14 May 49	3rd Air Division	MGEN Leon W Johnson	RAF Bushy Park	
15 May 49	1 May 51	3rd Air Division	MGEN Leon W Johnson	RAF South Ruislip	
20 Mar 51	23 Mar 51	7th Air Division	BGEN Paul T Cullen	RAF South Ruislip	Died in C-124 crash prior to arrival
26 Apr 51	23 May 51	7th Air Division	MGEN Archie J Old	RAF South Ruislip	Later SAC/DO, 15th AF/CC, retired as LGEN
24 May 51	13 Mar 53	7th Air Division	MGEN John P McConnell	RAF South Ruislip	Later VCINCSAC, AF CoS, retired as GEN
14 Mar 53	19 Jul 54	7th Air Division	BGEN James C Selser	RAF South Ruislip	Briefly acting 8th AF/CC
20 Jul 54	9 Jul 55	7th Air Division	BGEN Thomas C Musgrave	RAF South Ruislip	
10 Jul 55	24 Feb 57	7th Air Division	BGEN James H Walsh	RAF South Ruislip	Later SAC CoS, retired as MGEN
25 Feb 57	30 Jun 58	7th Air Division	MGEN William H Blanchard	RAF South Ruislip	Later SAC/DO, AF VCoS, retired as GEN
1 Jul 58	18 Jan 60	7th Air Division	MGEN William H Blanchard	RAF High Wycombe	
19 Jan 60	31 Jul 61	7th Air Division	MGEN Charles B Westover	RAF High Wycombe	Later TAC/CV, ADC/CV, retired as LGEN
1 Aug 61	17 Sep 62	7th Air Division	LGEN Edwin R Broadhurst	RAF High Wycombe	
18 Sep 62	27 Jul 64	7th Air Division	MGEN Charles M Eisenhart	RAF High Wycombe	Later SAC CoS, died in a KC-135 crash
28 Jul 64	8 Oct 64	7th Air Division	MGEN Delmar E Wilson	RAF High Wycombe	
9 Oct 64 inactivated	30 Jun 65	7th Air Division	Col Ervin Wursten	RAF High Wycombe	
1 Jul 78	16 Jul 78	7th Air Division	Col Doyle F Reynolds	Ramstein AB, FRG	
17 Jul 78	25 Jun 79	7th Air Division	BGEN Jerome R Barnes, Jr	Ramstein AB, FRG	
26 Jun 79	12 Feb 81	7th Air Division	BGEN Robert D Beckel	Ramstein AB, FRG	Retired as LGEN
13 Feb 81	30 Jan 83	7th Air Division	BGEN John J Doran, Jr	Ramstein AB, FRG	Later SAC DCS/LG, retired as MGEN
31 Jan 83	20 Jun 86	7th Air Division	BGEN Wayne W Lambert	Ramstein AB, FRG	
21 Jun 86	28 Feb 90	7th Air Division	BGEN Loring R Astorino	Ramstein AB, FRG	
1 Mar 90 inactivated	1 Feb 92	7th Air Division	BGEN Kenneth L Hagemann	Ramstein AB, FRG	Later Director DNA, retired as MGEN

ADC = Air Defense Command; CC = Commander; CV = Vice Commander; CoS = Chief of Staff; DCS/LG = Deputy Chief of Staff for Logistics; DNA = Defense Nuclear Agency; DO = Deputy Commander for Operations; n/a = not available

deployed to Giebelstadt AB in West Germany. Just *where* these B-29s would be based was a subject of considerable anxiety, as the RAF and SAC worried that there were 'only five B-29 compatible fields' in England. RAF Waddington, RAF Wyton, and even Heathrow Airport were considered and rejected, with the airplanes finally arriving at RAF Marham for a 'week-long stay.'

The first formal SAC deployments to the UK were to RAF Scampton, RAF Marham, and RAF Waddington during July 1948 as part of Operation FERRYBOAT, SAC's response to the Berlin Crisis. The 3rd AD (USAFE) command element was located at RAF Marham. All of these bases were less-than-optimal in terms of their ability to support B-29 operations, but there were few alternatives. RAF Lakenheath was added as the fourth base.

Concerned that future deployments required more suitable bases, SAC requested the use of four existing UK bases for wartime use beginning July 1949. These were to be located in Oxfordshire where they would benefit from British fighter protection from pre-emptive attack. Runways had to be at least 9,000ft (2,743m)

long and 200ft (61m) wide, although SAC preferred a width of 300ft (91m), and capable of accommodating 45 B-29s on paved hardstands. The RAF offered RAF Brize Norton, RAF Upper Heyford, and RAF Fairford, plus an 'unnamed'

SAC COMMANDERS

From	To	Name	Title
21 Mar 46	15 Oct 48	GEN George C Kenney	Commanding General, SAC
18 Oct 48	28 Oct 51	LGEN Curtis E LeMay	Commanding General, SAC
29 Oct 51	Jun 53	GEN Curtis E LeMay	Commanding General, SAC
Jun 53	31 Mar 55	GEN Curtis E LeMay	Commander, SAC
1 Apr 55	30 Jun 57	GEN Curtis E LeMay	Commander-in-Chief, SAC
1 Jul 57	30 Nov 64	GEN Thomas S Power	Commander-in-Chief, SAC
1 Dec 64	31 Jan 67	GEN John D Ryan	Commander-in-Chief, SAC
1 Feb 67	31 Jul 68	GEN Joseph J Nazzaro	Commander-in-Chief, SAC
1 Aug 68	30 Apr 72	GEN Bruce K Holloway	Commander-in-Chief, SAC
1 May 72	31 Jul 74	GEN John C Meyer	Commander-in-Chief, SAC
1 Aug 74	31 Jul 77	GEN Russell E Dougherty	Commander-in-Chief, SAC
1 Aug 77	31 Jul 81	GEN Richard H Ellis	Commander-in-Chief, SAC
1 Aug 81	31 Jul 85	GEN Bennie L Davis	Commander-in-Chief, SAC
1 Aug 85	22 Jun 86	GEN Larry D Welch	Commander-in-Chief, SAC
22 Jun 86	24 Jan 91	GEN John T Chain	Commander-in-Chief, SAC
25 Jan 91	1 Jun 92	GEN G Lee Butler	Commander-in-Chief, SAC

CINCSAC = Commander-in-Chief, SAC

Finding suitable B-29 bases in the UK was problematic, as runways were too short and other US Air Force assets, including SAC and USAFE fighters, competed for basing rights. *Terry Panopalis collection*

location, with the sly intent of having the US paying to upgrade them for joint use. Upon realizing that SAC intended these bases to be fully occupied in peacetime – not just wartime – by its bombers, the RAF demurred and instead offered RAF Marham, RAF Sculthorpe, and RAF Lakenheath in exchange for RAF Upper Heyford and RAF Brize Norton. In addition, RAF Greenham Common was identified as the fourth projected SAC base.

Locating SAC's B-29s in the UK during peacetime was especially problematic for the RAF, as it needed the same bases to house its soon-to-be-delivered Washington B.1 (B-29) bombers. Consequently, SAC swapped RAF Marham and RAF Sculthorpe for RAF Upper Heyford and RAF Brize Norton, later yielding RAF Lakenheath for RAF Fairford, with the fourth base (still identified as RAF Greenham Common) for wartime use only. In any event, these exchanges existed only on paper, with construction yet to begin on any of the SAC-dedicated bases. By the end

of 1949, SAC was using only RAF Marham, RAF Lakenheath, and RAF Sculthorpe.

In January 1950, SAC agreed to return RAF Marham to the RAF, and would not increase its bomber force in the UK until suitable arrangements were made to house both SAC and RAF B-29s. Britain committed funds to pay for extending the runways and building 45 hardstands at both RAF Brize Norton and RAF Upper Heyford, completing these two bases before working on any others. This changed as RAF Fairford became the second to upgrade with RAF Brize Norton third. Following the outbreak of the war in Korea, SAC bombers began using 'any available base', including RAF Oakington, RAF Burtonwood, and RAF Valley.

With the establishment of the 7th AD in March 1951, SAC was using only RAF Sculthorpe, RAF Lakenheath, and RAF Mildenhall for operations until the four 'Midland Bases' of RAF Brize Norton, RAF Fairford, RAF Upper Heyford, and RAF Greenham Common were ready. Other RAF bases, notably RAF Wyton, RAF Marham, RAF Bassingbourn, RAF Lindholme, and RAF Waddington (replaced by RAF Scampton, and later by RAF Full Sutton) were available as back-up venues, and were known as the FAMOUS bases. This code name changed to BLANKET, and four of the five bases returned to the RAF between January 1952 through November 1954. Three other RAF bases – RAF Swinderby, RAF Oakington, and RAF Lindholme – provided ad hoc coverage pending completion of construction at the Midland bases. Fortunately, SAC deployments to the FAMOUS and BLANKET bases, especially in the early years, produced few conflicts. In an effort to accelerate access to the Midland bases, SAC evaluated RAF Chelveston, RAF Gaydon, RAF Harrington, and RAF Polebrook as alternatives to RAF Greenham Common, but no action was taken.

The arrival of RAF Washingtons complicated the availability of British bases for SAC B-29s, and led to tensions between the two governments. It also resulted in the development of the four 'Midland Bases,' which proved fortuitous. *Author's collection*

Ready at Last

RAF Upper Heyford, RAF Fairford, and RAF Brize Norton all became operational in 1952, but construction at RAF Greenham Common, known by the 7th AD program name GALLOPER, had made little progress. SAC planned to deploy its bombers to these three bases while rotating its tankers and reconnaissance assets to RAF Lakenheath and RAF Mildenhall. Plans to expand the EWP by 1953 resulted in the possible addition of nine RAF bases to pre-strike locations, including RAF Blackbushe, RAF Bruntingthorpe, RAF Chelveston, RAF Stansted, RAF Desborough, RAF Gransden Lodge, RAF Chipping Norton, RAF Podington, and RAF Lasham. B-36 post-strike bases were considered at RAF Burtonwood, RAF Boscombe Down, and RAF St Mawgan. Few of these were actually included in the EWP.

Runways at all SAC bases remained a considerable problem, especially with the planned arrival of the B-47 beginning in 1953. SAC insisted in May 1952 that all B-47 bases have runways that were 11,300ft (3,444m) long to allow operations at high temperatures during the English summers. In the face of strong local opposition to acquiring additional land adjacent to these bases, SAC acquiesced to 10,000ft lengths with the understanding that peacetime B-47 operations would cease when temperatures peaked. At the time, only RAF Fairford and RAF Greenham Common had 10,000ft runways, although RAF Bruntingthorpe and RAF Chelveston could be so configured. RAF Brize Norton's runway was limited to 10,000ft but without any overruns, and RAF Upper Heyford was similarly constrained at 9,600ft (2,926m), also without overruns. The runways at RAF Sculthorpe, RAF Lakenheath, and RAF Mildenhall would not be extended beyond 9,000ft.

During the initial B-47 deployment to RAF Greenham Common, the new runway failed in March 1954, forcing the unit's hasty relocation to RAF Lakenheath, and RAF Greenham Common was removed from the EWP until October 1956. At the same time, RAF Mildenhall was closed for runway repairs through June 1956. Construction at other planned bomber bases was making slow progress, with little hope of early completion.

Changes to the EWP in 1955 resulted in the shift from pre-strike launches from British bases to post-strike reconstitution, resulting in a three-tier classification of Main Bases, Post-Strike Bases, and EWP-Only Bases. The main bases included RAF Brize Norton, RAF Greenham Common, RAF Upper Heyford, and RAF Lakenheath for bombers, and RAF Sturgate for fighters. Second-tier post-strike bases included RAF Fairford, RAF Mildenhall, and RAF Chelveston. War-only bases were RAF East Kirkby, RAF Homewood Park, RAF Lindholme, and RAF Full Sutton. Throughout the following year, many of these bases were dropped temporarily from the EWP due to construction or runway repairs, accounting for the shift of aircraft to other bases. Overall, these improvements led to an increase in EWP capacity at UK bases from 500 aircraft in 1955 to 650 in 1956. By 1957, SAC operations in England reached 'full maturity', with four main bomber, five post-strike, and a handful of EWP-only bases capable of fulfilling their assigned wartime roles.

REFLEX and RED RICHARD

With the 1958 advent of SAC's ground alert program, the need for extensive basing capacity in the UK decreased. Consequently, RAF East Kirkby, RAF Sturgate, and RAF Stansted were removed from 7th AD operations. The seven

Despite ongoing improvement efforts, when B-47s arrived at RAF Fairford in 1953 they found conditions were barely suitable and put the delicate airplanes at risk of damage from the rough runways. *Harold Siegfried*

B-47s sat REFLEX alert at a variety of bases throughout the UK, but the French decision to evict American nuclear-capable aircraft forced the consolidation of the WILDCAT bases.
Brian Baldwin

REFLEX alert bases (code named WILDCAT) were RAF Fairford, RAF Greenham Common, RAF Brize Norton, RAF Mildenhall, RAF Chelveston, RAF Bruntingthorpe, and RAF Upper Heyford. It appeared that SAC could at last use its many peacetime bases for small numbers of alert bombers while maintaining a robust post-strike capability at British bases, pleasing both American taxpayers and English residents.

Events in France, however, altered this equation. President Charles de Gaulle insisted on the departure of all nuclear-capable American aircraft from France in July 1959. The relocation of these units to West Germany and England under Operation RED RICHARD necessitated the transfer of four UK bases from SAC to USAFE. On 1st September 1959, RAF Bruntingthorpe, RAF Chelveston, RAF Lakenheath, and RAF Mildenhall were assigned to USAFE, and their REFLEX mission was terminated.

The planned elimination of REFLEX as part of the American effort to reduce its expensive overseas commitments resulted in the closure of RAF Fairford and RAF Greenham Common in 1964. The following year, RAF Brize Norton was transferred to the RAF and USAFE acquired RAF Upper Heyford, although SAC reconnaissance operations and tanker support continued there.

SAC's formal presence in the UK resumed with the reactivation of the 7th AD on 1st July 1978 at Ramstein AB, West Germany, and the transfer of the 306th SW transferred to RAF Mildenhall. As with prior SAC command elements, the 306th SW had no assigned combat aircraft, and oversaw tanker operations with the ETTF as well as reconnaissance missions. On 1st October 1982, RAF Alconbury became the only British base with an assigned operational SAC flying unit when the 95th RS, 17th RW was established there while flying TR-1s. The 17th RW was inactivated on 30th June 1991, and the 95th RS was reassigned without relocating to the 9th SRW at Beale AFB. The unit remained active at RAF Alconbury after the disestablishment of SAC, inactivating on 15th September 1993.

Primary SAC Aircraft Bases in the United Kingdom

RAF Alconbury I Huntingdon, Cambridgeshire
RAF Bassingbourn I Royston, Hertfordshire
RAF Boscombe Down I Amesbury, Wiltshire
RAF Brize Norton I Carterton, Oxfordshire
RAF Bruntingthorpe I Leicester, Leicestershire
RAF Burtonwood I Warrington, Lancashire
RAF Chelveston I Chelveston, Northamptonshire
RAF East Kirkby I East Kirkby, Lincolnshire
RAF Fairford I Fairford, Gloucestershire
RAF Greenham Common I Greenham, Berkshire
RAF Lakenheath I Lakenheath, Suffolk
RAF Manston I Kent
RAF Marham I Marham, Norfolk
RAF Mildenhall I Mildenhall, Suffolk
RAF Oakington I Oakington, Cambridgeshire
RAF Scampton I Scampton, Lincolnshire
RAF Sculthorpe I Fakenham, Norfolk
RAF Sturgate I Lincoln, Lincolnshire
RAF Upper Heyford I Upper Heyford, Oxfordshire
RAF Valley I Anglesey, Wales
RAF Waddington I Lincoln, Lincolnshire
RAF Wyton I St Ives, Cambridgeshire

TR-1s from the 17th RW at RAF Alconbury were the only SAC aircraft to be home-based in the UK. This followed a protracted turf war over operational ownership of the TR-1s, with USAFE providing mission tasking for exclusively European requirements.
Richard Vandervord

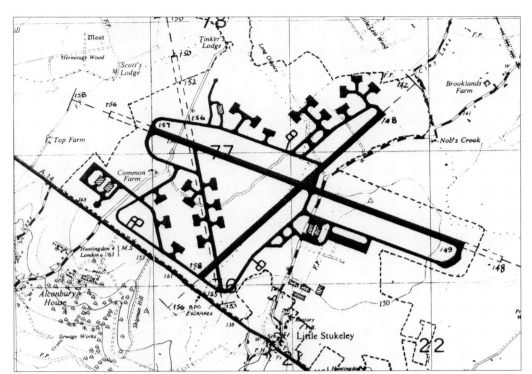

Site plan of RAF
Alconbury.

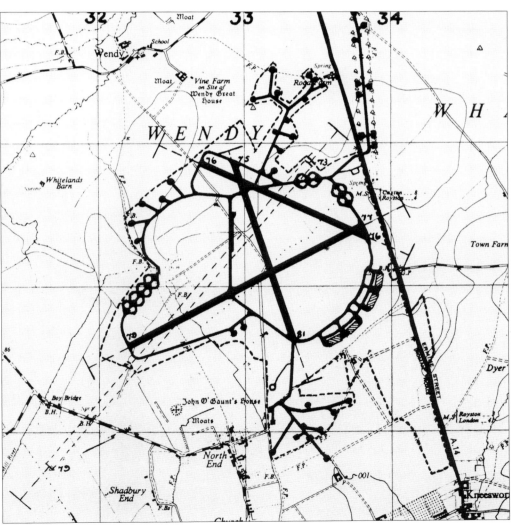

Site plan of RAF
Bassingbourn, one
of the five FAMOUS/
BLANKET bases.

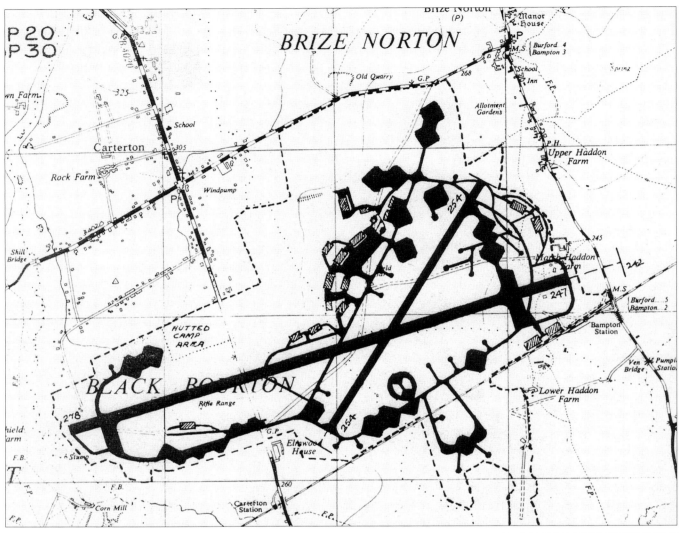

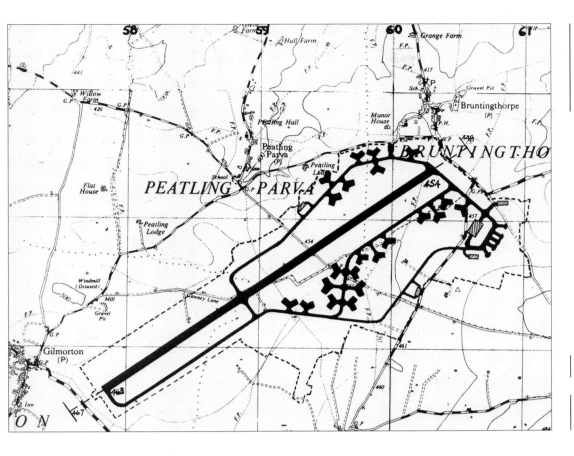

Site plan of RAF Bruntingthorpe, which reverted to USAFE under the RED RICHARD relocation from France.

Below: Site plan of RAF Burtonwood.

Opposite, top: Site plan of RAF Brize Norton.

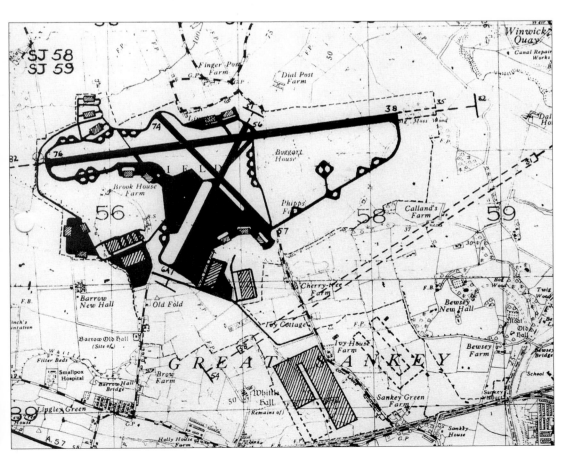

Photos opposite: Multiple B-47s were assigned over time as 'hacks' to Brize Norton. Aside from shuttling personnel, they enabled crews to maintain proficiency and training requirements. These included RB-47E 52-0791 and B-47Es 52-0496 and 52-0581. Note that the latter two have their guns and drop tanks removed. During the Cuban Missile Crisis, it was temporarily re-configured for its EWP mission, crewed by the 307th BW. *Mike Hooks via Nick Stroud/TAH (top). Brian Baldwin (left), and via Rod Simpson (right)*

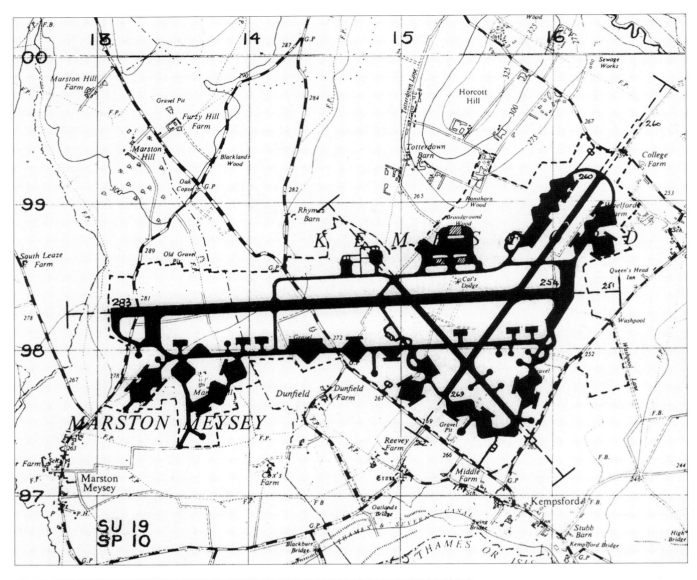

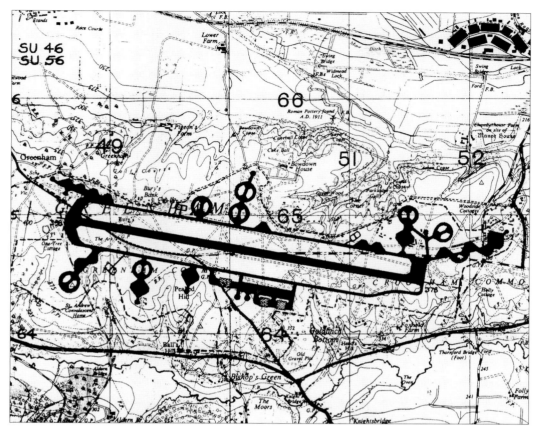

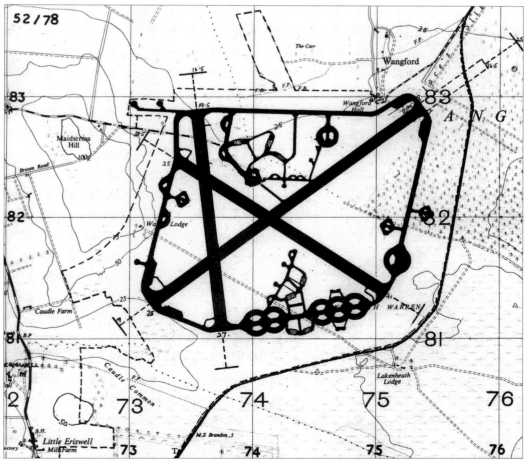

Left: Site plan of RAF Greenham Common.

Below: Site plan of RAF Lakenheath. From B-29s to F-111s, RAF Lakenheath's longevity spanned the entire history of SAC operations in the UK.

Opposite, top: Site plan of RAF Fairford.

Opposite, bottom: C-54G 45-0546 was based only briefly at RAF Fairford from April through August 1961, after which it was relocated to RAF Upper Heyford when seen here on 5th June 1963 at RAF Greenham Common. These transports provided free transport for REFLEX personnel throughout Europe – Copenhagen, Paris, Rome – for R&R.
Brian Baldwin

Site plan of
RAF Marham.
SAC's first UK visits
were to this base,
complicating RAF
plans to base its
own Washingtons
there.

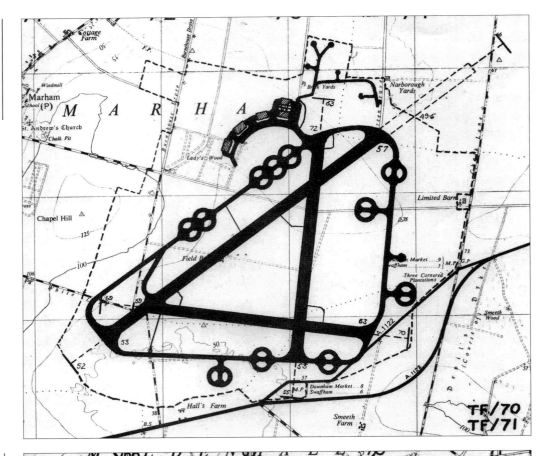

Site plan of
RAF Mildenhall.
The many parking
slots around the
perimeter allowed
ample space for
ETTF and Det 1
RC-135s.

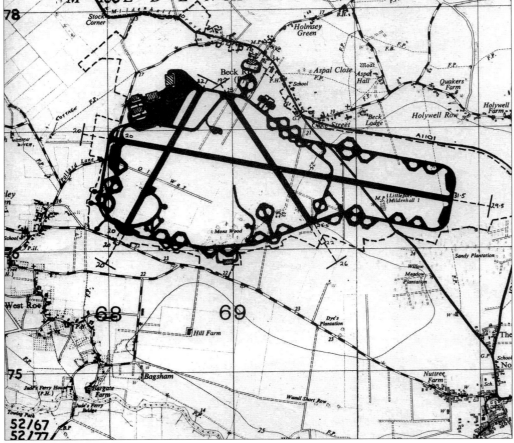

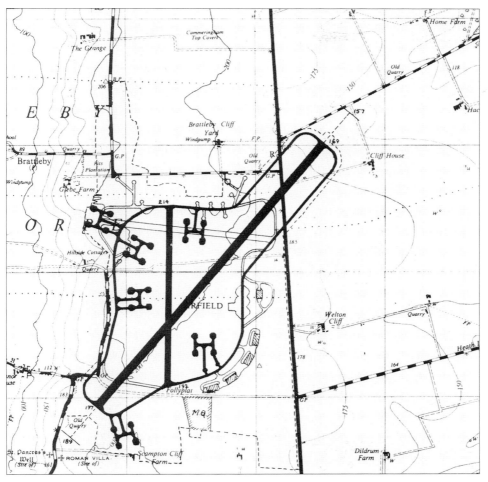

Site plan of
RAF Scampton.
The short runway
there severely
limited B-29
operations, and
were barely
tolerable for B-50
departures.

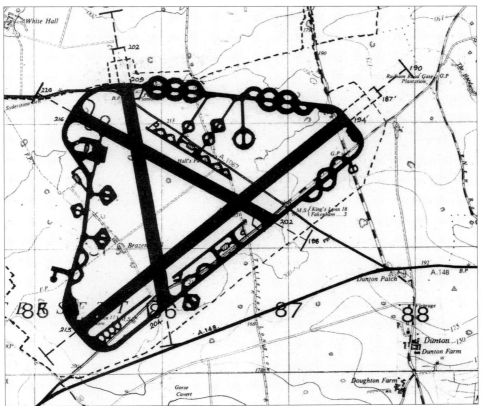

Site plan of
RAF Sculthorpe.
RAF RB-45s on
loan from SAC
departed here in
1952 for the first
JU JITSU overflight
of the Soviet
Union.

Site plan of RAF Upper Heyford. One of the four 'Midland Bases', operations at RAF Upper Heyford covered the complete spectrum of SAC missions: bombers, REFLEX, tankers, and reconnaissance.

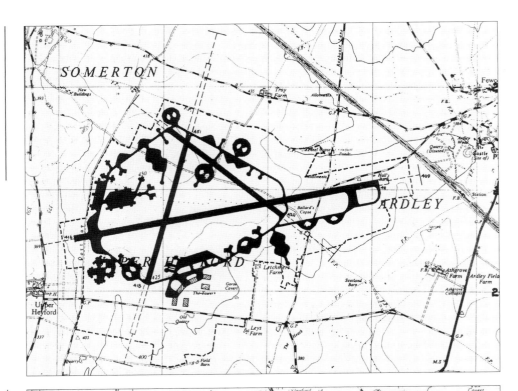

Site plan of RAF Waddinton. Lengthening the runways to accommodate SAC and RAF aircraft has been a perennial challenge for RAF bases.

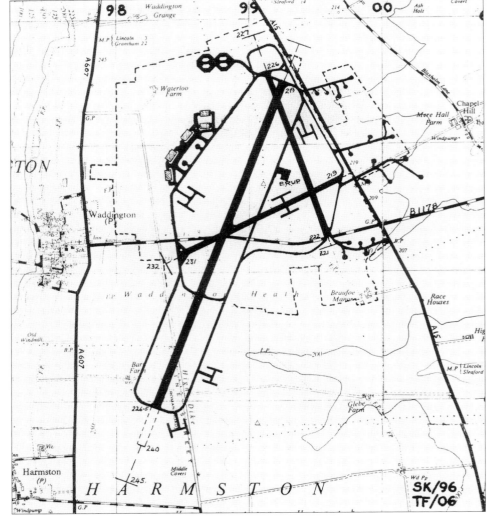

SAC AIRCRAFT ASSIGNED TO RAF BRIZE NORTON

Type	Serial	From	To	Comments
C-47A	42-24214	15 Dec 52	10 Jun 53	to RAF Fairford
C-47D	44-76600	23 Mar 53	27 Jun 53	to RAF Upper Heyford
C-47A	43-15352	9 Apr 53	9 Dec 55	to RAF Greenham Common
C-47D	43-49406	25 Sep 53	20 Jan 54	to RAF Sturgate
		25 Jul 58	8 Nov 58	to Torrejón AB
		18 Nov 58	1 Jan 59	to RAF Lakenheath
C-47A	43-15645	Dec 53	23 Mar 54	to RAF Fairford
C-47A	43-30678	4 Apr 54	19 Apr 54	to RAF Greenham Common
C-47D	43-48883	12 Apr 54	18 Jan 55	to RAF Mildenhall
C-47A	43-15943	14 Aug 54	11 Sep 54	to RAF Upper Heyford
		24 Nov 54	22 May 55	to RAF Sturgate
		2 Jun 55	24 Mar 61	to 305th CSG, Bunker Hill AFB
C-47A	43-16048	3 Oct 55	5 Aug 57	to Chateauroux AB
C-47D	43-16379	1 Nov 56	7 Feb 57	to RAF Burtonwood
C-47A	42-24172	29 Dec 56	6 Nov 58	to 92nd ABG, Fairchild AFB
C-47D	43-48318	4 Oct 57	1 Jul 58	to 7350th ABS Templehof
RB-47E	52-0760	11 Dec 57	7 Jun 61	to 2704th AFSDG, Davis-Monthan AFB
RB-47E	52-0791	11 Dec 57	27 Jun 61	to 2704th AFSDG, Davis-Monthan AFB
C-54G	45-0560	29 Sep 59	13 Jul 61	to RAF Upper Heyford
RB-47E	52-0777	19 Sep 60	12 Apr 62	to 2704th AFSDG, Davis-Monthan AFB
C-54D	42-72627	26 Mar 61	23 Jun 61	to OGMA Lisbon, then RAF Brize Norton
B-47E	52-0496	9 Jun 61	4 Jul 64	to 2704th AFSDG, Davis-Monthan AFB
B-47E	52-0581	10 Aug 61	22 Jul 64	to 2704th AFSDG, Davis-Monthan AFB
B-47E	52-0448	20 Apr 62	19 Mar 65	to 509th BW, Pease AFB
B-47E	52-0517	3 Apr 63	29 Jul 64	to 2704th AFSDG, Davis-Monthan AFB
B-47E	52-0518	4 Aug 64	4 Jan 65	to 2704th AFSDG, Davis-Monthan AFB
B-47E	53-1897	10 Jan 65	18 Mar 65	to 2704th AFSDG, Davis-Monthan AFB

SAC AIRCRAFT ASSIGNED TO RAF BRUNTINGTHORPE

Type	Serial	From	To	Comments
C-47D	43-30678	1 Aug 57	15 Jul 58	to 7310th SS at Templehof
		2 Feb 58	31 Aug 59	to 10th TRW at RAF Alconbury
C-47D	43-48673	8 Jun 59	31 Aug 59	to 10th TRW at RAF Alconbury

SAC AIRCRAFT ASSIGNED TO RAF CHELVESTON

Type	Serial	From	To	Comments
C-47A	43-15619	2 May 56	28 Sep 59	to RAF Mildenhall
C-47A	43-15352	29 Jan 57	12 Feb 57	to RAF Greenham Common
C-54D	42-72488	15 Apr 59	2 Sep 59	to RAF Upper Heyford

SAC AIRCRAFT ASSIGNED TO RAF EAST KIRKBY

Type	Serial	From	To	Comments
C-47D	43-49784	15 Oct 54	9 Nov 55	to RAF Sturgate
C-47A	42-24214	15 Apr 55	16 Jun 55	to RAF Lakenheath
C-47D	43-49406	29 Aug 57	25 Jul 58	to RAF Brize Norton

SAC AIRCRAFT ASSIGNED TO RAF FAIRFORD

Type	Serial	From	To	Comments
C-47A	43-15619	30 Aug 52	19 Aug 55	to RAF Upper Heyford
C-47A	43-15352	3 Feb 53	4 Mar 53	to RAF Mildenhall
C-47A	42-24214	10 Jun 53	28 Sep 53	to RAF Mildenhall
C-47A	43-15645	23 Mar 54	Oct 55	to RAF Greenham Common
C-47A	43-15289	18 Aug 54	1 Apr 55	to RAF Upper Heyford
		27 Jun 55	20 Apr 61	to MAP
C-54G	45-0505	15 Jul 57	1 Aug 61	to RAF Upper Heyford
C-47D	43-49406	30 Sep 59	20 Apr 61	sold to commercial buyer
C-54G	45-0546	20 Apr 61	1 Aug 61	to RAF Upper Heyford

MAP = Military Assistance Program

SAC AIRCRAFT ASSIGNED TO RAF GREENHAM COMMON

Type	Serial	From	To	Comments
C-47D	43-48318	7 Sep 53	4 Oct 57	to RAF Brize Norton
		19 Sep 58	20 Apr 61	to MAP
C-47A	43-30678	6 Dec 53	4 Apr 54	to RAF Brize Norton
		19 Apr 54	10 Jul 54	to RAF Sturgate
C-47A	43-15645	Oct 55	20 Apr 61	to MAP
C-47A	43-15352	9 Dec 55	29 Jan 57	to RAF Chelveston
		12 Feb 57	8 Sep 58	to RAF Lakenheath
C-54G	45-0555	7 Jul 58	1 Aug 61	to RAF Upper Heyford
C-47A	42-24214	29 Sep 59	25 Apr 60	to RAF Upper Heyford
C-47D	43-48883	19 Sep 59	15 Apr 60	to RAF Upper Heyford

MAP = Military Assistance Program

SAC AIRCRAFT ASSIGNED TO RAF LAKENHEATH

Type	Serial	From	To	Comments
C-47D	43-48803	16 May 51	10 Jul 53	collided with RNoAF F-84 at Sola AB, Norway
C-47A	43-15619	26 Jun 52	30 Aug 52	to RAF Fairford
C-47D	44-76600	14 Apr 52	7 May 52	to RAF Sculthorpe
C-47D	43-48318	14 Jul 52	7 Sep 53	to RAF Greenham Common
C-119C	49-0191	15 Apr 55	6 Feb 58	to 2578th RFCCN Ellington
C-47A	42-24172	15 Apr 55	29 Dec 56	to RAF Brize Norton
C-47A	42-24214	16 Jun 55	16 Feb 58	to Torrejón AB
		1 Mar 58	29 Sep 59	to RAF Greenham Common
T-33A	53-4961	10 May 56	23 Jul 56	to Wiesbaden AB
T-33A	53-4962	10 May 56	23 Jul 56	to Wiesbaden AB
C-47D	43-48883	11 Sep 56	6 Oct 56	loaned from RAF Upper Heyford
		29 Jan 58	29 Sep 59	to RAF Greenham Common
C-54G	45-0560	13 Jun 58	29 Sep 59	to RAF Brize Norton
C-47A	43-15352	8 Sep 58	30 Sep 59	to RAF Upper Heyford
C-47D	43-49406	1 Jan 59	30 Sep 59	to RAF Fairford
C-47D	43-49784	16 May 56	20 Sep 56	to RAF Mildenhall
		20 Nov 56	16 May 57	to RAF Mildenhall
		19 Jan 59	27 Mar 59	to Torrejón AB
		1 Apr 59	1 Sep 59	to RAF Mildenhall
C-47D	44-76600	8 Jun 59	30 Sep 59	to 48th TFW at Chaumont

SAC AIRCRAFT ASSIGNED TO RAF MANSTON

Type	Serial	From	To	Comments
C-47D	43-49784	1 Mar 51	20 Jul 51	to 12th FEW, RAF Manston
		28 Jul 51	11 Dec 51	to RAF Upper Heyford
		15 Jul 52	15 Oct 54	to RAF East Kirkby
C-47A	42-100912	16 May 51	5 May 52	destroyed at RAF Burtonwood by USN P2V
C-47D	43-48318	28 Jul 51	14 Mar 52	to RAF Upper Heyford

SAC AIRCRAFT ASSIGNED TO RAF MILDENHALL

Type	Serial	From	To	Comments
C-47A	42-24172	15 May 51	15 Apr 55	to RAF Lakenheath
C-47A	42-24214	15 May 51	7 Feb 52	to RAF Sculthorpe
		10 Oct 52	31 Oct 52	to RAF Upper Heyford
		28 Sep 53	15 Apr 55	to RAF East Kirkby
C-47A	43-15352	1 Jul 51	3 Feb 53	to RAF Fairford
		4 Mar 53	9 Apr 53	to RAF Brize Norton
C-47D	43-49406	1 Jul 51	3 Jun 52	to RAF Upper Heyford
C-54D	42-72721	22 Jan 52	1 Mar 55	fire damage at RAF Northolt and scrapped
C-47A	43-48096	2 Jun 52	29 Aug 52	to RAF Upper Heyford
KC-97E	51-0199	9 Jun 53	14 Jul 54	7th AD support, to Nouasseur AB
KC-97E	51-0205	9 Jun 53	19 May 54	7th AD support, to Nouasseur AB
VC-47A	43-16121	16 Jun 53	1 Feb 55	to RAF Upper Heyford
C-47A	43-30678	4 Apr 54	19 Apr 54	to RAF Greenham Common
		17 Apr 57	1 May 57	to RAF Upper Heyford
C-119C	49-0191	29 Jul 54	15 Apr 55	to RAF Lakenheath
KC-97F	51-0261	29 Sep 54	9 Nov 54	7th AD support, to 26th SRW
C-47D	43-48883	18 Jan 55	1 Feb 55	to RAF Upper Heyford
C-47D	43-49784	20 Sep 56	20 Nov 56	to RAF Lakenheath
		16 May 57	25 Nov 58	to 7350th SS at Templehof
		1 Sep 59		remained with 7513th ABG under USAFE
C-47A	43-15619	28 Sep 59		remained with 7513th ABG under USAFE
C-47A	43-15352	8 Sep 58	30 Sep 59	to RAF Upper Heyford

SAC AIRCRAFT ASSIGNED TO RAF SCULTHORPE

Type	Serial	From	To	Comments
C-47A	42-23356	16 May 51	5 Nov 51	to RAF Burtonwood
C-47D	44-76600	18 May 51	14 Apr 52	to RAF Lakenheath
		7 May 52	10 Jul 52	to RAF Upper Heyford
C-47A	42-24214	7 Feb 52	3 Jun 52	to RAF Upper Heyford

SAC AIRCRAFT ASSIGNED TO RAF STURGATE

Type	Serial	From	To	Comments
C-47D	43-49406	20 Jan 54	29 Aug 57	to RAF East Kirkby
C-47A	43-30678	10 Jul 54	17 Apr 57	to RAF Mildenhall
C-47A	43-15943	22 May 55	2 Jun 55	to RAF Brize Norton
C-47D	43-49784	9 Nov 55	16 May 56	to RAF Lakenheath

SAC AIRCRAFT ASSIGNED TO RAF UPPER HEYFORD

Type	Serial	From	To	Comments
C-47D	43-49784	11 Dec 51	15 Jul 52	to RAF Manston
C-47D	43-48318	14 Mar 52	14 Jul 52	to RAF Lakenheath
C-47A	42-24214	3 Jun 52	10 Oct 52	to RAF Mildenhall
		31 Oct 52	15 Dec 52	to RAF Brize Norton
		25 Apr 60	20 Apr 61	to MAP
C-47D	43-49406	3 Jun 52	25 Sep 53	to RAF Brize Norton
TB-17G	44-8891	29 Jun 52	31 Aug 53	to Air Materiel Command
C-47D	44-76600	10 Jul 52	23 Mar 53	to RAF Brize Norton
		27 Jun 53	24 Nov 54	multiple SAC bases; to RAF Burtonwood
		5 Apr 55	29 Jun 58	to Torrejón AB
C-47A	43-48096	29 Aug 52	21 Mar 61	to 305th CSG, Bunker Hill AFB
C-47D	43-48883	22 Dec 53	12 Apr 54	to RAF Brize Norton
		1 Feb 55	11 Sep 56	to RAF Lakenheath
		6 Oct 56	29 Jan 58	to RAF Lakenheath
		15 Apr 60	20 Apr 61	to MAP
C-47A	43-15943	11 Sep 54	24 Nov 54	to RAF Brize Norton
KC-97F	51-0261	11 Sep 54	29 Sep 54	to RAF Mildenhall
VC-47A	43-16121	1 Feb 55	4 Jun 56	to RAF Northolt
		1 Apr 60	20 Apr 61	to MAP
C-47A	43-15289	1 Apr 55	27 Jun 55	to RAF Fairford
C-47A	43-15619	19 Aug 55	2 May 56	to RAF Chelveston
C-54D	42-72489	9 Dec 55	3 Jan 56	to RAF Northolt
		5 May 60	3 Jul 65	to 499th AREFW, Westover AFB
C-47A	43-30678	1 May 57	1 Aug 57	to RAF Bruntingthorpe
C-54E	44-9054	29 Oct 57	1 Sep 58	to RAF Northolt
		2 Sep 60	12 May 61	damaged, SOC 18 Jul 61
C-54G	45-0487	12 Jun 58	14 Jan 65	to 2nd BW, Barksdale AFB
C-54D	42-72488	2 Sep 59	22 Feb 65	to 389th SMW, F E Warren AFB
C-47A	43-15352	30 Sep 59	20 Apr 61	to MAP
C-47A	42-100531	1 Apr 60	21 Aug 60	to 801st CSG, Lockbourne AFB
C-47A	43-48145	11 Apr 60	21 Apr 61	to 303rd CSG, Davis-Monthan AFB
C-47D	43-49207	12 May 60	20 Apr 61	to MAP
C-47D	44-76425	3 Jun 60	21 Aug 60	4081st CSG, Harmon AFB
C-54D	42-72529	28 Mar 61	1 Aug 63	to 2704th ASDGP, Davis-Monthan AFB
C-54D	42-72510	4 Apr 61	4 Aug 64	to 2704th ASDGP, Davis-Monthan AFB
C-54D	42-72753	5 Apr 61	4 Aug 64	to 2704th ASDGP, Davis-Monthan AFB
C-54G	45-0560	13 Jul 61	9 Jan 65	to 2nd BW, Barksdale AFB
C-54G	45-0505	1 Aug 61	1963	to 499th AREFW, Westover AFB
C-54G	45-0546	1 Aug 61	21 Jan 65	to 499th AREFW, Westover AFB
C-54G	45-0555	1 Aug 61	19 Feb 63	to 2704th ASDGP, Davis-Monthan AFB
C-54M	44-9048	26 Aug 61	5 Jan 65	to 2704th ASDGP, Davis-Monthan AFB
C-54D	42-72627	4 Nov 61	9 Feb 65	from OGMA Lisbon, to 306th BW, McCoy AFB
U-3B*	60-6048	10 May 63	1 Apr 65	to Torrejón AB

* Nominally at RAF Upper Heyford, but rotated routinely to other bases, notably RAF Booker; MAP = Military Assistance Program

Four B-47Es from the 384th BW sit REFLEX alert at RAF Upper Heyford in August 1963. Their actual strategic value had become debatable. *Adrian Balch*

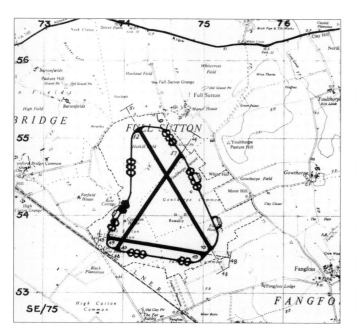

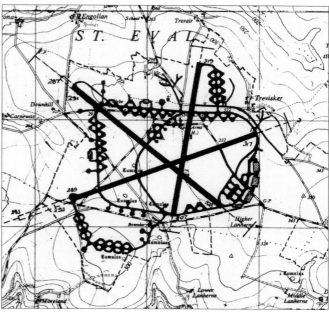

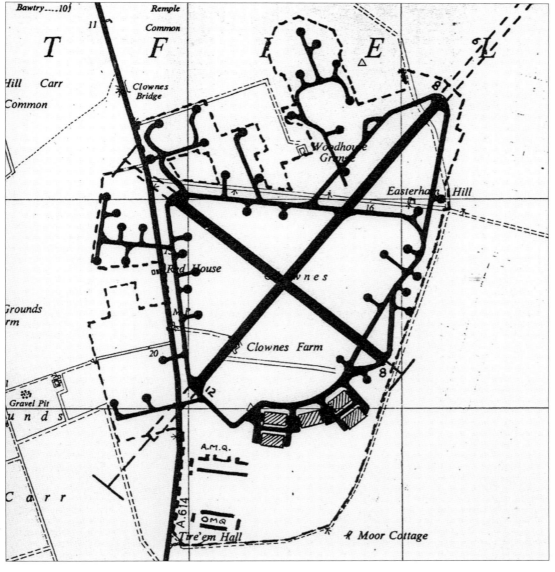

Bases like RAF Lindholme (bottom) and RAF Full Sutton (top left) were part of the FAMOUS/ BLANKET program, but were never operational. RAF St Eval (top right) was an important divert base for airplanes low on fuel after crossing the Atlantic.

Appendix II
SAC Losses in the UK

I t is ironic that the first aircraft loss associated with SAC operations in the United Kingdom crashed in Belgium on 3rd September 1948 while on a flight from RAF Lakenheath. Exactly two months later SAC lost two more airplanes, one at Lajes in the Azores returning to the United States from its deployment at RAF Waddington, and the other was the first crash within the UK in Derbyshire. The disparate geography of these losses raises the question of what constitutes the loss of a SAC aircraft affiliated with the United Kingdom.

Throughout the early years of SAC deployments to England, trans-Atlantic aviation was still an inherently risky operation, especially with the shortage of skilled mechanics in SAC to maintain the airplanes in top condition. Consequently, this section includes not only those airplanes operating from bases physically located within the UK, but SAC aircraft lost while en route to or from bases in the UK. The exception to this is the final SAC UK-related loss of U-2R 68-10330 on 7th December 1977 which crashed on takeoff from RAF Akrotiri, the British air base in Cyprus. This might sug-

Above: The wreckage of RB-29A 44-61999 remains in Derbyshire some 60 years after it struck high terrain on 3rd November 1948. *Rob Hall*

Right: B-36H 51-5729, which crashed near Goose AB on 14th February 1953, was one of 26 SAC airplanes lost flying to or from the UK, underscoring the hazards of these rotations. *via Dennis Jenkins*

gest that the last SAC loss associated with the UK should instead be the 3rd February 1991 crash of B-52G 59-2593 north of Diego Garcia in the British Indian Ocean Territory. The expansive American military presence there – including its runway – is subsumed by the US Naval Support Facility (NSF), and for purposes of this book is considered an American, rather than British, air base

Right: Transports such as C-54D 42-72721 moved personnel, supplies, and VIPs throughout the UK in support of SAC's mission. LeMay was a regular passenger prior to a fire at RAF Northolt on 1st March 1955 which led to scrapping of the airplane. *Photo P13610 courtesy Boeing*

Below: B-47E 53-6216 jettisoned a drop tank which struck a B-47E preparing to return to the CONUS from RAF Greenham Common on 28th February 1958, killing three. The blaze on 53-6204 burned for 18 hours, consumed a million gallons of water, and prompted fears of nuclear contamination. *Brian Baldwin*

Left: The loss of U-2C 56-6700 on 29th May 1975 in West Germany marred both the OLYMPIC JUMP and the CONSTANT TREAT programs. *Kurt Finger*

SAC LOSSES ASSOCIATED WITH UK OPERATIONS

Date	MDS	Serial	Location	Home Unit	Comments
3 Sep 48	B-29A	44-62100	20nm NE Brussels, Belgium	20th BS, 2nd BG, Davis-Monthan AFB, AZ	TDY to RAF Lakenheath, crew bailed out
3 Nov 48	B-29A	44-86356	Lajes Field, Azores	372nd BS, 307th BG, MacDill AFB	During redeployment from RAF Waddington
3 Nov 48	RB-29A	44-61999	Bleaklow, Derbyshire	16th PRS, 91st SRG, McGuire AFB, NJ	En route from RAF Scampton to RAF Burtonwood
17 Jan 49	B-29A	44-62276	Strachur near Dunoon, Argyll	32nd BS, 301st BG, Smokey Hill AFB, KS	Struck high ground in bad weather during attempted redeployment from RAF Scampton
26 Jan 49	B-29A	44-61775	35 miles S Canary Islands	341st BS, 97th BG, Biggs AFB, TX	Missing while TDY from RAF Marham
30 May 49	KB-29M	44-87770	RAF Marham	509th AREFS, 509th BG, Walker AFB, NM	Belly landing, used for fire practice
20 Jul 49	B-29A	44-62141	North of Wisbech, Cambridgeshire	344th BS, 98th BG, Spokane AFB, WA	Engine fire during the night of 20/21 July and crashed
13 Oct 49	B-50A	46-0060	Isleham, Cambridgeshire	65th BS, 43rd BG, Davis-Monthan AFB, AZ	Crashed after takeoff from RAF Lakenheath
16 Nov 49	B-29A	42-65289	300 miles E Kindley AFB, Bermuda	2nd BS, 22nd BG, March AFB, CA	Compass problems, lost, fuel exhaustion
17 May 50	KB-29M	44-69875	Lajes Field, Azores	301st AREFS, 301st BW, Barksdale AFB, LA	Crashed on landing en route RAF Lakenheath
7 Jun 50	RB-29A	42-94081	60 miles ENE of RAF Sculthorpe	72nd SRS(P), 5th SRW, Fairfield-Suisun AFB, CA	Shot its own engine during gunnery practice at 500ft while TDY to RAF Sculthorpe
16 Jun 50	B-29A	44-69861	RAF Lakenheath	32nd BS, 301st BW, Barksdale AFB, LA	Crashed on landing
13 Jul 50	B-50D	49-0267	Lebanon, OH	342nd BS, 97th BW, Biggs AFB, TX	Lightning strike en route RAF Sculthorpe
11 Aug 50	RB-29A	45-21763	RAF Mildenhall	72nd SRS(P), 5th SRW, Fairfield-Suisun AFB, CA	Crashed on runway; remains to RAF
10 Oct 50	B-50D	49-0318	RAF Mildenhall	329th BS, 93rd BW, Castle AFB, CA	Crashed on landing
15 Nov 50	B-50D	49-0277	15 miles NW Montpelier, France	342nd BS, 97th BW, Biggs AFB, TX	TDY to RAF Sculthorpe
31 Dec 50	T-33A	49-0945	Narsarsuaq, Greenland	307th FES, 31st FEW, Turner AFB, GA	Ground loss en route to RAF Manston
18 Jan 51	T-33A	49-0946	Near Ash, Kent	308th FES, 31st FEW, Turner AFB, GA	6 miles SW of RAF Manston
24 Jan 51	F-84E	49-2105	Margate, Kent	308th FES, 31st FEW, Turner AFB, GA	4 miles NE RAF Manston
3 Feb 51	B-50D	49-0270	RAF Bassingbourn	341st BS, 97th BW, Biggs AFB, TX	Crashed after takeoff
9 Mar 51	B-29A	45-21840	Mediterranean Sea off the Spanish Coast	393rd BS, 509th BW, Walker AFB, NM	
23 Mar 51	C-124A	49-0244	Atlantic Ocean W of Ireland	2nd SSS, Walker AFB, NM	Carrying BGEN Paul T Cullen and his 7th AD staff
26 Apr 51	KB-29M	44-87704	Lajes Field, Azores	509th AREFS, 509th BG, Walker AFB, NM	Crash landing after engine fire en route from RAF Mildenhall to Walker AFB
15 May 51	RB-45C	48-0026	RAF Sculthorpe	323rd SRS, 91st SRW Barksdale AFB, LA	Landed long and skidded off the runway
7 Jun 51	KB-29P	44-83950	Carsphairn, Kirkcudbrightshire	2nd AREFS, 2nd BW, Hunter AFB, GA	2.5 miles NW Carsphairn while TDY to RAF Lakenheath
21 Jun 51	F-84E	49-2079	RAF Manston	308th FES, 31st FEW, Turner AFB, GA	Taxying accident and fire
26 Jun 51	F-84E	49-2055	Dover, Kent	308th FES, 31st FEW, Turner AFB, GA	3.5 miles NE Dover TDY to RAF Manston
4 Aug 51	RB-45C	48-0032	Goose Bay, Labrador	324th SRS, 91st SRW, Barksdale AFB, LA	Hit trees while turning onto final approach en route to RAF Sculthorpe
25 Aug 51	F-84E	49-2346	3.5 miles SE Varde, Denmark	560th FES, 12th FEW, Bergstrom AFB, TX	Deployment from RAF Manston
29 Aug 51	F-84E	49-2034	RAF Mildenhall	560th FES, 12th FEW, Bergstrom AFB, TX	Struck parked 2nd BW B-50Ds 48-0066 and 48-0071 while TDY to RAF Manston
13 Sep 51	F-84E	49-2088	Near Dover, Kent	560th FES, 12th FEW, Bergstrom AFB, TX	Crashed in sea 20 miles S RAF Manston
18 Sep 51	F-84E	49-2368	Neubiberg AB, FRG	559th FES, 12th FEW, Bergstrom AFB, TX	Takeoff accident while TDY to RAF Manston
13 Oct 51	F-84E	51-0644	Wheelus AB, Libya	560th FES, 12th FEW, Bergstrom AFB, TX	Takeoff accident while TDY to RAF Manston
4 Dec 51	F-84E	49-2053	Vlandern, Luxembourg	167th FBS, 123rd FBW, Standiford Field, KY	TDY to RAF Manston
7 Dec 51	B-29A	44-62078	Lajes Field, Azores	33rd BS, 22nd BW, March AFB, CA	On takeoff en route RAF Wyton to March AFB
2 Mar 52	KB-29P	44-87600	Harmon Field, Newfoundland	97th AREFS, 97th BW, Biggs AFB, TX	Landing accident en route to RAF Upper Heyford
12 Mar 52	F-84E	49-2057	RAF Manston	167th FBS, 123rd FBW, Standiford Field, KY	Landing accident
1 Mar 52	B-45A	47-0043	RAF Sculthorpe	322nd SRS, 91st SRW, Lockbourne AFB, OH	Undercarriage collapsed on landing at RAF Sculthorpe and ground looped. Abandoned by SAC but eventually rebuilt for USAFE use
21 Mar 52	F-84E	49-2327	RAF Manston	156th FBS, 123rd FBW, Standiford Field, KY	Cockpit explosion during approach
26 Mar 52	RB-45C	48-0020	Goose Bay, Labrador	322nd SRS, 91st SRW, Lockbourne AFB, OH	Struck a snowbank landing short
27 Mar 52	F-84E	49-2044	Near Canterbury, Kent	167th FBS, 123rd FBW, Standiford Field, KY	TDY to RAF Manston
27 Apr 52	F-84E	49-2111	Near RAF Manston	167th FBS, 123rd FBW, Standiford Field, KY	Crashed into house after takeoff

Date	MDS	Serial	Location	Home Unit	Comments
1 May 52	C-47A	42-100912	RAF Burtonwood	3917th ABG RAF Manston	Struck by undershooting USN P2V
14 May 52	F-84E	49-2074	Near RAF Manston	156th FBS, 123rd FBW, Standiford Field, KY	Crashed into sea on approach
24 Jun 52	B-50D	49-0271	RAF Lakenheath	830th BS, 509th BW, Walker AFB, NM	Stalled and crashed
6 Nov 52	B-50D	48-0091	Great Dummow, Essex	49th BS, 2nd BW, Hunter AFB, GA	Crashed
2 Feb 53	B-29A	44-27261	Wheelus AB, Libya	352nd BS, 301st BW	Deployed from RAF Upper Heyford
7 Feb 53	B-36D	51-5719	Near Chippenham, Wiltshire	492nd BS, 7th BW, Carswell AFB, TX	Ran out of fuel en route RAF Fairford
14 Feb 53	B-36D	51-5729	Goose Bay, Labrador	9th BS, 7th BW, Carswell AFB, TX	Hit high ground returning from RAF Fairford
11 Mar 53	B-50A	46-0048	Harmon Field, Newfoundland	63rd BS, 43rd BW, Davis-Monthan AFB, AZ	Landing accident en route to RAF Brize Norton
2 Jul 53	B-47B	51-2267	RAF Upper Heyford	368th BS, 306th BW, MacDill AFB, FL	Stalled on final approach
10 Jul 53	C-47D	43-48803	Sola, Stavanger, Norway	3909th ABG, RAF Lakenheath	Collided with RNorAF F-84, personnel from 28th SRW
5 Aug 53	RB-36H	52-1369	Atlantic Ocean NW of Ireland	72nd SRS, 5th SRW, Travis AFB, CA	En route Travis to RAF Lakenheath
8 Feb 54	B-47E	52-0023	RAF Upper Heyford	2nd BS, 22nd BW, March AFB, CA	Stalled on final approach
8 Mar 54	B-47E	51-2416	Davis-Monthan AFB, NM	358th BS, 303rd BW, Davis-Monthan AFB, AZ	Crashed on takeoff for RAF Greenham Common
20 Jul 54	B-47E	51-17385	Near College Farm, Glouscestershire	51st BS, 68th BW, Lake Charles AFB, LA	Landed short at RAF Fairford
6 Aug 54	B-47E	51-2382	Radcot Lock, Oxfordshire	656th BS, 68th BW, Lake Charles AFB, LA	Stalled during takeoff from RAF Fairford
25 Nov 54	B-47E	52-0083	RAF Lakenheath	65th BS, 43rd BW, Davis-Monthan AFB, AZ	Overran the runway
10 Dec 54	B-47B	51-2100	Oulmes, French Morocco	445th BS, 321st BW, Pinecastle AFB, FL	Ran out of fuel en route RAF Lakenheath
1 Mar 55	C-54D	42-72721	RAF Northolt	3910th ABW, RAF Mildenhall	Damaged by fire and sold for salvage but later repaired for commerical use
1 May 55	B-47E	52-0386	RAF Fairford	359th BS, 303rd BW, Davis-Monthan AFB, AZ	Improper crosswind takeoff
4 May 55	KC-97G	53-0110	90 miles SW of Iceland	310th AREFS, 310th BW, Smoky Hill AFB, KS	Supporting 27th SFW to RAF Sturgate while TDY to RAF Brize Norton
29 Jun 55	F-84F	51-17070	RAF Sturgate	524th SRS, 27th SFW, Bergstrom AFB, TX	Runway hydroplaning
29 Jun 55	F-84F	51-9386	RAF Sturgate	522nd SRS, 27th SFW, Bergstrom AFB, TX	Runway hydroplaning; later scrapped
14 Jul 55	B-47E	52-0421	Barskdale AFB	376th BW, Barksdale AFB, LA	Departing to RAF Upper Heyford
2 Aug 55	B-47E	52-0397	RAF Upper Heyford	512th BS, 376th BW, Barksdale AFB, LA	Aborted takeoff
19 Aug 55	F-84F	51-9392	Near Bergstrom AFB, TX	522nd SRS, 27th SFW, Bergstrom AFB, TX	Returning from RAF Sturgate
24 Sep 55	SC-47D	43-16145	Burns, Wyoming	62nd ARS, Stead AFB, NV	Fuel starvation en route to RAF Greenham Common
5 Feb 56	B-47E	53-1831	Walker AFB, NM	715th BS, 509th BW, Walker AFB, NM	Stalled after takeoff deploying to RAF Upper Heyford
16 May 56	B-47E	51-2442	English Channel near Lands End, Cornwall	97th BW, Biggs AFB, TX	Engine failure while TDY
27 Jul 56	B-47E	53-4230	RAF Lakenheath	307th BW, Lincoln AFB, NE	BROKEN ARROW nuclear incident
10 Oct 56	R6D-1	131588	Atlantic Ocean 370 miles WSW of Lands End	VR-6 MATS Atlantic Division	MATS carrying 307th BW personnel en route to RAF Laenheath to Lincoln AFB via Lajes
28 Feb 58	B-47E	53-6204	RAF Greenham Common	307th BW, Lincoln AFB, NE	Destroyed by drop tanks from B-47E 53-2154
11 Jun 58	B-47E	53-1931	West Hills, VT	96th BS, 2nd BW, Hunter AFB, GA	REFLEX to RAF Brize Norton
27 Jun 58	KC-135A	56-3599	Westover AFB, MA	99th AREFS, 4050th AREFW, Westover AFB, MA	Trans-Atlantic speed record en route RAF Brize Norton
1 Jul 60	RB-47H	53-4281	Barents Sea	343rd SRS, 55th SRW, Forbes AFB, KS	Shot down by MiG-19; TDY to RAF Brize Norton
14 Sep 60	B-47E	51-7047	Atlantic Ocean 250nm West of Shannon	380th BW, Plattsburgh AFB, NY	REFLEX to RAF Brize Norton
12 May 61	C-54E	44-9054	RAF Upper Heyford	3918th CSG, RAF Upper Heyford	Damaged, SOC 18 Jul 61
5 Feb 63	B-47E	53-2134	RAF Greenham Common	307th BW, Lincoln AFB, NE	Crashed during go-around
26 May 64	B-47E	53-2296	RAF Upper Heyford	509th BW, Pease AFB, NH	Crashed while landing
26 May 64	B-47E	52-0525	RAF Upper Heyford	509th BW, Pease AFB, NH	Debris from 53-2296 hit 52-0525
29 May 75	U-2C	56-6700	Crashed 2.7nm from Winterberg, FRG	100th SRW, Davis-Monthan AFB, NM	TDY to RAF Wethersfield
7 Dec 77	U-2R	68-10330	RAF Akrotiri	9th SRW, Beale AFB, CA	Crashed on takeoff

Glossary

AAA	anti-aircraft artillery
AAB	Army Air Base
AAF	Army Air Force or Army Air Field
AASB	Arizona Aircraft Storage Branch
A&AEE	Aeroplane and Armament Experimental Establishment
AB	air base
ABG	Air Base Group
ABNCP	airborne command post
ABS	Air Base Squadron
ABW	Air Base Wing
AC	aircraft commander
ACC	Air Combat Command
ACM	Air Chief Marshal
ACRP	Airborne COMINT Reconnaissance Program
AD	Air Division
ADC	Air Defense Command
ADS	Air Defense Squadron or Aviation Depot Squadron
ADW	Aviation Depot Wing
AEC	Atomic Energy Commission
AEELS	Automatic ELINT Emitter Locator System
AF	Air Force
AFB	Air Force Base
AFDS	Air Fighting Development Squadron or Aviation Field Depot Squadron
AFFTC	Air Force Flight Test Center
AFHRA	Air Force Historical Research Agency
AFLC	Air Force Logistics Command
AFRES	Air Force Reserve
AFSC	Air Force Systems Command
AFSDG	Air Force Storage and Disposition Group
AFSS	Air Force Security Service
AFTAC	Air Force Technical Applications Center
AGL	above ground level
AI	airborne intercept [radar]
ALSS	Advanced Location Strike System
AMA	Air Materiel Area
AMC	Air Mobility Command or Air Materiel Command
ANG	Air National Guard
AO	Authentication Officer
AOCP	Aircraft Out of Commission for Parts
AP	Airport
APGC	Air Proving Ground Command

ARDC	Air Research and Development Command
AREFS	Air Refueling Squadron
AREFW	Air Refueling Wing
ARG	Air Rescue Group
ARS	Air Rescue Squadron
ASARS	Advanced Synthetic Aperture Radar System
ASD	Aeronautical Systems Division or Aircraft Storage Depot
ASDG	Aircraft Storage and Disposition Group
ASIP	Aircraft Structural Integrity Program
ASS	Aircraft Storage Squadron
ATC	air traffic control or Air Transport Command or Air Training Command
ATO	assisted takeoff
ATTG	Aerospace Technical Training Group
ATU	Air Transport Unit
AWE	Atomic Weapons Establishment
AWS	Air Weather Service
BDA	bomb damage assessment
BG	Bombardment Group
BMEWS	Ballistic Missile Early Warning Systems
BNS	bombing-navigation system
BS	Bombardment Squadron
BTS	Bombardment Training Squadron
BW	Bombardment Wing
C	Celsius
CAA	Civil Aeronautics Authority
CC	crew chief
CCTS	Combat Crew Transition School (later Combat Crew Training Squadron)
CCTW	Combat Crew Training Wing
CEA	circular error average
CENTO	Central Treaty Organization
CEP	circular error probable
cg	center of gravity
CG	Composite Group
CHOP	change operational control
CIA	Central Intelligence Agency
CINCSAC	Commander-in-Chief, Strategic Air Command
CINCUSAFE	Commander-in-Chief, US Air Forces Europe
cm	centimeter
CND	Campaign for Nuclear Disarmament

CNO	Chief of Naval Operations
COMINT	communications intelligence
COMTAC	Commander, Tactical Air Command
ConAC	Continental Air Command
CONUS	Continental United States
CP	copilot
CSG	Combat Support Group
CW	Composite Wing
DASA	Defense Atomic Support Agency
DCA	Defense Communications Agency
Det	Detachment
DEFCON	Defense Condition
DEW	Distant Early Warning
DF	direction finding
DIA	Defense Intelligence Agency
DoD	Department of Defense
DRG	Democratic Republic of Germany
DSCS	Defense Systems Communications Satellite
E	Execution time/hour
EAM	Emergency Action Message
ECM	electronic countermeasures
ELINT	electronic intelligence
EOB	electronic order of battle
ESC	Electronic Security Command
ETTF	European Tanker Task Force
EW	electronic warfare or electronic warfare officer or early warning
EWO	Emergency War Order or electronic warfare officer
EWP	Emergency War Plan
F	Fahrenheit
FBS	Fighter Bomber Squadron
FBW	Fighter Bomber Wing
FEBA	forward edge of the battle area
FES	Fighter Escort Squadron
FEW	Fighter Escort Wing
FG	Fighter Group
FIS	Fighter Interceptor Squadron
FM	frequency modulated
FOD	foreign object damage
fpm	feet per minute
FRG	Federal Republic of Germany
FS	Fighter Squadron
ft	feet
FW	Fighter Wing
FY	fiscal year
gal	gallon
GCA	ground-controlled approach
GCI	ground controlled intercept
GDR	German Democratic Republic

GIUK	Greenland-Iceland-United Kingdom	**MSL**	mean sea level	**SAFE**	semi-automatic ferret equipment
GLCM	ground launched cruise missile	**Mt**	megaton	**SAM**	surface-to-air missile
GMT	Greenwich Mean Time	**N**	navigator	**SAW**	Strategic Aerospace Wing
gpm	gallons per minute	**n/a**	not available	**SBAC**	Society of British Aerospace Companies
HASP	High Altitude Sampling Program	**NAA**	National Aeronautics Association	**SDF**	Special Duty Flight
HE	high explosive	**NAF**	Numbered Air Force	**SEA**	Southeast Asia
HF	high frequency	**NATO**	North Atlantic Treaty Organization	**SENSINT**	sensitive intelligence
HMG	Her Majesty's Government or His Majesty's Government	**NCA**	National Command Authorities	**SFW**	Strategic Fighter Wing
HQ	headquarters	**NEAC**	North East Air Command	**SHAFE**	Supreme Headquarters Allied Forces Europe
hr	hour	**NIE**	National Intelligence Estimate	**SIGINT**	signals intelligence
HRR	high-resolution radar	**nm**	nautical mile	**SIOP**	Single Integrated Operational Plan
IAP	International Airport	**NORAD**	North American Air Defense Command	**SLAR**	side-looking airborne radar
ICBM	intercontinental ballistic missile	**nr**	near	**SLBM**	sea-launched ballistic missile
IFF	Identification – Friend or Foe	**NSA**	National Security Agency	**SMW**	Strategic Missile Wing
IFR	instrument flight rules or in-flight refueling [receptacle]	**NSAM**	National Security Action Memorandum	**SOC**	stricken off charge
				SOI	signal of interest
ILS	instrument landing system	**NSC**	National Security Council	**SPF**	Strategic Projection Force
IMC	instrument meterological conditions	**NSF**	Naval Support Facility	**SRW**	Strategic Reconnaissance Wing
		NUDINT	nuclear detonation intelligence	**SS**	Support Squadron
in	inch	**O**	observer	**SSB**	single side band
IN	instructor navigator	**OL**	operating location	**SSS**	Strategic Support Squadron
INS	inertial navigation system	**OPEC**	Organization of Petroleum Exporting Countries	**SSU**	Strategic Support Unit
IP	instructor pilot or initial point	**OpOrd**	operational order	**STTF**	Spanish Tanker Task Force
IR	infrared	**ORI**	Operational Readiness Inspection	**SW**	Strategic Wing
IRA	Irish Republican Army	**P**	pilot or Provisional	**t**	ton
IRAN	inspect and repair as necessary			**TAC**	Tactical Air Command
IRBM	intermediate range ballistic missile	**PACAF**	Pacific Air Forces	**TACAN**	tactical aerial navigation
JATO	jet assisted takeoff	**PARPRO**	Peacetime Aerial Reconnaissance Program	**TCS**	Troop Carrier Squadron
JCS	Joint Chiefs of Staff			**TDY**	temporary duty
JRC	Joint Reconnaissance Center	**PBS**	Pilotless Bomb Squadron	**TELINT**	telemetry intelligence
KIAS	knots indicated air speed	**PDM**	programmed depot maintenance	**TFW**	Tactical Fighter Wing
kg	kilogram	**PHOTINT**	photographic intelligence	**TRW**	Tactical Reconnaissance Wing
km	kilometer	**PLSS**	Precision Location Strike System	**TS**	Training Squadron
kN	kilonewtons	**PM**	Prime Minister	**UEE**	unit essential equipment
kph	kilometers per hour	**ppm**	pounds per minute	**UHF**	ultra-high frequency
kt	kiloton	**PPMS**	precision parameter measurement system	**UK**	United Kingdom
KTAS	knots true air speed			**UN**	United Nations
l	liter	**PRC**	People's Republic of China	**US**	United States
L	local time	**PTBT**	Partial Test Ban Treaty	**USA**	United States of America
LABS	Low Altitude Bombing System	**QRC**	quick reaction capability	**USAAF**	United States Army Air Force
lb	pound	**RADINT**	radar intelligence	**USAF**	United States Air Force
LCO	Launch Control Officer	**RAE**	Royal Air Establishment	**USAFE**	United States Air Forces – Europe
LORAN	Long Range Navigation	**RAF**	Royal Air Force	**USCM**	Unit Simulated Combat Mission
LOX	liquid oxygen	**RAPCON**	Radar Approach Control	**USN**	United States Navy
LRDP	Long Range Detection Program	**RATO**	rocket-assisted takeoff	**USSR**	Union of Soviet Socialist Republics
LSS	Logistics Support Squadron	**RBS**	radar bomb scoring	**VAR**	Variable Angle Release
m	meter	**RFCCN**		**VFR**	visual flight rules
MAC	Military Airlift Command	**RG**	Reconnaissance Group	**VHF**	very high frequency
MAP	Military Assistance Program	**RIAT**	Royal International Air Tattoo	**VIP**	very important person
MASDC	Military Aircraft Storage and Disposition Center	**RNoAF**	Royal Norwegian Air Force	**VOR**	very high frequency omnidirectional radio
		RON	remain overnight		
MASINT	measurement and signature intelligence	**rpm**	revolutions per minute	**wfu**	withdrawn from use
		RS	Reconnaissance Squadron	**w/o**	written off
MATS	Military Air Transport Service	**RSO**	reconnaissance system operator	**WRM**	war reserve materiel
MiG	Mikoyan *i* Gurevich	**RTASS**	Remote Tactical Airborne SIGINT System	**WRS**	Weather Reconnaissance Squadron
MITO	minimum interval takeoff				
Mk	Mark	**RTG**	Reconnaissance Technical Group	**WS**	Weather Squadron
ml	milliliter	**RTS**	Reconnaissance Technical Squadron	**Z**	Zulu time (Greenwich Mean Time/ Universal Coordinated Time)
mm	millimeter	**RV**	re-entry vehicle		
MMS	Munitions Maintenance Squadron	**RW**	Reconnaissance Wing	**ZI**	Zone of the Interior
MP	Member of Parliament	**SAC**	Strategic Air Command		
MPC	Mobile Processing Center	**SACEUR**	Supreme Allied Commander, Europe		
mph	miles per hour				
MRBM	medium range ballistic missile	**SAD**	Strategic Aerospace Division		

Index

AIRCRAFT

Advanced Manned Strategic Aircraft (AMSA) 73
Avro CF-105 191
Avro Vulcan 112, 194
Beechcraft RC-12 151
Boeing B-17 9, 40
Boeing B-29 and variants
  B-29A 28, 35, 47, 118, 123, 218, 219
  B-29MR 28, 29, 39, 92-94, 96
  KB-29M 28, 29, 39, 92-96, 108, 109, 123, 176, 218
  KB-29P 29, 92-94, 96, 108, 124, 125, 176, 177, 218
  RB-29A 28, 118, 119, 123, 216, 218
  WB-29 32
  Washington 14, 15, 26, 37, 76, 200, 208
Boeing B-47 and variants
  B-47B 9, 48, 49, 51-54, 219
  B-47E 4, 17, 18, 52, 54-67, 97, 130, 137, 205, 214, 217, 219
  DB-47B 191
  EB-47E 4, 55, 56, 60, 61, 65, 66
  ERB-47H 109, 131-33, 136
  RB-47E 108, 120, 122, 124, 127-30, 136, 137, 146, 205, 211
  RB-47H 23, 109, 118, 124, 130-39, 197, 219
  YRB-47B 52-54, 129, 130
Boeing B-50 and variants
  B-50A 28, 35, 36, 37, 46, 92, 95, 96, 218, 219
  B-50D 17, 22, 35, 36, 38, 39, 93, 96, 174, 218, 219
  RB-50E 119, 120, 124, 130
  RB-50F 122-24
  RB-50G 95, 109, 123, 124, 130
Boeing B-52 and variants
  B-52B 68, 69, 100
  B-52C 70
  B-52D 69-72, 76, 78, 82-84, 187
  B-52E 76, 78, 103
  B-52F 69, 71, 76, 81
  B-52G 4, 32, 69, 71, 72, 78-91, 217
  B-52H 70, 71, 76, 78-82, 86, 87, 196
Boeing C-97 and variants
  C-97A 180, 182
  C-97E 188
  C-97G 135
  KC-97E 49, 92, 96, 97, 213
  KC-97F 4, 92, 98, 108, 128, 213, 214
  KC-97G 9, 52, 92, 96, 99, 100, 101, 102, 105, 109, 132, 178, 219
  VC-97D 188, 189
  YC-97 180, 182
  YC-97A 180, 182
Boeing E-3 87
Boeing E-4 110
Boeing KC-135 and variants
  EC-135C 109, 111
  EC-135G 109, 111
  JKC-135A 109, 136, 137
  KC-135A 4, 10, 11, 101, 103, 105-116, 133, 165, 170, 188, 219
  KC-135E 108, 112, 143, 170
  KC-135Q 24, 110, 112, 116, 158, 159, 161, 164, 165, 196
  KC-135R 25, 107, 108
  KC-135R (recon) 110, 136, 138, 140
  KC-135T (recon) 138, 140
  OC-135B 170
  RC-135B 137
  RC-135C 117, 137, 138, 141, 142
  RC-135D 112, 117, 137-39, 141, 142
  RC-135M 141, 143
  RC-135S 170
  RC-135U 131, 138, 140, 142, 160, 163
  RC-135V 141-43, 160

RC-135W 141
'RT-135' 112
TC-135W 143
WC-135B/C 170
Breguet Br.1150 163
British Aerospace Nimrod 163, 170
Cessna U-3B 198, 214
Convair B-36 and variants
  B-36D 42, 43, 45, 46, 219
  B-36H 43, 46, 216
  B-36J 46
  RB-36D 42, 43
  RB-36F 45, 120-22
  RB-36H 43, 120, 121, 123, 219
Convair B-58 10, 11, 32, 66, 73, 105, 197
Convair F-102 179
Convair F-106 191
de Havilland Vampire 119
Douglas A-4 157
Douglas C-124 11, 16, 22, 37, 42, 52, 145, 179, 182-87, 193, 199, 218
Douglas C-47 and variants
  C-47A 13, 190, 211-14
  C-47D 121, 211-14, 219
  SC-47A/D 190, 191, 219
  VC-47A 190, 213, 214
Douglas C-54 11, 28, 39, 52, 179-83, 189, 207, 211-14, 217, 219
English Electric Canberra 126, 148, 176-78
English Electric Lightning 105, 147
Fairchild C-119 133, 189, 212, 213
General Dynamics F-16 116
General Dynamics F-111 and variants
  EF-111A 112, 114-16
  F-111F 112, 114, 115
  FB-111A 73, 74, 76, 81
Gloster Javelin 191
Gloster Meteor F.4 45
Grumman EA-6B 114
Grumman KA-6D 114
Handley Page Victor 105, 113, 194
Lockheed A-12 147
Lockheed C-130 111-13, 116
Lockheed C-141B 112, 116, 148
Lockheed C-5 116
Lockheed F-117 116
Lockheed P/F-80 171, 172, 174
Lockheed SR-71 4, 11, 23, 24, 110, 116, 120, 135, 141, 143, 147, 151, 152, 157-70, 197, 198
Lockheed T-33 172, 174, 212, 218
Lockheed TR-1 23, 151, 152, 155-57, 164, 170, 202
Lockheed U-2 and variants
  U-2A 145
  U-2C 149-51, 155, 217, 219
  U-2G 147, 148
  U-2R 148, 151-55, 157, 161, 216, 219
LTV A-7D 107
Martin RB-57D 120, 130, 132, 133
McDonnell Douglas F-15 87
McDonnell Douglas F-4 11
McDonnell Douglas KC-10 4, 11, 23-25, 29, 107, 108, 110, 112-16
McDonnell F-101 171, 172
MiG-15 Fagot 47, 124, 128
MiG-17 Fresco 128, 129, 138, 140
MiG-19 Farmer 133, 134, 219
North American B-45A 44, 47, 125, 126, 218
North American RB-45C 11, 108, 124-27, 129, 130, 145, 146, 218
North American F-100 195
North American F-51 171, 172, 175
North American F-82 171, 172
North American F-86 47, 171
Republic F-84F 4, 99, 171, 172, 178, 179, 219
Republic F-84G 93, 96, 99, 121, 172,

176-78
Republic P-47 171
Rockwell B-1 73-75
Sikorsky RH-53D 111
Tupolev Tu-4 Bull 26
Vickers Valiant 80, 105, 194
Yakovlev Yak-3 13

COMPANIES AND CIVIL AGENCIES

Campaign for Nuclear Disarmament (CND) 23
Central Intelligence Agency (CIA) 23, 117, 133, 134, 138, 140, 145-49, 153
Five Eyes 197
Ford Motor Company 138
Glenn L Martin Company 137
Greenham Common Women's Peace Camp 23
Imperial War Museum—Duxford 82, 84
Irish Republican Army (IRA) 193
Loral 167
Molesworth People's Peace Camp 23
Organization of Petroleum Exporting Countries (OPEC) 158
RAF Museum Cosford 80
Society of British Aerospace Companies (SBAC) 76, 159
Strategic Air Command Museum 73

DEFENSE AGENCIES

Air Combat Command (ACC) 25, 75, 76, 144, 170, 196
Air Defense Command (ADC) 55, 199
Air Force Flight Test Center (AFFTC) 76
Air Materiel Command (AMC) 175, 176, 181, 187, 191
Air Mobility Command (AMC) 25, 116
Air Photographic and Charting Service (APCS) 120
Air Proving Ground Command (APGC) 13
Air Research and Development Command (ARDC) 177
Air Training Command (ATC) 189
Air Transport Command (ATC) 172
B-29 Task Force Command 14, 199
Continental Air Command (ConAC) 172-74
Defense Communications Agency (DCA) 154
Defense Intelligence Agency (DIA) 163
Defense Nuclear Agency (DNA) 199
Electronic Security Command (ESC) 151
European Tanker Task Force (ETTF) 11, 25, 106, 202, 208
Joint Chiefs of Staff (JCS) 20, 26, 117, 165
Joint Reconnaissance Center (JRC) 134, 135
Military Air Transport Service (MATS) 12, 39, 59, 122, 172, 176, 179, 185, 189, 219
National Security Agency (NSA) 117, 154, 165
North Atlantic Treaty Organization (NATO) 4, 17, 23, 26, 31, 32, 40, 61, 74, 82-84, 86, 87, 101, 106, 108, 112, 151, 158, 160-62, 165, 170, 197
North East Air Command (NEAC) 55
Pacific Air Force (PACAF) 187
RAF Bomber Command 32, 37, 54, 69, 192-95
RAF Strike Command 23
Royal Australian Air Force (RAAF) 76
Royal Navy 18, 146
Royal Norwegian Air Force (RNoAF) 121, 212
Spanish Tanker Task Force (STTF) 10, 11, 105, 106, 109, 110
Supreme Headquarters Allied Forces Europe (SHAFE) 164

Tactical Air Command (TAC) 4, 44, 84, 96, 99, 125, 127, 199
UK Ministry of Defence 168
US Air Force Reserve (AFRES) 106-108
US Air Forces Europe (USAFE) 4, 16, 21, 33, 40, 84, 98, 101, 106, 111, 112, 114, 125, 135, 149, 151, 155, 171, 173, 174, 177, 179, 187, 190, 194, 197, 199, 200, 202, 205, 213, 218
US Air National Guard (ANG) 93, 99, 106-108, 110-12, 123, 171, 172, 175
US Army Air Force (USAAF) 11, 13
US Army Corps of Engineers 15
US Department of Defense (DoD) 164
Warsaw Pact 11, 32, 82, 126, 129, 157, 162, 165, 166, 170, 196

EQUIPMENT, WEAPONS, AND SYSTEMS

Advanced Location Strike System (ALSS) 149, 150, 155, 156
Advanced Synthetic Aperture Radar System (ASARS) 155-57, 160, 167
AN/ALD-4 SILVER KING ELINT pod 136, 137
AN/ALQ-27 ECM suite 66
AN/APQ-24 radar 40
AN/ASD-1 Automatic ELINT system 136, 137
Automatic ELINT Emitter Locator System (AEELS) 141
BLUE CRADLE ECM pod 54, 55, 61, 62, 66
CBU-71/87/98 cluster bomb 90
Fat Man 20, 180
GEM 19-22, 28, 30, 35, 36, 96, 185
General Electric J35 engine 174, 179
Grand Slam 13
Ground-controlled approach (GCA) 10, 43, 44, 49, 52
High-resolution radar (HRR) 158, 162, 164, 165
Little Boy 20, 180
Litton LN-33 inertial navigation system (INS) 153
Low Altitude Bombing System (LABS) 177
Mark IV atomic weapon 19, 22, 27, 31, 180
Mark VI / Mk 6 atomic weapon 27, 30, 38, 39, 55, 180
Mk 7 nuclear weapon 38, 39, 177
Mk 36 nuclear weapon 38, 39
Mk 39 nuclear weapon 38, 39, 59
Mk 82 high explosive bomb 90
Mobile Processing Center (MPC) 162
ON TOP 20, 96
PAVE TACK 112
Phase V ECM 4, 55-57, 61, 62
Precision Location Strike System (PLSS) 155
Precision Parameter Measurement System (PPMS) 138
Project Emily 193
Remote Tactical Airborne SIGINT System (RTASS) 151
Rocket-assisted takeoff (RATO) 52, 59, 60, 65, 189
RURALIST 20, 28, 92, 93, 96
SADDLETREE 14, 19-22, 27, 28, 31, 35, 36, 93, 180, 185
Short-range Navigation (SHORAN) 122
SILVERPLATE 19-22, 28, 31, 180
SUPERMAN 92
System 320 SAFE (semi-automatic ferret equipment) 132
T-59 training 'shape' 55, 57
TEE TOWN ECM pod 4, 65, 66
Tsar Bomba 136
Ultra-high frequency radio (UHF) 10, 49, 52, 129
Very high frequency (VHF) radio 155

W-49 warhead 194
Yellow Sun 194

MEDIA
American Bomb in Britain 12, 21
American War Plans, 1945-1950 31
Black Tuesday Over Namsi 47
Daily Express 19
Daily Mail 18
Gulf War Air Power Survey (GWAPS) 87
International Dictionary of Intelligence 117
Lockheed Blackbird 158
New York Times 133
Oxford Mail 69
SAC Fighter Planes and Their Operations 177
Sunday Dispatch 19
The Silverplate Bombers 20
The Sun 159
Who Fears? 185

MISCELLANEOUS
Bird in Hand 15
Blue Steel Trophy 78, 79, 81
BROKEN ARROW 182, 219
Camrose Trophy 81
Mackay Trophy 174, 177
Mickey's Tea Bar 6
Paris Air Show 42, 43, 108
RAF Mildenhall *Air Fête* 74, 76
'Royal Gloucester Air Force' 89
Royal International Air Tatoo (RIAT) 4, 74-76
Tactical Fighter Meet 74
Tiger Meet 74

MISSILES AND RADARS
AGM-45 Shrike 114
Bell GAM-63 Rascal 191
Boeing LGM-30 Minuteman 195
Chrysler PGM-19 Jupiter 191, 194
Convair SM-65 Atlas 195
deHavilland Firestreak 147
Douglas PGM-17 Thor 12, 17, 38, 179, 191-95
Fan Song radar 149
Ground Launched Cruise Missiles (GLCM) 23, 156
Hen House radar 138, 140
Intercontinental Ballistic Missile (ICBM) 20, 21, 23, 25, 66, 191, 195
Intermediate Range Ballistic Missile (IRBM) 12, 17, 38, 66, 191, 192, 195, 197
Martin LGM-25 Titan II 195
McDonnell Douglas AGM-84 Harpoon 83, 87
Medium Range Ballistic Missile (MRBM) 193
North American AGM-28 Hound Dog 86
Northrop SM-62 Snark 191
Raytheon AGM-88A HARM 114
SA-2 *Guideline* 149
SA-3 *Goa* 149
SA-5 *Gammon* 162
SS-3 *Shyster* 193
SS-6 *Sapwood* 21

OPERATIONS AND MISSIONS
ALARM BELL 10, 32, 69-73, 111
APPLE CART 187
ARCTIC CANDY 138
BALTIC CANDY 138
BELL HOP 187
Berlin Airlift 21, 33, 35
BIG LEAGUE 51
BIG PUSH 130
BIG TEAM 117, 137, 138, 142
BILLY BOY 105
Black Buck 112, 113
BLANKET 200, 203, 215
BLUE BAT 57
BOILER MAKER 54
BOLD GUARD 83
BOOT CAMP 100
BORDERTOWN 132
BOTANY BAY 82
BOX TOP 130, 136, 137
BRAD 135
BRAVO 31
BRIAR PATCH 110, 130, 138, 140
BROWN FALCON 82
BURNING CANDY 110, 130
BURNING PIPE 110, 130, 137
BURNING PIPELINE 130
BURNING SKY 130, 137
BURNING WIND 130, 141, 143, 144, 170

BUSY BREWER 32, 72, 82-84, 86
BUSY PILOT 159
BUSY PLAYMATE 152
BUSY WARRIOR 84, 86, 87
CAN DO 46
CART MAN 135
CASH BOX 180, 184
CASTLE GATE 130, 133, 137
CENTRAL ENTERPRISE 157
CERTAIN SENTINEL 82
CHALICE 148
CHERRY PIE 46
CHICKENPOX 180, 182
CHROME DOME 69, 103, 104
CLEARWATER 20, 21, 64, 66, 68
CLOUDY CHORUS 82
COBRA BALL 170
COLD FIRE 82, 151, 161
COMBAT SENT 130, 138, 140
COMPASS COPE 155
CONGO MAIDEN 130
CONSTANT PHOENIX 170
CONSTANT TREAT 149, 217
CORONET 4
COTTON CANDY 137-39
CREEK PARTY 99
CREEK SPECTRE 156, 157
CROSSROADS 180, 181
CURTAIN RAISER 45
DAILY DOUBLE 105
DAMSEL FAIR 82
DAWN PATROL 82
DESERT SHIELD 24, 87, 116, 143
DESERT STORM 11, 24, 32, 87-91, 116, 143, 168, 170, 197
DIP STICK 133
DISPLAY DETERMINATION 82
DIVIDEND 53, 129
DOMINIC 187
DREAMY RIVER 187
DROPSHOT 31, 32
DUFFEL BAG 190
EAGLE CLAW 111, 112
EL DORADO CANYON 4, 11, 24, 112-15, 157, 160, 168
EVEN STEVEN 149
FAMOUS 200, 203, 215
FAST FLY 20
FERRYBOAT 21, 33, 199
FLINTLOCK 82
Foil 36
FORTUNE FINDER 146
FOX ABLE ONE 172, 174, 176
FOX ABLE TWO 172
FOX ABLE THREE 172-74
FOX ABLE FOUR 176
FOX ABLE SIX 173
FOX ABLE TEN 172, 174, 177, 178
FOX PETER ONE 176
FOX PETER TWO 176
FREEZE OUT 130
FROLIC 13, 31
FULL HOUSE 58
GALE 44
GALLOPER 201
GARLIC SALT 110, 136-38, 143
GEM 19-22, 28, 30, 35, 36, 96, 185
GENETRIX 146
GHOST RIDER 113
GIANT BATTLE 82, 84
GIANT REACH 152, 157-59, 163
GIANT STRIKE 4, 71, 74, 76, 78-81
GIANT VOICE 76, 81
GLASS BRICK 69
GLOWING HEAT 159
GOLDEN PHEASANT 136, 137
Granby 24, 90
GREEN GARTER 100, 108, 128
GYPSY 132
HALF BREED 132
HARVEST MOON 98
High Altitude Sampling Program (HASP) 146, 147, 151
HIGH GEAR 53, 58, 99
HIGH TIME 191
HOGMANAY 44
IDEALIST 147, 148
IRON BAR 92, 100, 129, 130
JU JITSU 108, 126-29, 146, 209
JUMPING BUG 190, 191
JUNE BUG 42
L A HIGHWAY 159
LEAP FROG 58, 99
LITTLE GUY 135
LOBSTER POT 54
LONG HAUL 92, 114
LONGSTRIDE 172, 175-77

LOW GEAR 190
LUCKY BOY 57
MABELS DIARY 99
MAIN ROAD 190
MAXIMUM EFFORT 39
MAYSHOT 195
MEADOW LARK 189
MEDITERRANEAN CANDY 138
MIDWINTER 124
MIGHTY WARRIOR 84, 86, 87
MILK BOTTLE 61
NIGHTCHECK 195
NORTHERN WEDDING 83
NOVEMBER MOON 97
OCEAN SAFARI 82
OFFICE BOY 110, 137, 139
OFFTACKLE 13, 26-31
OLIVE FARM 152
OLIVE HARVEST 152-54, 159
OLIVE TREE 145, 154, 159
OLYMPIC FLAME 151
OLYMPIC JUMP 149, 150, 217
OLYMPIC RACE 151
OLYMPIC TORCH 151, 152, 155
OMBRELLE 40
OPEN DOOR 130
OPEN FENCE 185
OPEN GATE 82
OPEN MIND 54, 98
OPEN SKIES 170
OXCART 147
PAUL REVERE 58
PAVE ONYX 149
PEA PATCH 189
Peacetime Aerial Reconnaissance Program (PARPRO) 117, 153, 154, 160-65, 170
PEP TALK 130
PEPSIN 127
PICKET FENCE 54
PIED PIPER 130, 132
PINCHER 31
PINK LADY 55
POOP DECK 82
PORT CALL 43, 46
POWER FLITE 68, 100
POWER HOUSE 57
PROUD ELTON 110, 137
QUICK STEP 189
QUICK SWITCH 53, 97
RAF Bombing and Navigation Competition 4, 69, 74, 76, 78, 187
RECLAIM 195
RED RICHARD 201, 202, 205
RED SETTER 131
REDHEAD 93
REDOUBLE 195
REFLEX ACTION 4, 11, 20, 21, 32, 46, 58-67, 69, 73, 100, 101, 103, 105, 132, 179, 187, 196, 197, 201, 202, 207, 210, 214, 219
RESPOND 195
RIVET BRASS 117, 137, 139
RIVET CARD 141, 143
RIVET JAW 138
RIVET JOINT 141-44, 162
RIVET STAND 138, 143
ROAD BLOCK 130
ROCK ISLAND 130
ROMEO 171
ROUGH GAME 69, 101 185, 187
ROUNDOUT 43, 46, 119-24, 128
RUBY 13
SADDLE ROCK 55
SAFARI 51
SAM SPADE 123, 130
SCOPE SAFE 147
SCOPE SAINT 148
SENIOR BALL 149
SENIOR BOOK 151
SENIOR GLASS 151
SENIOR LOOK 153, 157
SENIOR RUBY 151, 152, 156
SENIOR SPEAR 151, 154-56
SENIOR STRETCH 154
Short Granite 80
SHORT PUNT 61, 101, 134
SIGN BOARD 54
SILK PURSE 111, 112
Single Integrated Operations Plan (SIOP) 66, 74, 78, 84, 87, 163
SKUNK 132
SKY TRY 48
SLIP KNOT 130
SNEAK PLAY 99, 178
SNOW FLURRY 101
Soyuz-80 166
SPEED LIGHT 109, 136
SPRING CORN 190

STATEHOUSE 124
STEEL TRAP 103
Strategic Projection Force (SPF) 82, 163
STRIKE OUT 190
SUN DOG 131
SUNBEAM 135
SWIFT 135
TACOMA 134
TALL BOY 187
TAR PAIL 54
TEA PARTY 74
TEAMWORK 82, 151, 161
TEST MATCH 191
TEXAS LEAGUE 55
TEXAS STAR 130
TOP DRAWER 54
TOP SAIL 103
TROJAN 26
TROJAN HORSE 130, 131
TULSA 132
Unit Simulated Combat Mission (USCM) 44, 46, 97, 179, 185, 187
WACO 134
WALKING CANE 190, 191
WILDCAT 61, 202
WINTEX-CIMEX 86
WORLD SERIES 51
YELLOW COLE 136
YORKTOWN FIFTY 103
YUKON JAKE 54, 99

PEOPLE
Acheson, Dean 13, 26
Acklam, Joe 127
Adams, Harold B 159
Allen, Lew Jr 165
Alsop, Stewart 18
Anstee, Bob 127
Armstrong, Frank A 92
Aroney, Albert T 69
Astorino, Loring R 199
Attlee, Clement 13, 19, 27
Austin, Harold R 'Hal' 128, 129
Baring, Rowland 159
Barnes, Jerome R 199
Beagle, Philip H 11
Beckel, Robert D 199
Berringer, Lynn T 114
Bevan, Aneurin 'Nye' 19
Bevin, Ernest 13
Blair, Bill 127
Blanchard, William H 66, 199
Boyes, John 193-95
Boyle, Dermot A 69
Broadhurst, Edwin R 199
Broadhurst, Harry 'Broady' 69
Burchinal, David A 52, 53
Bush, George H W 90
Butler, G Lee 199
Callaghan, L James 23, 158, 159
Carter, James E 'Jimmy' 111, 162, 165
Chain, John T 'Jack' 83, 84, 86, 199
Chamoun, Camille 57
Christie, C E 11
Churchill, Winston 19, 22, 23, 126, 127, 146
Clay, Lucius D 33
Clements, Ben H 69
Cloke, Dick 148, 149
Cochrane, Ralph 126
Cooke, Walter D 69
Crabb, Lionel 'Buster' 146
Crampton, John 126, 127
Craxi, Benedetto 'Bettino' 112
Cremer, Gordon 127
Crickmore, Paul 158
Cross, Kenneth B 'Bing' 195
Cullen, Paul T 16, 182, 199, 218
Davis, Bennie L 199
de Gaulle, Charles 202
Dillon, C Douglas 20
Doran, John J 199
Dougherty, Russell E 82, 199
Douglas-Home, Alec 159
Drew, Harry 148, 149
Earhart, Pat 52
Eden, Anthony 23, 145, 146
Eisenhart, Charles M 199
Eisenhower, Dwight D 20, 57, 66, 134
Elliott, William 25
Ellis, Richard H 82, 162, 199
Ellis, Richard N 178
Ford, Gerald R 23
Forgan, David W 114
Franco, Stephen 52
Ghaddafi, Muammar 112
Goforth, Oscar L 134
Goyt, Gordon F 76

Greenslade, Don 127
Griffin, Hays F 69
Griswold, Francis H 'Butch' 18, 58
Hacks, James 11
Hagemann, Kenneth L 199
Halloran, Pat 158
Hamilton, Archie 154
Heath, Edward R G 'Ted' 23, 158
Henderson, Arthur 13, 36
Hill, John 127
Holloway, Bruce K 199
Holloway, James L 163
Holt, Carl 128
Hussein, Saddam 87, 90
Iddon, Don 18
Jiggens, Jim 168
Johnson, Dave 138
Johnson, Leon W 14, 199
Johnson, Louis 26
Johnson, Lyndon B 20, 23
Kennedy, John F 20, 64, 135, 136
Kennedy, Joseph P, Sr 20
Kenney, George C 33, 199
Khrushchev, Nikita S 146
King Faisal 57
King George VI 38
Kissinger, Henry A 148, 159, 160
Knutson, Marty 149
Lambert, Wayne W 199
LeMay, Curtis E 20, 21, 26, 28, 33, 46,
   48, 57, 58, 92, 97, 126, 145, 179, 185,
   199, 217
Lindsay, Bill 127
Lord Trenchard 36
Machorek, William C 159
Malenkov, Georgi 18
Marshall, George C 13, 33
McConnell, John P 16, 17, 199
McCoy, Forrest 52
McCoy, Michael N W 48, 49
McGill, Earl J 47
McKone, John 134, 135
McNamara, Robert S 10, 20, 21, 195
Meyer, John C 199
Miragon, Curtis L 21
Musgrave, Thomas C 199
Nazzarro, Joseph J 199
Nixon, Richard M 20, 158, 159
Old, Archie J, Jr 16, 69, 199
Olds, Thayer S 176
Olmstead, F Bruce 133-35
Os'kin, Dmitri P 47
Pahlavi, Mohammed Reza 111
Palm, Willard 'Bill' 132-34
Pattie, Geoffrey 159
Phillips, Dean B 134
Polyakov, Vasilii A 134
Posa, Eugene E 'Gene' 134
Power, Thomas S 11, 20, 51, 60, 66, 103,
   188, 199
Powers, Francis G 'Frank' 134, 147
Quarles, Donald A 191
Queen Elizabeth 38
Reagan, Ronald W 112, 165, 166, 168
Rendleman, Terry 150
Reynolds, Doyle F 199
Ridley, Nicholas 90
Robinson, Robbie 148
Ross, Steven T 31
Rouch, Thomas A 69
Ryan, John D 199
Sage, Harmon R 69
Sanders, Rex 127
Sayeed, Jonathan 90
Schilling, David C 176
Schlesinger, James R 159
Selser, James C 11, 199
Skorheim, Ernest C 69
Slessor, John C 27, 126
Smith, Colin 43, 58
Smorchkov, Alexsandr P 47
Spaatz, Carl A 'Toohey' 12, 13
Sullivan, James V 159
Symington, W Stuart 35
Taylor, Donald L 69
Tedder, Arthur W 12, 13, 35
Thatcher, Margaret 156, 168
Thorneycroft, Peter 195
Truman, Harry S 13, 22, 23, 26, 27, 36
Twining, Nathan F 49, 58
Vandenberg, Hoyt S 26, 27, 35, 126
Von Ins, Paul 11
Walsh, James H 199
Welch, Larry D 83, 199
Werrell, Kenneth 185
Westbrook, Sam W 114
Westover, Charles B 199
Wheless, Hewitt T 16

Widdifield, Noel F 159
Williams, Alan 89
Wilson, Cy 174, 176, 177
Wilson, Delmar 199
Wilson, J Harold 23, 158
Wray, Stanley T 14, 199
Young, Kevin 12, 17, 21
Zhukov, Georgi K 18

PERSONNEL
Air Officer Commanding-in-Chief Bomber
   Command 195
Authentication officer (AO) 194
Chief of Naval Operations (CNO) 163,
   164, 170
Commander-in-Chief, Strategic Air
   Command (CINCSAC) 11, 17, 20, 22,
   51, 60, 66, 82, 83, 86, 103, 162, 178,
   188, 199
Commander-in-Chief, US Air Forces
   Europe (CINCUSAFE) 16, 82, 162
Launch control officer (LCO) 194
Supreme Allied Commander, Europe
   (SACEUR) 17, 194

PLACES
Adana AB 118, 131
Andersen AFB 39, 87
Ben Guerir AB 39, 100, 101, 102
Bitburg AB 198
Bodø AB 133, 160, 165, 166
Cairo West AB 110, 112
Chambley 131
Dayton 28
Dhahran AB 30, 99, 118, 119
EA Harmon AFB 27, 49, 69, 98, 132, 189,
   214, 218, 219
Eniwetok 1764,
Fürstenfeldbruck AB 13, 33, 118, 172, 173
Gardermoen AB 54, 99, 177
Giebelstadt AB 13, 199
Goose AB 22, 27, 28, 39, 42, 68, 69, 161,
   172-76, 178-80, 188, 216, 218, 219
Greenland-Iceland-United Kingdom Gap
   (GIUK) 117, 122
Hahn AB 151
Heathrow AP 15, 28, 43, 54, 160
Heligoland 35, 42
Hellenikon AB 89, 141, 143
Heston RBS 10
Howard AFB 172
Incirlik AB 105, 118, 131, 133, 134, 158
Iwo Jima 176
Kadena AB 37, 39, 70, 73, 140, 157,
   162, 170
Keflavik AP 21, 93, 119, 172-79
Kindley AB 27, 37, 39, 93, 172, 177, 218
King Abdul Aziz IAP 87
Lajes Field 27, 39, 61, 93, 98, 100, 101,
   105, 112, 118, 119, 172, 177, 216, 218,
   219
Midway 176
Misawa AB 140, 176
Mont de Marsan AB 89
Morón AB 10, 32, 39, 62, 64, 87, 88, 91,
   100, 105, 106, 110
Namsi AB 47
Narsarssuak (Bluie West One / BW-1) 172,
   175
Neubiberg AB 172, 174, 218
Newbury 67
Nouasseur AB 39, 45, 51, 62, 97, 172,
   175-77, 213
NSF Diego Garcia 87, 90, 153, 217
Osan AB 151
Pilsen 9
Ploesti 14, 199
Prestwick AP 9, 98, 123, 172, 173, 176,
   188, 198
RAE Farnborough 76, 159, 160
RAF Akrotiri 105, 145, 147, 148, 152-54,
   159, 216, 219
RAF Bardney 192
RAF Bassingbourn 35, 40, 119, 200, 202,
   218
RAF Bentwaters 28, 172
RAF Binbrook 147
RAF Booker 198, 214
RAF Boscombe Down 43, 44, 75, 76,
   201, 202
RAF Bovingdon 172
RAF Breighton 192, 195
RAF Brize Norton throughout
RAF Bruntingthorpe 38, 55, 61, 62, 201,
   205, 211, 214
RAF Burtonwood 43, 46, 92, 119, 200,
   201, 202, 205, 211, 213, 214, 218, 219

RAF Bushy Park 14, 199
RAF Caistor 192
RAF Carnaby 192
RAF Catfoss 192
RAF Chelveston 9, 38, 54, 55, 61, 62,
   200-202, 211, 212, 214
RAF Chipping Norton 201
RAF Coleby Grange 192
RAF Cottesmore 192
RAF Desborough 201
RAF Driffield 38, 191-93
RAF East Kirkby 92, 100, 189-91, 201,
   202, 211, 213
RAF Fairford throughout
RAF Feltwell 38, 191, 192
RAF Folkingham 192
RAF Full Sutton 54, 55, 192, 200, 201, 215
RAF Gaydon 200
RAF Grafton Underwood 9
RAF Gransden Lodge 201
RAF Greenham Common throughout
RAF Harrington 192, 200
RAF Hemswell 38, 191-93
RAF High Wycombe 189, 198, 199
RAF Homewood Park 54, 55, 201
RAF Honington 38
RAF Kinloss 148, 172, 173
RAF Lakenheath throughout
RAF Lasham 201
RAF Leuchars 76
RAF Lindholme 54, 55, 200, 201, 215
RAF Ludford Magna 192, 195
RAF Lyneham 37
RAF Manston 35, 92, 108, 124, 172-75,
   178, 202, 213, 214, 218, 219
RAF Marham 4, 13-15, 28, 29, 33, 35-39,
   74, 76, 78, 80, 83, 84, 86, 92, 93, 96,
   119, 183, 199, 200, 202, 208, 218
RAF Melton Mowbray 192
RAF Mepal 192
RAF Methwold 191
RAF Middleton St George 147
RAF Mildenhall throughout
RAF North Luffenham 38, 192, 193
RAF North Pickenham 192
RAF Oakington 35, 200, 202
RAF Podington 201
RAF Polebrook 192, 200
RAF Scampton 13, 33-35, 108, 118, 183,
   192, 199, 200, 202, 209, 218
RAF Sculthorpe 15, 17, 22, 28, 35-39, 42-
   44, 82, 92, 96, 108, 119, 120, 125-27,
   146, 156, 173, 185, 200-202, 209, 212,
   213, 218
RAF Shepherds Grove 192, 195
RAF South Ruislip 14, 16, 194, 198, 199
RAF St Eval 37, 96, 215
RAF St Mawgan 87, 148, 201
RAF Stanstead 54, 156, 190, 201
RAF Stornoway 172
RAF Stradishall 192
RAF Sturgate 99, 177-79, 189-91, 201,
   202, 211-13, 219
RAF Swinderby 200
RAF Thorpe Abbotts 25
RAF Tuddenham 192
RAF Upper Heyford throughout
RAF Valley 35, 200, 202
RAF Waddington 35, 38, 74, 170, 199,
   200, 202, 216, 218
RAF Wattisham 148
RAF West Drayton 43
RAF Wethersfield 149, 150, 156, 161, 173,
   178, 219
RAF Wittering 108
RAF Woodbridge 172, 173, 178
RAF Wyton 35, 39, 92, 199, 200, 202, 218
Ramey AFB 27, 45, 108, 119, 122, 123,
   172
Ramstein AB 82, 106, 157, 189, 199, 202
Rhein-Main AB 13, 190
Riyadh AB 143
Rouen 9
Schierstein 158
Sembach AB 149
Sidi Slimane AB 10, 39, 52, 53, 58, 83,
   97, 99
Sola AB 54, 99, 121, 174, 177, 212, 219
St Nazaire 9
Taif AB 157
Taji 90
Thule AB 21, 39, 100, 130, 131, 163
Torrejón AB 10, 39, 64, 70, 105, 106, 151,
   158, 179, 211, 212, 214
Vernam AFB 172
Wake Island 176
Wheelus AB 49, 52, 99, 122, 134, 174,
   190, 218, 219

Wiesbaden AB 33, 135, 146, 212
Yokota AB 124, 130, 131, 198
Zaragoza AB 10, 39, 77, 106, 112, 165,
   179

POLICY AND INTELLIGENCE
1967 Six-Day War 147, 157
1973 October War 152, 157, 165
40 Committee 154
Berlin Crisis (1948) 4, 33, 36, 118, 199
Berlin Crisis (1961) 61, 63
Communications Intelligence
   (COMINT) 11, 117, 119, 137, 139, 141,
   142, 148, 151, 152, 154-56, 170
Cuban Missile Crisis 61, 69, 105, 136, 147,
   195, 205
Electronic Intelligence (ELINT) 11, 109,
   117, 122-24, 130-33, 135-38, 140-42,
   148, 149, 151, 152, 156-58, 162, 163,
   170
Hungarian Crisis 46
Korean War 19, 22, 34, 36-38, 40, 47, 76,
   93, 118, 119, 183
Lebanon Crisis 57, 58, 100
Marshall Plan 33
Measurement and Signature Intelligence
   (MASINT) 117
National Intelligence Estimate (NIE) 66
Nuclear Detonation Intelligence
   (NUDINT) 117
Partial Test Ban Treaty (PTBT) 137
Peace for Galilee 160, 168
Photographic Intelligence (PHOTINT) 11,
   117, 119, 120, 122-26, 130, 137, 148,
   151, 154, 155, 157, 158, 162, 164, 165
Polish Labor Crisis 160, 165-67
Prague Spring (1968) 166
Radar Intelligence (RADINT) 164, 170
Signals Intelligence (SIGINT) 117, 141, 143,
   151, 154, 162, 163, 170
Suez Crisis 46, 57, 153, 157

SHIPS AND SPACECRAFT
Ain Zaquit 112
Defense Systems Communications Satellite
   (DSCS) 154
Ordzhonikidze 146
RMS Queen Mary 9
USS America 114
USS Coral Sea 114
USS Harlan County 152
USS Indianapolis 180
USS Nimitz 152
USS Saratoga 147

UNIQUE NAMES AND CALL SIGNS
Ace in the Hole 75, 91
Apache Chieftain 183
Bad Penny 36
Blytheville Storm 88, 91
Bodonian Express 166
Bracer 14, 99
Can Do 73
Caribbean Queen 123
Cheri-Lynn 51
City of Turlock 69
Courage 88, 91
Daffy's Destruction 88, 91
El Diablo II 118
Equipoise II 89, 91
Flamingo Flier 76
Greased Lightning 10, 73, 105
High Roller 91
Homogenized Ethyl 95
Karma 52 114
Last Resort 97
Little Rascal 73
Panic Wagon 94
Persian Rug 70
Ramrod 105
Runner 11 69
Runner 22 68
Runner 33 69
Runner 44 68
Runner 55 69
Sa-Gua 49
Special Delivery 91
Tank 133
The Real McCoy! 48
The Shocker 107
Tillie the Tanker 109
Treasure Hunter 91
Up 'N Atom 95
Weedpatch 132
What's Up Doc? 88, 91